It Happened in the Seventies

A Memoir of Love, Colliding Worlds and

a House on a Hill

Dieter Lüske

LU Books – Australia

Copyright © 2022 by Dieter Lüske

All rights reserved.

No part of this publication may be reproduced or transmitted in any form or by any means, electronic or mechanical, including photocopying, recording or any other information storage and retrieval system, without the permission in writing from the publisher.

Disclaimer

This book is a memoir. It reflects the author's present recollections of experiences over time. While all the stories in this book are true, some names and characteristics have been changed, some events have been compressed, and some dialogue has been recreated to protect people's privacy.

Cover Design by Makani Lüske

Photography by Giselle

www.gallerygiselle.com

Edited by Lynne Lloyd at Lloyd Moss Publishing

www.lloydmosspublishing.com/

For my wife and my son
Giselle & Marly

Contents

1. A Christmas Encounter — 1
2. Sydney and Free to Go — 26
3. Getting Mobile — 41
4. Taking to the Road — 49
5. Gem Hunting Fever — 61
6. Chasing Adventures — 76
7. Tropical Dreams — 86
8. Meeting Dean — 94
9. Where the Music Plays — 105
10. The Road to Nowhere — 120
11. Melbourne — 127
12. Working Holiday — 136
13. The New Year - 1976 — 154
14. One Pear at a Time — 158
15. Moving On — 167
16. Fields of Dreams — 181
17. The Faceting Game — 191
18. The Enigma called Steve — 200
19. Life is a Beach — 212
20. All the Way to the Top — 220

21.	The Wild West	226
22.	The Sun Sets in Perth	230
23.	The Nullarbor Plain	234
24.	And Time Stood Still	245
25.	Back in the Old Country	259
26.	The Final Stretch	288
27.	Hunting the Dream	292
		303

Chapter 1

A Christmas Encounter

Christmas Day 1973 - Hamburg, West Germany

It was cold and waking up was painful. I liked sleeping with my window open, the central heating turned off. My left leg was frozen, my knee resting on the carpet, but there was a reward – fresh, crisp air.

My bed consisted of a custom-made foam rubber mattress fitted to the dimensions of my room. I had elevated the mattress off the floor with the help of some old wine crates. At my previous unit I found out it was not a good idea to lay a foam mattress directly onto the floor, it caused mould infestation.

I curled up once more, retrieved my frozen limb, and began warming it up on my other leg. I knew I should get up and close the window or jump up, open my bedroom door and escape into the warmth of the hallway and the rest of my bachelor pad of three bedrooms, an ample living space (partly used as my office) and the obligatory kitchen and bathroom. Instead I decided to lie still and have five more minutes. Clearing my mind, I reflected on the previous evening celebrating Christmas Eve with my parents.

Christmas dinner had been simple, like every year as far back as I could remember. That tradition started because my brother Herbert and I couldn't sit still and eat while waiting desperately to open our presents. Our Christmas dinner was frankfurters with potato salad and a slice of the German version of a baguette. We demolished it in no time and were allowed to leave the table to wait in eager anticipation to enter the candle-lit room, which was decorated in glorious Christmas attire.

To the sound of Christmas bells, we entered the room with eyes wide open in wonderment. First, a quick check on our Christmas plates loaded with sweets and pieces of fruit. As a special treat, we received an orange and a mandarin. Then we would delve into our presents, absorbed in a world of pleasures.

This Christmas was different. I made my parents leave the room; I had something special up my sleeve.

I opened the boxes I had brought up, revealing a stereo sound system complete with speakers, radio, and turntable. I set it up as fast as possible and put our traditional Christmas record on the turntable. The sound illuminated the warm room, enhancing the sweet smell of Christmas cookies and oranges. Pretty proud of myself, I rang the bell. My parents looked around like kids, searching for the presents until my dad started to laugh, pointed at the stereo and marvelled at the beautiful sound. - Mission accomplished.

That night I should have stayed longer and gone to sleep in my old bed, but that didn't happen. Shortly after 11 pm, I left the cosy atmosphere behind. My dad seemed OK, my mother less so. I didn't go back to my nice unit, but where I went probably too often - one of Hamburg's nightclubs. This time it was the Madhouse. Sounds mad all right to go there late on Christmas Eve but it was the time for young guys like me to hit the clubs. Before eleven was for kids; after midnight, things became serious.

As expected, the Madhouse wasn't crowded and only occupied by desperate singles. There was some dancing to progressive rock, or just head rocking in time to the beat and too much drinking, but not for me. I had changed my diet and drinking habits a couple of years ago. Not sure how long I stayed. I could have taken someone home, but I didn't feel like doing so. Back at my unit, I opened my bedroom window, and went to sleep.

Enough reflection; I rose from my bed, closed the window and ventured into the kitchen. I put on the kettle. I checked Bernd's bedroom, my friend and roommate, but he wasn't back. His dad had died a week before, and he had spent Christmas with his mum. He would arrive for the Christmas Day party in the afternoon.

Having breakfast in my office, I rang the answering service to check if someone needed me on Christmas Day. Nothing urgent. Relieved, I hung up. Slot machines, jukeboxes, pinballs, or any other amusement or arcade games had the unpleasant habit of breaking down at the most inappropriate times. But not that day.

I bought my first business not long after my twenty-first birthday. I had achieved the youngest ever Master's degree in electro technique, however my plan to take on a position in an electrical engineering company didn't work out. Various companies told me in no uncertain terms that I was too young and to come back in five years.

While studying, I worked for a repair shop, fixing amusement machines. My boss also owned slot machines, pinball and jukeboxes. He provided me with a car and I had to be on call fixing machines day or night. The job was well paid and suited my lifestyle. Not long after I graduated and coincidentally on a Christmas

Day three years previously, I crashed his car. The accident happened on a callout to fix a jukebox in Hamburg's famous red-light district, the Reeperbahn.

For a major disaster, this incident turned out to be a blessing in disguise. My boss, angry at first, didn't make me pay for a new car; instead, he suggested I buy his repair service shop. I took only one day to make up my mind. With no hope of scoring a top job at only twenty-one years of age, I was given the opportunity to buy his flourishing business. The answer was obvious: 'Yes.'

I had some savings and with the help of a bank loan took over his business. Even better, I had the loan arranged to cover the cost of a new car, a station wagon. I felt pleased with myself; here I was, a proud business owner, with a nice car, my own unit, and eager to get out and make some serious money. Business was good, money was coming in, and a few weeks later, I celebrated by rewarding myself by buying a watch. I had alternative motives. Apparently, girls liked guys with a good car and a good wristwatch, and one couldn't get much better than a Rolex Submariner. Driving my new car, window down, radio on and my hand holding onto the window frame flashing my Rolex, I was showing the world I had arrived.

·········

The upcoming Christmas coffee and cake party was at 3 pm. Susie had invited me, a girl I'd met at Madhouse a couple of years previously. She'd needed a lift home, and I was only too eager to oblige. Halfway there, I'd asked, "Like to come to my place?" "Why?" she asked. "I don't like sleeping by myself," I replied. She must have felt the same and off we went to my place. I drove her home after breakfast. That's how we came to know each other and we stayed friends, no further benefits attached.

Dressed in the style of that time - skin-tight jeans, T-shirt, and high-heel half boots that elevated me to a dizzying height of 190cm, I arrived punctually at Susie's place. One could expect nothing less from a boy influenced by the German Zeitgeist! Sure enough, other eager guests had arrived even earlier. I knew some of them from frequenting the same clubs and venues. A quick scan around and I parked myself next to the prettiest girl in the room. I had never met her before and couldn't keep my eyes off her. Barely avoiding the cliché, 'Where have you been all my life?' I politely introduced myself. Christmas cakes and cookies sampled, we indulged ourselves in carefree chit-chat, a nice comfy get-together celebrating the Christmas spirit. Speaking of spirit, it followed on from the coffee. Were there any hashish biscuits? It wouldn't be out of the question, but I don't think so.

Putting my funniest side forward, I kept talking to Giselle, the girl next to me. Did Susie intend to set me up with her? If she did, it was a bit naughty of her; she knew that Bernd and I had planned to go to Australia for a couple of years. I had no intention of getting seriously involved at this precarious and exciting time of my life. I was focused on getting out of my business to pursue a more creative side of my being.

Only a few people knew of my plans. Bernd, of course, and Mark, a friend of ours whose photography studio was situated next to my repair shop. Mark was originally from New Zealand but had lived in Sydney, Australia. I had met him three years before when he moved into a large open space of an old industrial factory building to set up his studio.

Mark had separated that space into a living area, bedroom and studio sections. He was also a black belt karate trainer. I had done judo and was looking for another sport to keep me fit. Mark invited me to train with him a few times a week and, a year later, when Bernd and two other guys joined us, training became serious. Bruce Lee, here we come! We watched one karate movie after the other, inspired to become mean lean fighting machines. We didn't, but we were getting fitter. It was Mark who sparked our interest to visit Australia.

Naturally, I slipped all this into my conversation with Giselle; the topic of going to Australia created lots of attention, and not only from Giselle who liked the idea. The other guests thought I had to be crazy to give up my business and lifestyle in Hamburg.

"What made you think of going to Australia?" Giselle asked, opening the lid of a treasure chest of deep and involved conversation. If this question had come up at a chat show, I would have said, "Thank you for your valuable question," but I didn't. I had asked myself the same question. I also had the answers, ranging from my previous lifestyle choices to my more ambitious future goals, creative pursuits, and a healthier, more meaningful lifestyle.

"I always wanted to get away, but was never sure where to go or what to do," I replied. "I nearly emigrated to South Africa."

Engrossed in our conversation, I nearly missed Bernd's arrival. Australia remained the topic, and Bernd contributed his motives, which received a more positive response.

As Susie's pad was comfy but tiny, I suggested we move on to mine which was more spacious and had better music.

I made sure I stayed close to Giselle; one could never be sure whether another keen guy would disrupt our fragile developing closeness. More people turned up and things got a bit out of hand. One guy decided to take a shower and came back walking around in the nude. Not sure why he was so proud of his physique. He received the undeserved approval of cheers and applause and proceeded to the kitchen to get stuck into the bread and cheese on offer, still naked.

I took my camera out, taking photos in the dim light, using no flash; long exposure was the arty way to go. Giselle was interested in photography. I took a beautiful photo of her and familiarized her with my camera gear.

Dancing took over from drinking and the music became louder. I noticed the doorbell ringing non-stop, accompanied by hard knocking. Anticipating our neighbours - two girls - wanting to join the fun, I opened the door. It was the police, two reasonable friendly officers. They merely asked if we could keep the music down and sniffed around for drugs. Luckily we were clean. I knew who had complained, the neighbour living above us, but not to worry, the party had run its course.

Susie and some others decided to meet for ice-skating the next day. I asked Giselle if she would like to join me. "Yes, that should be fun," she said.

Surely that was a good sign, as good as a date, but did it mean anything? I felt a touch of guilt, of not trusting myself. Was I leading her on? I didn't answer myself.

It was too late to drive Giselle home and I had too much to drink anyhow. I asked if she wanted to stay. But no luck, Giselle opted for home and I walked her to the taxi stand just down the road on the corner of Eppendorfer Marktplatz. A tender goodbye kiss brought this party and our first Christmas Day to a happy ending.

Refreshed from a good night's sleep under my open window, Bernd and I headed out to Hamburg's botanical gardens where the ice rink was winter's main attraction. In addition, there were the questionable nourishments of bratwurst and glühwein.

As an 'old pro' at ice-skating, I had brought my skates; the others hired theirs. I took Giselle's hand and we walked precariously on our skates over worn-out timber planks towards the rink. Sensing that Giselle was slightly hesitant, I held her hand as we glided onto the ice. We gently merged ourselves into the stream of skaters swirling around and around.

Holding hands is no match for the treacherous slipperiness of ice. Giselle's feet went up in the air while her beautiful body, wrapped in winter garments, came crashing down in free fall and she landed on her bottom. I knew how painful that was; no one in that situation could hold back tears. I knelt next to her, carefully helping her up while trying to get her away from passing skaters. The boundary of the ice rink was only a couple of meters away. We made it in one piece. Skates are lethal weapons. On this very rink, as a young boy, I had witnessed the cruel and cold way a girl lost her fingers, cut off clean by a speeding skater.

After resting a while on a bench, with Giselle still in pain, we decided to visit the hospital close to my unit to ensure she hadn't broken any bones. We didn't have to wait long to see a doctor. A physical examination and X-rays found no fractures, only severe bruising.

We went back to my place for a while but Giselle needed to get home and rest. Living close to the airport, she could see planes taking off from her 5th-floor unit which had gorgeous sunset views through insulated double-glazed windows. Not that I was going to see any of that. I wanted to bring Giselle up but that would not happen.

"Do you like living that close to the airport?" I asked, in a clumsy effort to have her remain a bit longer in my car.

"I love the airport; I need the feeling of freedom and the possibility of flying away on the spur of the moment," she said. Who could argue with that? We said our goodbyes, and I made sure to get her phone number; she already had mine.

The last week of the old year went by less eventfully, but something between us had definitely changed. We talked on the phone every day. It was apparent we liked talking to each other.

• • • • • • • • •

Bernd and I prepared for our big New Year's Eve Party. We bought a keg of beer and lots of wine which I bought from one of my clients, Herr Rehbein. He had poker machines in pubs and was a wholesaler in wine and spirits. He even drove by my parents' place and supplied them with brandy at cost price.

Why would he do that? Well, he was a nice guy but he also was indebted to me big time. Fixing his machines day or night wasn't the only service I was providing, I was also instrumental in obtaining a vital service for his lady and himself.

No spring chicken, Herr Rehbein was probably in his fifties and his lady was ten years his junior. It came as a shock to both of them to find they were 'expecting'. With Hamburg's red-light district supplying half my business, I had connections and could recommend a very competent doctor who applied his skills to the benefit of all concerned.

I am not boasting about my dubious connections which were not of my making. Working in such an environment, one can't help learning what people are up to. Seedy as this may sound, the camaraderie among the various bars and clubs, stripers, prostitutes, dealers, pimps and everyday folks working in that district was curiously harmonic, the occasional gang bust-ups excepted.

One morning after fixing a poker machine in a strip bar, close to where the Beatles played their gigs, I left my big bunch of keys behind, which opened 200 poker machines, giving free access to the money.

Arriving at my next job, I noticed to my shock and horror I did not have my keys. I panicked! Losing the keys meant replacing 400 locks at my expense. I rushed back to the Reeperbahn, parked close to the strip bar on the 'Grosse Freiheit,' and rushed up the flight of stairs, heading straight to the bar. A topless stripper smiled at me, handing me my keys, "You owe me one," she said. "Thank you, I will think of something" I replied. I ended up giving her a box of chocolate.

Considering that milieu, it borders on a miracle that nothing terrible ever happened to me. Funny stuff, yes, all the time, but never anything nasty. I knew that once one became accepted and stuck to an unspoken code of behaviour, life would be pretty easy-going. For me, it included leaving plenty of credits on pinball machines and jukeboxes. Other parts were being non-judgmental and not squeamish.

Smaller gay bars mainly had jukeboxes for their entertainment. Being greeted with 'Hello darling' meant I was accepted. I got along fine with most of the patrons. Being mounted while bending over a jukebox, changing records, and being 'assaulted' in a simulated act of pleasure, were all part of the game. As a thank you for the service bestowed onto me, I handed out a few of the replaced records and plenty of credit on the jukebox.

When I met some of them in neighbourhood bars across town, I pretended not to know them. They had to stay in their closet - we were still in the seventies. I was also on friendly terms with transvestites who performed in bars, not forgetting establishments where the working girls told me stories about their clients.

Cosy as all that sounds, I had to move on. I had enough of late nights and fixing machines, even if it was very good money and perks like free drinks and connections to get me anything I wanted from TVs to handguns. I had no idea where some of these items came from. Why was there a glut of toasters, electric can-openers, blenders and the like on the black market? I was smart enough not to ask and my mother was happy with her newfound kitchenware, as my friends were with theirs.

I had decided as far back as two years previously to find a way out of that lifestyle. It all started with my health, and once I was thinking about my ridiculous lifestyle, one thing led to another.

•••••••••

One day until our New Year's party and the No.1 priority was food. Without it, one can't survive drinking. Next to the obligatory loaves of bread and various cheeses, there were also 'rollmops', a pickled herring rolled up. The New Year's tradition was to get tiny half-size Rollmops floating in a sea of tomato sauce. I loved those little guys; they fitted perfectly into an open mouth without even biting into them. Plus they had a good reputation as a hangover antidote.

When the big day arrived, the only thing left to buy, and yet another German tradition, was fireworks. Once a year event, the efficient, punctual German citizens were let loose to buy fireworks galore. I came home with a couple of cardboard boxes full of outside and indoor fireworks. The indoor stuff was fun, little cylinders stuffed full of confetti and tiny toys that exploded into your face if you weren't careful. It was all about the bang, in this case, the 'bang for the bucks.'

The next-door neighbours, the two girls previously mentioned, helped with decorating. They had invited lots of their friends and the party would be in both of our units.

Arriving home from my work shift late in the afternoon on New Year's Eve, I had to ring the doorbell, having left my house keys in the car. A fellow I didn't know opened the door, "Are you invited?"

"Sure am; it's my unit," I answered, asking him if he was invited. He was, by Bernd. The party was already underway. Some guests had come early to fill up on free food; most would arrive much later. Time enough for me to have a leisurely hot bubble bath without further interruption.

I can't remember picking up Giselle, only that she was there and stayed until the early morning, disappearing into a taxi to take her home. Being used to girls being a bit easier made our slowly blossoming relationship all the more special.

As we hoped, the party went off with a bang. Before midnight, it was eating and drinking, interrupted by loud bangs from the table fireworks. As it was a combined party spread over two units, dancing went crazy due to the different music sources. My hi-fi equipment was the winner, judging by the number of dancers it attracted. Midnight came and went with fireworks exploding from absolutely everywhere for at least 30 minutes before the sounds slowly diminished and the city normalized once again.

We may have been young and cool but we still played traditional New Year's Eve games. One fun tradition was 'Bleigiessen', pouring molten tin into a cup of cold water and, from the resulting frozen shape, we read everyone's future for the coming year.

We kept celebrating, which included the expected visit by police, who responded once again to a complaint about loud music. We turned down the volume and continued partying into the early morning.

New Year's Day breakfast consisted of coffee. Guests were still sleeping it off in various rooms and positions, on chairs, couches and propped up with pillows on the carpet. No longer in party mood, I needed to get those people out sooner rather than later. By lunchtime, I had everything cleaned up, and the unit looked habitable again. Time to start my favourite part of that day, making New Year's resolutions. Mine didn't involve goals like losing weight or fitness activities but drawing up a precise account of the year gone and developing strategies of change for the new one. It had become a tradition I looked forward to.

I have always loved change and fresh starts, even more so if it involved a change of scenery. It has allowed me to reinvent myself. Often it involved not seeing certain people anymore when I felt that I had moved on or changed where I lived.

The first time I had this exciting feeling of renewal came about when my parents moved to a different suburb to a new unit. No one knew me, no one would know what type of kid I was before the age of nine. I instantly became more assertive, spurned on in part by my brother, Herbert, who was six years older.

After that glorifying life experience, I yearned for similar happenings again and again, and if they didn't come, I made them happen.

Study time, work experience, girlfriends and other friends, new scenes, new clubs and questionable lifestyle choices all came into it, all part of growing up.

One change I didn't see coming, it was dramatic and it was due. I should have known but I never gave my food intake much thought. I had been living on non-nutritional food for most of my young life.

Growing up in a baker's family sounds idyllic for a kid like me, living on cakes, bread and sugar. Skipping lunches in favour of chocolate cakes was undoubtedly a pleasurable experience. But it was a habit that contained the seeds of trouble, amplified once I lived in my own unit. Cooking wasn't my strong point; a soft-boiled egg and a pot of tea were the sum total of my cooking skills. Light meals were obtained in pubs, accompanied by either beer or Coke, depending on the time of the day.

The first repercussions from my dietary habits reared their ugly head at the age of twenty just before I moved into my unit. I made myself one of my super sandwiches, comprising generous slices of bread; loaded with butter, pepper salami and mayonnaise. Carrying my delicious food construction from the kitchen to the living room, settling down on the couch with my book and a glass of beer. How much better could life get? Not much, actually. Shortly after finishing my feast, I started to have stomach cramps. I took some antacids powder, a remedy my dad resorted to after nearly every meal. Was that a common condition for a baker? Even my brother had stomach problems and was on acid-reducing drugs. In his case, a stomach ulcer was suspected. His good doctor ordered a diet of milk, bread and pasta. It didn't help at all and made it worse, preventing my brother from becoming a baker.

I doubled over; the antacid relieved my cramps for a minute, only to start up even more severely. It was late at night but with the hospital only five minutes away, I dragged myself along to the emergency department. (How comforting a hospital can be if you need one.) A friendly doctor checked me out and injected some magic potion which quickly made me feel better. He advised me to stay around for a few hours before going home and seeing my GP in the morning.

The following day, too scared to even eat, I made myself a cup of chamomile tea. I was sure it would help. It seemed to be common knowledge, and not only in our family. Maybe it was a German thing. We stocked a variety of herbal teas at home. Every night Dad drank a herbal concoction to flood his kidneys with goodness preventing stones from developing.

Off to the doctor's, where I found about ten patients waiting patiently. No appointments or taking a number at this clinic. I came prepared - book in hand. "Who came last?" I asked. That was all it took to get sorted. Only a year later, my waiting times were over; I had my own business and could afford private insurance. Private patients received preferential treatment, but I still had to wait on this occasion. Deep into my book, I was called in to see the doctor. He didn't take long to prescribe milk, bread, pasta and medication to lower my acid levels. He told me I had a sensitive stomach, prone to gastritis and ulcers. Not yet ready to take his warning on board, I continued as before, except now with frequent interruptions from violent stomach cramps.

A couple of years down the road, I was still working day and night in my own business and living in my comfortable unit. I had a new doctor and the luxury that he made house calls whenever I needed him. All paid for by my private health insurance. On one 'final straw' day, I needed the excellent doctor urgently and after settling me down, he suggested I may have stomach ulcers and arranged a barium meal x-ray. Sure enough, it showed ulcers. He prescribed more tablets and issued a strict order: no coffee or alcohol.

On returning home that fateful day, I met Bernd's friend Jo, a ship's captain, who was on shore leave for a few days. Getting comfortable with a couple of beers and idle chat, it didn't take long before my ulcer diagnosis became our main talking point. And the answer to my sufferings came as a revelation.

Jo knew a lot about health and diets and when he began to share his expertise I gave him my full attention. For the rest of the afternoon and into the night - after taking my beer away - he bombarded me with everything I needed to know about the macrobiotic diet and its underlying philosophy.

I took to it all like a fish to water. It appealed to me; I was eager to try that diet and believed in Jo's promise that it would heal my ulcers. I was desperate enough to deprive myself of my favourite food and stop my drinking habits. I was ready for another momentous change in my life. And this time it had been delivered right to my door. Jo suggested a brown rice diet with a few vegetables along with unique teas and condiments I'd never heard of before.

The next morning I rushed out to visit a health food shop called 'Schwarzbrot'. Besides organic produce, it stocked books on nutrition, including one about my newfound interest, macrobiotics. It would become my go-to resource for everything I needed to kick-start my healthy new lifestyle. I bought Mu-tea, a blend of eleven invigorating and soothing oriental herbs, tahini, a sesame paste, *hatcho miso*, a fermented soy paste, *umeboshi*, a Japanese pickled and salted plum, and of course my new food stable, brown rice and sea salt.

The diet was a good fit for my cooking skills. All I had to learn was how to cook brown rice in a particular way to bring out the yang. Yin and Yang were the cornerstones of the philosophy behind the macrobiotic diet and lifestyle and appealed to me in a strangely familiar way, as though I had been looking for it. And I probably had, it worked in perfect harmony with my karate training and its teachings.

Fast-forward six weeks into my new diet of brown rice and vegetables: I had persevered and could report good news, no more stomach cramps or pain. I had lost weight, felt truly alive, and underwent a second barium meal test. My GP was surprised, to put it mildly - probably more correct to say - astonished. There were no signs of any ulcers. Never again did I have to consult him about my stomach.

· · · · ● · ● · · · ·

All this went through my mind as I sat in my kitchen sipping Mu-tea and contemplating strategic steps for my New Year's resolution. No doubt, if the diet and lifestyle changes I had made were big, my planning to go to Australia was far bigger. Even as I was thinking about making it all happen, I dreaded the next phone call telling me of another a broken jukebox and having to drive somewhere to fix it. I truly was over it. The faster I could quit this business of mine, the better.

My deadline to get out was the end of June. To make that happen, I had to find a buyer quickly. My list expanded with names of possible buyers to contact and spreading the word within this weird amusement machine environment.

Next item: finding someone who would take over my unit. I needed travelling money for Australia and anticipated good returns for my furniture and sound equipment. My final task was to complete the emigration papers for Australia, and I added taking some extra English lessons. My conservational English was pretty bad; no point lying about that. It consisted of what I'd learnt in primary school from a teacher who couldn't speak the language either. I knew technical English: I could read the English instruction manuals that came with the juke boxes. But how could I use terms like 'gear', 'cartridge', 'coil', 'pick-up', 'turntable' and 'slot' in ordinary conversation?

I made one more entry on my resolution list, 'Giselle.' Nothing else, no comment. What was I thinking? I liked her a lot. Our few encounters had been unlike anything I had felt before. Logic told me not to pursue a steady relationship while Bernd and I were in the middle of emigration procedures. I deliberately didn't decide anything that New Year's morning; I left it to fate.

After all this deep thinking, I rang Giselle, asking when she would have time to catch up for dinner. In the following weeks, we met often. I can't repeat our conversations, not because I don't want to, only because we talked non-stop. We were made for talking to each other. I had never found it so effortless to talk with someone; nor had I found someone who understood me so well.

I had relaxed my limited and strict macrobiotic diet and included some meat. The difference was the quality of food, no more sausages, salamis, or other processed smallgoods. It would have been challenging to take Giselle only to hippie-style macrobiotic eateries, slurping miso soup.

Instead, we met in trendy clubs, steakhouses and in top-flight restaurants, not too noisy to interfere with us talking our heads off.

Giselle had studied art, painted, loved ballet, theatre, photography and decorating. She worked in interior design around Hamburg and often in different cities. My mother referred to her as my arty girlfriend, implying she was too good for me. That came as a bit of a surprise, but then I put her remark down to a touch of jealousy.

It became evident that Giselle and I complemented each other in every sense; even so, we still hadn't consummated our blossoming relationship. I still wasn't allowed up into Giselle's unit. The topic was on our minds, and again we were on the same wavelength. We both had a variety of not going anywhere relationships and were not ready for something more serious, particularly not with the considerable roadblock of going to Australia.

Weekends became my preferred working time for far-out locations. Trips to Luneburg, Luebeck, Neumunster or even as far as Bremen or Hannover were much more enjoyable with a beautiful girl by my side. Giselle didn't have a car, I would pick her up, and we drove together into the sunset. No, not really, but there was a romantic element to it.

On our first trip together, we went to Luneburg. One of my clients, a friend of my parents, had a poker machine at the city's train station restaurant. I gave the machine the once-over, replaced some parts that looked a bit iffy, and the job was complete an hour later.

Giselle and I went walking and re-discovering Luneburg. I had been there many times and knew interesting stories about some of Luneburg's historical landmarks. I had brought along my camera, a Pentax Spotmatic, and showed Giselle how to use it. The camera was loaded with a black and white film, and we played around with ideas to take creative photos. I had my own darkroom equipment, and on returning home we would be busy developing the film. Not exactly a romantic sunset atmosphere, but something even deeper developed which hadn't been mentioned before: love.

· · · · ● · ● · · ·

At work, sitting behind my desk with a prehistoric Continental typewriter which had come with the business, my mornings were filled with writing invoices. Failing that, there were enough jukeboxes or other machines to work on. Jukeboxes like the AMI Continental, which looked like a spaceship, were great to work on. I would take them totally apart and replace all worn-out parts until in the end they looked like new. Same with old pinball machines, everything had been reconditioned. If coils were burned out, I rewired them to keep the feel of authenticity.

Considering all the different aspects of my business, I worked non-stop. My Dad even started to help, taking machines apart and cleaning their interiors for me to repair and reassemble them. It soon became apparent from the odd casual remark that he hoped to help out full-time in the business. So when I finally told my parents I wanted to sell up and go to Australia, they were shocked. And once the news spread, relatives and friends also told me I was a fool to leave all my achievements behind for the unknown that was Australia.

I had contacted and met with many of my fellow repair guys. Some with businesses like mine, but none were interested in spending money to expand. I hadn't considered this drawback and changed my strategy accordingly. The larger companies had their own workshops; mechanics employed there would be my new target. Whenever I needed a new machine or spare parts, I sounded these guys out if they were interested in setting up for themselves. Towards the end of February, I had a fair idea about who could be enticed to buy my business.

It was a cold rainy Friday night. The day had been hectic and I'd worked late. Coming home, all I wanted was a hot bath. I was thinking of calling Giselle when the phone rang, it was Giselle. 'What are you doing?' she asked.

"I just arrived home and am going to have a bath. Do you want to go somewhere, maybe have a late dinner?" I replied.

"No, I thought we could stay in tonight," she said.

"What? You mean, stay in? At your place?"

"Yes, let's stay in tonight."

"Sounds good; I'll see you soon; I'm on my way."

My luxurious soaking bath turned into a quick shower. I jumped into my tight jeans, threw on a T-shirt, and forgetting it was winter left without my jacket. From my street to hers was a fair distance and the fifteen minutes it took me for the journey wouldn't have disgraced a Formula One driver. Sixty km/h is too slow when you're in a hurry.

On arrival, I pressed the bell and waited for the buzzer to open the door. I found the lift and went up to the fifth floor. Giselle looked out, smiling, and invited me into her little kingdom of heaven. From the entrance I could see four doors. The one on my left led into the bathroom where one could sit in a tub and read (as I would soon discover). Next along on the left was a more important door, giving admittance to the living room where a bed fitted neatly into an alcove. How snug and comfortable the bed was, I would also find out soon enough. The door straight ahead led to a kitchenette.

Giselle gave me the Grand Tour. Everything reflected her exquisite taste. I admired the classy furniture, her state-of-the-art TV set, the chrome-and-glass table, and the comfy seating. "Wow", but I should have expected nothing less than cutting-edge modernity mixed with comfort; after all, Giselle worked in interior design.

We settled down with a glass of wine to talk about our day. But how much talking is possible in such an energy-hyped-up atmosphere? We moved from her comfortable furniture to her even comfier bed to continue the conversation. Until this point neither of us had been ready to take things further. For each of us, the relationship road had ended in disappointment. I had given up looking for a perfect partner and so had Giselle. All these considerations were forgotten being with Giselle. It felt so right. I could feel the tingling of anticipation, and I knew I wanted to keep that feeling. I wanted even more, and we both received more: love was in the air.

I stayed for breakfast.

"Now what?" I thought, driving back to work. I was in love, we were in love, but we didn't know where this was heading. We preferred to stay in the moment; it was easier. While I was looking for a suitable buyer for my business, Giselle was also busy. Before we met, she had booked a five-day holiday in Moscow at the beginning of May. It was too late for me to join her even if I'd had the time. We stayed off the headache-inducing topic of Australia; it was much more fun to plan Giselle's trip to the Soviet Union and how she would manage to take photos without creating an incident.

As luck would have, I received an excellent offer for my unit; one of my clients was looking for a spacious apartment in a good location. He also would take most of my furniture and even pay for the carpet my brother had laid throughout the unit when I moved in.

There was, however, a rather large fly in the ointment; my elusive landlord, with 'lord' being the correct expression. He owned the entire block my unit was part of and was widely known for keeping apartments empty and letting them fall into disrepair, demolishing the vacant buildings and starting afresh. His 'vision' had nothing to do with town planning or preserving history and he had no concern whatsoever for the residents under his roof. Still, I had to put all this in the back of my mind and write him a perfect, persuasive letter. So I sat down and did my best.

One week later, in mid-March, I received his answer. It was not the one I had hoped for but much worse. Not only was I forbidden to pass the unit on to someone else, but he demanded I clear all my belongings out, repaint, and even get rid of the carpet. That was not all; I had mentioned that I wanted to vacate the unit at the end of June. He made it very clear I must terminate my lease by the end of March. Not one to shed tears over spilt milk (or whatever the fitting metaphor may be), I sat down again, gazed at my trusty typewriter, mumbled into my beard and wrote a short letter complying with his demand. And that was that.

I passed the bad news on to my client. He wasn't too concerned and even offered to buy some of my furniture. Next morning, after arriving at work, I asked the neighbouring shop owner if he needed any furniture. A couple of days later, he stopped by my place and bought all my living-room shelving and cupboards.

Things were speeding up. Once I accepted there was no alternative, I actually found the activity of cleaning out my flat was fun. Once a month in Hamburg there was a kerbside rubbish pick-up service. That day was like Christmas for some people. Students, antique and second-hand dealers and even art dealers roamed the suburbs where people had dumped their rubbish onto the streets. In the past, I had driven around, scouting out old chairs and mirrors; now these items went back to the trash.

My first big cleanout was highly successful; everything I took out in the afternoon had acquired a new owner before the actual pick-up started early next morning. Some stuff was taken out of my hands before I could even put it down. People even asked if they could help carry out things. Good as all this was, it didn't earn me any cash.

My unit was empty, a curious and liberating feeling. Bernd didn't have much to throw out or sell but, like me, was happy to leave everything behind and 'travel light' in both the physical and mental senses.

One Saturday, as March was drawing to an end, Giselle and I ventured into the vibrant city centre for a spot of window shopping. We did buy a few things, including a record, and grabbed a table at our favourite café. Over a delicious torte and cups of coffee, with people on neighbouring tables immersed in their own little worlds, I knew this was the right time to pop the question.

"Why don't you come with me to Australia?" I asked, holding Giselle's hand.

She looked at me, "Let me think for a couple of minutes," took a sip of coffee and stared into the cup. Looking up after what seemed to be minutes of silence, she smiled: "Yes, I'd love to come."

I felt as if I'd asked her to marry me. The effect of Giselle's decisive answer must have shown on my face. Happy that the problem had been solved, I was also shocked at my audacity in asking the question.

"I think we need a brandy," she said.

I laughed. "Yes, please, we sure do!" And, planting a kiss on her cheek, I gestured the waitress over and ordered two brandies. Our talk was now infused with added energy. The café's background noise seemed muted; our world had changed and widened in scope.

Later that afternoon, with hours to think it over, Giselle called me, offering reassurance: "Don't worry about anything. I am sure we will be good but, if not, I can look after myself. I always have done."

I answered: "It will be great; I am OK, can't wait to make it happen."

That night we brainstormed how we would move forward. Giselle suggested I move in with her once my business and unit had been sold. It was as easy as that. Everything was easy now; no more hesitations or avoiding the topic of Australia. Instead, we immersed ourselves in planning every last practical detail for our emerging future together.

The next day I told Bernd. Naturally he was a bit taken aback but I talked the development up, depicting it in the most positive light. We could rent a unit in Sydney which would be more affordable with the three of us. Our friends took a less sunny view, predicting gloom and doom. Bernd will be a third wheel. When other people offered their thoughts on our plans, we – Bernd as much as I – put a positive spin on the situation. We convinced ourselves everything would work out perfectly for all concerned.

Telling Bernd or our friends was one thing; telling our parents quite another. Giselle's parents seemed to accept it, telling her; "From the moment you met Dieter, we knew you would go to Australia with him." They were supportive and seemed to like me - maybe not the fact that I would take their daughter away - but they regarded me as a polite, educated and successful person.

My mother wasn't at all happy. In her mind, it was Giselle's fault that we were going to the other end of the world. In her eyes, Giselle was a son-snatcher and I was accused of being a pantoffelheld, a German expression for someone who asks his wife's permission before doing anything. I didn't know whether to laugh, cry or defend myself; I was too busy pacifying Mum to seek out what Dad thought of our plan. Their concerns were perfectly understandable. For them it was a double whammy: first, the shock of giving up my business and, second, being confronted with the possibility I had found my life partner.

But my dad's perception must have been different; he liked Giselle and saw in her a beautiful new family member. My mother liked Giselle too, but at the same time saw her as a threat. One thing was sure; my parents were now taking this talk of going to Australia more seriously than before. And they were right because, right on cue, a new contender arose to take over my business.

I had met Peter a few times before. He was a technician working in the repair shop of a company warehouse where I bought poker machines. He had heard on the grapevine that my business was for sale. I had him earmarked as a potential buyer and we agreed to meet at my workshop. Peter turned up with his uncle whom he introduced as the investor who would run the show while Peter did the repairs and installed new machines.

That sounded like the perfect arrangement; they even agreed to my price after a bit of haggling. Sitting behind my desk discussing the transaction with these two operators, I felt the warm glow of satisfaction that comes when a difficult task is concluded. My successors were clearly excited about their brave new future. We shook hands on the deal and parted, intending to put everything down on paper. As part of the deal, Peter was going to quit his job and work in partnership with me for the whole month of June. From July on, I would be available for him to consult, should problems arise. A fortnight later the landlord of my shop, happy to have continuity of tenancy, presented a new five-year lease ready for signing.

•••••••••

Giselle left for her one-week sightseeing holiday in May. With my camera in hand, my lovely Giselle arrived in Moscow on May Day and couldn't wait to capture the spectacular 'Red May Celebration.'

City buildings were draped in huge red flags and the annual military parade proceeding past the Kremlin was a highlight. But there was also constant surveillance, and Giselle had to consider what scenes and objects were allowed to be captured on film.

A couple of days later, she managed to call me. the phone call had to be pre-booked, and Giselle had the uncanny feeling that someone was listening in to our conversation.

The black market in Moscow was thriving and proved to be a fascinating experience. The best place for these underhanded exchanges was the 'GUM' on Red Square, Moscow's leading department store. In 1974 it looked like an indoor marketplace where students and young kids were slyly trading items Giselle wanted in exchange for Western items unavailable through official channels. Giselle had brought stockings, ballpoint pens and other goods into the country, and as she walked the aisles of GUM's vast interior, her modern fashion sense sent a clear signal to the black marketeers that a Westerner was in their midst.

Giselle, whose dad collected coins and stamps, wanted a silver rouble. Soviet regulations banned the export of roubles, let alone silver ones, not that this would stop my Giselle.

She handed over the nylon stockings, doubtful of ever seeing a silver rouble in return. The hosiery disappeared into the crowd, handed from one student to the next. Five minutes later, someone bumped into her and she could feel the cold touch of a silver coin in her hand. Before she even could say thank you, the provider was gone. She deposited the valuable coin in her wallet, where it remained, mixed in with ordinary currency. If stopped by Customs, she would act clueless about it. A few days later, I had Giselle back in Hamburg in one piece, with everything she brought out of the communist state still in her possession, including a chessboard and records for me. I had good news for her.

We had received our emigration confirmation letter from the Australian consulate in Cologne, together with interview appointments. Encouraging as this news was, last-minute rejection was still a possibility. Neither of us had been to Cologne before. It would be our first holiday together, and we were more excited to see Cologne's cathedral than its Australian consulate.

We left on a Wednesday and had to be back by Sunday, ready for work on Monday. The trip was roughly 450 km each way – a piece of cake on a German autobahn. We hit the road before sunrise to the sounds of a Pink Floyd cassette on the car stereo and snacks to make our travel even more pleasurable. My Opel station wagon, sports edition, ran as good as new, even though I had been driving it for three years. Sticking to the autobahn, we could easily have made the distance in four hours, but we decided to try the scenic route and take plenty of coffee and sightseeing breaks.

Arriving in Cologne, it was a bit hectic but with Giselle's map-reading skills and directions we found the consulate easily. We spotted a suitable hotel not far away, deposited our belongings in our room and rushed straight out again to see the city sights.

Weighed down by the cool-looking but not-so-practical leather bag containing my camera gear, I started taking photos the moment we hit the street. A bunch of Hare Krishna devotees were among our first 'targets.' Giselle took over, snapping the neat stacks of market produce on street stalls close to the cathedral.

Cologne Cathedral towers gigantically over the human ants below. The dark, nearly pitch black, aged sandstone from which the world's third tallest church had been crafted added to the Gothic atmosphere. One couldn't help but be overwhelmed. Between us, Giselle and I must have photographed every square centimetre of its vast façade. Already we were proving that we were a fine team, each exhibiting a distinct taste and coming up with interesting variations on our chosen creative themes. Those few days in Cologne became our training ground in which we shared our views and skills and hatched the idea of making a book out of our future travels in Australia. Hardly any books about the southern continent were available in West Germany back then, sparking our vision to fill that gap with a coffee-table book with our stories and images.

•••••••••

'Nervous' sums up how we felt on approaching the consulate the following day. Our appointment involved much more than an informal chat. First, we each had to undergo a medical examination and chest X-rays. I seem to recall there was also a vaccination.

Next came the interview. The person in charge looked relaxed in his impressive office, his boots on his desk. I felt like an extra in a vintage cowboy movie.

This diplomat from 'down under' spoke no German, only English, but nothing remotely like the school English I knew. Overcoming a measure of incomprehension, I managed to answer his probing questions. His main concern was where we would live and how we would earn money to support ourselves.

We had decided to keep to ourselves that we intended to stay in Australia for only two years, travelling far and wide on an extended holiday. When I showed him my electrical engineering qualification, the attaché advised me to settle in Western Australia, where emerging enterprises were in great need of skilled labour.

He expressed concern about Giselle; what would happen if we split up and poor Giselle was left alone in the Australian wilderness? He obviously didn't know Giselle, and her answer, given in no uncertain terms, amply demonstrated her individuality and independence. Giselle's English put mine to shame, and impressed by her confidence, he signed the papers for our approval without any further hesitation.

This really was a red-letter day; not only were immigration visas stamped in our passports, but the Australian government graciously subsidised our outbound airfares. We would only have to pay 300 Deutschmarks each instead of some DM3000. The only catch was, we had to stay for two years. If we came back any earlier, we would have to repay the cost of the flight. Too easy, as the Aussies would say.

We were so elated we could have skipped out of the consulate but didn't act on the impulse to avoid attracting unfavourable attention and be declared unsuitable after all. Having cleared our main hurdle, we now had to wait a fortnight for the outcome of Bernd's interview before deciding on a flight date. If we were going to spend time in Australia together, we wanted to leave together.

With the formalities behind us, we turned our attention to pleasure. Several towns and villages around Cologne are renowned for their medieval fortifications. There was nothing more to keep us in Cologne so I said to Giselle: "Let's go. I want to see a castle." An hour later, we were in Brühl, booking a tour of its famous castle. Having never set foot in a castle before, I was suitably impressed; less so Giselle, who had visited a few of them, including some in Ireland.

At night, we found a small restaurant that doubled as a disco. As we finished our meal and polished off the wine, the venue filled with an eager dance crowd, the lights dimmed and a disco mirror ball began spinning overhead. After a couple of songs, I looked at Giselle, and she at me. This wasn't our thing. "How about we hit the road?" I said. "Great," was her reply, "maybe we can make it home in time to catch a late-night movie." A speedy three hours down the autobahn and we were home in time to snuggle up in bed watching TV after midnight.

· · · · • · • · · ·

Back in my repair shop, I looked around; only three more weeks and none of this would be mine anymore. The desk I could do without but I felt sad about leaving the jukeboxes and old pinball machines behind. I would also miss my workbench, wall-mounted instruments, oscillographs and power-regulating devices. Would I return in a couple of years to regret what I had done?

Before doubts could get the better of me, the phone rang. A poker machine was waiting to be fixed in Hanstedt, 40 km south of Hamburg.

I loved Hanstedt, where some of the happiest days of my childhood had been spent. It was the scene of our family's annual holidays. For six years, my parents rented the same one-roomed cottage for four weeks over the summer school vacation. Next door lived a family with eleven children I could play with; I even slept at their place (one kid more or less hardly made a difference). We played non-stop, soccer being our favourite game.

A few years later, and not long after I obtained my own business, the owner of our former holiday property contacted me and asked if I could maintain her machines. I couldn't be happier; she also hooked me up with a few more clients.

She was decidedly unhappy to learn that I had sold my business and even talked to my parents about it. Clearly, her trust and goodwill were in as much need of repair as her machines, the ones I had come to fix that morning. I promised her to visit again soon to let her know how the service would carry on under Peter.

Over the next couple of weeks, Peter and I went out on repair jobs together. I introduced most of my clients to him at this time. Fixing poker machines involved trust; I needed clients' consent to hand over the keys to their machines.

Understandably, some were reluctant to grant that consent, but they relied on my judgment that I had sold my business to another trustworthy person.

In my own mind - and I had confided this only to Giselle - I wasn't sure about Peter. But, as there was nothing wrong that I could put my finger on, I brushed my reservations aside.

June came and went in no time. Peter seemed capable of doing the work to the client's satisfaction. His uncle took care of the bookwork and incoming phone calls. Everything was going to plan. Only one thing was missing: my money. Peter and his uncle promised to have it by the end of June, leaving me no choice but to wait it out.

At month's end I handed over my keys and received half the money owed, with the other half now promised in August. Two days before I walked out of the shop for the final time, I had turned twenty-five. Now walking from the office to my car for the last time, I felt surprisingly light-hearted. Next stop would be my unit to hand over my apartment keys to an agent from the landlord's office.

Arriving shortly before the appointed time, I walked around the rooms of my familiar home, anticipating a mild attack of nostalgia. Nothing. Not even a slight tug of the heart. My scrupulous efforts to repaint everything white and pull out the carpets had eroded its once-cherished atmosphere. It looked dreadful. The doorbell rang, it was the agent. After a quick look around the unit, she seemed satisfied; I placed the keys in her outstretched hand and just in time I remembered; getting a screwdriver from my car; I unscrewed my nameplate from the front door and said goodbye.

Free! I was free of nearly everything except my car, which I had arranged to keep until we left Germany. I sold it back to the car dealer where I had bought it. I might have done better selling it privately, but this way was hassle-free, getting the money deposited straight into my bank account.

My birthday party, held at my parents' house, was inevitably also a going-away party. That must be why it wasn't quite the happy occasion a birthday party ought to be. In good German tradition, everyone arrived for coffee and cake. I can't remember if I received any gifts: I certainly didn't want anything cumbersome to carry to Australia (money would have been gratefully accepted).

The coffee party went off well. It was a lovely day, which lifted everyone's mood, and everyone at the gathering was chatting happily, in an atmosphere we Germans call *gemütlich* – cosy, familiar, warm and harmonious.

Present were my brother Herbert, sister-in-law Heike, a sprinkling of uncles and aunts, and two friends from my early teenage years, Freddy and Rolf. In the intervening years, we lost touch but they stayed close friends with my parents, mainly with my dad. Dad was a great guy; he got on well with most people. To Rolf and Freddy, who had a bad or no relationship with their respective fathers, my supportive and understanding Dad must have been a revelation. He played the accordion; I used to accompany him on guitar while still living at home. Even though Freddy knew only a few basic chords, he loved playing music with my Dad. But on this birthday of mine, there was no accordion music to be heard; instead, the note Freddy struck was one of discord. Without warning he launched into a tirade of accusations against Giselle's and my plan to head off to Australia.

Rolf's language was more subdued but no one understood why we would abandon our comfortable life at home for an unknown future in a strange land. And who could blame them? Here we had steady earnings, a career and almost guaranteed security. How could we throw all this away for what sounded like an overlong holiday excursion?

Bernd was at that party as well, and we hadn't expected the need to be so defensive, but we had formed a pact to speak in glowing terms about the possibilities that Australia and changing our lifestyle offered. Our upbeat tone seemed to inflame Freddy even more. I thought his aggression resulted from his frustration at not achieving what he wanted. Yet in the end, mellowed by a few glasses, we did part as friends.

Waking up next to Giselle nullified any adverse effects still presiding in my brain from the events of the previous evening.

The rest of our time in Hamburg was much less stressful than my birthday bash. I loved Giselle's unit. Each morning we took our time to have a comfortable breakfast in front of the double glazed windows watching the planes take off from the nearby airport. My strict diet had become less rigid; I was seduced by fresh bread rolls I bought every morning from the downstairs 'Spar' Supermarket. They also had beautiful fresh cut turkey slices and pepper salami.

Sitting in front of that window, slurping tea with too much sugar and lemon added, chewing on my break-feast opposite my beautiful Giselle, I felt the world had changed and was about to change even more drastically. I was reborn, free of every tie that bound me to my past. Material possessions weighed me down no more; Giselle and I felt a huge weight had been lifted from our shoulders. The future spread before us was going to be awesome. What could possibly go wrong?

· · · • · • · · ·

I was still busy in July helping Peter and his uncle run my old business. My motive was influenced by a nagging worry that they wouldn't come up with the second half of what they owed me. Giselle and I were keen to scrape any bit of money together that we could lay our hands on. I even helped former clients with rapid repairs to earn a few extra Deutschmarks.

Not everything went towards savings. I wanted to invest in better camera gear. Guided by Mark my photographer friend, I bought a 6x6-format Bronica camera with a couple of lenses, a tripod and a light meter. Acquiring the Bronica for myself allowed Giselle to use my Pentax, which came with five lenses.

All up, two heavy bags full of camera gear guaranteed that we could take photos in Australia to a professional standard.

In those final weeks in Hamburg, our plans took on more concrete form. We would stay awhile in Sydney and take hundreds of photos before taking off to travel around Australia with the ultimate goal of writing and publishing a book and selling photos to magazines.

The new equipment took a hefty bite out of my savings. We knew we would need to buy a reliable car to take us all the way around a continent almost the size of Europe. Giselle saved all her money and sold some of her interior decoration materials as well.

Throughout this time Bernd and I had kept up our karate training, and Giselle joined us. Mark's friends from Sydney, John and Ann, had arrived in Hamburg for a karate tournament. John took over from Mark, training us for a couple of weeks. He ran the YMCA karate club in Sydney and invited us to stay at his and Ann's house in Rose Bay, close to famous Bondi Beach.

We couldn't believe our luck; we hadn't even arrived in Sydney and already had somewhere to stay, at least for the first week. Before long, Bernd was also approved for immigration and we received our flight tickets. Departure day was September 23 from Frankfurt Airport. Unfortunately, Bernd would not be with us; his flight left the next morning.

Giselle and I must have been born under a lucky star. A company for which she had done interior design had a new employee from Düsseldorf who required accommodation. He came with his wife to inspect Giselle's unit; they liked it and signed a two-year rental lease that commenced on October 1. Surely this was more than coincidence?

I still hadn't received the final payment for my business. What's more, other so-called friends had not paid up either; they promised to pay directly into my bank account. There is a German expression for such dubious statements, "Wer es glaubt, wird seelig." Freely translated, "If you believe that, you'll believe anything."

And to make matters worse, quite a few of my clients had left their final invoices unpaid. Were they banking on I wouldn't come back?

• • • • • • • • • •

The big day finally arrived. All we had were two suitcases, handbags, camera gear and, most important, each other.

Being aware that I could carry all my worldly possessions in my own hands was a surreal feeling. Flooded with adrenalin and a sense of unlimited freedom with no other responsibilities was a new sensation for me.

It was the same for Giselle, except that she still owned her unit, a kind of security blanket for the two of us. We could always return to her place if something went wrong with our grand plan.

Bernd had arrived as well, suitcase in hand. Is that how one starts a new life? I think it is; we had created plenty of free space within ourselves, waiting to be filled with whatever came along.

Some of our mutual friends were already waiting for us at Hamburg Hauptbahnhof, our designated railway station. We farewelled them and Giselle's parents, who were experiencing mixed emotions. My parents and Heike arrived just in time; my mother later wrote of how furious she was not to have arrived much earlier. All these years later, I can still see the tears in our parents' eyes. Goodbyes are never easy.

Aboard the train to Frankfurt, our excitement gradually morphed into a calm, relaxed mood. We took a sentimental last long look as towns and landscapes sped by. Germany is beautiful, but we were heading forward, broadening our view, on a quest for meaning, expansion, independence and liberty for our life together.

Arriving at Frankfurt's huge central train station, we found the right connecting train that would allow us plenty of time before taking to the air. Sadly, we had to say goodbye to Bernd, who left to book himself into a hotel close to the airport for one night.

We were boarding the plane in the late afternoon. Nothing new for Giselle who was a seasoned flyer but I had never been on a plane. We were flying in a jumbo jet, whose enormous size gave me a sense of security; surely nothing could go wrong in something that size?

Flying in the Seventies was exciting; one felt special. Everyone was in a good mood. I think the seats were larger and more comfortable. We 'rented' two headphones for $2 each to listen to stereo music and follow the movie. The only movie was one with Henry Fonda, and that was the end of the onboard entertainment. People read or talked to each other, sharing their excitement and information about their destinations and adventures to come. Time literally flew by. We talked to a few passengers who were also on immigration visas, with the difference that they wanted to stay in Australia for good. They found it quite amusing that we immigrated to travel for an extended time.

The sights that greeted us on a stopover in Bahrain were memorable. After exiting the plane, we had to walk on the tarmac in steaming heat to the arrivals hall. Except for us passengers, everyone we saw wore glistening white robes. But, my hygienic self was in for a shock when I went to the toilet and found only a hole in the floor. How did those guys in white robes manage to squat without messing up their garments? That would be the only time in my life when I've preferred the cramped quarters of an aircraft toilet.

We were happy to return to the interior of our lovely big plane. For some reason, our take-off was delayed, so to reward the passengers' patience, we were all gifted packs of cards with the Malaysian Airlines logo. After we became airborne again, a group of travellers behind us became slightly unruly but the spirit of good humour prevailed. And that wasn't the only spirit in the air; we understood hardly a word of what they were saying. It took us a while to figure out that they were members of a Scottish football club who had brought their own whisky onto the plane.

We wrote our first letters home while still aloft over the Indian Ocean, ensuring our parents didn't have to wait too long to hear from us. The airmail paper was supplied as part of the excellent service.

The flight was even better after we landed in Melbourne. Our plane, now half empty, continued on to Sydney. The stewardess allowed us into the cockpit; what a privilege. On the approach to Sydney, the pilot announced that everyone should move over to the right side and look out of the window as he introduced the incredible views of the Harbour City. A bit later, there was a mass movement of passengers to the left side for more pilot information about the spectacular views. Then we had to return to our seats and put on our belts. I could feel my tummy tightening; the plane descended into landing mode, and our future rushed forward to meet us.

Chapter 2

Sydney and Free to Go

Stepping out of the plane, we were handed little pin buttons, tokens of our immigrant status. We were amazed at how easy it was to step onto Australian soil, so to speak, while still walking on the airport concrete floor towards the customs officers.

"Do you have an address to go to?" the officer asked.

"Yes," we chorused, showing John's address.

"Welcome to Australia," he smiled. And that was it; we were officially and legally in the Commonwealth of Australia.

We kept looking over our shoulders but no one was following us. We were two among many tourists. They didn't even check our suitcases. Being used to Germany's bureaucracy, we still suspected some paperwork being thrown at us any minute now. But nothing, we were free to go. Now what? Maybe we should grab something to eat. "Are you hungry?" I asked. Giselle had spotted a counter where food items were sold.

"Let's have a look," she suggested. We saw a food item we were not accustomed to, called a meat pie. But we settled for something more familiar and ordered a couple of sausages. We should have tried the pies; it couldn't have been any worse. One bite was enough; the taste had nothing in common with a German sausage. From that day forward, as long as we were in Australia, we never went in search of sausage again.

Time to venture out, leaving the security of the airport. With each step we took, we felt our level of excitement rising. Dragging our suitcases to the taxi stand, we were confronted with questions we didn't understand; we guessed he asked where we wanted to go. "Did you understand anything he was saying?" I asked Giselle.

"A little bit; it's the mumbling we don't get," she responded.

Fortunately, Giselle's English was better than mine. I could only hope my ears would adapt quickly. Australian English sounded nothing like what I had learnt. I handed the driver our piece of paper with the address. He said something which must have been 'No worries' or 'She'll be right, mate', phrases we both learnt quickly and off we went, faces pressed to the taxi window so we wouldn't miss any part of this alien world we were entering for the first time.

"Look, look, the ocean!" shouted Giselle, pointing in front of us. Later we learnt that this was the famous Bondi Beach. John and Ann lived a little further along the coast in Rose Bay, a slightly more affluent suburb. They had bought an old house which they were busy renovating.

Unloading our suitcases and paying off the driver, we survived our first hour in Australia. The sun was shining; the air was pleasantly warm, and it was springtime. We walked through a rusty iron gate towards the open front door. We knocked, "Halloo!" A guy came to the door, one of the workers helping John renovate. You could see at once that this chap was friendly; he recognised we were not fluent in English and deliberately talked slowly, a welcome gesture considering how tired we were.

He gave us Ann's work phone number and I left it to Giselle to talk to her. Ann suggested we use their bed to catch up on sleep. That sounded perfect, but we were too excited and went for a walk instead. We soon found ourselves at the face of a cliff. The ocean surf was splashing over rocks. It was mind-boggling to realise that just over a day ago, we were still in Hamburg, and now here we were right on the edge of the Pacific Ocean, our faces refreshed by the cool mist of salt water.

Back at John and Ann's house, we laid on their bed and slept soundly until 4pm when they arrived home and welcomed us. After a quick refresh in the half-renovated bathroom, John drove us to the airport to pick up Bernd. He had a similar experience, walking through customs without hassles. We returned to John's place, and finally for that eventful day, we settled down in an empty room except for some mattresses on the floor and went to sleep.

It was Wednesday, September 25.1974, the first morning we woke up in Australia. I became aware of the sea's endless, timeless roaring sound which I had never heard before.

No time to waste; we were keen to get going. The next shopping suburb was Bondi Junction; we boarded a bus and paid for three tickets. The bus went slowly, the engine coughing up the incline. Would it make it? Yes, we reached our destination in one piece.

We wandered around, taking in the new sounds and visual differences, shops, people, fashion and even funny-looking rubber footwear called thongs. Plenty to learn, but first, we needed to buy a few essentials like cups, plates and cutlery.

Our suitcases had been damaged en route, so we bought a metal trunk to store our belongings. Luckily it was empty and light enough to carry home.

We had asked John which bank we should use; he suggested the Commonwealth. Yes, we liked it, 'common' and 'wealth' make for a solid combination. Opening a joint savings account – our first – was remarkably easy, and we received a little booklet displaying our first cash entry.

By the time we left the bank, it had started to rain and was colder. We sought refuge in a pub. I ordered a cognac to warm Giselle up, not noticing the look of surprise on the bartender's face. I should have ordered brandy; the price difference was enormous.

I was constantly calculating the exchange rate; everything in Sydney seemed expensive. It was my turn to be surprised when a supermarket checkout lady called me 'love'. "Did you hear that?" I asked Giselle. "Did she say "Thanks, love?" My love replied, "I think so." Our confusion was cleared up over dinner at a Bondi restaurant when Ann and John explained that 'love' and 'honey' are everyday friendly expressions.

We also noticed men did not shake hands with women, and women didn't go into the pub but waited outside or in a lounge area to be served. Weirdest of all, you couldn't buy alcohol after 10pm. Not that we compared, but we couldn't help noticing.

The next day, Giselle and I bravely went out on our own. Bernd wanted to do his own thing. We boarded a double-decker bus; all the buses in the Sydney fleet seemed 100 years old. We were looking for sleeping bags, convenient for travelling, and useful meanwhile as bed covers.

As manager of the YMCA Kyokushin-style karate school in Sydney, John invited us to join his annual karate training camp in the Blue Mountains at the weekend. He warned us the nights would be cold. Luckily, we spotted a pair of green army-style sleeping bags that could be zipped open or even zipped together, making one giant bag. How good was that!

Happy with our purchases, we returned and met up with John and Bernd to check out real estate offices. We were keen to get out of John and Ann's hair as soon as possible; they had enough to do with their renovation.

Finding a suitable unit is never easy, and it was no different in Bondi where we wanted to live. We based our expectations on Germany's standards. In Hamburg, units are cosy, well furnished, spotless and – yes, the word applies again – gemütlich. John took time off work to drive us around to different places. It would have been impossible to do it ourselves, walking up and down those San Francisco-like hills around Bondi.

The first unit we saw, you could have heard our jaws drop. Whoever designed it appeared to have punishment rather than domestic comfort in mind. Forget about Gemütlichkeit. That carpet, was it really a carpet? Any second-hand dealer would have refused the furniture. We didn't even bother to go into the bedroom and quickly sought refuge in John's car.

Bondi Beach units fell way short of our expectations. People living here were lovers of the outdoor life and treated their apartment interiors accordingly.

Amazingly enough, we found an above-average exception to the rule, a suitable unit close to Bondi Beach. It was reasonably clean and sparsely furnished but relatively large. We loved the spectacular ocean view and didn't mind not having beautiful furniture. Yes, that would be our unit, within a 3-minute walk to the beach and in the only high-rise building around Bondi. It was a gem on the 5th floor, overlooking Bondi Beach. Rent was $34 per week, and we could move in on Monday, September 30.

The contrast between rainy grey Hamburg and glorious-looking Bondi Beach could not have been more stark.

Time to celebrate and thank John by inviting him for lunch. Not a big deal, we chose a modest snack bar and ordered hamburgers. Clearly, my dietary ambitions would have to wait for the time being.

The weekend training camp we were attending was perfect timing; instead of impatiently waiting to move into our unit, we would be busy with karate training.

Friday morning, bags packed, including our new sleeping bags, we headed in John's car for the Blue Mountains. The camp was in bushland, at a National Park camping ground. Most participants brought their own tents, but we would sleep comfortably in one of the on-site hut's bunk beds.

Once settled, we familiarized ourselves with the surroundings. A lake was a few meters from the campsite, and some kayaks were free to use.

John didn't give us much time to relax, pushing us promptly into our training regime. Tough enough to start with, it became even more challenging on day two for the forty or so participants, mainly men.

Night-time was cold – borderline freezing, in fact – but we slept in reasonable comfort, thanks to our sleeping bags.

Training recommenced bright and early with a twenty-minute meditation session on wet grass. Bruce Lee would have been in his element, but I was scarcely able to get to my feet after so long in the lotus position. We loosened up with a long run and only after that went to breakfast. Then the activities turned serious; if you can imagine one of those karate movies where everyone jumps around like crazy and takes on several combatants at once with punch-and-kick combinations. Next came Katas, precise movement forms that needed to be learnt and performed to perfection.

We used our free time to recuperate, paddling on the lake and hearing a kookaburra laugh. Our first thought was: Why is someone laughing at us?

We had a great time, full of new impressions, even if it was exhausting. Late in the afternoon, John drove us back, and we spent the last night at John and Ann's house.

・・・●・・●・・●・・

The last day of September found us busy packing up. At 11 am, we had a meeting with the landlord to finalise our lease. 'Landlord' was a new word to us; it sounded medieval. In our case, it was a French landlady with a curious fashion sense. She looked like she had just climbed out of bed. Was that a robe she had on or a loose-fitting dress? Her hair was uncombed, and she looked as if she hadn't slept last night, but she was very friendly, greeting us after we rang the bell and letting us into her house.

We paid two weeks in advance, plus electricity and bond money. The landlady went out of her way to make things easier, even opening an account for us with the electricity supplier. We received our keys and walked down towards our new home; her house was a short way up the road towards Bondi Junction.

The sun was shining as we arrived at the walkway leading to the building entrance on Sandridge Street. Opening the door to our unit, we were again captivated by the glorious views over Bondi Beach and the Pacific. We knew we had made the right choice; this was heaven.

The three of us had worked out how to split the $34 per week rent. Giselle and I would contribute $20, and Bernd $14. Bernd took the front lounge room with the balcony and kitchenette, while Giselle and I took the bedroom with ensuite bathroom. Both rooms had full-sized windows with those glorious ocean views.

We didn't stay long; there was more shopping to do. We needed pots, a frying pan and cleaning utensils. Back from shopping, we were busy cleaning the place up, assisted by a 'housewarming' bottle of wine.

It was apparent after the first couple of weeks; the three of us had different interests. We still explored a few things together, shopping for food, checking out the beach, and the nearby hotels which were basically pubs.

Bernd went out by himself, he loved the beach and wanted to learn surfing, and he loved hanging out in the hotels meeting girls. Once a week, Bernd and I went for karate training at John's club.

Giselle and I spent hours on long walks during which we would take photographs galore. When shopping, I was still comparing prices. Things we liked back home, such as camembert cheese, we couldn't find at all. Meat, however, was much cheaper, fruit and vegetables were plentiful, and we sampled new fruits such as rockmelon, pawpaw and avocado.

The butcher's shops had a dead meat smell we found hard to get used to, but from time to time, we bought enormous steaks for the weekend, enough for the three of us. On one of our walks to Bondi Junction, halfway up Bronte Road, we walked into a small shop we hadn't noticed before. To our surprise, behind its unassuming facade, we found a large delicatessen owned by Jewish people. Then, as now, Bondi was home to many Jewish people. To us, that shop was heaven-sent, full of foods we liked, all kinds of bread and cakes, and finally we could enjoy camembert again. When we walked in and asked the lady behind the counter if she had any, she laughed and pointed at a refrigerator full of camembert alongside other cheese varieties.

The walk up to Bondi Junction was short compared to other hikes we undertook around Sydney. Giselle and I set off nearly every morning loaded with camera gear and ready to be urban explorers. Most of the plants and trees we saw were new to us, and we loved the peculiar-looking letterboxes at the front of every house. At other times we took a bus to the city and systematically explored the CBD, leaving us with way too many photos of the Opera House and the Royal Botanic Garden.

We also wondered about those nurses in their lovely white uniforms, probably on some outing playing a ball game. Strangely enough, we saw women in identical outfits in most suburbs. Finally, I asked a passer-by on the footpath: 'What are those nurses playing?' He laughed or, more correctly, fell into a fit of hysterics: 'They're not nurses, they're LAWN BOWLERS! That's their bowling uniform: men wear white socks, shorts and shirts.' Now, we were laughing but still had no clue what this game's rules were but could see it resembled bocce, which we knew from Europe.

Naturally, we checked out Kings Cross and took photos of its fountain. We loved Paddington, admiring the rows of terrace buildings, some restored to their former glory. Gradually we acclimatised to our new environment and, with temperatures on the rise, we hoped for a day at the beach. One morning, feeling brave, we made our first official beach visit, taking towels and sun lotion. To protect ourselves from the wind, we hid behind a wall of sand we had dug out. Other brave beachgoers gave us funny looks. (*Didn't they know beach castles?*)

The next day was warm enough to get into the water. A stern-faced man approached us – he seemed to be a patrol officer or some other authority figure and told us off for getting undressed in public to change into our swimming gear. He pointed out the pavilion; apparently, one had to use the pavilion's dressing cabins. No nudity on Bondi Beach! It would take time for us to learn 'everything' about Australia.

The language continued to trip us up. Imagine our faces when we read the fine print on tins of food, 'Preservatives added.' In German, preservatives are condoms. Yes, indeed, we had a lot to learn. Everything was an adventure for us, including the language or the peculiar way it was used. We had noticed many 'Garage Sale' signs. Why was everyone selling their garage? Often adventures and fun go hand in hand, and more language adventures were coming up.

Bernd and I had established a routine of going to night-time karate classes in Pitt Street twice a week. After training, most of the boys went to a nearby pub for refreshments; naturally, we joined them. The Australian pub experience was still new for me, I scarcely knew how to order a beer, but I didn't have to; one of the karate guys handed me an ice-cold lager filled to the brim. A few minutes later, one of them told me, "Your shout!" I looked at him, clueless, and said, "What?" "It's your turn to shout beer," he insisted.

"OK, if you say so. BEE-ERRR!" John rescued me, handed me another glass of beer, and educated me in the fine art of ordering drinks and how to recognise a larrikin if you see one.

One of the guys was a German named Wolfgang; he had lived in Sydney for a couple of years. Incredibly, he came from the Hamburg suburb I'd grown up in, only two streets away, and had gone to the same church for confirmation classes. He had a car and drove us back to our unit. We invited him up and introduced him to Giselle. He told us about his Sydney experiences and promised to pick us up in the morning for a sightseeing tour. Next morning, he turned up and drove us far and wide through the suburbs, even as far as Manly Beach, where we visited the aquarium and saw sharks close up for the first time.

As the days became warmer, the beach became our main attraction. We didn't swim much but spent lots of time lying on the sand, reading and getting brown. We had seen a Chinese restaurant close to the beach with just six tables and the best part; they had a lunch meal for only $1.20, a once-a-week treat.

Out of the blue, we received a letter from the Australian Emigration Department. What did they want from us? We were naturally suspicious, but the letter merely contained friendly advice about free health benefits and work possibilities, with an address we could write to for more information.

Wolfgang had told us it was easy to rent a television. That sounded like a fun way to advance our English. We were already reading the newspaper every day with the help of a dictionary, so TV seemed the next logical step.

In a Bondi side street, we found a shop where you could buy or rent a set; the salesman was totally laid-back. "What's your name and address?" he asked us. We wrote it down – and that was it. We paid for the first month and the TV was ours to take away; no security measures, deposits or paperwork. All it had cost us was $9.40. Maybe we looked like people one could trust. Getting the TV back to our flat wasn't quite so easy. We had to carry it between us, occasionally stopping to catch our breath and collect our strength. There was no need to debate where it would go; we took it straight through to our bedroom, plugged it in and attached a portable aerial. Reception was good enough to watch a couple of channels. The news was on; a car company called Leyland – not a make of car we knew – had closed its doors. The news report said 3000 to 5000 workers had lost their jobs.

And something else was new, Australia's immigration policies had been changed, only well-qualified people were allowed in.

·····••·····

Bernd was spending more time doing his own thing. One day Giselle and I told Bernd that we were planning to drive around Australia by ourselves. He didn't seem to mind; he told us he was thinking of seeing more of the country, maybe going to Perth with friends for a couple of months. He was also looking for his own flat.

We continued our walking excursions around town. The variety of architectural styles – from inner-suburban terraces to low-roofed houses from the 1950s or buildings in the art deco style – amounted to a different 'cityscape' than we had known in Europe. It was combined with unusual creatures like goannas or lizards sunning themselves or lazy cats greeting us.

Every bit of green was called something-or-other park and most had barbecue areas which we didn't have in Germany. It was common to see public tennis courts and golf courses, something unthinkable in Hamburg where one had to be rich to join a tennis or golf club. Here, it seemed everyone played tennis; even school grounds had courts.

Giselle's birthday was creeping up, just a couple of days away. I had to do something. Mustering the limited culinary skills I inherited from Dad, I decided to bake her a cake. I tracked down the essential ingredients and baked a chocolate cake in a glass dish. It turned out a bit flat but smelt fantastic; obviously, Giselle had noticed my not-so-secret activities. It was official; we had our cake – and ate it too. It was yummy.

The money we transferred from Germany had still not arrived. What was going on with those banks? It couldn't be that hard to move a little bit of money. The cash we had with us was limited. Time to get serious; we paid the head office of the Commonwealth Bank a visit. After some slight communication issues, we obtained an agreement they would follow it up for us. Happy with our achievements, we returned to our unit. We told Bernd what we had done; his money hadn't arrived either.

After more phone calls and two more head-office visits, our money finally arrived. We never found out why it took so long but were relieved and glad it had. A pleasant surprise awaited us when we went to our local branch to collect it. During our protracted wait, the dollar had devaluated, gaining us much more for our hard-earned Deutschmarks. We splashed out and treated ourselves to a celebratory whisky and Coca-Cola even though we hardly ever drank whisky.

Bernd's money still hadn't arrived, and he had found a flat close by; we had to lend him $300 to pay the bond. He shared the flat with Jens, another German guy. Naturallly enough, we were invited to his house warming party. It wasen't the first party we were invited to. At our first party invitation, we were asked to bring a plate; we found it odd that they didn't have enough plates. Friendly as we were, we decided to take a few more plates. Luckily we found out beforehand what 'bring a plate' meant, sparing us major embarrassment.

A week after Bernd moved out, we had lunch in the sun-filled beer garden of the Bondi Hotel – steak, salad and, yes, beer. That day there was also a television crew filming happy hotel patrons and, even better, when we came home and switched on the telly that night, we watched ourselves on the screen.

It was getting hot by now, and we loved the freedom of leaving the unit dressed in only our swimwear and a towel wrapped around our bodies. We even adopted thongs as our favoured footwear. The two-minute walk to the beach warmed us up to a light sweat which meant we didn't need an invitation to cool down in the surf.

All this sun, sand and surf had made my face itchy. I shaved off my beard to give my face a treat. Giselle had never seen me without a beard, and there was a slight hesitation on my part, but no fear, Giselle took the scissors to cut away the scrub, and I cleaned up the rest with my shaver. I looked pretty weird; imagine a brown face with white patches where the beard used to be.

· · · · · · · · · ·

We loved the beach but were not the type to spend much time on it. It was a hot sandy environment and with our swimming skills not adapted to surf conditions, we were merely splashing around. We also had a hellish respect for sharks. I couldn't see very well without my glasses which contributed to my unease in the water. A swimming pool we passed on our walks down to the beach seemed worth checking out. Our typical swimming style, breaststroke, was best suited to calmer waters. As it happened, the pool was quite famous through its association with the Bondi Icebergs Club.

The following day we took our bath towels, went to that pool and paid 20cents entry fee each. It was a tidal pool filled with seawater and not chlorinated. Everything was concrete and natural rock; there were also wide concrete steps to sit on. Schoolchildren receiving their first swimming lessons had priority; then, it was our turn. We hopped in and swam the 50-metre length of the pool. At first, we only managed a couple of lengths but over the coming weeks, we eventually managed to swim 20 lengths.

On our second visit to the pool, we talked to the lady collecting the entry fee. Her name was Gabrielle. She and her husband Henry lived in a cottage next to the club as caretakers of the pool. We liked her; she was originally from France, grew up in Switzerland and spoke perfect German. That day, after the schoolchildren finished their lessons and left, Gabrielle invited us to her house. We kept talking into the late afternoon, and for the first time, we heard something positive about the aborigines and how they had been mistreated and misunderstood.

Gabrielle and Henry had travelled around Australia by car many years prior and had a passion for digging up precious stones. We knew instantly that gem hunting would be something for us in addition to photography when travelling around Australia.

They were also passionate about politics, against nuclear power and uranium mining and demanded better treatment for the Aboriginal population. Through them, we understood more about the political system and the then prime minister, Gough Whitlam.

Their creative spirit was prolific. They loved ballet and visual art and made jewellery out of the gemstones they had found or collected over the years; they even wrote poems and stories. They did everything we wanted to do; only they had done it thirty years ago. Before we left her home that afternoon, Gabrielle invited us to a recital at her friend's ballet school in the city. As if that weren't enough, she gave us two bath towels that had been left at the pool.

Every time we went back to the pool, Gabrielle had something new for us; that was how we ended up with a Gem Hunting Atlas of Australia. It whetted our appetite for digging up sapphires, topaz or amethyst, but also for opal, a gemstone we knew almost nothing about. She gave us one called a triplet which consisted of a thin layer of opal between a clear crystal top and a base that looked like plastic. Not a pure opal, more like an affordable version for the tourist trade, but we loved it.

She gave us another gift, something much more valuable than opals or any other gemstones. She told us that Giselle and I were soulmates, destined to be together, and our love for each other was not only obvious but rubbing off on the people we met.

We were touched by Gabrielle's observation, which profoundly influenced us. We knew we were well matched and hopelessly in love, but to hear that from someone else, particularly someone we liked and respected, heightened our awareness. We knew now that we were meant to be together.

Coming back to our unit and checking the mail brought us back to reality. We had mail from my mother and she was worried that nothing had been paid into my bank account. Many of my clients still hadn't paid their last invoices. We were less concerned and there were more imminent things to consider, like Christmas, but I knew I had to calm my mum's worries.

We were waiting for our parents' Christmas presents, hoping they would arrive in time. So far, it didn't even feel like Christmas. In Germany, seasonal decorations are everywhere, and Christmas markets invite you to overeat and drink too much glühwein. In Bondi, we hardly noticed that Christmas was five days away. The only decorations we saw were in the heart of the city, a giant Christmas tree in Martin Place and window decorations in the larger stores. We went to the carol singing in Hyde Park but still couldn't get that Christmas feeling. It was too warm for us.

Back at the unit, we decorated a branch of a native bush with Christmas decorations, courtesy of Gabrielle. At least it was something, and we were planning to buy glorious food for our festivities and a better brand of whisky. In the meantime, we were hanging out looking for the mailman to deliver our presents.

Another letter from my mother arrived three days before Christmas. My aunt had died. Aunty Hannie was my father's sister; Giselle had only met her once. So sad, we liked her, and she was fond of us. That dampened our Christmas spirit even more.

Christmas Eve, and not a sign of festivity anywhere. We still had not received our long-awaited Christmas parcels, but there was one more chance. We waited until 11 am before we walked to our local post office, "Has any parcel arrived for Luske or Uyma?" we asked. We didn't have to ask; she knew us and what we were waiting for. After disappearing into the next room, increasing our suspense, she emerged with two parcels and some mail. "Thank you, and Merry Christmas to you!" she greeted us. Happy, we grabbed our parcels and raced back to our unit.

We were good little kids, placing the parcels under our homemade Christmas tree and resisting the temptation to open them until night-time, a German tradition. To kill time, we went back to the pool to cool off. Gabrielle invited us in for a Christmas drink and gave us a present; we only had a card for her. We spent the rest of the afternoon walking around Bondi, buying more festive food. To our eyes, no one seemed to be in a Christmas mood; it was like any other day.

Time to get back to our unit, cook our dinner and prepare for our own Christmas Eve Party. After dinner, we opened our parcels and sampled some of the Christmas sweets our parents had sent us.

On Christmas morning, we had a bird's-eye view from our balcony of the Australian Christmas unfolding below us on Bondi Beach. Families were celebrating on the beach, a totally different Christmas experience. Something shifted in our perceptions that day. We missed Christmas in a cold climate but at the same time we could see how much fun it was to spend Christmas Day on the beach, even if we were only watching from afar.

We had no hope for a spectacular New Year's Eve but we were invited by Gabrielle's friends to a party somewhere in North Sydney, and it would be a costume affair. Time enough to prepare. Gabrielle had lots of suitable dresses and accessories stored in her cupboard. We tried various combinations until, with the help of a few cocktails, we finally found something ideal. Giselle would be going as a gypsy; I would be dressed as an Arab. No one cared about authenticity as long as we dressed up and brought a plate; by now, we knew what that meant. I would bake a chocolate cake for this grand occasion and deliver it on a plate.

We used the remaining few days of the year planning our future. I did my usual end-of-the-year activity, bringing the year purposefully to an end and starting something excitingly new. I was prone to spend considerable time on those tasks. I cheerfully indulged in my self-appreciation activities within the first few pages of my diary.

Planning our future endeavours was an intoxicating task. Giselle and I were sitting for hours plotting and scheming. Our long-term goal was to get our own house. In the short term (1975), we aimed to buy a car, find jobs to experience Australia's working conditions and to travel around Australia to write a book illustrated with our photographs.

Goals have unique ways of manifesting themselves. A part of our newfound lifestyle philosophy was to spot opportunities and make the best of them which included turning negatives into positives. We heard about Cyclone Tracy which devastated Darwin over Christmas. How could we turn that into something positive for us? We decided to start travelling later and work longer than intended, to save up more money.

We discussed those topics over our favourite breakfast, banana on toast with honey. Not sure how that started, but we had both developed a sweet tooth since arriving in Australia. Giselle became a chocoholic and was addicted to Toblerone.

Finally, the New Year's Eve party came along. It was at Avalon Beach, in a mansion high on a hill, surrounded by even more expensive-looking homes and gardens. We were amazed to see banana plants, citrus fruit and other exotics we had never encountered before. The balcony view overlooked a bay called Pittwater which was crowded with large numbers of sailing boats. My chocolate cake was well received, but the party was a bit of a non-event. It was all about eating and drinking; no dancing or fireworks.

Just days into the New Year, we noticed our skin was coming out in little red spots, mainly on our legs. We showed Gabrielle the affected areas, and she immediately knew what was afflicting us. "Those are sand flea bites," she explained, "You need to clean the carpet in your unit."

This meant a visit to our landlady. She looked horrific again, wearing a soiled white blouse over a swimsuit. Who could blame her, it was hot, but it didn't instil much confidence regarding our flea issue. We needn't have worried; she promised to come over the next day and take care of it.

That afternoon we went back to the pool; I had promised to help clean the pool, little realising what a tough job that would be. It turned out more like an extreme sport than a helping hand. By the time we arrived, Henry had already pumped the water out of the pool. What remained was a lot of sand, which needed to be swept and shovelled out. Giselle helped to sweep the pool.

Standing in the pool, we were confronted by a three-metre-high wall, with the ocean on the other side. Our challenge was to shovel all that sand back into the sea.

I still have no idea how Henry could do such hard work at his age. Despite being fit due to karate training, I was in pain for a few days after the ordeal. From then on, I helped him weekly but I concentrated on technique rather than showing off to Henry.

As promised, our landlady turned up with a man in tow. They vacuumed the whole place and sprayed the carpet with a lethal fluid. She swore it would do the trick.

It looked like the New Year was testing our positive philosophy. On a Saturday morning, we paid Gabrielle a visit. Her house was surrounded by a high wooden fence. To open the gate, you had to reach through a hole to turn the latch on the other side. We'd done that often but this time, as Giselle slipped her hand through, she screamed with pain. Gabrielle's dog, Tessie, must have been scared and bit Giselle's hand. Having heard her scream, Gabrielle rushed out and quickly daubed the wound with iodine, then gave her a painkiller and a sedative. Still in shock, Giselle was shaking. "Is it dangerous? Do I need to go to the doctor?" she asked Gabrielle who reassured her: "No, it will settle down. We don't have rabies in Australia."

Giselle calmed down and we even stayed for lunch; everything seemed fine, but she needed to lie down once we were back in our unit. Giselle got up for dinner, feeling better, but around eleven that night, the pain increased and we noticed a red line slowly creeping up to her elbow. Panic stations; what to do now? At this time of night, there was no alternative but to seek emergency attention. We went downstairs and hailed a taxi; the driver took us to St Vincent's Hospital. A nurse attended promptly to Giselle but I had to wait until 2 am before she came out, her arm in a sling, but smiling and feeling better. She received two injections and had to take penicillin tablets every six hours. The hospital treatment was free; we only paid $1.50 each way for the taxi. Another experience behind us, even though it took a couple of days for the discomfort to diminish.

• • • • • • • • • •

For Bernd, 1975 began with his handing over $140 for an old Holden station wagon that drove perfectly OK. We had our sights set a little higher; we needed a vehicle reliable enough to transport us around Australia. A station wagon would do us nicely, or a panel van, as we liked the idea of living and sleeping in the car.

On Saturdays, we followed a morning ritual; a quick walk to the newsagent's to buy the Sydney Morning Herald, Australia's oldest continuously published newspaper, and a magazine featuring a full seven-day program schedule, appropriately named TV Week.

We were ready to look for work but there were no suitable jobs to be found. Bernd was also looking for work, but January was not a good month as businesses were closed and life proceeded in slow motion.

In the meantime, we continued our leisurely life, I wrote a few short stories about our Australian life, accompanied by our photos while Giselle sketched scenes of Bondi.

In a letter to our friend Mark, I upset him inadvertently; I had voiced a few observations which may have sounded like I was criticising Sydney.

For instance, we had noticed that garbage trucks around Bondi drove from one collection point to the next without any covering and consequently a lot of rubbish fell off or blew off. Such comments infuriated Mark but we still continued writing to each other. Letter writing definitely helped to develop my English writing skills.

We also continued to take long walks during which we discovered new sights and took many photos. Each time we followed a specific route with clear intentions of what we wanted to photograph. Our most extensive hike took us all the way to La Perouse, a distance of around 26 kilometres..

A few times, we marched from Bondi, following the coastline, to Double Bay which was a rewarding photogenic walk with great views of the City, many little parks for a quick rest, and even a lighthouse. The highest vantage point is Bellevue Park, with spectacular views of Sydney's Harbor, South Head and Bondi Beach.

My not-too-distant past was catching up with me with every letter I received from my parents. Too many of my former clients and Peter, who bought my business, still had not paid. I had no choice but to pen some semi-nice threatening letters. It was a tricky business; they had to be neither too harsh nor too lenient. My aim was for the golden path, right in the middle. They knew how powerless I was to act from Australia; it is not called "down under" for nothing.

My poor parents were feeling the stress more than us. We remained in a happy holiday mood, eager to leave all the old stuff behind and march forward with our exciting future.

Talking about our holiday mood, we went horse riding with a group of friends.

Even before we arrived, I felt like a cowboy, stimulated by childhood memories of being a fearless cowboy. Now I could be a cowboy on a real horse.

But our first attempt at horse riding was a failure. The horses won! Since we had paid upfront, we decided to sit on the horse and take funny photos. In the end, we surrendered and dismounted, relieved to be still alive.

We knew Sydney and its surroundings pretty well by now. Wolfgang took us to many beaches around Sydney and another friend, Peter, a Swiss guy, also a keen photographer, took us chasing sunsets or other photo opportunities. It was time for us to get mobile and buy a car.

Chapter 3

Getting Mobile

It was time to buy a car and get serious about finding a job. Constantly reading the papers had paid off; we had found a few suitable cars to look at. Peter drove us to the various addresses. The first few were sub-standard or too small but the last one we checked out that Easter Good Friday had potential.

We already liked it when we saw it in the driveway, a big yellow panel van with black racing stripes. It was an XW Ford Falcon, the ideal travel car, large and in good condition. A fashionable car for surfers, only four years old, with sporty-looking attachments and a modified gear assembly, a racing floor-shift gearstick. After a bout of hard bargaining, the seller reduced the asking price from $1600 to $1300. We had the car we wanted; it would be our home for the next couple of years.

Now, we had to drive home. I asked Peter if he could lead the way, ensuring I would not drive on the wrong side of the road.

In the following days, driving around Sydney, more for practice than sightseeing, we noticed problems with that fancy gearshift stick. A mechanic from a nearby service station had a look and fixed it. Unfortunately, the repair put us back another $200. He also informed us that the modified gearshift would cause problems. Exposed to the road's dust and dirt, it would need constant cleaning.

Even though we had our international driver's licences, we decided to apply for Australian ones. We were required to sit for a theory test and were handed a little booklet to study Australian road rules. After the second attempt on the same day, one after the other, we both had our official permits to drive.

We had the car; now, we went in search of at least a month's work for the experience and to earn money to buy equipment for our planned journey. Some job ads in the papers looked promising; there was even work available for fashion models (unless that was a scam and one had to pay a fortune upfront to have one's photo taken). *Could we be fashion models?* Giselle definitely could; me, I don't think so!

Having run my own business, I had never experienced the nerve-racking process of asking for a job. I had collected addresses from businesses in the amusement machines industry, including jukeboxes, pinballs, poker machines, arcade games and the first video game consoles, such as Atari's Paddle series.

Bernd had given me addresses as well. He had found a job quickly and it was well paid. It felt weird to be applying for a job at the ripe age of twenty-five. It was a new feeling to be at the mercy of someone else's approval.

At the first business, which looked more like a garage workshop, I muddled up my English.

"Good day; I am looking for a job. Do you have anything for me?" I'd forgotten to introduce myself, let alone state what type of work I wanted. They could have thought my ambition was to clean their windows which I noticed certainly needed cleaning.

They declined my offer, "Sorry mate, nothing here for you."

My second interview ran more smoothly, but the employer had all the staff he needed but he gave me a promising address.

Boosted by that good experience, I boldly went for the third address. Giselle always waited in the car for me; she saw job hunting as an act of amusement. After all, we knew we would be quitting in four to six weeks.

The third job interview went splendidly; I said all the right things. It may have helped that the boss was German. He would have liked to hire me but had no position available. "Wait," he added, hopped on the phone and talked to another manager, also a German, and this development sounded promising. When he was off the phone, he gave me the address and urged me to drive there straightaway.

Fourth time lucky! The manager, Fred, showed me around, explaining everything as he went, and asked me if I liked it. I did.

He talked to the big boss, and I was hired on the spot, for $100 a week. That was good money. Fred told me it was the usual beginner's wage and would go up after a few months if they liked me. That was unlikely but I was glad to have that job. I would start on Monday: the hours were 9 am to 5.30. I learnt that the company had outlets in Melbourne and Perth. Who knows, there might be an opportunity for a job if our travel took us to those cities.

For my first day at work, we left early, and I dropped Giselle off in the city. She wanted to look for a job as a window dresser or something similar and had decided to walk from one shop to the next until she found a job.

I arrived early at my new workplace and couldn't help comparing it with my experiences in Germany. Here, it was less tidy, which was a polite way of putting it.

We had slowly grown used to Australians' fondness for four-letter words, the ones not taught in our school English curriculum. Talking to Gabrielle and Henry, we had never been confronted with terms like bloody, fuck or the like.

That morning was my initiation into a different language altogether. I was shown around the repair shop with comments like, "Over there, all machines are fucked; they need fixing." And apparently, most things seem to be "bloody."

I had slight difficulties getting all the meanings of what was said. Fred kept on enlightening me as we went around, "Don't worry mate, you get used to it."

The company covered a vast area, with different departments and rooms for repairing all kinds of amusement machines, even coin-operated kiddie rides and arcade games.

My first job was in a large room with at least 100 arcade games; I had to get ten of them working by cannibalising spare parts from the others. Most were car or bike racing games.

I had brought my own tools; other mechanics wandered over to check how I was coping. They loved my tools and repair gadgets, especially my soldering gun and precision pliers for gaining access to tricky spaces. They appeared to accept me and were clearly a friendly bunch. Even the boss dropped by to see how I was getting on before he led me to a large showroom crammed with new machines, including coin-operated pool tables.

That first day on the job was fun, with no hassles and the atmosphere was remarkably relaxed. I also learned new expressions to enrich my English word repertoire.

"Don't worry" and "She'll be right mate" were favourites.

Others I didn't understand at first, "Give us a lift mate". "What?" OK, got it.

On one occasion, I needed to carry something heavy to a workbench and asked one of the guys, "Can you give me a lift?" "Sure," he said and lifted me up. Those guys had their fun, and it wasn't the only time.

Driving home, I felt a bit like an Australian; even so, I didn't have a clue how they felt, but they were more laid-back than their German counterparts. They had a kind of connection – a camaraderie of sorts – that verged on the tribal. They were quick to recognise whether someone belonged to their ranks or not.

I couldn't wait to get home and tell Giselle everything. We talked for hours. After I left Giselle in the city, she went into any appropriate shop and asked for a job. In some shops, she received a simple "no" but in others, she had a conversation and was able to learn about the general business of decorating shop interiors and shop windows.

Finally, Giselle ended up at a huge department store called Farmers. Once she found the most suitable sales division, it was smooth sailing. They liked her experience and offered Giselle a position. She would be responsible for interior décor and window displays. Giselle would be well paid; her weekly wage would be $2 more than mine.

I had an exciting second working day. Seemingly impressed by my work on day one, the boss shifted me to a room where I had to fix pinball machines all day. The exciting bit came later when he told me they had sold a large consignment of machines to a guy who ran an amusement arcade in Narooma, a small seaside town on the South Coast of New South Wales. Someone would have to fly there to ensure all those machines were in working order. Guess who that someone was going to be! Could things get any more exciting? Flying in to do a repair job was a new one for me.

Wednesday was payday; the company secretary handed me an envelope with two days' pay, $39. I'd expected $40, but $1 was deducted for tax. I had forgotten about that. I realised that from the promised weekly wage of $100, I would see only $97.50, but I could live with that.

That afternoon, the manager from my third job application, Gerhard, visited me. I hadn't expected ever to see him again. What did he want? He told me that word gets around quickly in this industry and apparently I had become a desirable item. He couldn't say too much; he had come to tell me to call him the next day. I was intrigued.

At night, Giselle and I were competing over who would talk first. Giselle had similar experiences to mine and was enjoying her new job. Everyone at the store was friendly, easy-going and well-spoken.

When I phoned Gerhard before work the following day, he made me a fantastic offer, which I must admit went to my head a bit. He offered me the post of chief technician at $120 a week, and the position would come with a company car. My request for a couple of days to think about it didn't faze him. "Sure thing," Gerhard said, "take your time."

I liked where I was working, not that I could compare it to anything, but everyone was friendly and the working environment was comfortable. I also had to factor in that semi-promised plane trip to Narooma which was very tempting. An evil plan began to brew in my mind; I would try to leverage my worth to these rival bosses in order to jack up my earnings. Giselle thought this was a brilliant move; it was as if that extra $20 was already in my pocket.

Next day, Fred wasn't in the building. I asked a co-worker about Fred, and he muttered something like, "He had a piss-up last night." I wasn't sure what that meant. Did he have a bladder infection? No, apparently, Fred enjoyed a few too many beers. He'd be back tomorrow, "no worries".

The next day couldn't come quickly enough. After getting in to work, I wasted no time, taking Fred aside and confiding to him, "I've received a great offer from Gerhard – $120 per week and a company car. Do you think the boss would agree to give me a pay rise?"

"Let's find out," he said, and off we went to seek out the big boss but ended up talking to the company bookkeeper who thought it should be all right; he would consult the boss.

It all worked out. I didn't get a company car but then I didn't ask for one either, though deep down, I was hoping for a sweetener to make up for that part of the competition's offer.

For the following few weeks, work progressed smoothly, and we concentrated on getting our car in tip-top shape. I had bought a do-it-yourself car repair manual in preparation for fixing breakdowns in the middle of nowhere. During my half-hour lunch break, one of my workmates took me on his motorbike to shops and places where I bought every spare part I possibly would need for venturing deep into the outback. Fan belts, carburettor repair kits, radiator hoses, gaskets, air filter, a jerry can with petrol, and lots of bolts, nuts, clamps and whatever seemed handy.

Giselle was busy decorating the interior of our mobile home. We wanted it to be fully carpeted without spending heaps of money and came up with the idea of asking carpet shops for free samples or offcuts. It worked; after visiting only three shops, we had enough pieces to cover the van's interior in a 'psychedelic' variety of colours. It now felt super *gemütlich* and it muffled the external traffic noise. Better still, Giselle used her staff discount to buy fabric which she turned into makeshift storage bags. We fastened a row of bags to each wall of the van's interior to accommodate our belongings. Our car had become our home.

The van's undercarriage, where the spare tyre was meant to be became our cellar. Germans need their cellars. No Sydneysider had a cellar unless it was a wine cellar. We had one now and used it to store our tinned food. On top of the vehicle, two small racks screwed together made one rack spanning the length of the van. The spare tyre went up there, and we bought another in case we had two punctures on the long and lonely roads.

We had a friendly neighbour, a mechanic who had helped out doing some maintenance work on our car. A country boy, he knew the outback well and insisted we should buy ourselves a gun. "Everyone has a gun in the country," he said, and we would need one too. We had noticed guns were on sale even at Woolworths. Having no idea about firearms, we didn't see them as a priority. They were not as crucial as a car bench covering as we had been burnt several times on the hot plastic seating.

The front cabin, where we would spend most of our time, had a couch instead of bucket seats, and with our stereo equipment, cassette, car radio and an ashtray to keep small change in, it had an unmistakable lounge feel to it. The back of the van, with its floor carpets, cloth-bag wardrobe and sleeping quarters, became our bedroom. The likeness to a house on wheels didn't end there; the lower rear fold-down door was our balcony which doubled as a table and the fold-up section was our sunroof.

The car outfitting had cost more than expected. The foam mattress was pretty expensive and so were the gas bottle, camp cooker, pots and pans. The day of reckoning would come soon. I felt some apprehension about quitting my job. Giselle had fewer hesitations but I had become quite friendly with my work mates and they had no idea about our impending great escape.

One afternoon at work, Fred interrupted me and announced that the big boss wanted to see me. "What's it about?" I asked. His only reply was, "Don't worry, she'll be right."

But I did worry I had nicked some screws, wires, and other items I'd seen lying around which didn't look like they'd be of much use to anyone.

Fred was right; nothing to worry about, and the boss was in a good mood. That Narooma customer had placed an order for more machines and was standing right beside my boss. It was time to spring into action; they needed me to fly to Narooma.

That was how I met Tino. With the first sentence he uttered, I knew he was Italian. His English pronunciation was worse than mine. In other words, we understood each other perfectly.

He was a likeable guy; short, compact, full of energy, smiling, maybe ten years older than me and, as I would soon find out, very generous. Everything was arranged for me to fly down to Narooma a couple of days later. All I needed were my tools and the plane ticket.

Getting up with the sun in Bondi was a glorious experience. One hardly could see the ocean, a carpet of sun-instigated glitter disguising it. Each morning, we witnessed that spectacular light show unless we were still sleeping. But I didn't sleep that morning; I was wide awake, even before the sun rose. Could I feel a few butterflies in my stomach? I wasn't sure if I was nervous or excited; I had never before had the opportunity to fly to work.

I kissed Giselle goodbye; she was excited with me. Driving to the airport went smoothly. I had envisaged a complicated check-in process, but it was a piece of cake, I only had to show my ticket.

"Through that exit, please," said the check-in lady, pointing to a door. Walking hesitantly onto the tarmac, I was looking for the plane. Where was the plane? I was about to go back when another passenger behind me pointed to a toy plane, "Over there, that's ours." My confidence declined while my butterflies increased. I had expected a small plane, but not that small. I climbed up a couple of steps; the pilot sitting in his cockpit turned around and called out, "Just take a seat". That was the boarding procedure. I placed my tool bag in front of me and watched a few more passengers arrive, six in all, if I remember correctly.

"Everyone seated? Let's go," the pilot said and the plane slowly crept along the runway. Next minute, we were up; it was pretty painless, actually. Nice view; I didn't think we were flying very high. The pilot announced Narooma was 180km by air, about 1 hour of flight time. He was right. I had hardly settled down, admiring the view and the cockpit and we were landing. Kind of nice; I wouldn't mind flying to work more often.

Stepping out of the plane, I noticed I had come to a tiny country airstrip. It couldn't be called an airport, it was more like a garage but it had one of these windsocks which indicated it was an airport of some kind.

Tino walked over from the garage shed, greeting me, "How was the flight?'"

"Very nice," I replied. Actually, I would have liked to say, "Bloody fantastic," but I was still not comfortable answering the Australian way.

He pointed to a car; I put my tools into the boot, and off we went to his business premises. It was located right opposite a beach; two fishing boats were tied up at a pier, an idyllic scene.

Come the Christmas season, that beach would be packed. The holidays were Tino's top-earning weeks. For the rest of the year, his amusement parlour and milk bar relied on trade from the locals.

Tino made me feel at home, introducing his English wife, Jenny, and their four boys. First off, he made me a large milkshake; I think it was more ice cream than milk. "Help yourself to anything you like," he said, pointing to the shelves around the milk bar.

It was still early, mid-morning, when I started work. There were a dozen pinball machines to repair and, in addition, Tino wanted me to check, clean and adjust the coin slots for all the machines on the premises, including the pool tables.

The day went by much too fast; it felt more like fun than work. We even played pool and Tino invited me to the golf club for lunch where we played the pokies with 5 cent pieces. That night, work completed, Tino cooked a spaghetti dinner for the whole family, including me. Best spaghetti I ever had, authentic Italian, or maybe just Tino's way.

Over dinner, Tino questioned me about Giselle and what we had done before coming to Australia. I felt Tino was fishing for something specific and after I outlined the concept of our travel goals, he came out with his proposition. "Will you be back from your travels by Christmas?" he asked.

"We're not sure yet, but yes ... most likely, we will stay in Sydney before we take off again."

"Do you think you could stay here and work for the season?" he quizzed me and while I was considering, he continued, "You and Giselle could stay here for free, bed and all meals provided, and I will pay you in cash."

I hadn't seen that coming, it sounded perfect, exactly the opportunity we had been looking for – extra cash to finance another year's travel.

"Thanks, Tino, sounds great. I will talk to Giselle, but I am sure she will like the idea as well."

"When will you start travelling?" he asked.

I trusted him and answered accordingly, "Please don't say anything, but I will quit my job within the next couple of weeks, and we will hit the road a few days later."

Tino didn't miss an opportunity; "Why don't you stop here for a few days of work and maybe travel to Canberra? I have relatives there you could stay with."

"Sounds like another great idea; I'll let you know".

Shortly before 8 pm, we arrived at Narooma's fabulous airport – no check-in at all. It was like boarding a bus. The pilot looked at my ticket and invited me to sit next to him in the cockpit. Only two more passengers arrived and the toy plane went off into the night.

Coming home, Giselle was still awake, sitting on our bed, laying cards. I bombarded her with all my news. We agreed to go along with Tino's plan; it was an unexpected gift, and we couldn't be any happier; everything was going our way.

·•·•·•••·•·

Countdown to our take-off. Soon, we would exchange our unit for a car home, travelling and living free as birds. Now came the tricky part, I had to quit my job. The company had been good to me and would assume I had taken the position under false pretences.

I need not have worried; I forgot I was in Australia where people constantly change jobs, unlike in Germany where people stay for a lifetime.

The boss not only wished me all the best; he even gave me a good work reference. All too easy; I had to get used to the "she'll be right, mate" attitude. I worked through to the end of the week, collecting my final pay and reference on the Friday. Giselle experienced the same goodwill from her own employer.

We had already cancelled the unit lease and received our bond back on Friday. Our landlady was happy; she was getting her unit back in a better condition than when we arrived.

The last days were spent visiting friends, last-minute shopping, joining the NRMA (on Gabrielle's advice) for its road breakdown service; we even bought a fishing rod, not that we had any idea about fishing. The final purchase was a gold pan, and we saw ourselves already rich with gold and gemstones, we were overflowing with excitement and positivity.

Chapter 4

Taking to the Road

Autumn 1975 – Bondi, Sydney, NSW, Australia

We left on a Saturday morning and quickly stopped at Gabrielle and Henry's place to say goodbye. They were as excited as we were. At the last minute, Gabrielle handed me a warm jacket, explaining that it gets cold at night in the Outback. I found that hard to believe, but what would I know? In case we got bogged, they also gave us a piece of carpet to place under the tyres for traction. We hugged them one last time, hopped into our panel van and put Bondi firmly in our rear-view mirror.

What a feeling of freedom it was, seated in the front of our beloved van, music playing from our cassette collection; Manitas de Plata, our favourite flamenco guitarist, did his best to lift our good mood even more. Life was beautiful!

As the scene shifted from urban to country, we swapped de Plata for another cassette, Canned Heat's On the Road Again. We loved the sentiment and it became our theme song throughout our journey across the continent.

Our first stop, and our first night sleeping in the car, was at Kiama, a coastal town south of Sydney. It was a sleepy little town - obviously sleepy - we arrived late at around 7pm.

We found a caravan park and haggled with the manager about the fee which included the use of electricity, toilets and showers. Our point was we needed less space than a caravan; therefore, we should pay less. The caretaker, who appeared more amused than annoyed, reduced the fee from $1.60 to 60 cents. Before leaving Sydney, Giselle and I had vowed to be thrifty to last the distance. This was a good start.

We knew nothing about Kiama, but the caretaker was adamant we couldn't leave town without seeing its No. 1 tourist attraction, a 'blowhole.'

"A what?" I asked.

"A blowhole. Seawater shoots up through a hole in the rocks and blows out water."

"Hmm,' I replied, "OK, we will have a look tomorrow."

The first night went well, lying on our bed, reading with the help of an electric light plugged into an extension cord and into the power outlet which we had told the caretaker we wouldn't use. How naughty were we? We slept reasonably well but learned to make sure the car was parked dead level.

The emotions we felt that morning were something out of this world and possibly can only be experienced once in a lifetime. Here we were, happy as anything, after having refreshed ourselves at the shower block, not shaving, which was a thing of the past, and sitting down for breakfast.

Everything was a first for us including boiling tea and eggs on our one-ring gas cooker. We had never, ever gone camping before. But this was no camping; this was living! With the freedom we had gained, nothing could hold us back. Sitting next to our makeshift breakfast table (the van's rear door), we enjoyed our feast of tea, eggs, bread, butter, jam and yoghurt.

The sun had come up and it was still a bit nippy. I wore the jacket Gabrielle had given me at the last minute. Giselle wore a cardigan and, clasping a mug of tea in both hands, was cuddling up to me. We looked at each other and shared the feeling of deep contentment with life that comes from having no responsibilities to anyone but ourselves as well as a burning desire to experience life and our journey. Just then, a cat walked by, jumped on my lap, curled up and started purring, and so was I. "I think we have to get going soon. We should try to reach Narooma by lunchtime," I said. The cat, which must have been listening, stretched and jumped down but then jumped on to Giselle's lap. "Let's go," I said. The moment Giselle answered "OK," the cat jumped off.

Before driving to Narooma, we went to look at that famous blowhole. It didn't look like much but stepping closer to look down the hole, I learnt how it had acquired its name. With great force, water sprayed up through the hole and I had my second shower of the day. Giselle, who had kept her distance, laughed and handed me a towel.

We arrived at Narooma in time for lunch. Tino and Jenny welcomed us and introduced Tino's brother and wife who were staying for the day. Another brother arrived later with his family, wife, kids and father-in-law, all Italian.

Sitting in Tino and Jenny's kitchen and sharing lunch with this extended family, we felt Italian ourselves! Tino was grilling steaks and the kitchen table was laden with various salads and fresh bread. Father John arrived, the parish priest, and joined the table, completing the Italian atmosphere.

After lunch, Tino and I went next door to the amusement hall; we had work to do. It was full-on and it seemed we would need to stay longer than planned. Tino, cheekily, had anticipated this necessity and booked us into a local motel for the week.

No one could accuse Tino of having an all-work-and-no-play attitude. After work, we got ready to hit the town. Tino was a member of all Narooma's clubs – bowls, golf and something called the RSL. We found out later it was a club for servicemen who had been to war. Had Tino been a soldier, we wondered. No, he hadn't. It turned out that anyone could join the club. Tino paid for dinner, and then we hit the pokies followed by crazy dancing until 1am.

After one week of Italian family life, including Father John, we felt sad about leaving Narooma behind but were looking forward to seeing the national capital. There was no autobahn to Canberra; no autobahn anywhere. We had to get used to dirt tracks and gravel roads.

That week, Giselle and I transformed into an incredible fixing team. Together we reconditioned dilapidated pinball machines. I stripped them of their electrical and mechanical parts while Giselle cleaned and repainted the bodies and "resurfaced" the playing field by gluing a transparent plastic film on top to make the pinball go lightning fast. As a final touch, a good dose of polish from our friend 'Mr Sheen.' Tino didn't take Giselle's work for granted; he paid her as well.

Working together saved a lot of time and felt wonderful. We even daydreamed about one day opening an amusement hall of our own.

Jenny knew of our interest in digging for precious stones and introduced us to a friend who had a tumbling machine for polishing semi-precious stones like agates and jasper. We saw the finished product; beautiful, colourful pebble-like stones. It sounded like a good business idea and gave us even more reason to hunt for gems and other precious stones.

Before we left, Tino gave us a box of potatoes which ended up on the roof rack because the cellar was full. Potato dinners would be the norm for the next few weeks. We promised Jenny and Tino we would be back by mid-December and agreed to stay until the end of January.

Back on the road again. Consulting our gem hunting atlas, we knew we would pass fossicking opportunities on the way to Canberra. We felt like treasure hunters. Finding precious stones would give us exciting topics and great photos for our planned book.

We left Narooma early in the morning. The drive turned out to be beautiful, mainly pastures and winding roads up and down hills, with dirt or gravel road most of the way. We reached a picturesque valley with a tiny village called Araluen. According to our map, there was gold in those creeks, but it started to rain and turned cold so we decided to put our gold-panning careers on hold and drove straight to Canberra.

We arrived at the home of Tino's brother Silvio at around 8 pm; no one was home, and by now, it was freezing. We parked in the driveway and treated ourselves to a couple of glasses from a flagon of sherry. While we were waiting, we may have had a few too many and we went blissfully to sleep.

Loud knocking on the car door woke us up; it was Silvio! He invited us in for breakfast and to freshen up. In an instant, we found ourselves in Little Italy. The family had stayed at the house of Silvio's other brother overnight, and now everyone had come back with him. Italian, German, and broken English conversations were flying about. I have no idea exactly how, but we understood each other perfectly. Mind you, the parents-in-law spoke no English at all.

Silvio and his wife had given us a list of landmarks to see while in Canberra. Old Parliament House topped the list, which in 1975 was known simply as 'Parliament House.'

We left after breakfast, map in hand, and tried to make sense of the city's numerous roundabouts. 'Going round in circles' is more than a figure of speech in Canberra. So confused were we that we drove in the wrong direction at one point. No harm done, a bit of beeping and lights flashing and we realised our mistake and managed to turn around.

Parliament House is a grand old building and we took way too many photos.

Among other landmarks we visited were the Australian War Memorial, one or two galleries and some churches. We even looked at the German Embassy which resembled a 1950s-style government building, sterile German architecture. It may have been the first time we became aware of something looking distinctively German and somehow out of place.

In the afternoon, we came across a vast grassy space crowded with people looking at hot-air balloons of all shapes and sizes. It was quite a spectacle, never having been close to one such balloon, let alone fifty. Carloads of spectators were parked around this oval which was called a showground, something we didn't have in Germany.

We made it back in time for dinner; afterwards they took us to the movies. It was an all-Italian cinema and an original black and white Italian film. Even though we didn't understand the dialogue, we easily followed the plot. The cinema experience was more fun than the movie; it was a real family affair. Everyone was present, babies, young adults, parents and grandparents, all Italian. There was laughing, clapping and whistling. It was way after midnight when we went to bed.

Next morning after breakfast, we left for Sydney; it was raining, and we didn't make many stops. We returned to our old flat, now occupied by a friend of ours. He had collected our last mail. In the future, we would have our mail forwarded to whatever city was our next destination, care of the post office.

That night we slept at Bernd's place. The next morning, we bought an extension cord, a frying pan, a little broom, and more food, and then, we were on the road again, still raining, but travelling north, anticlockwise around Australia.

We stopped in Gosford and stayed at a caravan park. People live there; the caravans hadn't been moved for a while and we felt out of place. We hoped for opportunities to camp overnight off-road instead of paying a camping fee, a cost we hadn't budgeted for and more expensive than we anticipated.

We picked an unfortunate time for travelling. It had rained steadily for two weeks, and the forecast was for more rain. We left Gosford and continued north. Our gem hunting map indicated sapphire fields near Glen Innes.

Even with the rain, we enjoyed being on the move and the periodic stops for tea or coffee became our favourite pastime, catching up on letter writing, reading or simply relaxing. While camping overnight in Kempsey, it was so cold we hooked up to a power point and heated the van's interior with our hairdryer.

Heading up the Pacific Highway to Coffs Harbour, we passed many fruit and vegetable stalls on the roadside. Prices were low so we feasted on bananas and apples. Where else could one buy twenty bananas for 35 cents? In Coffs Harbour, we were greeted by the Big Banana, a gigantic statue alongside the highway. The surrounding landscape already looked tropical to us despite the rain. We stopped that night at a caravan park outside the town and drifted off to sleep, hoping the new day would bring us better weather.

Our wish was answered. The rain stopped and patches of blue sky were visible. We were heading away from the ocean and inland to Glen Innes where our map identified several sites to find gems. We climbed up to 1,000 metres above sea level and travelled through beautiful mountain scenery, nature reserves and national parks. It was getting colder, too cold for our liking, and the rain had started again. Never mind, we drove on until we reached a rocky, slippery track that took us to a fenced-off sapphire mine, obviously a private holding.

We drove back to look for a spot where we could dig a bit; maybe we would strike it lucky outside the designated mining zone. We used our little geo pick but didn't unearth anything spectacular. We took some pretty stones with us to have something to show, and drove on, slightly less motivated. Five minutes later we were back to our enthusiastic selves and looking forward to driving north where it would be warm and tropical.

We made it to Ballina after dark. The camping ground looked deserted. We got out of the car; someone was calling, "Who is there?" We couldn't see anyone.

Again, "Who is there?"

"Can we stay here for the night?" I shouted back at the invisible person. But again, "Who is there?"

By this time we had come closer to the house and saw an oversized birdcage. A galah hopped from one leg to the other, shouting, "Who is there?"

We stayed that night. Next morning, the caretaker knocked on our van; we explained our conversation with the galah. He seemed pleased and we were free to go; no money was exchanged.

Tweed Heads was next on our map. We stayed for a couple of days and even tried our luck fishing until a guy came and said, "No fish here, mate." I believed him.

Everything looked different from around Tweed Heads and further on as we left New South Wales and drove along the Gold Coast in Queensland with its high-rise buildings, golden beaches and places with enticing names such as Surfers Paradise. We walked around for a while admiring the beach before settling down for the night at a well-groomed camping ground on Main Beach.

After our brown rice and vegetable dinner, I developed a nasty toothache. I tried my home remedy of gargling with whisky to dull the pain when a fellow camper told me we could get free dental care in Brisbane. I didn't need to be told twice; we went straight to Brisbane the next morning.

We parked on a reasonably busy city street but worried someone might pinch belongings from our roof rack. We had no choice; I needed to see a dentist quickly; the pain had become unbearable. We asked our way through to the dental hospital. I couldn't believe my luck; they didn't mind treating tourists. Without waiting, they took me in, and 10 minutes later, the offending tooth was gone. Unbelievably, the cost for this operation was only $3.50; that's what I call affordable dental care. While waiting, Giselle talked to an elegantly-dressed lady. She looked like she had the money to pay for a dentist, but she preferred to attend the dental hospital.

Emergency over, we wandered the streets of Brisbane; not a modern city, but we liked it. It had the laid-back feel of a big country town and was certainly less hectic than Sydney.

We dressed casually, cut-off jeans, a t-shirt and thongs. Having stopped shaving, I also sported a sparsely developing full beard and still had my shoulder-length hair. We were not dressed to impress. No wonder we were surprised when from a passing car someone waved at us. It was a well-dressed guy we didn't know. He stopped and called out to us, "You are Germans, aren't you?" Oh my God, do we look that much like Germans? We had nothing against Germans but thought we looked unique and special. He turned out to be Austrian and invited us for coffee in the afternoon. "Please call me in one hour, my wife and I will be home by then," he said, handing me a card with his phone number, and drove on.

Giselle and I looked at each other. Was that for real? Maybe he was a serial killer, or wanted to share more than coffee. His invitation took a while to digest, but in the end, we made that call from a phone booth. A minute later, we had their details and street directions and went on our way to visit Gerd and Heike.

We found their house and parked on the driveway, as instructed. It was an old Queenslander, high set, with plenty of space underneath between concrete stumps. We walked up the wooden staircase; Heike and Gerd were at the door to greet us. Apart from beams of light streaming in from the doorways, the hallway was dimly lit. The whole set-up was a bit spooky.

We sat at their large kitchen table drinking coffee, chatting animatedly. We seemed to hit it off nicely, and they decided we had to stay for dinner. We obliged. Gerd left to buy beer while we talked to Heike and their two young kids.

He returned with the beer, each 500ml bottle disguised by a brown paper bag. The first bottle came out of the bag. Was it Victoria Bitter or was it Foster's Lager? It was a brand we had sampled before. We cheered each other while Heike cooked up a storm.

That dinner was especially welcome, not only because it was delicious but also it was our first home-cooked meal in quite a while.

By now it was dark and the house appeared even spookier than before, though now I was sure this impression was due to its period feel with stucco ceilings and ornate doorways. Even the furniture had a touch of the ghostly about it, couches and chairs with dark-red faded covers.

The children were asleep and we were comfortably settled in the living room, drinking more beers while our topics gradually switched to the spirit world. We had an affinity for ghost stories and the supernatural; no wonder our stories became more involved and took on a reality of their own. Giselle and I exchanged glances which revealed our initial unease about Gerd and Heike had not entirely vanished. They were friendly enough, and we were having a good time, but something in Gerd's demeanour stopped us from feeling fully relaxed.

Gerd was a representative for a pharmaceutical company. His job was to convince doctors that the drugs he represented were superior. The subject of 'the pill' came up. Gerd clearly felt strongly about it, warning us of the terrible side effects it would cause. He showed us research papers he was not supposed to have. Giselle had been taking the Pill for several years and Gerd's arguments were clearly directed at getting her off it. What he said affected both of us. I didn't want Giselle popping those nasty-sounding drugs.

We decided right there in that spooky living room to stop the pill. And sure enough, the conversation was taking on a slightly sexy topic, discussing alternative contraception.

Come bedtime, we would happily have returned to our car's comfort, but our hosts insisted we use the spare bedroom. As we lay there with mixed feelings in bed in a strange house, could we allow ourselves to go to sleep? After 10 minutes of listening for possible suspicious noises, we decided it was probably safe to fall asleep.

I woke up hearing footsteps. "Did you hear that?" I asked, waking Giselle. "What?" she asked.

"Psssss – someone is walking, listen." There it was again, definitely footsteps. I got out of bed, crept to the door, and listened intensely. I couldn't hear or see a thing; it was pitch dark. I went back to bed, "It must have been something else; I don't think it was Gerd sneaking around," I said.

"It came from the ceiling," Giselle said.

We couldn't entirely dismiss the possibility that the house was haunted. We kept listening but eventually must have dozed off. We woke up still alive, the sun shining into our room.

When we shared the story of our disturbed sleep to Gerd and Heike over the breakfast table, they agreed it must be a ghost but they had stopped worrying.

As Gerd had the day off, he offered to give us a sightseeing tour of Brisbane. It was a proper family outing, kids in tow; we visited parks, rivers and an old water tower and indulged in ice cream.

Late that afternoon, we parted and left Brisbane for Redcliffe, on Moreton Bay, where we stayed overnight in a caravan park, again one with no manager in sight. Next morning we left without paying and resumed our drive north. We found a nice spot to camp on a beach, close to Caloundra, where we stayed the whole day to have a good rest and to soak up the sunshine.

Driving slowly for a few days, from one beach to the next, we arrived at Coolum Beach and found the ideal camping spot; it felt like being on an island, very romantic. We looked for somewhere to have my birthday celebration dinner and went to the only restaurant we could find; pleasant enough, but nothing to get excited about. We joked we wouldn't come here again. We stayed two more days and used our four by four metre annexe to cover our rear van door for extra comfort.

At night we tried something new. With Giselle not being on the Pill anymore, it was time to try one of Gerd's recommended alternatives. It was a new vaginal spermicide or, to use plain language, contraceptive foam. Maybe we should have asked Gerd if he and Heike had tried it themselves? Not to worry. The product came with instructions.

Here we were, not to forget it was my birthday; I thought I deserved a bit of sizzle. I still can picture it, sitting in the back of our car on our foam mattress, dim lighting, the sound of the surf, music playing, and my beautiful Giselle reading the instructions on preventing pregnancy. Shaking the bottle vigorously, as per the instructions, attaching the applicator, inserting that thing where it belongs and finally pressing the button to release the foam, how could anything go wrong?

In two explosive seconds, foam splattered in all directions; Giselle was covered, as was our bed. Even the ceiling was not spared, and neither was I. We couldn't stop laughing. It took a while to clean up that mess, with the can of foam landing in the rubbish bin. That was the end of my birthday party.

We stayed another day feeling like kids in paradise, surrounded by palms and the waves gently rolling up the beach. We walked along that beach for hours, struggled up the dunes only to slide down again, and repeated the activity until we ran out of puff.

A family travelling in an old Sydney bus camped not far from us. Kids were running around, the dad was playing the guitar, and mum was cooking; very idyllic. No wonder we were getting hungry. I tried to light a campfire but the fire was not cooperative. It kept going out and I resorted to our fallback equipment, the gas cooker, which worked every time.

We often talked to fellow travellers and heard tall stories about fruit picking and earning good money. Couples, even whole families, travelled from farm to farm, season-to-season, picking fruit or vegetables. The kids were home schooled and received all their teaching materials by mail. We wanted to try fruit picking ourselves. Travelling further north would bring us to large farms for picking opportunities. We learnt that Bowen was the place for tomato picking.

For the moment, however, we were enjoying ourselves too much to think about hard work. Lying on the beach with a good book was much more enticing.

We had been reading a lot; it helped our English, particularly our vocabulary. I bought some paperbacks on supernatural themes; they were fun, easy to read and worked well with our belief in positivity, healthy living and mind power. I also found a new book about macrobiotics, deepening our understanding of the yin and yang philosophy.

We left our beach paradise a couple of days later and continued north. We kept to the coastline, exploring small villages and towns, Noosa, Tewantin, Eumundi, and Nambour, taking photos of whatever we found unique or attractive.

Coming to Nambour we were confronted by a big Pineapple, another tourist attraction, similar to Coffs Harbour's Big Banana. Giant fibreglass replicas seemed to be an Australian peculiarity.

Further on, we found a secluded beach at Hervey Bay that made an ideal free campsite. Next morning, we noticed it was not as secluded as we thought. The outgoing tide had transformed the beach into a mudflat. Locals were out in force hunting for mud crabs with a device that looked like an oversized bicycle pump. We watched the locals for a while before we left the mudflat beach with its fantastic scenery of calm blue waters surrounded by mountain ranges and travelled on to Howard, Childers, Bundaberg, and Bargara. After a couple of days of sightseeing, we arrived in Gin Gin.

The fields of sugarcane were immense, stretching as far as the eye could see. Anything not cultivated was bushland and occupied by grazing cattle. We felt like extras in an American cowboy movie. The men riding amongst the cattle looked like cowboys but were called stockmen.

Giselle and I were still coming to terms with Australia's immensity. From Hamburg to the Swiss city of Basel is 800 km, spanning almost all of Germany north to south. Since leaving Narooma two months earlier, we had travelled twice that distance. Yet, looking at the map of Australia, we had hardly covered any ground at all.

We were still in Gin Gin. Appetizing name for a town, but the name had nothing to do with gin; like many towns, it was an Aboriginal name, possibly meaning red soil and thick bush or scrub. There wasn't much to see in Gin Gin, and we left for Gladstone.

On that stretch of road, we had our first minor emergency, a puncture. Not a big deal; we were well prepared, carrying two spare tyres tied up on the roof rack. After fitting one of the spares, I followed up with a German profanity, "Scheisse!" which immediately caught Giselle's attention.

"What is it?" she asked.

"The spare is flat," I grumbled in reply.

"What about the other one?"

Luckily, the second spare was fine.

We didn't see a single car until Miriam Vale, where we had both tyres fixed, before driving on to Gladstone. What would we have done without that second spare?

Gladstone was too industrial for us and we drove inland to Biloela, another 120 km. Only the first few kilometres of the route were sealed before it turned into a bumpy gravel road, but we made it safely to our new destination. We strolled around town to stretch our legs and stocked up on essentials at the local shops. We found everything we needed, but at a higher cost, including petrol.

We liked the Biloela camping ground, it was surrounded by gum trees offering their shade. We found a cosy spot not too far away from the shower blocks. We craved a hot shower. Giselle went first while I set up the camp stove, ready for cooking our dinner.

Giselle came back with good news; she had met a woman who was just back from Sapphire, the aptly named town in the middle of the region's gem fields. That woman actually had found sapphires. All one had to do, was to obtain a 'MINER'S RIGHT' which was available from a police station for $3. It would entitle us to set up camp in the middle of the bush, even on land owned by cattle farmers, and commence digging without getting into trouble.

Next morning, before 7 am, someone knocked on our car door. It was the husband of that lovely woman we had dubbed 'sapphire lady'. He invited us over to their caravan to inspect their treasures and give us a few tips for finding similar beauties ourselves.

We were ready to go in no time. Their caravan was spacious enough to fit all of us, with the table in the middle covered with gemstones in all shapes and sizes. Unremarkable-looking in their uncut state, the glint of colour in each stone was visible if you held it up to the light. Others were pitch black; those were 'spinels' and not very valuable. Yellow-coloured stones were most likely zircons.

A vital piece of equipment we still needed was a large wood-framed sieve for washing and sifting the sand and dirt from the stones. Wetting the gravel made the gems easier to recognise.

Anticipation now at fever pitch, we lost all interest in inspecting old shop fronts or taking photos of period architecture and prehistoric petrol pumps. No time to waste; fortunes were waiting.

We drove on to a village called Banana. Who calls a town Banana? There was no Banana in sight. We were curious about the name but had no time to find out; our unfound sapphires were beckoning.

All this driving had made us hungry, and we decided to have lunch in Emerald, the next town. That name could only mean one thing; there must be emeralds waiting to be picked up. About 30km before we hit the town, a swarm of grasshoppers attacked us, but they didn't hop; they flew right into our windscreen. Within a couple of minutes, we were driving blind. A yellowish substance covered our windscreen. We waited until the cloud had passed before we inspected our car. *What had hit us?* Our wire windscreen protector had cut those grasshoppers into pieces before the dismantled bodies splashed onto the windscreen. Using our precious drinking water, we cleaned a small section, barely enough to keep driving the last few kilometres to Emerald.

We were allowed to wash our car at a service station and learnt our attackers were not grasshoppers but locusts, a plague and nightmare for farmers. For us, it felt like we were extras in a Hitchcock movie. The service station guy urged us to clean the radiator as well.

We had sufficiently recovered from our shock and horror and went for lunch; our appetites had not suffered.

Back on the road, driving the final stretch to Sapphire. We tried to buy a big sieve for our sapphire hunt but they had sold out. Was there an onslaught of sapphire crazy tourists? We stopped in Anakie where we walked into the police station, paid $1.50 each and received our 'Miners Right 'and a 'Magistrates Court Office' receipt. We were now the official owners of a Miners Right License, numbers 27571 and 27572. As it was getting late; we stayed the night in Anakie.

We left the camping site by 8 am, stopped at the service station to fill up our car, and as luck would have it, they had the sieve we were looking for, in the right size, 50cm in diameter. We also received advice to look for sapphires in Rubyvale and only to use Sapphire for essential shopping.

Chapter 5

Gem Hunting Fever

Rubyvale was a tiny village, looking like a western gold rush town on the American frontier. There were only a handful of buildings, and I expected Wyatt Earp to step out of the post office. Across the junction was a pub. Was that the pub from the song, "A Pub with No Beer?" On the opposite side was a caravan park with what looked like an old locomotive steam engine next to the toilet and shower blog.

Off to the left stood a row of houses, occupied mainly by gem cutters. Near the post office were huts that were used by Taiwanese sapphire dealers as offices.

We parked outside the post office. In a village this size, the postmaster knows everything; in this one, the postmaster was a postmistress, and she did. First, we had our mail redirected to Rubyvale; we planned on staying for two weeks. Having completed the postal business, she gave us the vital village information. We could shower at the village campground for 30 cents a time. If we wanted meat, we had to order it from the shop; delivery was on Wednesdays and Saturdays. If we found sapphires, we could sell them to the Taiwanese dealers. The only English phrase they knew was 'Dig more, dig deeper, more digging,' and they were keen to buy up everything, even tiny or cracked sapphires.

Finally, she gave us a hot tip: drive 3 km out of Rubyvale before setting up camp. On no account should we stake our claim too close to someone else's. Shouting distance would be reasonable. That way, we could call hello to see if they were friendly or hostile.

As we thanked her and left the post office, a mean-looking bloke dismounted his motorbike; we noticed a holster with a gun sticking out from behind his saddlebags. This wasn't Wyatt Earp, but we couldn't help feeling that Earp's services might soon be required from the look of him.

A few kilometres out of town, we found what looked like a suitable spot to camp. Another car drew up and the driver called, "Can I help you?"

"Thanks, we are fine; we're looking for a nice spot to camp."

"Like to come to my camp for a cup of tea? Follow me."

A couple of minutes later we reached his camp, a permanent set-up. It consisted of a big caravan with annexes, huts and sheds. Heavy machinery and equipment completed the picture, and we could hear a generator humming. He introduced himself as Ryan, and his wife as Kath. A German Shepherd and two cats followed her; they also wanted to be introduced.

We sat down, the cats snuggling up on our laps. Kath made tea and we talked our heads off. They were from New Zealand and had been in Rubyvale for a couple of years, along with Ryan's two brothers.

They weren't amateur fossickers but into serious digging. They had a massive truck with drilling equipment to bore mining shafts about 60 cm wide. After reaching what they called a wash, they would dig with jackhammers and shovel the dirt into buckets, which automatically went up the shaft high above the ground and down again into an arrangement of drums for washing, sorting and sieving. At the end of the day, they checked their catchment container for any 'colour,' sapphires or other gems. Not as romantic as we envisaged, but still exciting.

Ryan showed us some beautiful cut sapphires and tins full of smaller rough gems. We talked about where to find stones and establish our little claim site. Ryan lent us a 44-gallon drum cut in half so we would have a container to wash the dirt in. The sieve we'd bought fitted perfectly into the drum. For good measure, he gave us a shovel and a pick.

It was getting late, and we were keen to dig for at least one hour. Driving back, we spotted an ideal campsite and parked between three trees in the perfect position to tie our tarp to. We took our chairs out, made a cup of tea, and relaxed. It felt right; it was a nice campsite. The carpet from Gabrielle and Henry came in handy and made the camp look neat. We set up a proper campfire using rocks and our barbeque plate.

It was 4 pm before we picked a spot to dig. Not as easy as we thought. The top 20 cm was easy digging, but it became more challenging after that. One hour later, we were pretty much buggered. We hadn't done much physical work for a while. Looking back at the fruit of our labour, we had nothing. So far, we hadn't found anything resembling a gemstone.

Ryan had told us about a trick to check if a stone was a gem. We should take the stone into our mouth, and if it stays cold, it is a gemstone. Every few minutes, we tasted little stones, but all became warm. All we had to show for our efforts was a mouth full of sand and gravel.

Almost on dinnertime, people from the next campsite called out to us, "Any colour?" Colour, as we knew from Ryan, referred to sapphires.

"No," we called back, "nothing yet."

The following day we were up early; sapphire fever had taken hold. After an enjoyable breakfast of freshly toasted bread, courtesy of the campfire, we were ready to dig. We continued where we left off the day before. But when we dug about 30 cm down, we hit clay and the going got tough. I was about to take a rest when I noticed something unusual looking.

"Schatz, (Darling) I have something," Giselle stopped digging and rushed over.

We looked in amazement at this thumbnail-sized, heavy, cold, dark stone. Could we be this lucky on our first full day of digging? I cleaned the stone and placed it in my mouth. Seconds of suspense, then I mumbled; "It's staying cold." I held it up to the light. Would a pristine blue sapphire shine back at us?

"I can't see much," said Giselle. "Can you?" All we could see was darkness, cracks in the mineral and maybe a glint of blue at the edges. We walked over to our neighbours, who were packing up camp.

"Got anything?" they greeted us.

"Not sure," I answered. "Could you have a look? What is it?" I handed him the stone, and he held it to the light.

"That's corundum," he said, explaining that it was a sapphire but too compact and not of gemstone quality. Our level of excitement dropped accordingly.

"Keep digging," the neighbour suggested, "wherever there is corundum, sapphires will not be far away."

We returned with renewed energy, sure that we would strike it rich any minute now. Another hour's punishing digging dampened our excitement considerably. The only thing we unearthed was a dark stone which we knew was called 'blackjack,' a spinel often used in men's rings. This was better than nothing, but by now, we were aching all over from the effort. Our picks and shovels were getting heavier by the minute. Time for lunch.

In the afternoon, we felt like a shower. That was the only drawback of camping wild, no shower facilities.

"Let's go to the dam; we can wash there," was Giselle's solution.

The dam was a short distance away. With no one else around, I stripped off and stood under a water tank next to the dam, with refreshing cold water pouring down. Giselle was about to follow suit when a couple of cars drove past, blowing their horns. Giselle stayed dressed and washed herself as well as she could.

That night, I played guitar as we sat around the campfire, had a drink, and dreamed of the 'big one,' being happy despite our sore backs.

We woke up in the dead of night. "Did you hear that?" Giselle asked. I did; someone was walking and tripping over our pots and pans. We had locked our car but still felt uneasy. Was it one of those scruffy-looking guys with a gun? We peeked through the rear curtain but couldn't see anything in the dark. Whoever it was had retreated. We were waiting for something to happen, but nothing did. Eventually, we drifted off to sleep.

At first daylight, we carefully left the car; nothing was missing, although some pots were turned over. "Have you seen these droppings before?" I asked Giselle, pointing to something on the ground. Our razor-sharp deduction skills, worthy of Sherlock Holmes, produced only one possible solution, a kangaroo must have visited us. We had seen a few hopping around.

Much calmer and after a strengthening breakfast, we returned to work and persevered until about 1 pm but found nothing worth mentioning. That Sunday, no one seemed to be working; quite a few people came around, saying hello and the usual question, "Any colour?" Everyone showed off their findings, stimulating each other's enthusiasm to keep digging. We presented our gigantic corundum; it was suitably admired. And why not? It looked impressive at first glance.

Tomorrow would be our lucky day for sure.

We had to drive to Rubyvale but needed to venture all the way to Sapphire to get what we wanted. Leaving our camp and equipment took all the trust in humanity we could muster. On returning, nothing had been disturbed; we felt rewarded. However, our digging efforts and perseverance went sadly unrewarded; what we were doing wrong? We convinced ourselves we had been digging in the wrong spot.

Our neighbours had packed up and left but a new couple was already digging in their place. Our turn to go over and ask, "Any colour?" They showed us a few bits and pieces but were also looking for another spot. They were friendly people, in their fifties and from Melbourne. They stayed at the camping grounds in town and came with their truck for digging whenever they felt like it.

We'd had enough of digging for the day and drove off to see Ryan. Maybe he could suggest a more promising spot. He wasn't home but his brothers were. One was up on the truck monitoring the washing and sieving; the other was down in the mineshaft, drilling away with a jackhammer. I asked if I could go down the shaft and have a look. No problems. Down I went. Good thing I wasn't claustrophobic.

The jackhammer worked by air pressure from hoses above ground connected to a noisy compressor. I had a go with the jackhammer. It was not something I would like to do for a living. The thing was heavy and its hammering action shook my whole upper body. Five minutes at the rock face convinced me I would never become a miner.

Enough excitement for one day. Giselle and I returned to the serenity of our camp. I played the guitar, the fire was burning, and dinner was coming up; another idyllic night.

Tuesday morning, the lovely couple we met the day before dropped by. Bob and Joan had sold their service station in Melbourne, bought the roomiest caravan on the market and began their long-dreamt-of road trip right around Australia, the first generation of 'grey nomads.'

They drove a 1970 Ford F100 V8 ute, powerful enough to tow their large caravan and all of Bob's tools, including a generator and jackhammer. They suggested we work together, use Bob's jackhammer and dig deeper to find something decent for a change. Great idea, and we agreed.

After looking around for a while, we settled on a new spot. With Bob's help, we shifted our water drum and to make washing the gravel easier, we constructed a seesaw device. To one end, we attached the sieve, hovering over the drum with the water; the other end acted as a lever raising and lowering the contraption, achieving a washing action. It worked; no more backbreaking manual lifting, shifting and sifting.

Shovelling and jackhammering, Bob and I dug a hole four by two metres and one metre deep. Giselle and Joan operated the sieving contraption and inspected the washed stones.

Not far from us, another couple were digging. Unexpectedly, the lady yelled, "Eureka!" I looked over at Bob. "What does that mean?"

"They must have found something," he replied.

We walked over; they had unearthed a partly-coloured sapphire, about one cm in diameter, a good size, with no cracks; it would look fantastic as a cut stone. They had worked hard for it.

Looking at the hole, I could see they'd found the 'wash' at a depth of three metres. Sapphires were definitely there, waiting to be discovered. To think, they nearly gave up. At that moment, we all experienced a burst of energy; if they can do it, so can we.

That night, we were exhausted. And what did we have to show for it? A few measly stones, too tiny for cutting, one good-sized zircon and several blackjacks.

Wednesday, meat delivery day, and we hoped for mail. We were in luck; all our mail had arrived. Some of it was still for my birthday; my parents had sent a cake mix. We were keen to try baking a cake over our campfire. We picked up our meat and drove back to our camp, ready to start digging.

Bob and Joan had arrived as well. The digging fun continued; we enlarged our hole in all dimensions with refreshed vitality. We had a couple of steaks for lunch, courtesy of our meat order. Not having a fridge, we had to eat our meat fast. At 4 pm, we called it quits. Bob had picked a green sapphire from the wall where he was digging. We didn't find anything worthwhile, but there was enough smallish stuff to keep the spirit going.

Bob and Joan invited us for dinner. We were happy to be on the receiving end of their hospitality and arrived by 5 pm. Their caravan was more like a house on wheels. It had everything, a perfect kitchen, bathroom and shower, a living room and a bedroom. But first, we paid 60 cents for the luxury of a steaming hot shower provided by the caravan park's old steam engine. Being all washed and fresh, we walked back to Bob and Joan's caravan and used their bathroom and hairdryer before we were rewarded with pre-dinner cocktails, a very civilised touch.

What a night; fish, chips and salad, followed by peaches and ice cream. And it didn't stop there; beer and wine flowed freely, with no police to stop us on the way home and test our breath. Bob had trouble pronouncing Giselle's name and decided to call her Fred, "Here you go, Fred," he said, giving Giselle a couple of opals from his collection.

Bob had been in Rubyvale long enough to know a bit of its history. He told us big miners had arrived here early in the 1970s with heavy machinery such as bulldozers. We weren't surprised to hear this, having seen the devastated landscape they left behind. The small miners wanted to preserve the gem fields and develop a tourist industry. We heard on the grapevine that an outbreak of hostilities was a possibility. That was probably why guys had been running around with guns. Would this idyllic environment be destroyed by greed?

Still not happy with our current mine, we climbed a fence hoping for better conditions on the other side. What's the saying? 'The grass is always greener on the other side.' Well, it wasn't, only some cattle curiously eyeing us and a lot of cow manure. "Maybe we should go into gardening," Giselle suggested. "Look at all this bullshit." Bob cracked up while Joan blushed. Apparently 'bullshit' was not ladylike language.

We called it quits that day and went to town to check for mail. A letter from my brother Herbert kept me up to date on family matters.

Tomorrow would be our washing day which was a real challenge in the absence of fresh water. Giselle had soaked our washing in a water drum before breakfast, only to see that everything had turned brown, looking dirtier than before.

In desperation, she chucked the whole lot onto the floor. I know I shouldn't have laughed, but in my defence, it looked funny. I helped pick our laundry up and we started again using our precious drinking water for the final rinse. It worked, and the world was in order again. Drying was a piece of cake; we hung the washing on a line stretched between two trees.

Late in the morning, Bob showed us yet another spot. We shifted our equipment and began digging. Would our luck turn? For the first two hours, it didn't, but a bit further over where someone had dug before us the ground looked different, sandy with gravel mixed in. The digging was easier and before long we found a blackjack, then a few more and, at last, some actual colour. The more we dug, the more precious stones we came up with, even a few bigger ones. This may not have been a 'Eureka' moment, but it inspired Bob to fetch a bottle of blackberry liqueur from his truck. We celebrated our newfound success in style. I would have settled for a cold beer.

After work, we went to the dam, stripped down and showered under the overflow of the water tank. Ryan drove past, blowing his horn, but didn't stop. A minute later, at least ten horses galloped along the road. We couldn't believe our eyes. They didn't stop to look at us either.

Our mining adventure continued, spurred on by those early finds. We kept finding little gems but the big one we longed for avoided us. We decided to skip a day of work and relax instead.

It was Sunday and we attempted to bake Dr Oetker's 'Sonntagskuchen,' the one we had received from Hamburg. Our campfire became the designated baking station. With the addition of more rocks and suitable timber to create charcoal and keep the heat steady for longer, our trusty campfire was converted into a bakehouse oven. Keeping in mind the book we aimed to write, we used all thirty-six exposures of a film to photograph the complete baking process, not forgetting the consumption of the finished product.

The cake-mix manufacturer had thought of everything, including a measuring device and a foil-lined cardboard-and-aluminium baking pan. Thirty minutes in, with the oven at the right temperature, we poured the mix into the pan and placed it on a metal tray. Holding our breath, we carefully slid it into the oven, onto the glowing charcoals. So far, so good. We were thinking we should cover the oven opening with aluminium foil when the cake pan caught fire, and the cake mix tried to escape.

"Quick, do something!" Giselle yelled.

"(^^%$^&&,.." I said, grabbed a shovel and rescued the cake. We transferred the cake mix into a saucepan. That was a good idea, wasn't it? Back into the oven it went. But now, the saucepan handle threatened to burst into flame. "Don't worry, the cake is more important, I said and placed foil on top. Twenty minutes later, we thought the cake should be pretty much ready. For the final photos, we set up a make-shift table, of course with a table cloth as Germans do at their traditional 3 pm coffee and cake time.

"OK, let's have a look now," I snatched the cake away from the fire.

"Oh no, it's all burned," Giselle exclaimed.

"We can cut off the black stuff, I said. We sacrificed at least a quarter of the cake, but the rest looked edible.

Tripod and camera ready, we had our coffee and cake and could eat it too. Staying in style, we played a game of chess; Giselle won.

More mail awaited us in town on the Monday. A letter from my mother was very worrying; it sounded confused and all over the place. Before we left Germany, she had been in hospital with circulation problems. There were no facilities to make an international call; we could only hope she would be all right.

Back at work by 10 am, we found more blackjacks and little green and blue coloured sapphires. Giselle and I were happy with what we had found. Bob was less so; he wanted something of a decent size. We had lost our gem fever and were less serious but the appeal of finding great riches kept us amused. With the onset of colder weather, we had an excellent excuse to stay in our cosy bed longer, followed by breakfast next to the campfire.

At night we had dinner with Bob and Joan. They had begun packing and were looking forward to their next destination, Cairns. Bob eagerly gave us tips about car repairs, travel and even work. He wrote out the address of a Victorian orchard where they needed fruit pickers.

Before leaving next morning, Bob adjusted a few items on our panel van and filled the engine with some special oil. Later, Bob and I went to one of those Taiwanese dealers who looked at our collection, brushed them to one side and said, "Dig more, dig deeper. No deal." Back on site, Bob and Joan plucked out three of the stones, shifting all the others across to us. As they did, Bob said, "Here you go, all yours." We thanked him with a genuine feeling of gratitude at having met such lovely people. The goodbye was sad but we knew we would meet again soon.

Walking back to our car, we overheard a couple speaking German. They were not sure where to set up camp. Introducing ourselves, we suggested a site not far from us. It was an older couple from Melbourne on holiday, wanting to try their luck.

Still early, we went back to our own spot, digging for a couple of hours and finding more little gems for our collection. We hardly noticed when the German guy, Friedrich, came over to chat and invited us to their camp. We seemed to be magnetically attracting older couples. They told us half their life story. Friedrich had a heart problem and spent most of his time pottering around the home. His wife, Margot, worked at a food-processing factory and gave us a handful of one-serve jam jars. We wondered how they would dig if he had a heart problem. They even gave us their address and wanted us to visit them in Melbourne. We thought we would probably take them up on that offer.

The next day's breakfast was a treat, five slices of toast with the jam our new friends had given us.

More digging. We were like kids playing in their sandpits. Giselle was sitting on the ground and sorting through the washed stones. Even though it was cold at night, it warmed up quickly during the day. I did the digging and washing, and in between, we rested, sunning ourselves and relishing our peaceful laziness.

An emu must have liked that serene scene and came walking over to us. We met the bird's hypnotic gaze with blank stares, stunned by its close attention, sitting still and hoping not to be pecked by its enormous beak. Its curiosity satisfied, the emu resumed its journey.

Another week had gone, such a free way of living; time meant nothing. Occasionally, we heard someone calling 'Eureka!' reminding us that one can get lucky which stimulated us to keep digging. We went to another spot closer to Margot and Friedrich. They wanted to leave in a couple of days, and we had promised to help them dig for a couple of hours but didn't find anything. They were doing more talking than digging. We loved a good conversation but were overwhelmed by their non-stop talk about diseases, war and how terrible everything was.

A couple of days later, after they had moved on, we kept digging and unearthed two golden zircons which we knew would make beautiful cut stones.

The next day, we went to Rubyvale and Sapphire for shopping. The essentials were cheaper in Sapphire. We filled our tank, bought plenty of postcards and a Sara Lee cheesecake. We spent the afternoon having coffee and cake and talking about new ideas. We wanted to tie the knot, get married when back in Hamburg and have a honeymoon in Venice. Giselle had been to Venice with her parents when she was only sixteen and had dreamt ever since of going there again.

At night, we visited Ryan and Kath. They were keen to see our slides and Ryan wanted to get tips on photography techniques, and have a guitar lesson. He knew only a few chords. Finally, I could show off my skills, I wasn't much better but I did know my chords.

Ryan told us they had found a new location to drill for sapphires. His younger brother was skilled in the art of divining. He couldn't even wear a watch because it would stop working and at airports he triggered the alarm when walking through the metal detector.

It wasn't precisely sapphires that he could locate, it was the wash where they were supposed to be. By drilling where he told them, they had found many valuable stones; after all, the whole family lived off their mining proceeds.

Ryan also warned us not to go walking around at night. Apparently, people mysteriously went missing. They may have fallen into an uncovered mining shaft. I am not sure if that story was true but many old shafts were unsecured. Ryan and Kath's toilet was built over one of those shafts, it never fills up, and I can assure anyone, there was no smell.

When we were about to leave, Ryan mentioned a friend of his, Rudolf, who lived in town with his wife and kids. He was one of the best gem cutters around the gem fields and came originally from Austria. We had the idea of having one of our stones cut.

Up early next morning, we saw our camp had received a visitor while we slept. A bag of flour and a packet of pea soup had been taken from our storage box, dragged along the ground, opened and half consumed. Whoever the intruder was, it was clearly a fussy eater. Was it a kangaroo? We never found out; it didn't leave a calling card.

We drove to town and went to the gem cutter Ryan had mentioned. We found his property; it looked well cared for with two cottages, the cutting shop and the living space. The door to the cutting shop was open. A guy sat in front of something that looked like a record player, moving the arm of that gadget gently back and forth.

"Hi, are you Rudolf?" I asked.

He looked up, "Yes, what can I do for you?"

"We're friends of Kath and Ryan; we wanted to have a look at how to cut gemstones." Almost immediately, we were chatting away in a mixture of German and English. Rudolf could not have been more friendly; he invited us in for coffee and introduced us to his wife, Susanne.

Rudolf and his family had been living in Rubyvale for a few years. He had a bad accident, his mine collapsed, and he broke his hips and back. After a slow recovery, leaving him partly disabled, Rudolf could walk only on crutches. He went into the cutting business and became quite an expert, well-known and respected. Two other cutters worked alongside him in his studio cabin, with a three-phase diesel generator providing the required power.

He picked out two zircons to cut from the collection of stones we had excavated. He could have taken the undersized sapphires, but he pointed out that the cutting would be more expensive than the values of the stones. He showed us his precious collection of different gems and cuts for sale and what we had to look for under a magnifying glass to determine their quality. We picked out a small blue sapphire worth $70 and bought it for $20. We also bought a little box designed for holding gemstones.

We stayed awhile and watched Rudolf working on a large sapphire. It's a slow process needing a delicate touch, with each phase requiring a different grade of diamond dust to cut and then polish the precious object. If the gem sustained even a slight scratch, polishing would have to start all over again. No wonder gems are expensive. Rudolf's precision hand-cut stones were of much higher quality than machine-cut stones. We learnt a lot that day and came away feeling like experts.

"I reckon we should buy more stones," Giselle whispered.

"What do you mean?" I asked.

"..... we could sell them when we are back in Hamburg."

"Hmm, could be a good idea. Maybe we should wait until we come back next year."

That night we couldn't shut up. One idea followed the other; life was too exciting. Writing, photography, selling stories, dealing in gemstones, maybe even designing jewellery, painting; the ideas came lightning fast.

We even had another nocturnal visit; we saw two possums checking out our goods. One had the audacity to sit in our frying pan, licking out the fat. They were cute, but we decided to store our food and utensils in a safer place to prevent any future raids.

Next night we didn't get much sleep either, this time due to a non-stop heavy, pounding torrential downpour, the first rain we'd had since arriving in Rubyvale. As we couldn't get out of our car without being drenched, we stayed in the van until 1 pm, when the sun finally came out to play. It felt like a hothouse. We attempted to drive on the muddy road; we became bogged a few times but eventually made it into town. A letter had arrived from my Dad, who didn't write all that often. I was worried. *Was my Mum OK?* She didn't sound good judging by her last letter, but my Dad didn't mention anything.

We made it back to camp as it started raining again. The sky was full of dark clouds, and the rain soon became heavier, followed by lightning and thunder. There would be no hot dinner tonight, and we didn't even have any bread. All we had to nibble on were our emergency rations of crispbread. It kept on raining, so it was breakfast in the car again. We managed to boil eggs and water for instant coffee, another fallback. Not fans of the instant stuff, we should have opted for tea.

It was mid-morning when the rain finally ceased. We wandered around, focusing on the ground, even found a few gems glittering on the wet gravel road. Locals call it *noodling*, walking around after rain and spotting gemstones.

That night we had a warm dinner, beans and fried eggs with tinned peaches for dessert, spoiling ourselves while playing chess. I was in fine form or Giselle didn't try very hard; I won 3 matches. Giselle sulked, or maybe she was only pretending. I had to make my darling happy again and swung into action. I straightened myself out, lying stiff on my back with my elbows pointing to each side of my body. Giselle kept looking at me suspiciously. "What are you playing?" "I am a submarine, stranded on the beach waiting for the sea to come back." My silly stunt worked.

We wasted no time getting to town next morning, eager to see our freshly cut zircons. How would they come up? We couldn't wait. Rudolf ushered us into the kitchen, and there they were – two beautiful cut gems. To us, they looked like diamonds. The conversion from what had resembled fragments of dirty glass to these fantastic sparkling creations was striking. "Thank you; they look fantastic. Hard to believe they're the same stones we brought you." Rudolf smiled.

We told Rudolf we would leave Rubyvale within a couple of days. He and Susanne had spent more than a year travelling around Australia, and they gave us some great travel tips and locations where fruit pickers might be in demand. The next likely town would be Bowen, renowned for its tomatoes, cucumbers and beans.

Before we left, Rudolf handed us a few pieces of quartz and amethyst; our gem collection was growing. They invited us to come back for a night of watching slides. We looked forward to seeing our slides in a large format. Upon returning, we dismantled our camp and prepared to leave Rubyvale. The prospect of going was bittersweet. We drove to visit Ryan and Kath for the last time, returning their tools and the water drum. Tea and cookies turned the occasion into a two-hour goodbye. We promised to stay in touch. On the way out, Ryan mentioned the sapphire we bought from Rudolf was a steal (a bargain). *Maybe we should buy more sapphires from Rudolf next year?*

Rubyvale led Giselle and me to notice how different life situations can change people in even a short period, let alone over a lifetime. Talking to Ryan and Kath, we realised how much we had changed. Not even a year in this unfamiliar land and our former life seemed unreal. Our Weltanschauung, (worldview) had shifted. We had developed new perspectives and new attitudes and were essentially new people.

When we arrived back at our camp for the last time, we had visitors, two guys who had heard about us from Rudolf. Gerhard came from Berlin and Fred from

Vienna. They looked like hardcore bush types; maybe it was a test from the Universe to see if we were still judging a book by its cover?

We just had that discussion with Ryan and Kath and now those two guys arrived and talked about alternative philosophies and lifestyles. Gerhard looked like someone you would hire to scare your worst enemy, but he was into minimalism and aimed to own as little as possible. He and Rubyvale were a perfect match.

Gerhard had led a nomadic existence for most of his adult life and now lived in his car. He was an intelligent and gentle soul who shared his philosophy without trying to convince anyone. Fred offered us a lifestyle prediction for free, "If you stay here longer than a year, you won't be able to live in normal society anymore. You'll be unable to cope with people, regular work or city life." Giselle and I had given this possibility some thought, wondering whether our old selves could ever enjoy life in Hamburg after the transformation we had undergone in Australia.

We changed the subject to sapphires and what their actual value was. Showing us a box with about fifty sparkling gemstones of different colours and cuts, Gerhard quizzed us; "What do you think they're worth?" We guessed about $2000. Gerhard laughed, "Some are only quartz or topaz. Very few are sapphires, but tourists don't know that." He paused for dramatic emphasis; "Their real value is about $600; the more naive the tourist, the more expensive the stones."

Next morning, our last breakfast felt like the last supper. By noon we arrived in Rubyvale, collected our mail and booked ourselves into the caravan park. We dropped by Rudolf's in the afternoon but he wasn't home. His neighbour came over to ask if he could help. From his accent, we knew at once he was from Hamburg. Sure enough, he had left there as a fifteen-year-old kid in 1946. He went to sea and eventually jumped ship in Sydney. His full name was probably Wolfgang, but everyone called him Wally.

Wally was yet another of those characters who had chosen Rubyvale because he could enjoy a lifestyle of obscurity. Wally, his wife and kids, occupied a comfortable house he had built with his own hands; they were not short of money.

He asked us to get him a cassette from Hans Alberts, a Hamburg singer and actor who was Germany's most prominent male movie star between 1930 and 1945.

That night at Rudolf's, we were joined by a few more visitors; they all gathered around the projector and watched our slides. So far, we were happy with our photographic output, and the others liked our photos as well.

During the evening, Rudolf told us about another German resident who had lived there forever, an octogenarian who was quite famous locally. Years ago, he found one of the largest sapphires ever to come from the Rubyvale area but refused to sell it. He preferred to carry it around and show it off to tourists. It was stolen once but was eventually given back. We planned to squeeze him into our tight schedule to take photos of him; it would be a good section for our book.

Walking to the Post Office the next morning, we ran into Fred and Gerhard and stayed talking right in the middle of the junction. No one bothered us, and cars simply drove around us. Even for us, accustomed to the bush lifestyle, standing there, we kept wondering why no one complained. On leaving this tolerant junction, still alive, Gerhard gave us two German news magazines; Stern and Der Spiegel. The latter is similar to The Times. We looked forward to hours of reading pleasure.

Driving to Rudolf's for a quick final goodbye didn't work out as planned. More people arrived, including Fred and Gerhard. We had to stay. The conversation turned to natural health and diet. Everyone seemed impressed with my incredible story of how I healed myself and my stomach ulcers with the macrobiotic diet.

We left by 4 pm, still in time to visit Mr Stonebridge, the guy who had unearthed the famous sapphire. He didn't speak German anymore, having lived in Rubyvale for fifty-one years. Incredibly, he had lived in the same camp all this time and kept it spick and span. The way he had stacked his firewood was a work of art. With his goatee and long white hair, he strongly resembled Colonel Harland Sanders, the guy from Kentucky Fried Chicken. Holding up his priceless sapphire, as he must have done many times before, he posed for the camera. We were only another couple of tourists to him; one couldn't expect him to look at us in any other light.

Even now, we weren't ready to push off as we had promised Fred we would come to see his half-built house and meet his wife, Linda. Sure enough, Gerhard dropped in a little while later and with him came Bob, another cutter at Rudolf's establishment, a man with a constant smile on his face but given to very few words, except when the topic of music came up. He liked electronic music and was glad to hear that we enjoyed it (none of the others were into electronic or avant-garde music). We were big fans of Kraftwerk, a German electropop band formed in 1970, and Giselle loved the electronic ballet music of Maurice Béjart and Pierre Henry.

We all stayed for dinner and talked about lifestyle philosophy topics into the early morning when we dropped off to sleep in our van.

On the last day of July we escaped the gravitational pull of Rubyvale. We had been there for four glorious weeks, made countless friends, learnt a lot, had not found the big one, but were compensated with the freedom to do whatever we wanted.

Those four weeks had instigated a shift in our thinking, perspective and attitude. We had become even more positive, more tolerant. Most amazingly of all, after living and being together 24/7 every day for the past nine months, we hadn't had even one cross word. Deep within ourselves, we recognised how fortunate we were to have found each other. Gabrielle had been right when she told us, "You are soulmates." We felt the universe was on our side.

And here we were, 'on the road again' heading for Rockhampton. Arriving around 4pm, we liked what we saw, a pretty town consisting of mainly low-set houses, a lovely church and an unusually high amount of traffic from our bush dweller perspective. All the town's shops closed at 5pm, so we had no time to do anything more than a quick 'food run' and book into the first caravan park we came across, which was located behind a big bridge. After dinner, we attempted to catch up on letter writing, processing our impressions from the past four weeks, but we could hardly keep our eyes open and went to sleep early.

Chapter 6

Chasing Adventures

We slept through for twelve hours straight. Sightseeing and shopping occupied the morning, filling our pantry with tins of food bought at a reasonably-priced supermarket, much cheaper than in Sapphire, not to mention Rubyvale. We left with several large brown paper bags filled with goodies. Next on our list was to buy a book about faceting, but we couldn't find anything; instead, we purchased 'Ballet in Australia,' only $2, a bargain.

Shopping done, we left Rockhampton and drove to Emu Park, a small town where we fully expected emus to be running around. But no emus in sight, not even at the caravan park.

Unpacking our goodies to prepare for dinner, we had a heart-stopping moment, one of our bags was missing. Giselle remembered putting it aside to make space for another. The bag was filled with tins of food, and its loss would be costly. We decided to try our luck and drive back to Rocky the following day.

We would have to be fast; the shops would close at 1 pm. Our nerves were on edge as we re-entered the supermarket, but we were lucky again. They had stored our bag, being sure we would collect it. They were right, and we were happy.

Back to Emu Park, there was something we wanted to see. Bob and Joan had told us about a sailing-boat landmark with pipes as masts, which made musical sounds when the wind blew. We found it, the wind was blowing, and the music was playing. The monument, known as the Singing Ship, was placed at the highest point on the coast, where the wind blew constantly. We took a few photos, and classified them as tourist snapshots. Most of the time, we took photos with our Pentax; it was so much easier than carrying the large-format Bronica camera around. We planned to sell or exchange the Bronica in Melbourne for a Nikon.

We left Emu Park for Yeppoon, driving leisurely and looking at the scenery. We were lucky to find a space to camp right on the beach; it was only 3pm, the perfect time to enjoy a cup of tea and read those German magazines we'd been given. We read them from cover to cover as they were the first German magazines we'd seen since leaving Sydney. In the mood for even more reading, I started a book by Patrick White titled 'Voss.' It was about a German explorer who had disappeared in the Australian Outback; obviously, I hoped that, in our case, life was not going to imitate art! It was not an easy read; I needed my dictionary to make progress.

We were not in our usual upbeat travelling mood, leaving early next morning for Mackay. Stories we heard made us apprehensive. It was a long stretch of road, with bush on both sides and nothing much else in sight. It was this section of road that had prompted people to urge us to carry a gun. And now here we were, unarmed. If no one had told us about people being murdered along here, we would have had a relaxed trip. We estimated the distance at about 400 km and were anxious to make it to Mackay before dark. We made one stop, in Marlborough, the last town to get petrol. It's not the same spelling, but the country around here looked like Marlboro Country.

There was a fair bit of traffic around; not an ideal situation to murder us, too many witnesses. We relaxed and even stopped for a cup of tea and a sandwich.

About 100km from Mackay, we had a puncture. Climbing up to the roof rack to get down the spare, I noticed a car way behind us had pulled over to the roadside. Why did they stop? While I changed the tyre, Giselle kept an eye on that waiting car.

"Someone's getting out," she alerted me. I stood up and looked; sure enough, two guys were walking around. Opening the rear of the car, I brought out our fishing rod. From afar, it would look like a gun. I handed it to Giselle. " Carry it casually as if it was a gun," I said and went back to changing the tyre.

"They're getting back into the car," she called out.

I had finished, "Let's go, all done," I said.

When we hit the road again, the car was still by the roadside, a diminishing object in the rear-view mirror. I kept checking, but that was the last we saw of them. Maybe they never meant to harm us at all.

"They probably heard the same gruesome stories we heard," I said. Too much excitement for us; we needed a drink, a sip of brandy for medicinal reasons.

We made it to Mackay without being killed. We had expected a beautiful beach where we could camp under tropical palms, but nothing like that. It was still early enough to drive to Shute Harbor, where we camped in a National Park. At the entrance, we were confronted by a sign stating, "Not allowed to stay without a permit." We had no idea where to get a permit, so we drove straight in. The campsite consisted of a toilet block with a cold-water shower. We didn't mind; it was free, and that's what counted. The park was beautiful, with a view of the harbour's calm, clear blue waters and the Whitsunday Islands providing a picture-perfect background.

It had rained overnight but we woke to a blue sky. Driving around like proper tourists, we found great vantage points for viewing and taking photos of the harbour. Later we shopped for provisions and booked a boat tour to the islands for the next day before driving back to the free camping park. Would there be anyone to check if we had a permit? No one bothered us.

Our boat accommodated sixty passengers, was well patronised by senior citizens. We'd had no idea what to expect but apart from tourists of retirement age and a few Americans, we were the only young people on board. The trip was pleasant, the sea like a pond and the stop for lunch at Lindeman Island was thoroughly enjoyable. We were supposed to proceed to Daydream Island but the weather turned bad, and the boat returned to the harbour an hour and a half early.

That night at the camping ground, talking to fellow travellers, we heard that a trip on a sailing boat was a more befitting atmosphere. That would be right, but it was too late now; at least we had seen this pristine environment close up.

· · · · · · · · · ·

Our touristy time came to an end; no more leisurely sightseeing; fruit picking was on the agenda. We drove to Bowen with the hope of finding a tomato picking job. After the obligatory post-office visit, we walked around town, asked for jobs and collected a few addresses. We found a caravan park, but to our minds, it was costly, $2.50 for the night. Not much we could do about it, so we had an extra-long shower to make up for it.

We left early the next morning for job hunting. A couple of unsuccessful hours later, we came to a large farm, growing tomatoes, cucumbers and beans. Judging by the large packing shed on the property, it looked promising. Lucky at last, we found ourselves a job.

The farm was a family affair – father and son both no-nonsense, down-to-earth blokes. Their preference would have been for Giselle and me to work for the whole season, but when we told them we only wanted to stay two or three weeks, they offered us a mixture of weeding and fruit picking for two weeks on lower wages instead. "Work's from 8 am to 5pm and you'll be paid $20 a day," the son said. Camping, toilet, showers, and laundry is free behind the house; You can start tomorrow morning."

"Thank you, that sounds good; it's what we were looking for," I said.

We had only just set up our farm stay camp when our immediate neighbours, Rose and Colin, returned from work along with their six-year-old daughter, Debbie.

After dinner, we began talking with them. Rose and Colin were professionals, travelling around Australia from one picking season to the next. They would stay in Bowen until November before moving on.

We asked how that lifestyle affected their daughter's education; "Debbie is home schooled; we receive her learning materials by mail," Rose said and showed us the materials. Everything a schoolchild would need was included: pencil, eraser, books and exercise sheet. Debbie was clever, inquisitive, and outgoing, a sweet and well-behaved girl; home school obviously suited her.

Colin didn't say much; he was busy drinking and offered us a beer.

"Colin's a gun picker," Rose said.

"What's that?" I asked.

"He picks very fast and gets paid by the amount he picks," Rose explained. "The faster you pick, the more you earn. I work mainly in the packing shed, and Debbie helps out a bit or plays where I can keep an eye on her."

Colin piped up, "We'll do that for a few more years before we can buy our own farm."

Slowly we understood, it was a different lifestyle altogether, like nothing we had ever experienced. Farmers needed those travelling professional pickers; there never seemed to be enough workers living around the farm. Local people needed full-time work, which was not limited to a season.

It rained all night long; we lay on the bed wondering how this would affect our first day on the job. Colin came over first thing in the morning, "No work today."

He didn't look upset; as he put it, the rain had come at the right time to guarantee a bumper crop. After breakfast, it had stopped raining, and we took a long walk with Colin, Debbie and Michael, another farmhand. The fields of tomato, cucumber and beans looked magnificent. The sun had come out and made the tomato leaves sparkle, a breathtaking view over the mile-long fields with mountain ranges in the background.

Back at the farm, I had a ride on Michael's dirt bike; mud was flying behind me as I rode on the tracks beside the fields of tomatoes. Later, I saw the old farmer sitting on the bike, upright and proud-looking, his hat flapping in the wind, riding along and inspecting the fields of his labour.

Colin and Michael urged us to come to town with them; they wanted to help us buy a gun. They had convinced us we needed a gun to help them shoot kangaroos. That sounded ghastly and was against everything we believed in, but apparently there were too many kangaroos. A bumper crop is one thing; seeing it consumed by 'roo' in 'plague proportions' was another.

Roos weren't the only threat to the farmer's crops; birds were another. Next to his tomato fields, he had placed gas containers attached to a firearm of some description that automatically fired blanks to frighten off cockatoos. I don't think it worked; a cockatoo, perched on one of them, just hopped into the air whenever it 'went off' and returned to its position a few seconds later, unruffled. It would have made an excellent comic strip. Once a week, the farmhand and a couple of boys would go out at night shooting. "Why at night time, why don't you sit somewhere hidden on the edge of a field and wait for the kangaroos?" I asked Colin.

"It's easier at night; we drive around in a ute, standing on the tray at the back. One operates a spotlight, and the other guys shoot. Roos, when seeing the light, will look into it, and stand still which allows a clean shoot and the 'roo' will not suffer", Colin explained patiently.

"What do you think, should we get a gun?" I asked Giselle.

At the shop, Colin showed us a few guns and, seeing we lacked the necessary knowledge to make a sound decision, recommended we acquire a double-barrelled shotgun. The price tag put us off, and we ended up with a .22 (whatever that meant). It looked similar to the air rifles I used when I was a kid, and it was also light enough for Giselle to handle. Together with bullets and a rifle bag, our purchase cost $60. Colin reassured us; "Don't worry, you can always sell it again for the same amount, the shop owner gave you a good deal."

"I can't believe we bought a gun," I said to Giselle.

"I don't want to believe it," Giselle laughed.

Although we didn't have much cash left, we bought a carton of beer, another first for us. Sitting around a barbecue, drinking after a hard day's work, was the done thing and we couldn't go on accepting freebies from Colin. Sure enough, back at the farm, we were invited for a barbecue. Another guy staying on the farm returned from a successful day's angling; a fresh fish dinner was washed down with plenty of beer.

The conversation turned to guns. "Are you a good shot?" Michael asked.

"I used to be OK with an air rifle," I replied modestly "but honestly, I have never fired a real gun."

Colin said something along the lines of, "You'll get your chance tomorrow night. We're off on a roo shoot."

We went to bed dreaming about shootouts.

Next morning, a sunny Saturday, we were up and ready to start work at eight. Up we went into the top paddock to tackle the waiting cucumbers. No speed picking was needed for this plot, only a good eye to pick the right cucumber size. Colin raced along, and cucumbers were flying into his crate. Now we knew what a gun picker was.

Another young couple went along at a more comfortable speed. We slowly followed. It was not long before our backs were aching. Not a moment too soon, Colin called out 'smoko'; although we saw no smoke, we welcomed the break, resting on the ground and gulping down water. After the next break, half an hour for lunch, we struggled to stand upright, but there was no further relief until around 3pm when Colin called out, "Enough cucumbers." He knew how many boxes were needed for the market; the 'quota' had been filled.

Our day's work wasn't done, though. Handing us each a hoe and directing us to the tomato beds, he instructed us to get busy with the weeding. At least we didn't have to bend down to do that, but the work was tedious beyond belief, and by 5 pm, we declared ourselves officially dead.

A hot shower revived our spirits and body. Everyone gathered together for dinner, eating and having beers. We understood what the beer was for. Not only was the day hot, and one felt like a cold one, but it was also necessary to numb the backache. Jeff, the other picker, must have had a lot of backaches; he became pretty drunk, not funny anymore.

That very night, the shooting excursion was planned. I wondered, 'Would Jeff come too?'

One hour later, we sped off into the moonless night, standing on the open tray at the back of the ute. We were eight people, the guy driving, one operating the spotlight, and six others, five of whom had lethal weapons, including Jeff.

My inner pacifist, like Giselle's, was lying low. As a roo bounded into a patch of land illuminated by the spotlight, I sent the innocent-looking creature a telepathic message: 'Hop away!' Michael, an experienced shooter, aimed and fired. A clean kill, as they call it.

Colin's and Jeff's trigger fingers were getting itchy now. The second target wasn't as lucky as the first; they both fired at it, badly injuring but not killing the poor creature. Too sad to see; we didn't like the whole thing anymore. It had gone past an adventure and it was not safe with Colin and Jeff firing haphazardly.

We drove on, spotlight searching. I saw Colin reloading his double-barrelled shotgun. Getting worried, I raised my voice, "Hi Colin, do you have your safety on?"

He gave me a look as if to say, "What do you know?" but answered, "Sure I have." As he raised the shotgun, he pulled the trigger and a deafening bang shook my world. My ears rang like church bells; the shell just missed my head. I nearly collapsed in shock. Giselle was crying, and I, realising how close I had come to being killed, was shouting insults at Colin.

This was the first time I ever used the f-word. "Are you fucking crazy?" I screamed. I recall thinking he was bound to lose his temper and punch me but he turned really quiet and didn't say a word. Fortunately, his silence enabled me to calm down.

I took Giselle into my arms. We'd had enough for one night.

The driver called out, "Let's head back, it's no good tonight." As he turned the ute around, it stalled, and then he flattened the battery trying to restart it. In the end, we climbed out and trotted back to our quarters on foot.

A comfy bed awaited us, and we needed peace, no more shooting for us.

Waking up was painful; we crawled out of the car to alleviate our stiff muscles under a hot shower. No Sunday rest for us, at 8 am we were ready.

Hacking away at the weeds on rows of tomato bushes was the order of the day. Colin and Debbie were with us, Colin subdued, looking properly embarrassed about nearly killing me. I tried to lighten the mood with a few jokes, and at first with Giselle, then with Debbie pitching in, made up a few songs to help the day go more smoothly. After what had happened, there were no hard feelings. We weren't setting any speed records that day, but we were steady workers and I noticed even Colin was going more slowly as the day wore on. We kept chipping away until 5 pm. Two days completed, $80 in our hands.

It was freshly picked beans, steak and beer for dinner. We were allowed to eat all we could from the farm produce, even fresh milk, and tried our hand at milking Dora, the happy cow. Not as easy as it sounds. We both had a go but were happy enough to let the farmer's son take over. He filled up the bucket in no time.

Here we were on an idyllic farm, surrounded by nature and contented people. Cows to be milked, ducklings running around, little Debbie chasing after the chicks, dogs and cats clamouring for attention, something wholesome for everyone. The work was hard but the rewards were plentiful.

Hacking away at weeds was a never-ending job. Giselle had help on this task from two women who usually worked in the packing shed. I went into another field with Colin and Michael to spray the weeds with poison dispensed from a truck.

The beer we shared after work was more than a drinking session; it was a kind of celebration, saluting each other on a job well done. More than that even, it was an act of comradeship, or, as I increasingly came to call it, mateship. Had I become a mate? I would say yes, but at other times I was aware of being the outsider. Some of the blokes stared at me; it was a look that told me I wasn't a real mate. They were friendly enough but the feeling they regarded you as a mate was absent.

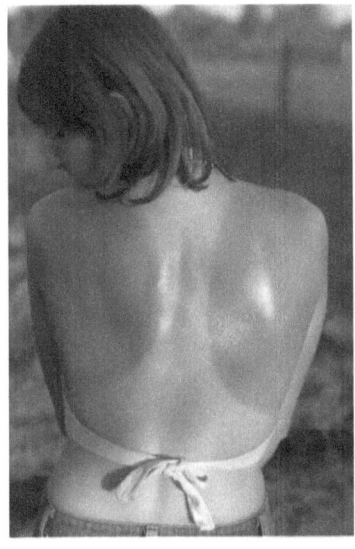

The next day, Giselle came back from work badly sunburnt. She had worn only a seamless singlet, and her shoulders and upper back were bright red and swollen. She felt feverish. I applied a spray for the sunburn we had from Gerd - I alternated the spray with cream every 30 minutes. Giselle never wore a bra; she didn't even own a bra. A bra strap would have irritated the burned skin. She wore a t-shirt and had to sleep on her tummy that night.

Giselle felt better in the morning. I took a photo of her back; it was fire red. I felt guilty she had been picking tomatoes all day long while I was spraying weeds which was a lazy job, despite having to walk fast while carrying the spray gun and hose.

One night, Rose and Colin invited us to dinner. Colin had baked a meat pie. He was a practical and versatile guy and I took it as his way of offering amends for the shooting incident. For our part, Giselle and I had sworn never to have a meat pie again, but this one – being home-made with quality meat – was different, and we liked it. We even had tomato sauce with it.

Payday arrived, and $85 for each of us, followed by a trip to town, shopping and picking up mail. My mother had written, the letter was over two weeks old, and the news was alarming. She was in hospital with thrombosis and a lung infection. We felt utterly helpless, with no choice but to sit it out and hope for the best.

Next morning, the heavens opened and work was cancelled for the day, so we drove to town, heading straight to the post office to book a call to West Germany. We were advised to make the call back at the farmhouse; the post office closed at 1pm, not enough time to book a phone call and not the right time to call Germany.

Meeting up with Colin and Michael, we went to the pub. I had three beers; that shouting beer ritual makes one drink too much. Giselle was clever, she had ordered a shandy. We didn't know the term, but Giselle had asked Colin what a mixture of beer and lemonade was called. In Hamburg we called it *Alsterwasser*.

If I'd been as clever as Giselle, I'd have ordered the same, but I couldn't, could I? It is regarded as a ladies' drink.

I was fit again for dinner, our regular barbeque. Beforehand, I talked to the farmer's wife about a possible phone call. "Yes, of course, no problem, the telephone operator is a friend of mine," she assured me. "When would you like to book it for?" "Half past five, straight after work, would be good." I answered, giving her my parent's number in Hamburg.

I went back to Giselle, "Phone call is booked, too easy, we should have thought about that before".

It was Sunday, just another working day, we didn't take a break, working right through until 5 pm. Walking into the house, the farmer's wife was on the phone, talking to her friend, the operator. She glanced over at us, said, "Won't be long" and pointed to the chairs.

We sat down. We had to sit down, having never been in a grand old-style 'Queenslander'; we were simply stunned. It took us a while to digest the stark contrast between the rough-and-ready appearance of the farm outside these walls and this interior, spotlessly clean with antique furniture, stained-glass windows, doorway arches and finely crafted timberwork. We felt as if we should go out, change into our best clothes and come back.

Still in shock and deep thoughts, we could hear a muffled voice, "It's ringing, I'll put you through." The farmer's wife handed me the receiver; I could hear it ringing. – My dad was answering.

"Dad, it's me, Dieter, how are you, how is Mum?"

Hearing the echo of my voice, Dad must have said something at the same time.

"Can you hear me?" he yelled.

"Yes Dad, how is Mum?"

"Mum is much better, but she needs to stay in hospital for another four weeks."

We continued talking over each other's echoes for a couple of minutes.

"Bye Dad, love to Mum, a letter is on the way," I said, finishing the call.

"Bye son" and a few more distorted sounding words – click.

"That went better than I expected," I said to Giselle. "He sounded OK." We were relieved. There was no emergency; it seemed everything would turn out all right. It would take time for my Mum to recuperate fully.

The operator called back, it was six minutes, but she only charged for three. "The line wasn't ideal, no charge for the first 3 minutes."

We paid our hosts, thanked them and remarked on their beautiful house.

Dinner and beer waited for us with our fellow pickers. Rose and Colin had prepared a proper German meal; it may have been from a tin but we appreciated the gesture, sauerkraut, potatoes and frankfurters which called for another beer. Tensions subsided; we went to bed early and slept like babies.

8 am sharp, and we were ready for work. We had to pick ten buckets full of cucumbers, an order for a local shop. It took us about one hour. We should have picked slower; we were sent back weeding the endless rows of tomatoes.

We had lost our enthusiasm. "Should we leave already on Wednesday?" I asked Giselle.

"Yes, let's stop; I've had enough," she replied.

But it was even better; after work, while I was under the shower, Neville (the older farmer) spoke to Giselle.

"Guess what?" Giselle asked when I came back.

"What?" I said.

"We are done, no more work for us, today was our last day, Neville just told me," Giselle said.

We hugged; we had survived another adventure. "I think the family like us," Giselle said, "Mrs Jones said we should come over for a drink."

"How nice," I said, "OK, let's go."

Mrs Jones certainly could talk. We knew everything about the family after one hour. Maybe it was the sherries; she must have refilled the glasses 3 or 4 times.

That night most of the guys went shooting again. We politely declined. "Sorry, too much to do" was the white lie I dished out. To make matters worse, Colin was half drunk and Michael was dressed like a big game hunter, wearing a white headband and a belt across his chest, holding cartridges for his sawn-off shotgun.

On the day of our departure we slept in, had a late breakfast and cleaned up around our camp. We were relaxed, happy and relieved, no more weeding for us – ever. We took more photos, looking for the best spots to capture the beauty of the place and convey the feeling of what it was like to stand in seemingly endless rows of tomato plants.

The farm's owner came over to us. (This was a first.) He handed us two cheques, amounting to more than we had expected. We talked for a while; this was also unusual for a man of few words. Unexpectedly, his hand shot out, "Goodbye," he said awkwardly. We were touched; he must have liked us.

Saying our goodbyes to everyone took some time. It was a bit like in Rubyvale, sad to go, leaving those friendly people behind, while at the same time happy to move on.

Before we finally went, we received a generous parting gift, cartons of carefully-sorted tomatoes in different stages of ripeness, cucumbers, beans, and eggs. Fresh food for weeks to come. A quick exchange of addresses, and off we went, "*On the Road Again.*"

Chapter 7

Tropical Dreams

The drive was uneventful but beautiful, kilometre after kilometre of sugarcane against a backdrop of mountain ranges. We arrived in Townsville in time for lunch. Something had changed; the air felt different, or was it our imagination? Was it the beginning of the tropics?

Rewarding ourselves for surviving as farmhands, we went to a Chinese restaurant before exploring the town. We saw the book we were looking for at a well-stocked bookstore, "Australia Yesterday." As the name suggested, it was a short history lesson with pictures. Enough for a better understanding of Australia's past.

A brief sightseeing tour comprising a quick drive up Castle Hill for great 360-degree views and photo opportunities completed our Townsville experience.

Before looking for a caravan park, we went down to the beach. It was a scene we had dreamt about, sitting and leaning against a palm tree, breathing the warm air and relaxing in harmony with waves flowing in and out.

Townsville was only supposed to be a stopover, so the beachside caravan park at an affordable $2 a night suited us perfectly.

Snuggling up in the van with our new book, we read about Australia's history and learnt in heartbreaking detail how the Indigenous population had been treated atrociously. Hopefully, we would meet some aborigines and would be able to talk to them.

At 11am next day, we set out on the northbound road to Cairns, a distance of some 360 km. The scenery was greener, lusher, but still dominated by sugarcane fields and mountainous terrain. We had a picnic lunch at a secluded beach near the coastal town of Cardwell. Hinchinbrook Island was so close to the mainland that we felt we could almost reach out and touch it.

Next stop Innisfail, where we saw a charming cottage for sale. During the past few months, our dream of buying a house had bloomed into earnest intent and the sight of this one had us indulging the fantasy that we might make an offer and end our travels there. We had written to our parents that we wanted to buy a house once back in Germany; not sure if we were trying to fool them or ourselves.

Deep down, the idea of staying in Australia crept into our consciousness. Would we return, how sure were we?

Fantasies can have real-life consequences. We looked at that little house so long that the post office and most of the shops were closed by the time we made it into Cairns. Next morning we found that the only mail for us at the post office was a letter from Bob and Joan, our gem hunter friends, directing us to the caravan park where they were staying.

A warm greeting awaited us and they handed us a bunch of letters they had collected for us. There was good news. My mum was home and had fully recovered. To celebrate, Bob and Joan took us to lunch at a nice restaurant, where we caught up on a month's worth of each other's news. We pitched in with a bottle of champagne, not the real one, the sparkling wine variation.

Finally they drove us to Ellis Beach, a special spot they were sure we would like. Once again, we were being given a vision of paradise. Our chosen camping spot was right on the beach, between swaying coconut palms. Ahead of us were the glistening turquoise waters of the Pacific; behind us mountains blanketed in rainforest. We had the best of both worlds. The caravan park manager told us that a food truck would make a stop here every day, selling fruit and veg, and sometimes fish or meat. We loved everything and booked for a whole week. Imagine $12 for a week in paradise! We sat behind our car, relaxing and overlooking the beach with a view of a small island called Double Island which appeared to be within swimming distance.

The only plan we made that day was that we would do nothing tomorrow. We slept in and missed what was no doubt a sunrise worth seeing. A lazy breakfast was followed by an even lazier couple of hours lounging around.

Eventually we pulled ourselves out of our chairs and took a long walk along the beach, kicking up sand, picking up shells, pebbles and even some pumice. In Germany, we had to buy those little volcanic rocks to keep our feet free of calluses. We picked up quite a few; one never knew when calluses would strike again.

Hot after the long walk, we jumped into the water and stayed there for a whole hour. The longest time we had ever spent in the ocean.

On the third day of the self-proclaimed, doing nothing holiday, we resumed activities. We needed creativity and suitable photos for our planned book. Still eager to do more, we finished all our letter writing and had a dreamlike discussion about our future. Dreams can come true.

That afternoon, we decided I should become an author. I had always loved writing; it was the lofty decision to become an author which was new. Giselle loved all my little stories which was enough encouragement for me to think about writing full-time.

Becoming an author was a bit of a joke; most of my short stories were somewhat ridiculous. I wasn't ready to become a novelist, but I did have a theme; I had to develop a good story to sell our book about Australia.

"I can't write without a good notebook," I said.

"That's a nice excuse to buy something," Giselle laughed. She knew I loved buying notebooks and diaries.

Fired up, I wrote a short story that night. Satisfied with my effort, I relaxed playing the guitar, dreaming about my new career while Giselle sang. No country music that night; it was Beatles all the way.

Woken up by the sound of the food truck's horn beeping, I emerged, bleary-eyed, from the car in time to buy fresh bread, cheese and tomatoes. The dreamy sleep of a night in paradise was followed by a heavenly breakfast.

Still exuberant about my decision to be an author, Giselle and I began brainstorming other ideas, half of them bordering on the delusional. We worked on the principle of letting thoughts go wild before focusing on what was possible. Developing our own philosophy, we came up with our new motto: *In attempting the impossible, one is meaningfully occupied.*

Bob and Joan came for a visit and brought our mail. My mum wrote that a radio station in Hamburg looked for short travel stories. Excitement took hold of me. I had written about Rubyvale already but it required shortening. My brain went into overdrive. Giselle came up with more suggestions. Time for bed and creative dreaming.

Armed with paper and a pencil, we took another long beach walk after breakfast next morning, and brainstormed story ideas. Most of them were discarded after a refreshing dip in the ocean. Some survived, and I wrote one down. All that was left to do was edit it and copy it in my best handwriting.

After lunch and a satisfying nap, I wrote another story about the treatment of aborigines. Our experience of Indigenous Australians was still limited, but our impression was they were the victims of disturbing and widespread intolerance. My views in this new story expressed how we had been thinking.

"I don't think we should show it to anyone. It may be too one-sided," Giselle said.

"I know, it's just between us," I replied, "It's too early for us to weigh in with our opinions on such a controversial topic. The main thing is to keep writing about it."

That night we read more from our 'Australia Yesterday' book. The first Australians' mistreatment was certainly well portrayed, but in our view, it was more disturbing that the government had no solution. Politicians knew something was wrong, but nothing constructive was done to remedy the situation, and throwing money at the problem seemed counter-productive.

Our time at our beach paradise ended; we dismantled our camp, ready for departure after one blissful week. We had Port Douglas in our sights and, further north, Cooktown. We were curious to see where Captain Cook found refuge for his damaged ship, the Endeavour, after running aground on the Great Barrier Reef in 1770. We had read that this was where the English word 'kangaroo' was first used, transcribed from the Aboriginal gangurru.

As it turned out, Port Douglas was as far as we could go; the road to Cooktown was passable only by four-wheel drive vehicles. Instead, we had a hearty, good-value lunch comprising a large steak, chips and salad at a Port Douglas pub. Since there wasn't much to see in Port Douglas, we turned around, heading back to Cairns to see more of it. Our first impressions had been somewhat underwhelming. The yacht marina was quite picturesque but you couldn't say the same about the rest of the town, as Cairns had no natural beach or surf.

We stayed in Cairns and camped close to Bob and Joan's caravan park and joined them next morning on an outing to the local flea market. We bought a couple of polished gems and a pipe that once belonged to a bagpipe.

Bob introduced us to one stallholder he knew. "Meet Ron," he said, "he is into leathercraft, an artist and musician." Giselle, of course, was interested in leathercraft and happy to receive hot tips on what to buy and how to start.

Giselle was especially interested in creating what she called; mini bags. Not knowing the exact English word for what she had in mind, Giselle sketched it out. "Yes, they're easy to make," Ron told her. "You need the leather, something to cut it with, a needle and string as well as a tool to punch a hole in the leather before you do the stitching. That's pretty much it."

Ron was also a keen collector of original Australian folk music. He had published two books containing the lyrics of the vast majority of folk songs ever sung in Australia. We couldn't curb our enthusiasm, bought both his books and had them signed. I was looking forward to learning some of the pieces. I could picture us sitting around a campfire, Giselle singing and me on guitar.

On Sunday afternoon, we bought an Aboriginal-created newspaper, something we'd never encountered before. I thought my opinion piece about the treatment of Aboriginals was harsh but it was nothing compared to this paper's frankness.

Monday, September 1 – A new day, another week, another month and, in this part of the world, the first day of Spring. For us, all this was a sign of good things to come. What did the planet have in store for us?

Green Island; we chose to be tourists for one day. Coral was nothing new to us but Green Island was supposed to be unique. It had a coral foundation and the island was formed by waves depositing sand, debris and vegetation.

Bob and Joan drove us to the jetty. Two tickets richer, and $11 poorer, we were allowed onto the boat. Reading the latest mail from Hamburg, I barely noticed the ship had left the harbour. Giselle's parents had enclosed the newspaper clipping of an article about a couple travelling around Australia. I was fuming; how come they were published and we weren't? Was it because we hadn't written any articles yet? My clear case of jealousy amused me, and I was so involved that I hardly noticed the boat trip. With the initial anger dissolving, motivation was setting in and I was eager to get our own story published.

I should have stayed involved; now, I was experiencing the boat trip which meant getting seasick. Once before, when I was about twenty, on a boat trip from Hamburg to the island of Heligoland, I was seasick. I was fine while the boat was still on the river Elbe but the open waters of the North Sea were too rough for my sensitive stomach.

That memorable boat trip focused on young people, disco dancing, plenty of duty-free drinks, and flirting. While dancing, I hardly noticed the rocking sea. That changed after I had more drinks and too much to eat on the island before shipping back to Hamburg. Was it the food or the whisky? After 5 minutes back on the boat, my stomach contents were liberated and I stayed sick for the rest of the trip, no dancing or flirting anymore for young Dieter.

We were coming in to Green Island when my colour changed to light green. Luckily, my seasickness was not enough to throw up. We arrived and I was rescued; the solid ground under my feet, fresh air, even though it was like a hothouse, and a brisk walk gave me back my healthy complexion. A spot of lunch, cold chicken, and lots of fresh salad which was complimentary and served on the boat completed my recovery.

We walked around the island once; yes, it was that small and there was no point doing it a second time. We did what everyone did, looking around, licking ice cream and visiting the underwater observatory, where pretty little fish swimming among the corals were enjoying their natural habitat; unaware they were the attraction.

The trip back went surprisingly smoothly; my green colour did not return. Bob and Joan drove us back to the caravan park for a fish barbeque.

The following day Giselle was unwell. Was it the trip, too much sun, the food, or a combination? We had no idea but now my darling was off the Pill, the answer might be something else altogether. Naturally, we had talked about children and we weren't keen on having any. There was still too much we wanted to do. Simply put, being pregnant while planning to travel for another two years would be highly inconvenient.

After a cup of tea and toast, Giselle felt well enough for a leisurely drive up to the Atherton Tablelands, a must for anyone who loves tropical rainforests. At

Kuranda, a small village high on the range, we could have done our sightseeing from an old train servicing the tourist trade. We preferred to walk, guaranteeing a close-up view of the perfect scenery, which featured waterfalls, steep cliff faces and rainforest.

These beautiful sights inspired us to create more ideas for telling the story of Australia. At one point I said to Giselle, "Maybe we could publish a book on Australia's most beautiful waterfalls?"

"Yes, I was thinking the same thing, and we could add some of my sketches," she said.

Obviously, we had no time for kids as yet.

It was the third of September, my mother's birthday. 'Happy Birthday Mama, hope you are well,' I thought. There is not much else one could do; it was too hard to book an overseas phone call from a caravan park.

We had more meaningful things to pursue. Bob and Joan drove us to a nearby Aboriginal mission. We felt hesitant; Bob mentioned we would need a permit, but we tried our luck and drove on, slowly, very slowly. Kids were playing cricket and some adults were making pottery which was not really what we had expected. Buildings on both sides of the street looked good and people seemed busy and friendly. They were waving at us and we waved back. No one asked us for a permit.

We drove on until we came to a secluded beach, half sand, half rocks covered with oysters. Bob was excited, took out his fishing knife and helped himself to a few of the rock oysters. Giselle and Joan had a couple while I politely declined, being averse to swallowing something alive and slimy-looking. To me, the oysters looked like space aliens plotting to take over the world. 'Maybe I should turn my hand to writing science fiction?' I mused. 'Or, maybe I've read too many science-fiction stories!'

As there was no one else around and it was pretty hot by now, we went for a swim. Giselle went topless, as she often did, and Joan copied the spirit of Giselle's sixties bra-burning attitude as she, probably for the first time in her life, discarded her top as well. Bob wasn't sure where to look!

After our swim, we settled down for a picnic. A bit further away, we saw an Aboriginal guy standing still in the water for what seemed an eternity. He was holding a spear above the water all this time as if he were a mere statue when with fierce suddenness, he thrust the spear into the water and brought up a fish. It was better than a movie, an aborigine in full action. This hardy black man looked like an Aboriginal warrior. How wrong our first impression was!

Giselle and I waved to him and walked over. He waved back quite casually. 'Would he speak English?' I wondered.

"Hi," he greeted us, and that's how a long conversation started, as easy as that.

For the next hour, we talked. He was a very knowledgeable guy and knew how to communicate his knowledge. He had been a schoolteacher but was suspended after being labelled a troublemaker.

His version of how 'whites' treated' blacks' struck us as authentic. In his view, the government was deliberately suppressing Aborigines' rights.

To the average person on the street, he said, it might seem that the government was trying to help, spending money on houses and welfare payments. In reality, the government kept the black man suppressed rather than support self-determination.

Aboriginals were being dictated to and pressured to adopt the lifestyle followed by white society. Their know-how was totally disregarded. We could only sympathise with this viewpoint.

"What do white politicians think, that 40,000 years (new data; 65,000) of culture is not worth anything, is nothing to learn from?" he said. "Many of us have been condemned to live on white-run missions where we have no self-regulation. We always have to do what the white man is telling us."

What astounded us was not what he said; I suspect we felt angrier than he did, but the calmness with which he made his points.

He went on, speaking even more calmly. "The government is deliberately suppressing us; out of fear we will rise to power and want our land back. They also fear we may get encouraged by the American black power movement which, by the way, we are not." He went on, "It all comes down to the fact that we have to do whatever politicians want, and they don't listen to what we want."

With that last statement, he finished his explanations. He moved a couple of steps away and, casually bending down, dug a large spider shell out of the wet sand which he handed to Giselle.

"We sell a lot of these to the tourists," he laughed. Instructions followed; we had to store it in a bucket of sand and give it two weeks to dry out. After that, it would be ready for cleaning and displaying.

Saying goodbye, Giselle and I both felt privileged to have been given an insight into what an Aboriginal man had to say about his people's experience. We felt that we had gained and lost a friend, all in the space of one hour.

We talked about our newfound knowledge. Could it be like the aboriginal teacher explained? Bob half agreed but thought the government was acting out of misunderstanding and ignorance rather than plotting to suppress Aboriginal voices.

One thing the teacher said I had never considered before. I shared that thought with Giselle; "Could Aboriginals ask for their land back? After all, it is their country and has been for tens of thousands of years. They must have some rights, mustn't they?"

We didn't have a clue but something was wrong with how the government was handling aborigines.

His main objective seemed simple enough; to find ways in which black people could achieve equality and full recognition in their ancestral lands.

One sentence he said stuck in our minds; "We are thinking with our hearts and feeling with our minds."

We didn't take photos on the way back through the mission; we felt too much like tourists taking photos of attractions; it seemed degrading.

After an early rise, we prepared for the road again. Having packed the car for travelling, we stayed a while longer, writing letters. Giselle wrote to her parents, asking them to find out about house prices in Hamburg. She knew they would see her question as assurance that we would return.

We left the Caravan Park by noon, driving into Cairns, picking up mail, getting cash from the bank and shouting ourselves lunch at a Chinese restaurant as a last goodbye.

I'm not sure what possessed me, probably because I was ready to travel and it was hot. I went into the restaurant barefoot and shirtless. Giselle was very casually dressed as well. The waiter looked at us sceptically but served us, nevertheless.

It was mid-afternoon when we got under way, singing '*On The Road Again*' at the top of our lungs. Our destination of the day was Ravenshoe, about 120 km inland, where we hoped to dig up some agate. We drove up into the mountainous rainforest, and admired a lake created by an asteroid smashing a massive hole into the ground. We had exchanged the stifling humidity of Cairns for clear mountain air and the perfect' temperature of 22 degrees.

Chapter 8

Meeting Dean

We found a camping ground just before dark. At the manager's office, they had agates for sale; we bought a piece for $1.50 just in case we didn't find any.

It had turned dark by the time we had our camp set up. A young guy camping next to us came over to lend us a torch. "You can give it back to me in the morning; I've got another one," he said. Some people are just nice.

At breakfast time our camping neighbour brought us a cup of tea. He was a geologist and worked for a German company looking for uranium, the 'Deutsche Uranium Gesellschaft.' We found out his name was Dean and he was travelling to his next job destination. Besides looking for something we didn't like, he played the guitar and was about our age.

His skills as a guitarist were not that great but neither were mine. I could play a few songs, and he knew a few too. That was all we had on offer, but it suited the atmosphere, campfire and guitar, always a good match. We parted as friends, exchanging addresses; he wanted to visit us one day in Germany.

Driving on, we looked where to find agates, but they were always hiding on private properties where we had to pay to enter. We gave up and travelled to Mt. Garnet. As the name suggested, it was a possibility for finding garnets, not that we had high hopes of success. The town was known for mining tin, zinc, copper and garnet. Actually, we didn't even know what garnet looked like, but it was mentioned in our Gem Hunting Map.

On the road to Mt. Garnet, we noticed Dean's vehicle behind us. We stopped in Mt. Garnet and got talking. Dean had an exciting offer for us. He needed someone for his next job and we fitted the job description. We would drive with him to a place called 'Robin Hood Station,' leave our car there, and travel further by Dean's four-wheel drive to his base camp. We had to check the radio transmission at certain times of the day and bring messages and food to where he was camping, about a 5 km long march. He wouldn't be at the camp during the day, only at night, and would leave rock samples for us to take back.

That sounded like an easy job, except the walking part. He would pay us $15 per day, not a lot, but seeing it was basically a walking holiday, we didn't complain. "Thanks, Dean; sounds like a deal. Yes, we will take the job," we said.

He had to drive ahead. We agreed to meet him in Georgetown the following night at the only camping ground.

With Dean gone, we became a touch suspicious. Funny, we were always so positive but still harboured negative thoughts. Maybe for self-preservation?

"I don't think he's an axe murderer," I said.

Giselle laughed, "Maybe he wants to hijack our car?"

In the end, our suspicions waned and we agreed that he and the job were for real. It was still early in the day. We decided to give the garnets a miss and drove to Mt. Surprise to look for topaz.

We arrived at Mt Surprise, filled our tank, and asked where to find topaz. They suggested we ask in the pub. We had noticed previously that whenever we went into a country pub, it would only be a few minutes, and someone would start to chat and ask where we came from. Sure enough, we hardly had lifted our glasses before we had company. After some small talk, Giselle asked the big question, "Where can we look for topaz?" That guy wasn't even surprised. He gave us the location and described how to get there and mentioned, "Drive very carefully, it's a bad rocky track." That wasn't all; he advised us to stay a fair distance away from other miners who camped out there. Some of them could get pretty nasty and all of them had guns to protect their precious finds.

He issued one more warning: "The topaz is found in the riverbed under large rocks and boulders."

"Thank you; we will try our best," I said innocently, not expecting what would come next."

"And the guys use dynamite to blow rocks out of the riverbed. You better watch out," he warned us.

I think we got the message, or maybe not, because after we shouted him a beer, we took off. We found the track easily enough but soon knew what he meant. The track consisted of sand and rocks, and we couldn't even go back; there was no space to turn the car. Our car didn't drive, it hobbled, rocks everywhere. We crossed a few creeks and were happy there were rocks, and surprisingly enough, we made it. It took over 2 hours of driving in suspense. It was Mt. Surprise for sure!

We saw a couple of scary-looking older guys at a fair distance from where we set up camp. We didn't feel much like digging or looking; it was late, and we were tired. After a quick dinner, we had an early night. The other guys had vanished into their tents. No nightlife at this location!

We didn't want to stay there long and had an early breakfast. As we looked around, we saw crystals and even topazes lying around. Someone must have discarded them, but they were good enough for us.

We went up the dry creek bed, kicked some rocks around, dug a little bit and even shifted a boulder with the help of a dead tree branch. All to no avail, no topaz showed its pretty face.

One of the miners must have watched what we were up to and he waved us over. "You won't find anything here," he said.

"Where should we go?" I asked.

"Nowhere, unless you have better equipment to shift large rocks much further up the creek," he replied.

I couldn't help feeling curious and enquired, "Have you found any?"

He looked at us for a moment, sat down and took off his left boot. He had a false leg; we had noticed he was limping. It got better. He tipped out the contents of his boot, a heap of large topazes. He picked up a few to show us the different colours. "We are after the blue ones; that's where the money is," he said.

We knew what he meant and could see that we wouldn't have a chance to find anything just by looking around. "Thanks, and thank you for showing us," we both said. "I think we'll leave it to you; we haven't got time to stay another day anyhow. Bye then, and good luck," I said.

Just as we turned around, he said, "Wait," and went to his tent and returned with a jar of smaller topazes. "Here you go, take some as proof you've been here," he said.

Lucky again, we happily took our gems away with us. He may have looked scruffy but was a nice guy after all.

Now the hard part; we had to drive back. We managed and arrived safe and sound in Mt. Surprise, continuing straight to Georgetown, a 90km long trip. Dean was right, there was only one caravan park, easy to spot, and he was easy to find as well.

We had tea with Dean and talked about the job and the terrain we would have to traverse. He invited us for dinner at the pub. We stayed quite a while, talking about all kinds of things, as one does when one is getting to know each other, including our experience with the Aboriginal teacher we had met in Cairns. Dean had a lot of respect for Aborigines and promised to show us original rock paintings nobody other than him and the farmers had seen. His base camp was at an oasis of rock pools with plenty of fish. We would sleep in a large tent on camp beds. It sounded fantastic; we couldn't wait to get there.

Having breakfast with Dean, he surprised us with his self-baked bread. What a versatile guy! We drove on a worn-out gravel road to a small village called Forsayth which used to be a gold mining town. Dean had old maps showing the location of the early mines. He wanted to find them, "You can find old bottles, porcelain, coins and even bits of gold," he said. That was right up our alley. Anything with gem or treasure hunting worked for us.

We drove on looking for one of the old gold mines. We found one which looked like no one had been there for ages. The gravel tracks were overgrown with grass. The mine was littered with giant, rusted, broken mining equipment including old steam engines, gears in various proportions, looking like someone's enormous watch had exploded.

Dean knew his business. Even though the old houses and sheds had disappeared, he made us aware of what the mine and surrounding area would have looked like. Carefully we walked around, trying not to fall into an old mine shaft. The shafts were open and supported only by rotten timber.

Dean looked for an indication of where the rubbish tip was. He pointed to an area towards one side which sloped downhill, "Let's have a dig there," he said. It only took scraping off the topsoil and our spades hit something hard. He found bits of glass, "That's it, we found the rubbish tip," he exclaimed. All three of us kept digging, gently parting the soil, moving the first layer of broken items, and some little treasures made their appearance. Giselle found a couple of ink glasses, some broken, some perfect, and a porcelain dish.

Different sections had other rubbish, and it was even more exciting once we found something unexpected, at least for us. Dean knew what those clay vessels were. We had found a large deposit of mainly unbroken gold-melting crucibles. We had finally found our treasure; some crucibles had tiny pearls of gold still in them. We had no idea how many there were; we dug out about 50 and stored them in our cars, but many more were still buried. We found other clay dishes, smaller, with natural glazes like molten glass or enamel.

We would have loved to dig more but had to leave to get to 'Robin Hood,' the cattle station. We arrived with plenty of daylight left. Our car was parked in a shed, locked away for safekeeping. We met the owner; he looked like a pioneer-spirited honourable man. We knew instantly he could be trusted, not only with our car but also with everything, a very impressive man. We were captivated by his aura and authenticity.

Dean was ready; we hopped into his car and drove to his camp. It started to rain. There was no road to speak of and with the rain coming down hard, it felt like we were driving in an undetermined direction right through the bush.

We arrived in one piece, the rain had calmed, and we quickly brought whatever was needed into his house tent.

The rain had stopped, and Dean lit a fire and started his generator. What a comfort, fire and electricity, we could have a pot of tea and a special dinner. Giselle sorted through Dean's tinned food collection. He liked German food. Tonight's treat was sauerkraut, sausages and mashed potatoes. Giselle had outdone herself.

For the next couple of days, we familiarized ourselves with the surroundings. And what beautiful surroundings we were living in. Even the knowledge that hardly anyone knew this place added a magical perspective to it. The rain was gone and we realized we had found yet another paradise. We had travelled from one paradise to another.

This paradise was unusual; it was an oasis in the middle of rugged bushland, with two-meter high magnetic termite mounds dotting the landscape. Distinctive Swiss cheese look-alike mountain ranges surrounded us. Wild pigs in the far distance and other wildlife everywhere we looked. Our oasis had tall trees and a bushy undercover; the large rock pool teemed with fish, turtles and, yes, crocodiles.

"Don't worry, they are sweet water crocodiles; they are very timid. One loud noise and they slip into the water," Dean said.

"Don't worry? We will do our best," I said.

At night in the moonshine, looking over the lake, one could see crocodile eyes everywhere. No point counting them; too many.

Butterflies, we had never seen so many butterflies. Walking just ten meters away from the tent towards the flowering bushes, we went through clouds of butterflies to reach one of the baby rock pools we used as our private bathtubs.

We spent our days fishing, preparing fish and eating fish. I didn't know anything about fishing but it was too easy. I just chucked in my line, and nothing else was needed to catch a fish.

Dean told us to throw back the smaller ones and only keep decent-sized fish. We also could have had turtle soup by the gallon; the turtles liked our fishing line. We couldn't, of course, keep or kill a turtle; back they went into the water. Whenever a crocodile took a bite, there was a sudden jerk and the line would snap.

Dean was busy making daily batches of fresh bread, and he even brewed beer. Before he went walkabout, he taught us how to handle the radio, finding the right frequency for staying in contact with the mining company and listening to the 'School of the Air'. Kids from remote cattle stations, who had no other way of getting to a school, would be on the radio at a set time. Their teacher talked to them, knowing everyone by name and handing out different lessons to different kids. If a kid had to go to the toilet, they asked to be excused, "Could I go to the toilet?" little Jimmy asked. "Yes, you can, let me know when you are back," the teacher answered. It was also the first time we used a camp shower. It was a large canvas bag with a shower rose on one end and a robe on the other. The whole contraption hung over a tree branch.

Dean certainly knew how to live in the bush. He even had a gym. Each morning, we would do weightlifting, some yoga and other exercises, and all that before breakfast.

We never dreamt living in the bush could be that comfortable. But of course, it was more than bush; it was an oasis.

Enough of this leisurely lifestyle, we had to work; after all, Dean paid us. It got serious; we had to walk with Dean to his second camp, about 2 hours away. Dean and I carried large backpacks, Giselle a smaller one. We also took some water and food for the walk back.

Dean alerted us to pay special attention to the landscape. We had to recognize the dried-out creek beds we crossed, on which side of the mountain ranges we walked, and even more critical, where we could walk between those mountain ranges back to the camp.

We memorized specific rock formations and were pretty sure we would find our way back. It seemed straightforward.

The walk was not easy; the grass was high and partly dried out. We had to dodge twisted and thorny shrubs, fallen trees and branches, and avoid wild pigs. Kangaroos jumped out from behind the bushes but the wild pigs needed most of our attention; they were vicious if they had young ones. We saw a few snakes and plenty of lizards and goannas, and we had never seen such giant spiders. Some of their webs stretched 5 to 10 metres, and we were caught a few times. Luckily, those spiders didn't like human flesh. Dean just brushed the webs away as he walked ahead.

Finally, we reached his camp. It wasn't much of a set-up; Dean knew how to rough it. A hammock spanned between two trees with a canvas slung over the top. A campfire and a natural spring he had discovered completed his camp. After clearing away sand, the water from the spring sparkled up. That was all he needed, somewhere to sleep, fresh water, plenty of food and his tools to look for rock samples.

Having had a little rest, a drink and food, we were ready to walk and find our way back. We only carried the empty backpacks. We would come back with food and collect his rock samples in two days. At least that was the plan. "See you in two days," we waved Dean goodbye.

It was hot by now; noon was not the best time to set out for our second long walk of the day. Not that we had much choice if we wanted to get back before dark.

The first half-hour was easy, even though we worked up a sweat. We had a good feeling that we would make it in record time. We hid behind bushes several times to avoid wild pigs coming too close for comfort. The boar always walked ahead of the family, the mama next, followed by the little ones, which were not that little either. The boar demanded respect, not just from his family, but also from us. The size of that beast was impressive; a domestic swine would look tiny beside it.

One hour went by, and we were still marching, not quite as cheerfully as in the beginning. We had crossed a few dried-out creek beds, but were we still on the right path?

"Next time, we will take more water," I said.

"... and maybe mix up some Staminade," Giselle said. We had become fond of this lemon-lime drink to replenish body salts, something we hadn't even been aware of in Germany. Gabrielle and Henry introduced us to it in Sydney. They claimed everyone who sweats needs it. And in Australia's summers, everyone sweats! No wonder it had become the National Australian Electrolyte Sports Drink.

How long had we been walking? Having a little rest, we realized it was already three hours. We should have been back at least half an hour ago. We were getting worried. Our water was gone; and we were tired, having walked the whole day in hot conditions. And we had no idea why we were not back at the camp yet.

"We must have missed the gap where we needed to walk into our valley," I said, "I think we are walking in circles."

"I don't want to sleep here. Should we go back to Dean's place?" Giselle asked.

"We've still got enough time; we always can go back; let's walk a bit more to the left," I said.

We didn't get very far. We walked for another half hour or more when Giselle had to sit down, feeling light-headed and close to passing out. We urgently needed water; we were exhausted. I sat next to Giselle for a while, trying to make sense of where we were. Trying to keep the anxiety out of my voice, I asked Giselle, "Do you think we are on the wrong side of the mountain range?"

She nodded, "Let's go back; we can sleep at Dean's camp; at least he's got enough water," Giselle said.

I was stubborn; I didn't feel like going back to Dean's camp. I would feel stupid to admit I couldn't find the way back. We were here to help, not to be a burden.

"Let's try one more thing," I said.

"What?" Giselle asked.

"I will get up that hill; I will have a good view from up there; maybe it will give us a better idea where we are," I said.

"I can't anymore," Giselle said.

"You stay here and rest; I will go up. It should only take 10 minutes," I said.

"Please be careful and don't lose me," Giselle answered.

I went as fast as I could muster with my last bit of strength. Uphill was a challenge. I turned around often; I had to make sure I could see Giselle. So far, I couldn't see any solution to our predicament. I needed to get up to the ridge to look over to the other side. I went on, 10 minutes were gone already, but I still could see Giselle resting against a tree trunk. On I went, right up to the top, I made it. Looking straight ahead, I couldn't make out anything specific. The sun had nearly gone down and the view was out of focus. Turning around, I looked back to where Giselle was resting. I envisaged that as 12 o'clock. I stared in that direction for a while, trying to make out something familiar. Nothing! I turned to 1 p.m., again looking for clues, nothing, and it went on, 2, 3, and 4 o'clock, which was where I guessed Dean's camp should be, but I couldn't see anything, 5 o'clock, 6 o'clock, still nothing, 7 o'clock, nothing, 8 o'clock, was there something?

I had seen a dim reflection when I turned; I kept turning my head from left to right. Yes, there was something. Squinting and holding my fingers around my eyes to focus better, I could just make out Dean's four-wheel drive. "Schatz, I got it! I got it!" I screamed.

She didn't hear me.

I looked around further and could see clearly where we went wrong and where we should have made a sharper left turn to go into our valley. I walked, stumbled, jumped and ran down as fast as possible on the rough ground. Every few metres, I screamed, "I got it, I got it!"

I saw Giselle getting up; she must have heard me and waved. A couple of minutes later, I took her into my arms. "I know where to go; it's not far; it's on the other side of the hill," I said. "Can you walk another 20 minutes?" I asked.

"Yes, I am OK now, let's go," she said.

We went back a short distance to where we had missed the turn-off. From there, it was straight ahead. We saw the familiar termite mounds in front of our camp. Not much later, we arrived. Slumping into our camp chairs, we drank as much water as we could. It had never tasted that good. We stripped down and had a shower before we celebrated with one of Dean's home brews. But, it was no celebration; it was warm and tasted odd. We had some cans of lemonade stored in cool water. We mixed the beer with the lemonade; it was good enough to drink. Wanting to try another bottle the next day, we used an old bush trick Dean had shown us. We tied a string around the bottle's neck, wrapped wet toilet paper around the bottle, and hung it up a tree branch for the wind to do its magic cooling action. We had done it before, and it did work, but you need to drink it just before the paper dries up.

On daybreak, we felt good again. Our close encounter of being lost in the bush had become just another adventure. We had plenty of time to plan our next walk. I checked the beer bottle; it was warm and hanging there with dried-out toilet paper in full sun. We knew what we had to do. We took a couple of beers and lemonade cans and placed them into one of the baby rock pools to keep them cool. We would pick them up in the afternoon and try the toilet paper trick again. We have used this cooling trick since we started travelling. Our canvas water bag was hanging from the front bumper bar of our car. That way, we always had cold water for our Staminade.

For the next two days, we amused ourselves with taking photos, lazing about, trying our hand baking bread using Dean's recipe, and generally just being Adam and Eve. It felt liberating to walk around naked, plunging into a rock pool to cool down and getting dried by the sun again.

The excitement mounted for our next walk. We woke up early in anticipation. It was a Friday, and we were singing, "Friday on my Mind," it certainly was. We listened to the two-way radio, and sure enough, there was a message for Dean. We had to wait till 9 am to get the message. We had planned to leave early to avoid the heat; never mind, we left the camp at 9:15 am. We were well prepared and dressed for the occasion, carrying water, tea, Staminade and food. This time we took matches, our camera and our secret weapon, a compass. Why didn't we take it the first time? The second backpack contained food for Dean.

The second time it was easier. We had become accustomed to the language of the bush and allowed it to talk to us. At first glance, everything looked the same, but one learns to differentiate after a while. I recognized the hill I had used as a lookout two days before, and we could distinguish the many dried-out creek beds and even the various trees. The tall dead ones were excellent directional pointers. And there was one close to where we needed to do a right turn to get to Dean's camp. We found his camp in record time, 1 hour and 45 minutes. And we hadn't even used the compass.

Dean had left us a note; he had found more Aboriginal paintings in caves about 4 hours walk from his camp. Too far for us, but we would have loved to see them. He did show us rock paintings closer to our camp. He had sworn us to secrecy even before we had seen those paintings. Even if we wanted, we could never have found our way back without Dean.

Loading our backpacks with Dean's rock samples, we got underway. We were not even nervous; we knew we would find our way easily enough. We used the compass, trying to find the shortest route. It paid off and we made it back to the mother camp in 1 hour and 30 minutes. We were pretty proud of ourselves; we deserved a cold beer. This time the cooling system worked well, but it didn't improve the taste.

It shouldn't have mattered to us what day of the week it was, but we still felt different on the weekends. It was Saturday, no work, and we stayed in bed till 9 am.

We got our bodies up from our camp beds and looked forward to a delicious breakfast. We boiled water for tea and eggs and set up a breakfast table with freshly baked bread, butter, marmalade and honey. We even had a tablecloth; actually, it was a tea towel, but it looked the part.

In the afternoon, we went fishing and managed to catch our dinner. Later we went back to the rock pool with our cameras, trying to catch those crocs on film. They really were extremely shy, just one footstep on a rock and they were gone.

We found a suitable spot to hide and lay still. About 20 minutes later, on the opposite side of the rock pool, two crocs slid silently out of the water and onto the rocks, sunning themselves. Naturally, we took some photos which we knew were mediocre. The crocodiles were so well camouflaged against the rocky surface that they were hardly visible. Time for dinner, and afterwards we practised playing and singing folk songs from the music books we bought in Cairns. We needed a lot more practice.

Sunday would most likely be the last day we had to hike to Dean's camp. We prepared a few things to be ready in the morning. Paradise or not, once again, we felt itchy to move on.

We didn't want to get out of bed; the bushwalking excitement had left us. We hoped it would be the last time; the blisters on our feet hoped the same. Dean had no further radio messages and we left before 9 am. We had taken the cameras, and while trudging along, we looked for opportunities to take photos of wild pigs, kangaroos and birds.

We arrived at Dean's camp early, a new record, and we had even paused to take photos. Dean was still in his camp; he had more explorations to do. We went back by ourselves; Dean would come a few hours behind us.

The way back was punishment, our blisters were screaming, and the novelty of bushwalking the same track had lost its attraction.

Dean arrived late in the afternoon. He checked the radio; he was waiting for instructions, but still, nothing had come.

We had a leisurely rest of the day, talking about my pet topic, the macrobiotic diet, and how to adapt it to different environments and growing seasons. We also tried to catch fish for dinner, but we caught a crocodile instead, and it went off with our last hook and sinker. Never mind, we had enough food.

Early next morning, the radio message Dean had been waiting for arrived. He had to go to Townsville, and more instructions would follow in the afternoon.

Our time in paradise had come to an end. We prepared to leave, but Dean wanted to do a little project. He wanted to build a lampshade for the naked light bulb in his tent. The light bulb would not be naked much longer. Dean had all he needed, a ball of garden string, wallpaper glue and an air balloon. He soaked the string in white glue, blew up the balloon and wrapped the glue-saturated string around it.

Waiting for his creative project to dry, he was getting ready for Townsville, writing reports, doing bookwork, and writing us a cheque for $120. We had hardly spent any money in September, and with Dean's cheque, our budget was looking good.

The follow-up radio message came at 3 pm; he had to be at the Townsville airport by 3:15 pm the following day. He would have to step on it to make it on time. Unperturbed, he prepared for our last dinner together.

He checked on the lampshade. The string structure felt dry and stiff; the moment of truth had come; carefully, he let out the air from the balloon. It worked; he had produced a string ball lampshade, with an opening large enough to insert the light bulb.

That night we had dinner inside the tent; the newly shaded-lightbulb provided a homely atmosphere.

We had to get up at 5 am but Dean was still half asleep and didn't feel like getting up. We got ready, prepared breakfast and tried to get him going. He still didn't want to go, but we had to leave the camp by 6 am. Eventually, he got up, still in his sleeping bag, and wandered around the camp. We all had to laugh, but in the end, we managed to leave the camp by 7 am.

We arrived at Robin Hood Station and quickly took our stuff from Dean's car, including our share of gold cubicles. It was another tough goodbye; he left quickly.

Chapter 9

Where the Music Plays

We stayed behind, re-packing our car and talking to the farmer. He showed us around and explained how the station worked. We found it hard to comprehend the sheer size of the land of many thousands of hectares belonging to one pioneering multigenerational family.

By 10 am, we were on the road to Forsayth. We went straight to the pub Dean mentioned. It was an old corrugated shed, but they had a fantastic agate collection. We knew what we wanted. We had a new secret weapon to advance our gem collection. Our devious plan was to exchange gold-crucibles for whatever we could get. Bravely, not knowing how someone would react to our exchange ideas, we approached the pub owner. We showed him one of our crucibles and asked if he would be interested in swopping it for some pieces of agate. He was intrigued and went straight to a cupboard and brought out a few beautiful pieces. How easy it was! We had caught the swopping bug. We drove back to the mine and picked up more un-broken crucibles to top up our exchange currency.

The next stop was Georgetown. We collected our mail and went for a pub lunch and returned to the caravan park we had camped before. Dean had given us most of his canned food, and we enjoyed our dinner courtesy of Dean.

We were still excited about last night's bartering, so we gave it another go. We went to a gem shop; the owner was a German lady. A bit of small talk before directing our conversation to our gold crucibles. Once again lucky; she had never seen any and wanted three of them, offering us $30 worth of agates. Back 'on the Road again' to Normanton, a 300km trip on a gravel and sand road with not too many potholes. Nevertheless, halfway to Normanton, we heard a loud bang from underneath the car followed by a rattling noise. We stopped and checked, "We've lost our exhaust," I called. I needed to secure the loose hanging pipe; a bit of wire did the trick. We drove back about 100 metres, where we found our muffler. "What now?" Giselle asked. "Why don't we have a tin of rice pudding?" I said.

"What? I can't eat anything now," Giselle said.

"I need a tin to fix the pipe," I answered.

We brought our camping chairs out and sat down on the side of the road, eating rice pudding. Satisfactorily strengthened, I crawled under the car, hooked up the muffler on its rubber suspensions, wrapped the flattened tin around the joining pipes, and fastened it with wires. It worked, and we made it into Normanton. It was too late to check into a service station. We bought beer and lemonade at the pub before continuing to the only camping ground, followed by drinks and dinner as we watched the sunset.

A guy was sitting cross-legged on the ground playing guitar close by. Not what one would hear every day in a remote country town. His playing sounded like a classical guitar piece. But it wasn't; he was only practising; playing relentlessly, ascending and descending scales in time to a metronome. Up and down, switching from one key to another. He was dedicated.

We invited him to have a beer with us. He was a Canadian hitchhiking around Australia, backpacker style. He never knew, but between Giselle and I, we called him "Schneider Meck Meck," a character from a fairy tale by Wilhelm Busch. Imagine an older tailor, sitting cross-legged, sewing a garment.

We talked until late and played guitar as well. He wanted to hitchhike to Darwin. We were not keen to have someone else on board as we didn't have the space; the front seat was just a bench, comfortable for the two of us. We decided to leave Normanton late in the morning, hoping someone else would have taken him by that time.

We still had Schneider Meck, Meck on our mind but his real name was Stan. We stayed in bed longer and saw him leaving with his backpack and guitar. A long breakfast continued our go-slow tactic, followed by driving, sightseeing and taking a couple of photos. Giselle did sketches and I went to a service station and bought different sizes of stainless steel screw clamps in case I had to fix the muffler pipe again.

It was already past 10 am, and we were sure someone would have picked up Stan by then. We left town heading for Cloncurry, and who was sitting cross-legged on the side of the road? Stan the man. What could we do? We had to pick him up. A long hot drive, no aircon, nothing much to look at, it was a desert out there. But it wasn't too bad. Stan was an intelligent guy and we had lots of deep conversations. Music, of course, but he was also on a health kick, and we discussed health and diet, comparing our ideas and knowledge.

After driving for an hour, the muffler decided to go its own way again. I was prepared, using the spare parts to fix it properly and secured everything with two screw clamps.

Our next stop was a short distance before Cloncurry at a roadhouse pub for a cold beer. Thirty minutes later we arrived in Cloncurry, had a quick lunch, and went straight on to Mt. Isa. We made it before 5 pm and rushed off to the post office for our mail.

Stan went for a walk and came back with a salad he bought. He invited us for dinner; we had salad and rye bread. How healthy was that?

We showed him our slides and shared our adventures. He wanted to travel to Darwin. "Are you aware you may not be allowed in?" I asked. "It should be OK," he reassured us. We were sure Darwin was still cleaning up and rebuilding after the cyclone. We agreed to take Stan up to the 'crossroads,' where the road north goes to Darwin, and south to Alice Springs, our destination.

The next morning we walked around the Cloncurry shops and bought film for our cameras. We also found a gem shop to exchange more gold crucibles. We checked what we would like before we approached the owner. We were pleased with a large piece of amethyst, two pieces of colourful cooper, and some crystals. Our collection had become quite respectable.

The following day we made it into Camooweal after another mechanical breakdown. This time the fan belt snapped; I had two spare fanbelts and fixed it in no time.

The camping ground was easy to find. A hot shower was urgently needed after the long drive and fixing the car. All freshened up, we ventured into the town; a collection of old buildings, a general store, pub and service station. At the pub, we ordered drinks and sat down when another couple joined us. They came from Alice Springs.

How do these things always happen to us? Another coincidence, or is the universe looking out for us? They invited us to visit them in Alice Springs.

A few aborigines joined us as well; we talked, laughed, and had a good time. No one was drunk, everyone was happy, and no one was bothering anyone. The pub owner must have thought differently. He approached us, looking aggressive and angry, and shouted at the aborigines to leave immediately or sit in a different room. Apparently, they were not allowed to sit or talk to us, and arguing with the publican made it worse. The aborigines politely said good-bye.

Our companions calmed us down, "Don't worry, it's normal here, nothing you can do, many white folks around here don't like aboriginals."

"That's terrible, and there is nothing one can do?" I asked.

"Not really, it has been going on forever; it's best not to interfere," they said.

We talked more about aborigines and racism and decided to ask the aborigines back to our table. They were genuinely friendly guys; proud stockmen. We had many questions and wanted to know about 'pointing the bone,' bush tucker, and 'walkabout.'

The pub owner must have been fed up with us. We wondered why he didn't come back to our table when the door sprang open and the local policeman stormed in, "Out", he shouted at the aborigines. "Out now, go home", he yelled and walked away.

"He is getting his gun," said one of the aborigines on his way out. Sure enough, the constable came back, gun at hand, calling out to us, "Don't talk to these animals," and left. We were too stunned to do anything.

We stayed a few minutes longer only to promise to visit the couple in Alice Spring before we walked back to the camp where Stan was practising his scales. "You should have come with us to the pub," I said, and told him the whole story. He said that Australians were known for their white Australia policies. The policy was officially stopped in 1973 under the Whitlam Labor government, but racism continued. We confessed that we had no idea about that. We were deeply upset about the visible oppression of aborigines and keener than ever to write about it from our perspective.

Waking up to Stan playing his tunes was getting on our nerves. He was a polite fellow, and sat further away rather than leaning against our car. Conflict dissolved.

We stayed most of the day at the camping ground. Plenty of trees provided welcome shade, and an opportunity for me to work on the car while Giselle wrote letters.

At lunchtime, I started writing a story about last night's incident. Stan helped by writing the same story from his recollection of what we had told him. His version was well written; I was impressed and asked him to re-write my story in proper English.

Over a cup of tea, I hinted to Steve about playing something other than scales. To our surprise, he could play some easy classical pieces which helped our ears recuperate. Giselle copied the notes of two of his pieces while I learned to play them.

In the evening we felt brave enough to visit the pub again; Stan came too. It was a surprisingly cheerful atmosphere, nothing compared to the night before. It was a mix of locals, tourists and travellers. Two guests proudly showed agates they had found, which unfortunately were only ordinary rocks, prompting many tall story jokes. Three young stockmen, real larrikins, were the absolute attraction of the night. They cracked one joke after the other, some of their expressions we didn't know, but everyone was laughing which was very contagious. We stayed until the pub closed at 10 pm. There were no aborigines to be seen.

Our goal was to reach Tennant Creek, a town a few kilometres south from the crossroads where Stan would leave us to hitchhike to Darwin.

With having Stan around playing the guitar and the folk music books we bought in Cairns, music had taken over as our primary focus. The couple from Alice Spring mentioned a folk music festival in Alice but had no details. Would we be lucky enough to attend a folk festival?

We left Camooweal early to make it to Tennant Creek. The road condition was better than expected, but the scenery rather bare, grass burned to a crisp from the hot sun. Our car didn't like the heat either, with the temperature gauge approaching red.

A long trip, finally a road sign interrupted the deserted landscape; Beer and Petrol, just what we needed. It looked like a pub with a petrol pump. A few cars were parked, and sure enough, as happened so often, inside were people we had met before.

Here we were, standing in the middle of nowhere with people we knew, in the shade under the pub's verandah, dressed in the barest of barest, which in Giselle's case was a bikini. Men wore shorts and a singlet. Cold beers hit the right spot, but petrol was too expensive. Refreshed, we drove the final stretch to Tennant Creek.

We arrived late afternoon, time enough for a quick drive around town. At the camping ground, a refreshing shower, and we were ready to relax with a cool drink. Stan was still determined to get to Darwin, it would be the last night we would sit together.

Time for dinner, Stan called it the last supper. He must have felt sad. Even his scale practising sounded sad.

· · · · · · · · · ·

Positive thinking was one vital element to the philosophy and emerging lifestyle Giselle and I had adopted. Believing we could influence reality with our thinking was equally strong. And here we were, encountering one coincidence after another, meeting people who helped us to actualise our ideas.

In the distance someone else played the guitar, obviously more talented than any of us. He joined us and introduced himself as Peter from England. He was travelling around Australia, living in his station wagon, which was packed to the rim with music instruments, even a sitar.

Stan and I played a few easy pieces before asking him to play. After that, we didn't say much; we listened. He was a superb guitar player. Was meeting him another coincidence?

"You should come to the folk club; it's every Tuesday night," he said. I looked at Giselle; it had happened again. Giselle nodded, "Yes, we would love to," we said.

"I'll let you finish your dinner, will be back later," Peter said.

"Yes, please, and don't forget your guitar," I said.

It was an hour before Peter came back carrying a petroleum lamp which looked like it had been nicked from a building site. Illuminated by the soft light, we had a spirited conversation about anything music related, while Peter kept playing the guitar until late at night, or was it morning?

Tennant Creek was hot. A cold shower was a must when one woke up. That Monday, we needed five cold showers. We didn't do much other than wait for Tuesday night's folk music meeting. Stan had left early, to hitch hike to Darwin. On Tuesday, we went shopping and I found an oil switch to stop the car from overheating.

We met up with Peter; he had a few people sitting around his campsite, two couples and a guy from England. Speaking English non-stop was still a challenge for us, especially if everyone spoke at once and in different accents. The English guy's name was Jimmy, a mean Banjo player. An intriguing character, he was driving around Australia in a Mini Moke. He had modified the passenger's left front and back seat as his bed; most of the time, he didn't even put up the top. He loved sleeping under the stars.

Jimmy was interested in photography and seemed captivated by our 6x6 format camera and our tripod, which had a special attachment to swivel the camera in all directions. We offered but he had no money to buy it off us.

After dinner, the four of us went to the pub, where the folk club was meeting. We were early and had a beer. A short time later, the organiser showed up, an Irish guy. More people arrived, and we shifted into an adjoining room where we sat around a large table. Without further ado, the singing began, helped with jugs of beer.

The nameless organiser set the tone with an excellent rendition of an Irish song; the others joined in. We knew Irish music from the radio, but this was different; a powerful and moving experience. Around the table, everyone would sing a song. And sure enough, after Peter sang a couple and Jimmy a few more, it was our turn. Help! We both were shell shocked and even ashamed we had nothing to offer. The only German folk songs we knew were those from school at grade two or three. Not something we wanted to repeat at this club, not even with the help of a jug of beer. But it got even better. Everyone knew we were Germans and they all wanted to hear the haunting song from that movie 'Cabaret.' We knew that movie; it was released in 1973 when we were still in Germany. And even at the time of watching it, the song in question made us feel uneasy. It portrayed the Nazi Hitler Youth, sung by a supposedly typical blond German boy in an outdoor café setting, made even more potent after others joined the singing, until at the end everyone was singing. Eerie.

That was the song they wanted to hear; it was called "Tomorrow Belongs To Me." Even if we had been able to sing it, we would have politely declined. We had to make up for it somehow. The folk music books we had brought along came to the rescue, "Have you seen these books? All Australian folksongs." I said. It worked; we were off the hook and everyone kept singing and drinking late into the night.

We slept in, not that it made any difference. But we were keen to reach Alice Springs for an actual folk festival in a valley close to the town. Peter left early, followed by Jimmy and finally, we sleepyheads. We knew we would catch up eventually. Jimmy's Mini Moke was not the fastest car.

About an hour's drive after Tennant Creek, the scenery changed. The landscape was littered with huge boulders. It was only later that we found out that the location is called 'Devil's Marbles,' a fair description.

The Devil's Marbles were the most intriguing sight but we frequently stopped to take photos of flowering shrubs and something that looked like watermelons. We never investigated if the fruit was fit for human consumption, and we were not game to try; after all, we had only just passed the Devil's Marbles. Eventually, we caught up to Jimmy and drove on to a tiny place called Barrow Creek where Peter waited for us. We were thirsty and so were our cars. Having filled up, we looked for a campsite to stay the night, planning to drive the final 300km the next day.

There was nowhere to camp close to the Roadhouse. We drove on and ten minutes later, we located a campsite behind some bushes. It was an isolated spot, remote from civilisation. Only aborigines would know how to stay alive in those desolate areas; we would die within a few days.

Luckily, we had matches. We made a small fire from collected deadwood and cooked dinner and boiled water for tea. The days were hot while the nights were cold. We crawled into our private sphere, catching up with letter writing.

Peter and Jimmy were having a heated discussion related to politics in England - not our expertise - and it grew too argumentative to butt in with my funny comments.

Early next morning, we left for the final three-hour stretch to Alice. Out of the blue, a sign came up. That term, 'out of the blue,' probably has been coined in Australia. If one drives for miles and miles on a dead straight road, with only blue sky above and on the horizon, whatever comes up in your field of vision, appears suddenly, "out of the blue."

A few more miles of driving through a gap in a mountain range and Alice Springs popped up before us. Even so, the sky was forever blue; everything else was tinted in hundreds of different shades of red.

Alice Springs is in a valley surrounded by a mountain range. One could drive up to top of the mountain range and view the whole town.

We parked our car next to the dry Todd River. Where did we find Jimmy and Peter? At the pub, which is always the central meeting place and source of information.

Where would we stay the night? We couldn't camp close to the river; it was the preferred sleeping place for aborigines who also slept there during the day when they had too much to drink.

We met up with the others at a caravan park called Green Leaves, which was rather optimistic as there were no trees. We didn't like this location; it was an open grassed area. Peter joined us for dinner. As likeable as he was, he was also a recluse and often talked to himself, but we enjoyed his musical company.

The next morning we picked up our mail. A letter had arrived from Gabrielle and Henry; they had retired from their Bondi pool management and relocated to Perth. Gabrielle went by train, while Henry drove a truck with their possessions from Sydney to Perth, a gigantic trip of about 4000 km. "That's a long trip," I said more to myself than to Giselle.

"What is?"

"Henry drove all the way to Perth," I thought about it and added, "We will drive the same distance and even more next year."

"We should visit them," Giselle said

"Yes, I am sure we could stay for a few days and explore Perth," I answered.

In the meantime, Peter and Jimmy had found out the details about the folk festival. It was the following day at Trephina George, 70 km away. The main event would be at night, and there was a $1.00 entry fee. We had to bring our own drinks but there would be food, grilled steak, sausages, and salads.

The same afternoon Eric, who we had met in Camooweal, visited us at the caravan park. He had seen our car and looked for us at various camping grounds. We told him about the festival and promised to see them next week.

• • • • • • • • • •

Before we went to Trephina George, we stocked up on camping essentials. Kerosene for our lamp, a music notebook, fresh bread, beer and lemonade. We arrived at the festival campsite at 2 pm and secured a sheltered spot for camping overnight. We were greeted by an enthusiastic crowd, more hippy than folk. We matched that look but didn't feel like hippies, considering ourselves 'creative travellers with a purpose.'

Having paid our entry fee and chatted to a few people, we joined them for a drive to a nearby waterhole. Peter arrived and offered to drive us there.

Is nudity a German thing? We hadn't contemplated that question before. Here we were, a group of free-spirited people, looking like loving hippies, and how did they go for a swim? As we were undressing, everyone else went into the water fully clothed. Giselle looked at me, "I think we need to keep our clothes on."

"Looks like it, but I can't be bothered getting my clothes wet," I said. And so we stayed dry. Peter didn't go in either.

It was crowded back at the camp; more people had arrived, with kids, dogs, and sausages. The festival took off in earnest at sunset, singing, eating, drinking and dancing all night long. There were a couple of surprisingly fine singers. How come they were not famous? We listened in awe to one lady holding her baby while singing with a distinctive country voice. Unfortunately, the enthusiasm waned with the onset of rain. People scrambled for cover; others didn't bother and cleaned up the place, getting ready for breakfast. The rain stopped towards the morning. The fire was started again, and the aroma of bacon and eggs tempted people out of their tents.

Slowly the crowd dissolved; there were some last-minute address exchanges, with promises to meet. That's how we found out that Sunday night was performance night at the Folk Club in Alice, a small but busy venue. And Bob, the festival's organiser, invited us to his party at 3 pm.

We left the camp with the help of a push. The sandy ground had turned muddy during the night and it needed muscle power to get out of it.

Back in Alice we found a more suitable caravan park. I erected a tent-like structure for extra comfort; we planned to stay a couple of weeks.

When we arrived at Bob's place, I delved into his collection of sheet music, not only folk, but also country and blues, and copied pieces from Leonard Cohen. I wanted to learn to play 'Suzanne'. Giselle talked with Bob about his pet kangaroo which hopped around and begged for a handful of beer from the guests. Bob showed us how to do it. He poured beer into his cubed hand and the young kangaroo lapped it up - what a happy kangaroo.

At night, we went to the folk club venue; it was packed. The highlight was a performance by Peter and Jimmy, playing the famous duelling guitar and banjo piece from the movie 'Deliverance.' They outperformed themselves, playing that track for nearly 15 minutes at an ever-increasing speed, helped by the crowd cheering them on.

The following morning, I looked out of the car: it had rained, and my fantastic tent structure had collapsed. "Damn!" Not the best start for the new week. Time to relax and play guitar. I had promised myself to play and practise two hours daily. After seeing Peter and Jimmy at their performance, I was determined to get up to speed myself, and Giselle encouraged me. I wanted to perfect Cohen's finger-picking guitar style to play 'Suzanne.' Giselle loved that song, and that was all I needed to know.

In town that afternoon, we saw Peter. We hardly recognized him without his bucket hat, with his hair combed, and wearing a clean long-sleeved shirt and long trousers. "Peter, what happened?" I asked.

"I am going for job interviews," he said.

"Ahh, that explains your outfit; let us know how you go. Good luck."

We drove on to Eric and Elizabeth's place. It was past 3 pm; Elizabeth and her two kids were home. She invited us in. "Eric is still at work; he will be home soon," she said.

We looked around the house when she asked, "Will you stay for tea?"

"Yes, sure, we will stay," we said.

She went into the kitchen while we talked to the kids who showed us their homework. Expecting a cup of tea any minute, we wondered why it took so long. Then we heard the front door and she called out, "Back in a moment, just watch the kids."

We looked at each other.

"That's strange," Giselle said in German.

"I know. What is going on, leaving us here with the kids?" I said.

Not much later, Eric arrived; he looked happy to see us. "Where is Elizabeth?"

"She just went out," I said.

And that question again: "Will you stay for tea?"

"Yes," I said, "we thought Elizabeth was making tea, but she went out."

"She probably needed something extra to buy," he said.

"Have you ever been to the Alice Springs Folk Festival?" I asked.

He hadn't, and we talked about Alice Springs and the festival we attended until Elizabeth came home, proceeding straight into the kitchen.

It became weirder by the minute. Eric went to the kitchen as well; we could hear muffled voices. Returning, he set the table for dinner, and said, "Tea will be ready soon."

That's when the penny dropped. "So sorry, Eric, we misunderstood; we thought we were invited for a cup of tea; we didn't know you meant dinner," I explained.

We stayed for dinner or tea, as it was called. It must be said we didn't hit it off; the conversation was awkward, and we left pretty soon after 'tea'. They didn't invite us again.

We slept in; it was raining again. When we finally rose out of bed, we had a shower before having breakfast in the car. To bring the rain into perspective, it did not rain in Alice very often. We sheltered in the car. We loved our car house and could sit upright on our comfy bed. I played guitar and Giselle wrote letters, a homely atmosphere, we didn't mind a rainy day. But the change in weather affected us; after the hot days, we couldn't get warm enough. Even during the day, the temperature had dropped, and at night it was freezing.

Next on the list for the following day was a short drive to a nearby sanctuary called Pitchi Ritchi. We loved it! Carved sandstone sculptures, showing the immense creativity of William Ricketts. About 20 sculptures were arranged in a native bush setting, classed as a tourist attraction. Luckily, there were no tourists. We took our time, admiring the work and sentiments expressed. The sculptures represented William Ricketts himself, in symbiosis with nature and the Indigenous people of the land.

We wanted to buy Aboriginal artefacts and looked at two shops when we returned to Alice. We soon discarded the idea; everything looked mass-produced and inauthentic.

The following day we went to the address Dean had given us. A bit apprehensive, we knocked at the door. An older man opened it, the father of Dean's friend. He tried to speak English but we quickly rescued him, answering in German. "Karin and Ulli are still at work," he informed us. "Come in; they will be home soon."

He wanted to know about us and we gave him our introductory talk. He was easy to talk to, a friendly guy, and best of all, an artist.

Half an hour later, Karin came home. She was only a few years older than us. Conservatively dressed, with matching behaviour, polite and friendly. She was accepting of us, despite our bush-influenced dress sense.

Shortly after, her husband arrived. I am afraid I labelled him instantly with a befitting derogative German term, loosely translated as bourgeois or conservative, a narrow-minded person. He hardly noticed us and behaved as if he was extremely busy and important and left with the excuse he had to go back to work. He didn't smile once. In all fairness, they were busy planning to travel to Canada. We talked mainly to his dad and even stayed for lunch. Art and life in Australia were the main topics. We could tell Karin appreciated how we were getting on well with her father-in-law. We had the suspicion she might invite us again to keep him company and for him to have the opportunity to converse in German. On the way out, Karin mentioned we should come again - please.

· · · • • · • • · ·

It had rained non-stop for the last three days; we were even wet in our car. For the last couple of weeks, I had practised two to three hours of guitar daily. My nimble fingers had become more nimble, and I was particularly proud of my ability to play classical guitar pieces and having mastered 'Suzanne,' with Giselle singing to it.

One afternoon, the weather had cleared enough that we could drive to the folk club to copy more sheet music. Bob told us developers wanted to pull down the clubhouse and convert the surrounding land into small house blocks.

According to Bob, everyone was against it. He asked us to join the protest meeting the next day. "Count us in," we replied.

Back at the camp, we went to Peter and the gang, but they had become friendly with a group of girls. No time for us anymore.

Three pm sharp, and we were at the folk club to support the demonstration. One hour later, it was absolutely crowded. Everyone signed a petition and listened to speeches. We recognised a few fellow travellers staying at the various camping grounds around the town. Like us, they all signed as well – was that legal? Who knows, but it felt like doing something for a good cause. The demonstration turned into a party with music and dancing into the night. It felt more like a folk festival than a demonstration. Was the development stopped? We never found out.

The relentless rain continued; even the usually dry bed of the Todd River was carrying water. According to the traveller's grapevine, the road to Port Augusta was already too muddy to travel by car and even Ayers Rock (Uluru) couldn't be reached with a car like ours. In other words, we were stuck in Alice for at least another week.

The rain had mercy on us and stopped for a while. We went to town and had our car serviced. While waiting, we walked around the shops, bought a book about silver craft and yet another book about aborigines. We picked up our car by 4 pm. New brake pads, sparkplugs, oil change, and of course, a new exhaust pipe. I felt the difference driving it. We knew we wouldn't have to worry about crossing the desert to Port Augusta.

Finally, blue sky. We left early; it was a day for long-distance excursions. The Hermannsburg Mission was a 100 km trip, and on the way, we wanted to stop at Stanley Chasm. It may sound too much, but we were enchanted by the beauty and magic of the West MacDonnell Ranges, their colour variations, and flowering bushes, courtesy of the rain.

We turned off to drive to Jay Creek. We parked the car, there were no people around anywhere and we went for a long walk to Stanley Chasm. I had an orange singlet on, the same colour as the chasm.

We drove to the end of Jay Creek, to the location of a Lutheran Mission. Rocks and Aboriginal rock paintings surrounded the old Mission. They looked re-painted or even new. It's hard to tell; we felt they were not authentic and had only been done recently.

The next stop was Hermannsburg Mission. We were disappointed, having expected an active mission with potteries and studios for painting, art and craftwork, but nothing. There was one ordinary grocery shop, some old empty buildings and a church. An Aboriginal man sat on the ground outside the shop, selling his carvings. We bought a lizard carving from him. Despite being disappointed, we thought it was worth the trip to see a piece of history of what was once a Lutheran Mission. (*It's now heritage listed*)

Having bought the lizard carving, we were keen to buy a boomerang. One of the shops in Alice had authentic-looking artefacts among the touristy stuff. We selected two boomerangs. The first one was for throwing, typically shaped, very thin and aerodynamic. The other, a more straight and heavy one, was meant for hitting someone over the head.

Our time in Alice was coming to an end. We planned on leaving but gave it a few more days for the roads to dry up. We went back to the German guy, and knocked at the door at 3 pm, the typically German coffee hour. We knew Dave's friends wouldn't be home; we wanted to visit their dad. He showed us his paintings of landscapes from around Alice. We liked them, but he was less enthusiastic about his work. He was from Munich which is surrounded by spectacularly beautiful scenery and Alice Springs couldn't be more different. "Everything is red, orange or brown here; I can't get the hang of it," he said.

Giselle told him, "We have been to those locations you painted after the rain; they look very different. Vibrant colours from the bush flowers now complement the strong earth colours."

He was a bit grumpy, "It's still too much red," he complained. With that, we switched topics and started to express our various opinions about aborigines. We were concerned about what we had seen and heard. There was a steady influx of aborigines into Alice Springs who did not speak English. Once they arrived, other aborigines welcomed them and encouraged to collect their welfare payment. We hadn't figured out if it was an unemployment payment or an allowance specifically for Aboriginal people. Whatever payment it was, it was paid straight away. The next stop was the pub and the money was spent shouting beer for other aborigines.

Giselle and I were moderate in our opinions. We didn't like what was happening, but we were hopeful the Government would fix that situation and regulate the payment support more effectively, but our opinion wasn't appreciated. He came up with a much stronger statement, much less trusting about the government actions and Aboriginal affairs policies. He firmly believed the Government handed out the payment with the complete understanding that aborigines would drink themselves to death. That was a strong statement, and it sounded to us like a conspiracy theory. He noticed our doubt. "Every day it is happening; more and more aborigines are getting drunk and sleeping it off at the Todd River," he proclaimed. "There is no other support," he continued.

"Maybe the Government doesn't know what to do. If they don't give money, they are accused of not helping; if they do, they are accused of killing them off," was my half-hearted argument.

"Surely there must be another way," Giselle said. We all agreed but had no solution other than better conversations and finding out what aborigines wanted.

That was an intense afternoon. When we left, he gave us a pile of German magazines. We knew what we would do that night.

We had also received mail from my parents; I had asked for music notes. My dad is a naturally talented musician who can play everything he hears, contrary to my music skills. He had sent us old and new folk music books. We showed them to Peter, who sorted them out and asked us to translate the German text into English. That morning we gave Peter the fruit of our labour. "Great stuff, I will rewrite it to make it easier to sing and show you later how to play it," he said.

At night, Peter invited us to his camp for dinner which was the first time he had done so. We had lots of chicken and salad, which we thought must have cost a fortune, "It's free from the restaurant I am working in," he explained.

Peter returned from work the next day frustrated; he couldn't stand washing plates all day long. The free chicken was good, but not enough. He sat in his car to get drunk. We kept talking to him for a while, trying to pep him up. It didn't help. That night, we went to the Folk Club for the last time and were allowed in without paying.

On our last day in Alice, we stocked up on what we needed for the big trip. Afterwards we drove to Bob's, but he wasn't home. A neighbour mentioned he was coaching a netball team in town. We had never seen a netball game and went to check it out. He wasn't coaching; he was refereeing. Paying 80 cents to be admitted, we watched all the games, took photos and talked to other onlookers. Later we went back with Bob to his home and had another drink before a final goodbye.

Chapter 10

The Road to Nowhere

We were excited and ready for a new adventure: Ayers Rock, here we come. A quick trip to the post office, only one letter from Susie, our friend from Hamburg. She had hilarious news. She was now an item with Stephan, a friend of Bernd and mine. We genuinely hoped that Stephan would be the right man for her.

On the road again, cassette playing. So far in our big adventure, we had experienced incredible luck in meeting the best people and opportunities. What awaited us now?

The first stretch of the road was sealed and sound. No problems with flooding or bad road conditions. That changed dramatically after the turnoff to Ayers Rock which was a gravel road compromised with mud and water.

It was a long stretch to Ayers Rock, longer than expected. We were awed by the beauty of the landscape; the rain had done its magic: carpets of flowers stretched for kilometres with colour changes from yellow to purple. We often stopped to take close up photos of the different flowers, shrubs and bushes.

To our left, we saw a mountain which looked like Ayers Rock but it was another mountain range. Eventually, we saw the massive monolith of Uluru, it looked as if a giant had hurled a huge rock into the desert. We arrived after 6 pm and camped under a tree, having paid for two nights. We were the proud owners of an official-looking entry permit, stating 'Ayers Rock – Mount Olga National Park – Number A 09364,' and being $5.00 poorer.

We were among the very few brave enough to drive after the rain. Tourist buses would not attempt to come with road conditions as bad as they were. We had Ayers Rock to ourselves. To get up early and take photos of the Rock at sunrise, we went to bed straight after dinner.

It rained half the night; would we ever get out of here again? There was no visible sunrise that morning. We stayed in bed till after 9 am. The rain had stopped, and it was dry enough to sit outside for a spectacular breakfast.

We bathed in the calm, spiritual atmosphere of the Rock, captivated by its beauty and feeling of power. An hour later, we went for a slow, prolonged drive circumventing it, stopping and driving, and inspecting and photographing every little nook and cranny. It was more than a rock; it was an entity talking in an ancient sign language.

Stopping the car, we wandered over to a cave-like crack in the rock. We knew the Aboriginal people had names for different parts of the rock, and we felt we understood the spirituality of the place. We sat down and meditated in front of a cave, but only until we felt energized enough. Sitting on the moist ground, we were getting wet bottoms.

By 1 pm, we stood before the spot where the climb started. We should have attempted the climb earlier, not in the heat of the day. In retrospect, we were sorry we had climbed Ayers Rock but also happy we were allowed to do so. At the time, we were not aware that the correct name was Uluru and there was no indication that climbing Uluru was disrespectful.

We noticed three bronze plaques, remembering people who died climbing the Rock. It was a steep climb, and I was wearing thongs, not a good choice. Once on top, we walked barefoot to feel connected to this influential force on our planet. The first stretch was easy, the second stretch steeper, but we were helped by a chain provided to aid the climbers. The final leg was also easy but very long. It took us one and a half hours to get to the top, and like proper tourists, we signed ourselves into the visitor's book.

We stayed for a while absorbing and deeply appreciating the never-ending view. It felt eerie to watch over this planet, not seeing anything that could be considered civilization. Had we landed in a different world, looking around for the first time? Were we the only inhabitants? That must have been the feeling the aborigines had when they stood on top and looked into the distance.

Coming back to earth within our minds, we took more photos. The Olgas looked incredible from on top of the Rock; we couldn't wait to see them close up. Reluctantly, we made our slippery way down to reality, and attempted to drive to the Olgas, but sadly had to turn around halfway as the road was flooded.

It was getting late and nearing sunset photography time. To capture Uluru in the best spectacular light, one needs to find a good position and hope for the best. Tripod and cameras at hand, we situated ourselves at the best spot possible. Being early, we sat down on our camping chairs and waited for things to come. What came were tourists; a bus had arrived after all. Slowly the area filled up with people and their cameras. Our stillness and spiritual feelings dissipated, and were replaced by an urge to get out of there. The sunset spectacular tourist show ended as quickly as it had arrived.

Tired but determined to capture the Rock from a different direction at sunrise, I dragged myself out of the car. Conditions were sublime; I positioned the tripod and camera, ready for 6.15 am. The tourist bus had left, and only a couple of people had ventured out.

After taking a few more photos, we drove around the Rock to honour its spirits and say goodbye, and off we went. The road was still good, despite the extra rain. As usual, we took it easy, admiring the bush flowers, resembling botanical garden beds in gigantic proportions.

Late afternoon we arrived in Kulgera, the first or last petrol station in the Northern Territory, depending on the direction one was driving. The South Australia border was only a few miles ahead of us.

We filled up and parked away from the station, there was no camping ground, too isolated. Someone was sitting on a bench outside the service station, looking worse for wear, "Are you OK?" I asked.

"I've been bitten by a brown snake, waiting for the Flying Doctor," he revealed, showing no obvious concern.

"Anything we can do?" I asked.

"No worries, all good," he answered.

We were up early the next morning as we planned to drive to Coober Pedy, a long stretch of 500km and all on a dirt road. The car was well prepared for the dusty trip, having used tape to seal up the windows and rear door. The fine red dust was getting everywhere; even our bed sheets were not spared.

The landscape was flat and monotonous, changing only in its vegetation of different coloured flowering grasses and bushes. We only stopped once at an undersized service station to fill up. After driving for another four hours, we caught sight of Coober Pedy from afar. It was a bizarre landscape with distinctive white hills and no trees as far as one could see. This was no place for the fainthearted. It looked like a demolition yard. The white gravel 'hills' were tailings from former opal mines which were everywhere along with demolished car wrecks, and nothing else.

We had arrived on Mars, and we were the aliens.

It wasn't all bad; where else could one visit an underground church? Cooper Pedy's inhabitants had turned old mine shafts and dugouts into good news stories. The dugouts were nice and cool, a perfect place to live, with signs like 'Don't walk on my roof.'

We found a caravan park; it was a sizeable bare plot, white gravel ground, fenced, no shade. Outside the fence perimeters, it looked like a rubbish tip.

No choice; we needed to camp somewhere and longed for a shower. That's where we headed first but came back straightaway. It was clean enough, but we needed money to feed the water meter. Back we went, coins at hand. What we didn't know was we needed more than one 20cent piece. And here I was, having paid, all soaped up, including my hair, when the water stopped. Eyes closed and no water to wash off the soap, I carefully peered out of one eye and tiptoed my way to feed the meter with two more twenty cents pieces, all I had.

I completed my shower experience without further ado and had water to spare. I heard swearing from the shower cubicle next to mine and saw a guy blinded by soap looking for his coins. "Try my shower; it's still going," I said. He let out a few expletives, which I will not repeat, but I felt the same way.

Back at the car, Giselle cooked our dinner. "How was your shower?" I asked innocently.

"It was OK, but I ran out of water; luckily, a lady next to me called me to use her shower," she said. "How did you go?"

We were marvelling how friendly the people were as we ate our first spoon of rice mixed with veggies. My usual response would have been, "Yummy," but not this time. I spat it out, "Yuk, what was that!" Giselle had a smaller portion but with a similar result.

A neighbouring camper laughed, "You used the wrong water tap," he called out to us.

"It's saltwater, not for drinking or cooking."

"Is there any drinking water anywhere? I asked.

"Yes, behind the shower block," he said.

"Thank you," but it left us minus a dinner. We made up for it with a couple of slices of bread and cheese, followed by a tin of rice pudding.

It was Sunday, should we go to the underground church? It certainly would be nice and cool. The father or pastor guarded the church door, greeting his regulars, and looked at us, as to say, "Come in, my children." We declined, and wandered the streets to view the dugout opal shops.

One shop owner was particularly friendly; he told us about the different kinds of opals and how they were turned into jewellery. We loved gemstones but opals were not high on our agenda. After taking a few more photos, we were on our way again, hoping to make it to Port Augusta, another 500 km trip.

The first stop was in Kingoonya, more or less an abandoned town. Petrol was expensive but we had no choice. I checked the car, oil and water were good, but was shocked when I looked at our tyres. Miles and miles on washboard gravel road had taken its toll. The tyres were badly worn; wires sticking out, and hardly any rubber left.

"We need new tyres; I hope we make it to Port Augusta," I said to Giselle. We slowed down; as long as we didn't hit anything sharp, we should be OK, and we still had two spares.

We took two more stops; one was at Lake Hart. It was spooky; we walked a few steps towards the lake; it was salt with a tiny bit of water shimmering in the distance. It may have even been a mirage. There was no sound, no bird or animal. We were the only ones standing on what could have been a dead planet. But that was not the only spooky thing. We took a turn to a place called Woomera. After a few kilometres, there was a sign we should have taken notice of, but we drove on. We came to a fence and could see buildings, but once again, everything looked dead. There was no one; the whole area was absolutely desolate.

"Let's get out of here; it doesn't feel right," I said, turning the car carefully; we didn't want to get a puncture in this remote area. Sometime later, we were back on the so-called highway, the Stuart Highway. As we came closer to Port Augusta, the road was better. Ironically, during that long trip, we had seen parts of a newly-sealed road not far away from us.

Late afternoon we arrived in Port Augusta; the tyres had lasted the distance. The first caravan park we saw was ours. The bed was begging; it had been a long day.

· · · · · · · · ·

We were getting ready to continue our trip down the South Coast. At a service station we asked for tyres. We worked out a deal, which included a much needed super cleaning; the red dust combined with driving in the rain had turned the car red. One hour later, it was recognizable again: washed, vacuumed and polished inside and out. While waiting in the Shell restaurant, drinking tea, we planned where to go next.

The weather came as a shock after many weeks in warm to hot conditions; Port Augusta gave us a hard time with cool uncomfortable windy weather. The forecast wasn't any better. We decided to drive on to the Barossa Valley.

We picked up the car, explored Port Augusta and took a few photos. We met a lovely couple from Adelaide and they asked us to visit them. They informed us that tyres were cheaper in Adelaide (We didn't need to know that!) After a late lunch, we left for Port Pirie where we stayed overnight.

The change in weather affected us. We missed the sun and couldn't wait to explore the Barossa Valley and its wineries. Our first stop was for lunch at a pleasant park in Clare. Still feeling the cold, we cooked up a hearty meal of fried potatoes, eggs and Salami pieces.

Driving in the Barossa, the landscape reminded us of Germany. No wonder Germans settled here. The rolling hills were covered with grapevines, only interrupted by old buildings, churches and wineries. But as much as we liked it, we felt like tourists going for a Sunday afternoon drive rather than participating actively.

We liked Sevenhill, a small town in the Clare Valley, with the beautiful St. Aloysius Church. We took many photographs. We drove on passing Watervale, Auburn, Tarlee, Greenock, and finally to Nuriootpa where we stayed the night. All these towns and villages had their attraction, be it wineries, good restaurants, impressive churches or old graveyards.

In Nuriootpa, an Aboriginal name, meaning "meeting place," we walked up and down the main street and bought something in a second-hand shop. The owner was German, and he invited us to come to his house at night. But after we settled in the caravan park and had something to eat, we were too tired and lazy to go somewhere else. The sherry we had enjoyed didn't help either.

Before arriving in Adelaide, we continued our small town and village tour. The first town we came to was Angaston, from there back to Nuriootpa, and further on to Dorrien and Tanynda. By about 4 pm, we arrived in Adelaide, with enough time to walk through the city. We had an early dinner at a Chinese restaurant before we went to look for a caravan park.

We woke up to the sound of rain. What better to do on a rainy day than to visit the couple who had given us their address? It was easy enough to find: a hilly, well-cared suburb, and a lovely house. But it was empty; no one answered the doorbell.

Giselle, map in hand, guided us out of Adelaide. "Let's drive to Hahndorf," she said.

"How far is it?" I asked.

"Only a few more kilometres."

"Maybe they have a German bakery with fresh bread rolls," I said.

In Hahndorf we, walked around Australia's oldest surviving German settlement. It was established by Lutheran immigrants and we admired the German architecture. We came across a bakery with a German-sounding name. It felt weird to see German-looking buildings and shops filled with familiar tasty foods, delicious loaves of bread, cheeses, sliced meats, and everything we hadn't seen or tasted for over a year. At the bakery, some of the staff even spoke German. We couldn't resist; we bought more than we needed. The neighbouring shop was a German butcher, it smelt like you wanted to stay and start eating. And that was even before you saw all the beautifully- presented small goods.

We left Hahndorf and its culinary temptations and drove to our next destination. We had bought enough 'real bread' to last us a week.

Leaving Hahndorf behind, the rain became heavier and we decided to take the inland road to Melbourne. We could travel along the Coast the next year.

It kept raining heavily, with nothing much to see along the road, one small village after the other. It was getting late, five hours of driving, and we were tired and hungry. We stopped in Horsham and went to the first restaurant we saw. We stayed for an hour, eating and slurping Chinese tea. We decided we'd had enough for the day and would stay the night. The rain was so heavy, we didn't bother leaving our car. We climbed from the front seat into our cosy bed. At once, our eyes closed, "Please let us wake up to sunshine" was our last thought for the day.

Chapter 11

Melbourne

We woke up and listened - no rain. No time to waste, we jumped out of the car and were getting ready for breakfast when it started to rain again.

I stepped on it; we wanted to get to Melbourne before the banks closed. We had a quick stop for lunch at a rest spot eating chicken soup and dunking bread and still made it to Melbourne by 2:30 pm.

Stepping out of the car, we were struck by the loud noises of that hectic big city, causing us physical pain. Had we become too sensitive? Feeling jittery and nervous, I checked my pulse; it was right up, over 80.

The situation became even more stressful when we couldn't find a parking spot. In desperation, we parked in a car park before racing to the nearest Commonwealth Bank. Only minutes later, we were cashed up again. Being calmer, having money to spend, we walked through the city. There still was this invisible element that gave us the jitters. We went for a cup of coffee to settle down, and to enquire where to buy shoes. They pointed us in the right direction, and we discovered that Friday was late night shopping, open until 9 pm. Shopping was our bespoke therapy; we calmed right down.

Back to the car park, we retrieved our car and paid a fortune, $2.50. That was hefty; never mind, we were composed again and looked for a place where we could park for free. It was still raining but we started to enjoy the city which had an atmosphere we liked. In a narrow street, we saw at least ten Chinese restaurants; going with our gut feeling, we picked the right one for us. Great food; we felt re-energised and ventured out to buy shoes.

It must have been the afternoon rush hour; traffic was heavy. A Rolls Royce beat the odds and was being driven leisurely towards the Town Hall. It helped that it was escorted by a number of police cars and bikes. Must have been someone important in that Rolls Royce; why else would it need police protection?

"I can't believe it," Giselle said.

"What?" I asked.

"I think it is Princess Margaret," Giselle replied.

Sure enough, some bystanders mentioned her name and waved to the car. I didn't know much about her, other than she was supposed to be somewhat unorthodox. Apparently, she had visited the National Gallery of Victoria and was on her way to the town hall to meet the Lord Mayor, councillors and wives. With that excitement over, we could finally concentrate on the more vital issue of buying shoes.

At the fourth or fifth shoe shop, I found what I wanted I asked the sales guy if he had a spray to protect my new shows from the rain; I wanted to wear them straight away. He had never heard of such a thing; it took ages before he reappeared with shoe cream and a brush. Giselle, who had designed the interior of a few shoe shops, knew about shoes and told him, "That is not going to work; it's the wrong cream and brush." He looked at Giselle, didn't know what to say, and applied the cream. The shoes ended up with three different coloured blotches.

"I will not buy them like this," I said. The poor sales guy became nervous and tried to even out the blotches which was not successful. We came to an agreement; I bought the shoes at a reduced price. Giselle looked for a dress but couldn't find any she liked. In the meantime, my feet started to get painful. After months of wearing thongs, my feet were in shock.

We still had to find a caravan park, and it was dark and raining. The one we found was closed. We stayed at their car park, and no one seemed to mind.

Lying in bed, we were still jittery, a new feeling for both of us. Was that an induced city stress reaction? It wasn't the excitement of seeing Princess Margaret.

We woke up by knocks on our car. We knew what that meant; it wasn't the first time. I scrambled out of bed and leaned over to the window.

"Yes?" I asked.

"What are you doing here? This is private property!" It was the proprietor from the caravan park, and he was not happy. "Get out of here at once," he continued. I couldn't get a word in. Not sure why it was such a big issue.

"Your park was closed, and we didn't know where to go," I explained. I could tell we would not become friends. "Out, out of here at once or I'll get the police," he raved on, not listening to what I said. He marched off, maybe to call the police.

I climbed into the driver's seat, and gone we were, no problems. We found a public park with a clean toilet block for us to freshen up. We stayed at the park for breakfast, planning the rest of the day while still laughing about that angry guy.

It was only 9 am when we arrived back in the city, at the same free parking spot as before.

Our main project was to sell our Bronica camera equipment. We had been to a camera shop the day before, and they knew we were coming. They seemed interested. The same guy, plus two more staff members, greeted us. They looked serious.

They checked the camera and lenses, went away for discussions, and returned with their offer. We would get a Nikon, the newest model, but they wanted an additional $500. We bargained for a while but could not agree. I was mad with myself; why did I ever buy that heavy thing.

We still had other things to do, something happier, looking for wedding rings. We had the genius plan to get engaged and had designed a ring we wanted but couldn't find anything like it.

Having had enough of the city for one day, we decided to visit the Germans we had met in Rubyvale. They lived a fair way away, and we had lunch first, McDonald's; we were fond of the matchstick chips and the thick shakes.

Satisfactorily nourished, we drove to the Germans' home. They were not home, but someone else was, a guy who rented their basement flat. He seemed to like us and suggested we stay under the carport as long as we wanted. There was a toilet and shower we could use. Perfect, and no cost involved.

We made ourselves comfortable, fired up the wood boiler for hot water and had a shower. Clean and refreshed, we continued our conversation with the lodger.

A car arrived, it was the German couple's son who came to check on the property. He looked like he disapproved of us which was understandable really.

Slowly, while we told him the whole story of meeting his parents in Rubyvale, his scepticism dissolved and he became quite friendly. He must have decided he liked us and invited us to come to his house and meet his wife. He drove us to his place, quite a distance away. Now it was his wife's turn to be sceptical and reserved; she needed time to warm up to us as well. We were our friendly selves, and in the end, we had a lovely evening with the help of a couple of bottles of wine and an apple strudel. It was also the first time we had come across someone born in Australia by German parents who couldn't speak German but could understand everything.

It was rather late when we arrived back, nearly midnight. Settling down for the night, I thought out loud, "Do you think the lodger called the son to check up on us?"

"I had my suspicions; it was too coincidental," Giselle said.

"Yes, a bit weird, and he didn't check or do anything around the house," I added.

"He must have approved of us," Giselle said.

"Even his wife was nice at the end; it's good we are always nice to everyone," I said. Happy with ourselves, we went to sleep.

Waking up at noon, we didn't bother to have breakfast and had lunch instead, which is allowed on a Sunday. The rain had stopped, and slowly the sun made an appearance. It felt like Sunday, we even bought a cake and stayed at the house, sitting on the verandah for the rest of the day, reading magazines, planning our next steps, and finalizing the design of our wedding rings.

Selling the Bronica remained our main focus. We tried many shops but however we argued and bargained, we couldn't get what we wanted. Next on our list were the wedding rings. We even found rings we liked but the price was too hefty, $100 each, and for our specific design, it would be double that amount. We were keen on a simple wedding band and decided on a square shape in white gold, 18 carat. Finally, luck was on our side; a large jewellery shop had exactly that ring for $60 each. We bought it without hesitation. Those were our rings, no question. At a nearby café, we sat down and put them on - yes, beautiful, we loved those rings.

We loved each other anyhow; it was not that we needed to get engaged or married. But we wished to make our parents happy and rather mischievously thought they would celebrate our engagement and get closer as a family unit. Another thought, only discussed in whispers, was to receive hard cash as engagement gifts.

In the evening we shouted ourselves tickets for a movie. What a luxury at $3.50 each, plus something to 'nasch.' It was a double feature, two movies for the price of one. The one we wanted to see was 'Goldfinger.'

We realized we liked Melbourne. Sydney had better beaches and a magnificent harbour, but Melbourne suited us more. It had more cafés and a thriving art and music scene.

More shopping, Giselle found a dress she liked, a blue, bell-shaped frock which was perfect on her. We must have looked in at least twenty dress shops.

The next night we went to the movies again and watched 'The Towering Inferno,' an exciting disaster film. What had happened to us, spending our hard-earned money on movies and, wait for it, another two cheeseburgers at McDonald's? Our diet was now totally out the window.

Gabrielle and Henry wrote us a lovely letter; they had bought a house in Perth and invited us to stay with them for at least three months. We couldn't imagine staying that long, but a week or two in Perth sounded great.

We left the inner city for the outer suburbs to visit Dean's wife Simone, but no one was home. We tried again at night and were lucky. Simone opened the door. We liked her straight away, and even better, she recognized us from photos Dean had taken. No awkwardness introducing ourselves; we were instant friends.

The house looked warm and comfortable like a European home. Simone lived there with her mother, Rita, a lovely lady from The Netherlands.

Dean was still in Queensland which was no doubt why Simone lived with her mother. Dave wasn't home much. Most of his work as a geologist was far from home. We couldn't imagine having such a lifestyle, being apart from each other. We loved being together 24/7.

We had visited at a good time; after talking and getting to know each other, the neighbour knocked on the door and invited us to his house for a barbeque. Actually, we had the feeling there was a touch of romance between the neighbour and Rita. He was from the Netherlands as well and his daughter lived with him.

It was wonderful company, easy-flowing conversation and lots of laughter. Simone suggested we should all go to the Melbourne Cup together. We had no idea what that was, and knew nothing about horse racing.

Everyone seemed excited, and it sounded like the whole of Melbourne would be attending the Cup. The big day was Tuesday, the 4th of November. It meant staying longer in Melbourne than planned.

Rita and Simone invited us to stay at their place. They showed us the guest room, absolutely luxurious for us, a queen-size bed, a large room and even our own bathroom.

It was 11 pm by the time we left, driving back for one last night sleeping under the carport. In the morning, we said goodbye to the friendly lodger. It didn't take long to clean and re-pack our car. We made sure everything we used around and in the house was left as we had found it.

It started to rain again. Did it always rain in Melbourne? We bought gifts for Simone and Rita. Would they still be happy seeing us? Maybe they had changed their minds about their invitation? Not at all, we were greeted like old friends and moved our essentials into the new accommodation.

The smell of freshly brewed coffee was wafting through the house, and the neighbours came with apple pie for another talkfest. That night we rested our tired bodies in a real bed for the first time after six months of travelling.

How nice it was to wake up in a proper bed. Simone and Rita were at work, and we had the place to ourselves. Giselle and I knew this was what we wanted, our own house, a short distance out of the city and on a bit of land. Where would it be, in Germany or Australia?

We sat at a table in the roomy kitchen, having breakfast and reading the paper. Why do simple things often feel absolutely perfect?

For lunch, we drove to the city. What happened to us? Had we forgotten our nutritional ideals? Yes, we went to Mc Donald's again. I quickly stopped at the post office. Giselle jumped out to collect the mail, while I drove around the block before I picked her up again. Melbourne felt now as familiar as Sydney, no more panic or anxieties driving around the big city.

The suburb to visit was Box Hill where Joan and Bob had lived before travelling around Australia. At least we knew now where our friends had lived.

We arrived back at our new home. Simone was cooking dinner and we had brought a bottle of wine. It was a party house; by 9:30 pm, everyone was sitting together again, including Rita and the neighbour Rudi. Not much later, Simone's brother and wife joined us bringing more wine - no wonder we were happy.

Sleeping until 11 am had become the new normal. We blamed the late nights and too much wine. Simone and Rita came back from work early, and Simone brought her boss. He used to work in a camera shop. We told him about our Bronica dilemma and he gave us the address of a place to try on Monday. He promised to call them.

In the late afternoon, the whole crowd had arrived again. Before leaving for a restaurant, we had already finished two bottles of wine. We were not sure how long we would survive, given that we were not used to consuming alcohol in such quantities.

They drove with us to an Indonesian Restaurant. Everyone ordered bits and pieces for sharing, all very yummy, and of course, more wine.

That lasted to 11 pm, and that's when the fun really started. We went to a country music club where a trio was performing.

I can only blame the wine but we thought the trio needed our help singing. My singing is not good at the best times but being accompanied by Simone and her crew, we did our best to outdo the trio. It worsened; we hassled them to sing Australian folk songs, and we even started singing without their approval. Reluctantly they joined in. The rest of the patrons were less amused but we had a ball. Eventually, we curbed our enthusiasm; it was past 2 am before we went home.

Our new friends took control of our activities. Vera from next door was in charge; she took us and everyone else to the flea market. It was huge and busy; we stayed for a few hours and still hadn't seen everything. There were a lot of things we would have loved to buy. We had to stop ourselves from going overboard. In the end, we went home with art deco silver salt and pepper shakers and an old-fashioned glass paperweight depicting a Brisbane Hotel. Simone urged everyone to finish up and return home. She had planned a roast lamb dinner.

We had never eaten a lamb roast; I wasn't sure if I should look forward to it. Everyone made jokes about little lambs, calling out "Bahhh" every few minutes between the sips of wine. It turned out to be a tasty meal served with roasted potato and pumpkin and more wine, of course.

The evening progressed with playing games and showing tricks, coffee and cheesecake, another night in bed past midnight. It was OK for us, we would sleep in, but they had to go to work.

The bed was too comfortable; we slept in again and crawled out of bed past 10 am. By the time we had breakfast and cleaned up, it was noon.

We drove into the city, a few letters had arrived and a $50 engagement gift from my parents.

Where was the camera store? Would we be lucky this time? We carried our trendy metal case with the precious Bronica. We were slightly anxious but hopeful. Walking in, we asked for Michael, "That's me," he said.

"We are the people with the Bronica, has Ron called you?" I asked.

"Yes, show me what you have."

'So far, so good,' I thought.

We opened the case; he took out the Bronica and tested it for what seemed like forever.

"OK, looks good, I can give you a Nikon for that but I need $100 in addition."

I looked at Giselle; that's all I had to do to see she agreed.

"Yes, we can agree to that," I said.

"I don't have the new model Nikon in my shop; it will be here by 4 pm, is that OK?" He asked.

Yes, that was OK for us; good timing, we felt like a coffee anyhow. I grabbed the case with the Bronica. We were elated! Finally we would be rid of that heavy contraption. Come 4 pm sharp and we were back at the shop. Holding the Nikon in my hand was such a nice feeling, just the right weight, and I loved the look of it. He explained the new functions, far more possibilities than the Pentax. I handed him the Bronica, paid the additional $100 but kept the case for the Nikon. We went out in a hurry, worried he would call us back and cancel the deal. But no, we escaped and were convinced we had the better deal.

No party that night, the camera was more important. I studied everything about it. Not having a flash didn't stop me from taking the first few shots.

The big day arrived. Melbourne Cup day was a public holiday and everyone was at the Flemington Racecourse.

Simone called out, "Come on, children, we have to get moving."

We were nine adults, two cars, nine bottles of chilled Champagne, and a ton of chicken drumsticks. That was another thing we learnt; race day is Champagne and chicken.

It was a typical Melbourne day, cup or no cup; it was raining. Simone had told us, "It's always raining on Melbourne Cup." She was right, but it wasn't that bad, we had umbrellas, and the rain came in short showers to cool off the overheated temperaments.

Sufficient to say, we had never seen anything like it, the party started already in the car park. People's car boots were open, revealing picnic baskets with Champagne and chicken.

All of that continued in the high fashion on the racing grounds. We couldn't get enough, what should we take photos of first. Simone had explained the dress tradition, but one had to see it to believe it. There were the wealthy society patrons decked out in the most extravagant designer outfits whereas the rest of us went for the fun fashion style, some with their top half in tailcoat and top hat, the bottom half in football shorts, socks and boots. Transvestites proudly showed off their most beautiful dresses and mascara. We didn't see much of the races; we walked, looked and took photos.

Finally, the big race. Who would be the winner of the 1976 Melbourne Cup?

We were not betting people but made an exception on such a prestigious day and had a bet of $3.00, an outrageously high amount for us.

We had a good position on the fence line, close to the track. Bang, the race started, not that we saw a lot of it; we could see only a short stretch from our viewpoint. Vera used her binoculars to get a first glimpse when the horses came out of the curve into our straight track. They came, and they were gone.

We didn't win; we blew the lot. We should have guessed the winning horse; it had the right name for a winner. And the winner was 'Think Big.' Vera told us the horse had won the 1974 Cup as well. It was a New Zealand bred horse, and to complete the winner's information, Harry White was the jockey.

There was a lot of horse talk that day; we learned that the first Aboriginal jockey to ride a winner was Frank Reys; he won the Melbourne Cup in 1973.

Our crowd went back to Simone's home turf just in time for dinner. Rudi revealed he won and shouted four bottles of Champagne which we had finished in no time. What a well-celebrated day it was. Good night, everyone; we were off to bed.

•••••••••

We decided to stay another week to celebrate Giselle's birthday and the official day of our engagement, Sunday the 9th of November, and would leave Melbourne on the 10th.

Giselle's birthday breakfast was enhanced with a gift from Simone and Rita. They were at work but had left a parcel and a beautifully written card. Later we went to the city, hoping for more birthday letters.

My mother had sent a lovely silver necklace and Giselle's parents a card with $100. How perfect was that? We were both happy and it wasn't even my birthday, but Giselle and I had pooled our money long ago. We didn't go by hers or mine; everything was our money.

Loaded up with cash, we could afford to buy ten new rolls of Kodak Chrome slide films. Whenever we bought a large number of films, we put on our bargaining hat to get a few dollars off.

We bought other little things, a cake, flowers and more Champagne, to celebrate at night with Simone and company.

The birthday dinner was at a Chinese restaurant. However, I felt terrible after it: palpitation, hot flushes, and stomach cramps which saw me hastily looking for a toilet. Playing doctor, I prescribed myself a B-complex which we bought at a pharmacy. At the time, I did not know about monosodium glutamate (MSG) in Chinese food and related symptoms.

Back to Simone's place where we celebrated for the rest of the night, eating cake, drinking Champagne and listening to Rita's German records. One cake is not enough; Simone went to the kitchen and returned with another cake ablaze with candles. Giselle blew them out and her wish came true.

Friday; last day driving to the post office before leaving Melbourne. The day went fast, and by the time I had written a six-page letter to my brother, it was time for the official engagement celebration dinner.

Simone had booked a table at an Indian restaurant for friends and relatives. By 8 pm, the feast was underway; we were thirteen people.

It was a fun gathering; even the people who didn't know us treated us like old friends. Having great food and too much to drink, conversation tended to be mainly funny, with hints that finally we were allowed to sleep together. As the night progressed, everyone encouraged us to pinch something as a souvenir and a memento of our special pre-engagement night.

And we did. We pinched our table sets, distinctively Indian. I knew there was no excuse, but we invented a new policy; *tourists were permitted to pinch three items per capital city or one item per small town.*

After dividing the hefty bill, we went to one of the guests' houses. At the appropriate time, one minute past midnight, everyone saluted with a glass of Champagne to our union of love. That was it; we were now officially engaged in the presence of eleven witnesses. We knew our parents would also meet on the 9th of November to celebrate our momentous event.

9.11 – Sunday – On our official engagement day, we prepared for our non-stop drive to Narooma. We were packing up, getting the car ready, everything washed, including us, and relishing our last day with Simone and Rita.

Chapter 12

Working Holiday

With the engagement as good as forgotten, we managed to get up early. We were raring to go, yes, on the road again - our theme song continued.

I had figured out how to drive to get back to the highway in the direction of Narooma. We were determined to make this long trip in one go, with only short stops taking photos.

The road went over Warragul, named after an Aboriginal word meaning "wild dog," although we didn't see any. Bairnsdale was next, where we admired a church with a surprisingly high tower, followed by driving to Lakes Entrance. If time had permitted, we would have stayed; lots of waterways and a very long beach, made it an attractive town. Sixty kilometres later, we arrived in Orbost, and 200 km later in Eden, already in NSW. To celebrate, we sang, "Here we are in NSW." Bega was next, and finally, after a 10 hour drive, we arrived in Narooma.

Jenny, Tino, and even the kids couldn't have been more welcoming. We felt at home with Tino dishing up his authentic Italian spaghetti dinner.

They had mail for us, and we gave them our presents. We should have bought something for the kids. Little Timmy, with his seven-year-old questioning eyes, indicated expectations.

A letter from Giselle's parents was particularly well-received; wrapped in aluminium foil, we found $250 as our engagement present.

"Look, we are engaged," I said to Jenny, showing our rings. I could see she wasn't impressed. It wasn't the kind of ring she expected, no sparkle.

There was more mail; 11 developed slide films. We would have loved to check them on the spot, but 400 slides deserved all our attention at a more appropriate time.

Tino wanted to discuss the financial arrangement. He took me aside and proposed to pay me $100 per week, fixing and maintaining the amusement machines for two months, and to live free of charge in their house. Breakfast, lunch and dinner - all free. And finally, Tino had secured a job for Giselle next door at the service station restaurant, for table service as well as being in charge of drinks. They had no alcohol license; drinks meant coffee, ice coffee, tea and soft drinks.

We were happy with everything but exhausted. Our bedroom was begging. It was an inside room without windows, no fresh air. We feared it could get hot and sticky with summer on its way. That night we didn't care and dropped off to sleep, happy and with great expectations for the coming weeks.

I rose first, woken by unfamiliar busy house noises. Thirty minutes later, we had breakfast in the kitchen. The kids were already at school, courtesy of Jenny as the designated driver and Tino was delivering potatoes to surrounding shops.

We relaxed at the kitchen table as long it took for an extra cup of tea and planned our next steps. We unpacked the car; everything went into our bedroom. It took us half the day, but the car was empty, our bedroom overcrowded, and the car washed and ready.

Giselle went next door to the restaurant and introduced herself. Unfortunately, no job yet. Work would start at the beginning of the holiday season. The manager assured Giselle the job was hers. Slightly disappointed, we drove to town and asked at the hotel, but no luck, it was the same story.

Sitting in our tiny bedroom, we wondered if we would last the distance. The room had no fresh air and was dark and gloomy. Our items occupied most of the available space, with a double bed, a chair, and an old-fashioned dresser taking up the rest. We had to do something with the light; it was a naked light bulb.

Sitting in the kitchen waiting for dinner, I showed Timmy my guitar and let him play but he either was too small, or the guitar was too big.

Jenny had cooked steak and vegetables; we were the only ones eating; everyone was busy. The kids were fighting and running around the house. Mark was missing and Tino was looking for him. We didn't know what to do and kept eating our free dinner. It was our introduction to Jenny and Tino's hectic family life.

They ran their own businesses: the amusement hall, a laundromat, and a potato delivery service. Combined with four boys, aged 8 to 14, and there we have it, utter chaos, at least from our sheltered life perspective. We consoled ourselves by concentrating on our goal; earning and saving as much as possible.

Going for a walk after dinner, we inspected the beach and a jetty for fishing boats, an idyllic holiday place. There wouldn't be much holidaying for us; work would start as soon as we were back from our planned trip to Sydney.

· · · · · · · · · ·

We left early the next morning for Sydney. The car was driving well, probably because it was empty. Driving into Sydney was a slow process, and when we arrived at Bondi Junction, it was 4 pm, and our favourite Chinese restaurant was closed. No problems, or as we had learnt to say, "No worries." We did some shopping on our hungry stomachs, never a good idea but before we knew it, the restaurant had opened up for dinner. I am sure we ate too much, but no one was complaining. It was late when we arrived at Bernd's comfortable two-bedroom unit.

There was much to catch up on; conversation flowed easily, aided by beer and wine. Between the 3 of us, we finished twelve cans of beer and two bottles of wine. Too much for Giselle and me; we were drunk when we went to bed at 2 am.

Poor Bernd, he had to get up early for work, but he was in surprisingly good condition. I couldn't say the same of us; we felt dreadful, not even a cold shower helped.

When Giselle tried to get up, she fell back onto the bed. She stayed in bed while I went out, buying fresh bread rolls. We felt better after breakfast, but it took a few more hours and a long walk to our bank to get back to normal. The bank had a happy surprise for us, $50 of interest, which didn't last long; it was gone after a late lunch and more shopping. The sensible thing would have been to have an early night, but no thank you, too dull; after all, we were not often in Sydney.

We met up with Bernd at our favourite pizzeria at Bondi Beach, and from there to the Bondi Hotel for a few beers before checking out a club and partaking in some animated disco dancing. It was past midnight when Giselle and I went back to Bernd's place. He came home much later.

We were not the only ones who had changed; Bernd had changed as well; he told us he would probably stay in Australia for good. It was a big step. We felt the same but needed to go back to Hamburg for a reality check, and of course, we had to take care of Giselle's unit.

Digging deep into our bank account on the promise of soon earning good money, we bought a new exhaust system. The car had to last for another trip around Australia.

Saturday was market day in Paddington which was a leisure activity we enjoyed. We checked out the stalls and talked to people. Whenever we mentioned we were travelling around Australia, people became interested and wanted to know more. From Paddington, we went over to North Sydney and Luna Park. Next was the Argyll Centre at the Rocks. Very trendy. We found a lovely cafe and had an apple strudel, too expensive, but we deserved a treat.

The day was nearly gone, only one thing left to do, we went to our favourite Chinese restaurant for the last time. Back at Bernd's place, we sorted out the stuff we had in our blue metal trunk. We gave Bernd some pots, cups and glasses before loading the trunk into our car. Bye, bye Sydney; it had been a good time, and we loved Sydney.

Narooma had us back. We unloaded the trunk, settled down, and read a letter from my brother. He loved what we were doing and, reading between the lines, he would have loved to join us in Australia. Our parents had written as well; they held an engagement party on our behalf. It must have gone well; they were calling each other by their first names now, a pleasing development and what we had hoped would happen.

The next morning, my work commenced. I opened the back door to the amusement hall which was to be my workplace for the next couple of months. It was a large hall; 20 pinball machines were lined up to the right. Most of the repair work was on pinball machines. Something always breaks down, even if it is one of the rubber bands which bounces the ball across the playfield. I planned to spend a considerable amount of time refurbishing those machines. My concept was to stop them from breaking down for another year.

The middle of the room was taken up with early "arcade video games," basically TVs in a box, the forerunners of Nintendo and the like. There was a TV-table tennis game called Ping Ponk, consisting only of a square blob, the imagined ball, and a right and left paddle to bounce the ball back and forth. Another game showed a brick wall which had to be demolished. Mechanical arcade games featuring car and bike races also came into the mix.

Two billiard tables provided more entertainment. Giselle and I played nearly every night. Obviously, we didn't have to pay; I had all the keys.

There was an extra room at the back of the hall, my repair shop. I had it set up to my liking, my tools where I needed them, and lots of props to rest machine parts on, ready for repair, as well as shelves with spare parts.

One pinball machine was waiting for me already. Tino had removed it from the hall after he couldn't fix it. A technician from Sydney had tried fixing it but was unsuccessful. I could read Tino's smirking face; he believed it would challenge me.

I had my own methods of working and fixing machines no one could repair. Whenever I had a machine in my workshop, free from spying eyes, I would do a whole reconditioning job instead of looking for the problem.

"Don't worry, Tino, we will fix it," I said. "The machine needs to be overhauled; I will overhaul it first and fix it once it is cleaned up."

"OK, you go ahead, I have to do a potato run," Tino said.

I was in my element, no one around to interfere. I liked to work alone in peace, with only the radio on.

The pinball machine brand in question was a 'Gottlieb,' an iconic name for pinball machines. The broken and supposedly unfixable machine was a 'High Hand.' It was reasonably new, having come into production in 1973 and Tino had bought it in 1974.

I dove right into it and diving was the correct expression. I opened it, removed the glass, and tilted the playfield against the lightbox, the head of the machine. Now I had easy access to the inner parts, a big deep box full of relays, and electrical circuits. It took me only one hour and I had all contacts cleaned and adjusted. Often, these processes were enough for a machine to function again.

No luck this time, the fault was still present. No problems, I was ready for part two of the refurbishment, and I re-soldered all connections which took another 30 minutes. I checked; yes, it had done the trick; the problem had been a 'cold' solder joint. The pinball machine was working fine now. Without looking for the problem, it took me two hours to fix.

I continued the refurbishment with new rubber rings and lots of other adjustments and refinements. Giselle came to help with cleaning and polishing. The machine was ready to go back into the amusement hall.

After lunch, I started on the next one. It was a 'King Cool,' another Gottlieb, one year older than the High Hand. Tino had bought it second hand and it broke down immediately. I checked it and I don't know how it had ever worked. I told Tino to return it. He was a good customer; they wouldn't mind exchanging it for a better one.

Tino shouted cheesecake and coffee, pleased that I fixed the High Hand in record time. We played billiards until it was time for dinner. What a fantastic first day of work!

The priest had come for dinner; we met him the year before. He came often and was always fed well. He had a good life; we wondered if he ever cooked for himself.

He told us he was into fishing and diving and was interested in buying my flippers, mask and snorkel. His offer was unexpected but most welcome, and now we liked him too. He was a friendly chap, and never tried to convert us or even tempt us to come to church. "Thank you, Father."

Nine am, and I was at it again, another pinball, 'Lawman,' a 1971 Gottlieb. It was older, and it looked older. It needed serious intervention. It took most of the day to get it working and looking like new. It was late afternoon when I brought the next pinball into my workshop. It was a 'Darling,' yes that was its name, and this time it was another iconic brand, 'Williams.' It was only a year old; it would be a quick job to get it back into top condition.

At dinner time Jenny handed us a belated engagement present, an Australian motif tablecloth.

That night we were learning how to serve customers by observing Jenny at the shop. Just as she was closing up, the hotel owner came to ask if Giselle could work the next day, starting at 7 am. The hotel had 20 rooms, a large kitchen and a restaurant; surely, more work would come Giselle's way.

The alarm went off at 6 am to which we were not accustomed. Slightly bewildered, we staggered out of bed. I took Jenny's car and drove Giselle to work. We made it in time to spare. Jenny's car was lethal. It had power brakes and, as I touched the pedal, we nearly flew through the windscreen.

I was naughty; I drove back, went to bed, and slept until 8:30 am. At 9 am, I was ready for work.

I picked up Giselle after lunch. "How was it?" I asked.

"Pretty relaxed, it's easy, I can do that any time," she said. It was good news for our bank account.

Giselle's work consisted of cleaning and preparing breakfasts for 17 occupied rooms. Two other girls and a chef were working as well. All those trays had to be carried to the rooms, preferably without spilling anything. Afterwards, it was breakfast for the staff who could eat whatever they wanted, all free.

After a week, we had established a routine. We worked in the mornings, enjoyed a lazy lunch, had enough time to do whatever we liked and worked more in the afternoons and nights.

For exercise, we included swimming in our routine. I went full out the first time, 500 meters at full speed. I shouldn't have because after the swim I was totally buggered. Giselle took it easy and felt better for it. We committed to go swimming three times a week.

One night Giselle had to do waitressing at the hotel restaurant, "How was it?" I asked when I picked her up.

"Quite fun; I have to get used to taking the orders; some guests were hard to understand. It wasn't busy yet, but a good start for the upcoming season." Giselle said.

"Any tips?" I asked.

"Not much, $1.20, Australians don't tip much. Nearly forgot, I have to work tomorrow morning as well, starting at 7 am."

No choice, we had to get up early. I drove Giselle to work, had a quick breakfast and started work but not for long. Tino needed me to help him box up potatoes. It took me a few back-breaking hours, packing and lifting all the boxes onto the truck.

We had to laugh, we were both highly qualified, had owned businesses, and now we packed potatoes and cleaned rooms. And the best of it, we still thought how lucky we were.

That day, it was my time to open the hall at 4 pm sharp, the first time I was the shopkeeper. Milkshakes were my speciality; I may have been too generous in my portioning of ice cream, but no one complained. However, I had problems understanding some of the orders.

"Two bob worth of lollies."

"What?" I asked.

The customer insisted, "Two bob," until I asked what he meant.

Two times 20 cents worth, "Why didn't you say so?" I queried.

"I did," I heard back.

I survived my first standalone shopkeeper experience, and as a reward, I made myself a milkshake with a triple scoop of ice cream. Tino joined me, and once everyone was gone, we played a few games of pool. He was too skilled for me.

· · · · · · · · · ·

Giselle went with Jenny on a "girls night out" to the golf club; it was dinner with thirteen other women, plenty of Champagne, and they partied on past midnight.

"I missed you, it was fun, but I was missing you the whole evening," Giselle said.

"I missed you more," I said.

We playfully argued about who had missed the other one the most for a while before I told Giselle she had to get up by 6 am. The hotel manager had called once again.

Six am, and we were seriously tired, particularly Giselle, who had only six hours sleep. I had to admit, I was cheating again; after taking Giselle to work, I went back to bed and slept way too long.

I hurried to get into my workshop. I had decided to adjust every tilt switch on all pinball machines. A tilt sensor switch will close a circuit if a machine is shaken, terminating the game. Some players were too enthusiastic in their shaking habits.

Shortly before lunch, Giselle came home, laid down and slept right through to dinnertime. That night Giselle and I were looking after the shop. We did well; I had told her about the slang words and pronunciations of the different flavours of ice creams. We closed up at 10 pm, but not before playing a few games of pool.

The next day, after delivering my darling to earn money, I went straight to church. Yes, I was going to church, and it was not any old church; it was a Catholic Church. Young Timmy had some kind of ritual to endure to be a member of the Catholic Church.

He had been carefully prepared. Tino, who had been a hairdresser earlier in his life, cut Timmy's hair and made him look respectable - kind of.

I had agreed to be the official photographer for Timmy's big moment. I was not used to the Catholic Church rituals, and this first insight didn't convince me I should join up. Instead, it stirred up deep thinking about life, church, religion, and God, including Jesus. I questioned my belief system.

Giselle and I believed there was something more profound; maybe it was God, but we had no particular trust or belief in a church or religion. We found the many different religions fascinating but corrupted by ego, money, politics and alternative motives. And we believed something else; if there was a God, we were convinced he or she wouldn't mind if we stuck to our own religion. God would know we respected a deeper meaning of life without making the ridiculous choice to pick one religion as the right one. We had decided our church was within us.

Witnessing the rituals performed for Timmy and his mates was quite something and surely had some distinct meaning, but it wasn't for us.

I must confess something else: I never understood the Jesus story, the one where he died for us. I simply don't get it. I am sure he was a nice guy, and I thought he would have been more valuable alive. And talking about confessions, here is another one: I have never understood the violence, greed, power play and destruction on this planet, despite all the glorious religions preaching love and peace. Where and when did we get it so wrong? Surely it would be better for everyone to understand and support each other, rather than killing each other.

I was interrupted in my deep thoughts by more present matters; Tino suggested I should do a whole refurbishing act on another pinball machine. Thank you, Tino, for letting me escape into the reassuring world of technology.

When Giselle came back, I told her all about the church business. Later we drove to the nearby golf course. It was well situated, close to the coastline with majestic views, the perfect place for a walk and to revive one's mind while taking photos of the golfers.

At night, we showed our prowess, playing billiards like the pros. We definitely had improved by playing every night.

The next day was mapped out, and I commenced overhauling the jukebox, an old-model AMI. In Hamburg, I was known as the specialist for AMI jukeboxes. Tino's AMI was a model K; it had impressive chrome work on the front grill, quite mean looking. The only part hard to renew, in case it would break, was the wraparound glass panel; everything else could either be fixed or restored with spare parts.

Tino's jukebox had another problem; the side panels had lost their lustre, all scratched, faded and broken. I suggested repainting the whole thing. Tino wanted intense primary colours. The result was slightly unconventional, the side panels were brilliant blue, and the head section was red. It was one heck of a bright jukebox. No one would ask anymore, "Have you got a jukebox?"

But Tino wasn't happy with his blue jukebox after all and decided on yellow. And it was not the only paint job. After my beloved AMI, Giselle and I started painting the bowling alley. It was not a quick job; it was five metres long and tricky to paint. We were not happy with the yellow repainted jukebox either and wondered if it would be painted for the third time.

Tino brought us our mail in the afternoon, one little packet from Giselle's parents with Christmas stories. We nearly forgot the first of Advent was coming up heralding the Christmas season. We wondered how Tino's family would celebrate Christmas.

A magazine in the parcel had a story about Peter Alexander, an Austrian singer and actor. Very popular in Germany, but not in our age group; we were more into Pink Floyd and Santana. The story came with a competition; one had to write a short story about an unusual Christmas celebration. Unusual? It sounded like us, and we were warming up to the idea, literally; after all, it was summer.

Painting the bowling alley took longer than I anticipated. I was carried away and painted large areas brown. When Giselle came to admire my work, she didn't. "Too dark, much too dark," she said. And of course, she was right.

Tino had a tape recorder which didn't work - Dieter to the rescue. Come to think of it, I loved fixing things; it's a great moment of accomplishment when you have solved the problem and fixed something. I am a compulsive fixer-upper!

To make me feel even better, particularly after the still unresolved bowling alley painting project, I went on to fixing the family's television. I found a shortage within the channel selection knob. I was pretty proud of myself. Now everyone in the family, particularly the kids, loved me even more.

In the afternoon, I distracted myself, getting away from fixing and painting for a while. I sat down next to Giselle who was sunning herself. I had brought my guitar and attempted to serenade Giselle. I shouldn't have sung. "Please play some classical pieces," Giselle suggested. An excellent way of not saying, "Please stop singing." I played for nearly an hour while Giselle drifted off into a refreshing afternoon nap.

It wasn't dinner yet; we had enough time to drive quickly to the hotel and pick up Giselle's pay. She didn't know what her after-tax pay would be. We were pleasantly surprised, $99.00 - we were getting rich.

The next morning getting our breakfast, twenty cent coins were all over the kitchen table as Jenny and Tino counted the week's proceeds. It hadn't been a good week; even so, there was a slight increase from the week before. But heading for the Christmas season, Tino was hoping for a better cash intake.

In the afternoon, Giselle and I decided to act upon the idea to write a short story for the Christmas competition. It took about an hour to write and we rushed it off to the post office. Would we hear back from that magazine or Peter Alexander, or win a prize?

Next to the hall, Tino had his laundromat business. He also owned a small farm, where he grew potatoes. He had done well. The laundromat, while taking in some money from locals, was yet another seasonal business. With the beach across the road and camping close by, a steady supply of dirty washing was secured.

I had already fixed the washing machines and dryers' money slots, and now I was asked to repair one of the gas dryers. I felt like an all-around fixing machine. I managed to get it going but advised Tino to get a gas fitter to exchange a valve. I didn't particularly appreciate playing with gas. I had a traumatic gas-related memory. As a 13-year-old boy coming home from school, I found my grandmother with her head in the gas oven. She had killed herself. I was in shock for some time. I knew she was sick and in pain, but I could never have imagined she would end her own life.

It was the 30.11, a Sunday, and the first of Advent. We grew up with the custom to light one candle to celebrate the first Advent before Christmas. Maybe Tino and his family did celebrate Advent, but we didn't notice. Instead, they had a large family picnic outside Narooma. Forty people were expected and they had prepared food to feed a thousand. Giselle looked after the hall while I put a few final touches of paint on the well-mentioned bowling alley, which at last looked acceptable.

"Thank you, darling," Giselle had brought my lunch to the shop. There were only a few guys in the amusement hall. One of them ordered a milkshake which I mastered to his satisfaction. He noticed our accent and started the usual conversation, "Where are you from?" We obliged and chatted casually about countries, politics and eventually about aborigines.

It was refreshing to hear a positive angle. He was knowledgeable and impressed by the Aboriginal culture, telling us about their Dreamtime stories. We already had a marvellous book about it, but now we understood a deeper aspect and how individual stories affected clans or tribes. There are over five hundred different clan groups, also called 'nations' in Australia. Most had different cultures, languages and Dreamtime stories. Many languages had been lost, but elders made an effort to write down and teach languages to the younger generation. We must have talked for over an hour before he left, but not without giving us his address so we could visit him in Canberra.

• • • • • • • • •

The first of December was the first day of a new week and a new month, a combination which always feels promising. There was excitement in the air, the holiday season had started and Tino expected bumper business. We were ready and the machines were in top condition. The shop was fully stocked, with more goodies in the storeroom. Everything was cleaned or repainted; even the laundromat looked refreshed.

We had an early morning wake-up knock on our bedroom door, "Giselle, could you be at work by 7 am?" Tino called out. "Yes, thank you, Tino," and out of bed we went. I dropped Giselle off at work, and it would continue in a similar pattern for the rest of the season. Giselle had to work much harder than I did.

Back at my workshop, Tino talked about the possibility of freshening up the milk bar counter. It had been painted white, but we decided to sand it back to get a smoother surface. I used sandpaper but it was too hard to get the paint off. I went out and bought a volatile paint stripper. It did the trick. After painting it onto the surface, the liquid turned alien, bubbling up and consuming more and more paint as time progressed. Thirty minutes later and the counter looked a total mess. I applied full strength and attacked the surface with a spatula. The paint came off like butter, revealing the original fifties look and a new character. I liked it and continued scraping and cleaning until I was satisfied and game enough to show Tino. He liked it as well, a surprisingly fresh-looking, greenish iconic designed Laminex surface, fake marble top.

In the afternoon, Giselle and I had a new project in mind. It was time to dress up the naked light bulb in our bedroom. Driving to the town's only hardware store, we bought an inflatable beach ball, wallpaper glue and rough garden string. Yes, we aimed at replicating the 'string lampshade' we had made with Dean. It didn't take long, and the strings were covered in glue and wrapped in attractive patterns around the ball. We left it to dry for 24 hours. I also bought a few large metal nuts, which I wanted to grind down and file into ring designs. We were not the only ones thinking creatively. Tino had decorative ideas in mind and asked if we could transform the amusement hall's large windows into a proper Christmas scene.

My ring designs had to wait. Giselle and I started on the windows. Tino handed me a box with Christmas lights and decorations to hang up. Giselle went for the more complicated stuff, writing and painting a Merry Christmas Scene onto the window. We had enough paint leftover from painting the bowling alley, and conveniently red was in oversupply.

Giselle did a fantastic job; everyone came and marvelled at how beautiful the windows looked. No one mentioned my lights; maybe I would get my time in the limelight at nightfall.

Our lampshade was waiting to actualize its purpose. The glue had dried. Carefully, I deflated the ball; voilà, we had a lampshade. It came out better than the previous one. Our bedroom would never be the same again. It took only minutes, and the lampshade dressed the naked light bulb, illuminating the room and throwing abstract patterns on the walls.

Our creative minds were teasing out more projects. We had seen homemade shoes at markets and thought we could do those as well. Giselle was good at leathercraft and the shoes were made out of old tyres.

"Hi Tino, can I cut up one of your old tyres, we want to make sandals out of it?" I pointed at a heap of worn-out tyres he had stored in his shed. He looked intrigued, answering, "Go for it."

We looked for a suitable tyre and picked one showing some profile. I used my pocketknife and attacked the tyre, intending to follow the outline Giselle had drawn. Not a chance; either my knife was blunt or the tyre too tough. I needed different tools and decided on a hacksaw. Better, but not effortless; it took ages and lots of sweat before I had cut out two 'soles' to be made into sandals with leather strips which Giselle had prepared. It took the rest of the day to get something resembling a sandal. I was now the proud owner of a pair of the toughest sandals ever made. It was time for a test run. I put them on, and I took them off. I decided right there we were not shoemakers. The sandals were terrible, too hard, too heavy, too stiff, too uncomfortable; in other words, too awful to wear.

Next project, please. Giselle was in her arty element, creating the most beautiful Christmas Cards for our parents, much better than bought ones.

I sneaked into the workshop and put my creative hat on, transforming those large nuts into designer rings. I didn't call it jewellery making; I decided on a new term, 'jewellery sculpturing.' It was a reductionist process, cutting and filing away what was not needed, and ending up with a delicate piece of jewellery, finely polished to make it look like silver.

Time to check the approval score. I put on all three rings and proceeded to walk to our room. Would Giselle like them?

"Look," I said, extending my beringed fingers, "What do you think?"

"Oh wow, I love them, I can't believe it, how did you make them. And how come they are so shiny?" Giselle asked.

It was exactly the response I needed and had hoped for. I explained how I mastered the craft of producing 'nut rings' in great detail.

"There is only one thing," I said.

"What is it? Giselle asked.

"They will get rusty over time," I replied.

Saturday was the day of the race meeting in Maruya, a town close to Narooma. Jenny and Tino went with Ricky in tow. Giselle had to work in the hotel, and I looked after the hall and shop.

Jenny had lent me a book to read, 'The Godfather.' She shouldn't have given it to me; I couldn't put it down. I even took it with me to the shop, reading it between serving customers.

Giselle was back from her work. She planned to do Jenny a favour and went to the kitchen, emptied the fridge, and cleaned it. It looked like new. However, not all good intentions have good outcomes. Jenny and Tino came home in time to cook dinner. As Jenny opened the fridge, she froze and murmured something like, "What the … ?"

I don't think Jenny ever thanked Giselle; we were surprised to learn that unasked cleaning could be perceived as an insult.

While Giselle was working hard, I was reading. The Godfather commanded attention, and I was submissive. 10 am late breakfast, more reading. I was still sitting at the breakfast table reading when Giselle came home early.

I was in a trance; I grabbed a deckchair and sat outside in the shade, and kept on reading. Someone, please take this book away from me. Giselle brought my lunch; I was still reading until I had to stop as it was my shift to look after the shop.

I had planned to take the book and read it under the counter, but mustered enough willpower and left it in our bedroom. I am glad I did; otherwise, I may have missed who was walking through the door. Giselle spotted him first. "Look who is coming," she said.

"Dean!" I called out, "I can't believe it; what are you doing here?"

"Checking on you," he said. We hugged, how nice to see him, totally out of the blue. We talked for a while; exchanged our latest happenings before he went to find a motel for the night. We invited him for dinner at the golf club.

We met up with Dean for dinner and stayed much longer over drinks and animated conversation. We even played the pokies, but as usual and predictably, no large winnings to retire on. We talked until 1 o'clock in the morning when it was time to say goodbye.

I was back in the grips of the 'Godfather' and Giselle was reading as well. We had the reading bug. Tino interrupted me; he had bought two second-hand television sets. He must have been in a betting mood because both sets were not working, but he bought them cheap and calculated on me fixing those damn things.

I repaired one of the sets working without new parts, but the second one needed a new valve. I wrote everything down, and Tino went to get it.

Over lunch, I fitted in more reading, but by 2 pm, we had to be on our way to the airport in Maruya. I had to post a broken pc-board to the company I used to work for in Sydney for them to either exchange or fix it. We stayed in Maruya, looking for a Christmas present for Jenny and Tino. They always had problems with blunt knives. We found an electric carving knife we liked. We thought it was a fabulous idea; we couldn't have been more wrong. We also bought a book for Terry, the oldest son, 'The Hotel'. Jenny collected teaspoons from different locations. Giselle had written to her parents, and they would buy a Hamburg touristy teaspoon and send it to us.

We were back in time for dinner. Later we watched TV until midnight, but I was still addicted to 'The Godfather' and kept reading to nearly 3 am.

When I wasn't reading, I congratulated myself on my multiple skills. In addition to fixing amusement machines, anything laundry associated, televisions, tape recorders, and skilled at potato bagging and packing, I had also become a nanny and supervised getting the kids ready and taking them to school, watching them enter the building in safety.

••••••••••

Friday, the 12th of December 1975, the day Tino had looked forward to, the official beginning of the holiday season. School had finished, and we opened the shop at 10 am sharp.

What a difference a day makes; kids were waiting for the hall to open. It turned out to be one of the hottest days in many years, 36 degrees in the shade. Poor kids, the hall was not air-conditioned.

I attended the shop and fixed a few minor faults caused by over-enthusiastic kids. Later, Jenny and Tino took over, and Giselle and I went to the beach to cool down. The water was just right. Not bad living opposite a beach; it's like having your own colossal swimming pool.

For dinner, it was steak. Jenny and Tino never noticed but most of our steaks went into feeding the cats under the kitchen table. We couldn't eat so much meat anymore.

I had finished reading 'The Godfather;' would it ever be made into a movie? I was now reading 'Hotel.' I had to finish it before Christmas.

One night after dinner, and the cats getting fatter, we watched the election results on TV. We were not allowed to vote; we were still Germans. But we followed what the politicians were up to. We had discussed politics with Gabrielle and Henry way back in Sydney. They were strong supporters of Whitlam, and we knew how disappointed they were by his dismissal and the demise of his short-lived Labor government.

As most had expected, the Liberals with Malcolm Fraser had won in a landslide. The next morning, I thought Jenny would talk about the election, but no one said a word. Maybe because it was Sunday, and politics were not discussed?

We didn't talk much about politics either. Giselle thought more about our future while she was at work. No wonder; cleaning rooms was not the most inspiring work. Despite countless marvellous ideas, we hadn't decided on where we would live or how we would earn money. Would we go back to our previous professions or start something new? We still hoped to make money from writing and photography, combined with other creative pursuits, such as jewellery, leathercraft, and Giselle's forte, painting. However, we also contemplated if we stayed in Germany, I could start my business again.

All the thinking and talking made us hungry, and we made dinner and relaxed watching TV, a movie with Robert Redford followed by the Dick Emery Show.

Mark, the second eldest son, came home with the priest in tow. They had been fishing together. We didn't quite get it; why was a pastor going fishing with a 14-year-old boy, then coming home with him and watching TV?

We couldn't put our finger on it, but somehow he was a bit strange. On the other hand, we didn't know any other Catholic priests; maybe it was the way they were.

It was creeping towards Christmas, and we talked about it at great length - were we getting homesick? We talked more about Christmas than we ever did in Hamburg. In Hamburg, we were surrounded by it in Narooma one had to search for the Christmas spirit. Only one week to go to Christmas, and we still didn't feel the spirit.

Jenny and Tino took the next morning off, and Giselle and I opened the amusement hall. Excitement arrived in the form of the postman. He had mail for us, a film and a letter from Dean and Simone, one from my mother, but the best one was a check, my tax refund, we were now $104.00 richer. What a wonderful Christmas present! In between, I had driven Giselle to her work. In the afternoon, Giselle came back with a bottle of Champagne, her Christmas gift from the hotel owner. Thank you, much appreciated from the both of us.

Finally the Christmas spirit arrived in the form of Tino bringing something remotely resembling a Christmas tree into the house. It was erected in a bucket of sand in the living room. We were honoured with the task of dressing it up. Tino provided a large cardboard box full of Christmas decorations. We were still clinging to our own Christmas decoration ideas but we couldn't find anything suitable for creating the kind of tree we desired; nevertheless, we accepted the challenge. After dinner, we threw ourselves with gusto into the decoration; we couldn't have done it without Giselle's bottle of Champagne.

I am deliberately not showing a picture of the finished product. But surprise, the family loved it, or maybe they were being polite.

It was the fourth of Advent, the last Sunday before Christmas. Giselle had to work but was back early, and we could explore more of the surrounding towns and villages. We drove to Bega and back over to Tilba Tilba. We admired the stunning landscapes and beaches on the way back and even thought we could live here. Maybe a piece of land not too far from Narooma; and I could keep working for Tino.

Tino wanted us back next year, and we were happy about it, but we didn't want to stay in their house. We needed our private space, and so did they. We were sure living somewhere else would be easier for all concerned.

Some of Tino's relatives had arrived for their Christmas holidays. They stayed at the caravan park close to the beach, and more relatives were expected for the Christmas Day celebration.

Christmas Eve arrived, and we had a craving for real Christmas feelings and traditional German Christmas sweets, but the mailman had nothing for us. No parcels, no Christmas presents. Instead, we opened our parents' Christmas letters.

After lunch, we went into our room and opened our mail. Giselle's parents' card included more than their Christmas wishes. Who said money couldn't make you happy!

Despite the happy mood, a couple of hours later, my beautiful Giselle had an emotional meltdown; a combination of homesickness, Christmas and the chaos around us. It didn't last long; I held Giselle in my arms until her tears were spent and all was good again.

At night, we noticed everyone was busy beautifying themselves and getting dressed up. Did we miss something? We didn't know anything until Tino asked if we were ready. "Ready for what?" I asked.

"Hasn't Jenny told you? We are going to the club, celebrating Christmas Eve," Tino said. I didn't say anything; I shook my head.

Tino said, "She must have forgotten to tell you. You were invited, of course."

"We'll get ready," I said.

It didn't take long to change into our best outfits; we didn't have much for dressing up. A short time later, we went with two cars and the whole family to the club, had lots of Champagne, fun with five cent poker machines and stayed until midnight. Jenny never mentioned anything and acted friendly and happy. Maybe she really had forgotten.

That was it; we had survived a day full of emotions. All was good, and with Christmas Eve behind us, we were excited to be off soon for another adventure.

While it meant less for us, Christmas Day was the main event for everyone else and it was our first real Australian Christmas experience. The kids were out of bed early looking for the presents waiting for them under the Christmas tree.

We didn't understand the whole thing. We thought parents loved seeing their kids excited and unwrapping presents. Not here. When we arrived for breakfast, everyone had opened their presents already. Only Jenny and Tino opened their presents at the breakfast table which is when a minor disaster occurred. Jenny was upset about the electric knife we had ever so proudly given her. It took a moment for us to understand; apparently, it was an absolute no-no to give a knife as a present, even an electric knife. For Jenny, it was a disaster; it meant it would sever a friendship. Luckily, there was a remedy; we had to add a penny to the knife and give it to her again. And Jenny gave us back the penny, as a symbol of payment for the knife. Such complicated superstitions!

With breakfast finished and disaster narrowly avoided, we could partake in the hectic activities setting up tables and chairs for a huge Christmas party. We even felt Christmassy now. More presents were laid out around the Christmas tree in the amusement hall. We were unsure what tradition we were following now, probably something between Italian, English and Australian.

The area at the back of the amusement hall was transformed into an Italian eating feast. Long makeshift tables with tablecloths, loaded with food and 24 chairs. By and by, the visitors arrived with even more food. There hardly was a space left; everything was covered with glorious home cooking. There was the turkey and ham in addition to the more traditional Italian dishes and countless salads.

The Christmas feast officially started at noon. Food and drinks galore, only interrupted by collecting presents and shouts of pleasure and gratitude.

It was unlike anything we had experienced before. Most of the relatives were Tino's, only a few were English. Games were the order for the rest of the afternoon. We knew most of them which were ones we played as kids at birthday parties. Spinning the bottle seemed to be the most favourite game, and no, not the stripping one. We played the kissing one. One of the guests was a pretty girl, 18 years old, Italian, and everyone tried to manipulate spinning the bottle to kiss her.

Christmas was well and truly over, and the next day the holidaymakers were flocking in to be amused at Tino's amusement hall. All games were working well, which gave me time to help little Timmy. He had received a junior guitar but he was a left-hander and couldn't play a right-handed guitar. I quickly restrung his guitar and showed him a couple of chords.

It became busy in the town with people everywhere. Giselle had to work next door at the restaurant in addition to her other work. At night she even missed dinner because of work. Tino and I cleaned up the kitchen while Jenny minded the shop. Tino and I had a chance to talk privately. I asked if he wanted us back for next year. "Yes, absolutely; what makes you ask that ?" he replied. I told him about our concern that Jenny seemed unhappy about us being there. We talked about it for a while and Tino decided he would hire a caravan for us to live in for the next season.

Late at night, when Giselle was back home, I told her about the caravan solution and that Jenny liked us; everything else was due to the stress of the season.

I realised why Tino needed me for the holiday season. Four pinball machines broke down; how did that happen? I watched the young guys for a while. They were pretty rough, shaking and banging, even lifting the machines and dropping them if something didn't go their way.

Giselle worked every day, morning and night shifts, until the end of the season. I usually opened the hall early. Jenny and Tino also attended; it was so busy it needed the three of us.

The weather had changed; it was raining, bringing even more people into the hall, when a power blackout interrupted the fun. Nothing worked, but people stayed and bought milkshakes which we made with a handheld shaker. I felt like a bar attendant mixing cocktails. One hour later, the power was back. Everyone clapped, machines fired up, at least for a while. The power outages continued throughout the day, but everyone behaved well.

The big day had arrived, New Year's Eve; we wondered how it would play out. When I was a kid, it was an unbelievably exciting day. It started in the morning when the shops opened to sell fireworks. Even kids could buy fireworks, but only those allowed for the under 18s.

In Narooma - nothing. During the day, one wouldn't even know it was the last day of the year.

My shift started at 5 pm, and Giselle's job was from 5:30 pm. I closed the hall at 10 pm, nothing was happening, and no one seemed to celebrate New Year's Eve.

Giselle was back and had showered when Tino invited us to the bowling club. What can I say? It was lame, absolutely dull, sitting around and nursing a beer. Tino invited us to play a round of snooker on a gigantic table, which provided the only excitement of the day.

"Happy New Year, darling; I love you. Are you excited for the New Year?" I asked Giselle.

"I love you; Happy New Year; I can't wait to sleep in our car and start to travel," she said.

The year had finished, and a new one started, but we missed the fanfare. Shortly after midnight, the club closed its doors; we couldn't believe it.

Chapter 13

The New Year - 1976

The next morning we were glad New Years' Eve was not a late-night party. Giselle had to get up at 6 am, and I started work at 9 am.

By noon I was finished and needed to rest as I had caught a cold. When Giselle returned from work, she brought me a packet of throat lozenges.

It was official; I had a bad cold or flu. I still managed to take Giselle to work and even fixed some machines, but I was half dead after that.

Tino supplied flu tablets. Not sure if it was the tablets, but after I had slept for an hour, I woke up and came up with hilarious sentences, and Giselle joined in. Some sentences were silly; others sounded deep and meaningful but meant nothing. Giselle had a good one; here is the translation: "The flexible fear of a crackdown is the hypnosis of the present."

My best one was a lame joke: "If you can look right through a mirror, it is most likely a window." We stayed in bed, laughing until we finally dozed off.

I began to feel better and drove Giselle to work, but only a few hours later, I relapsed and could hardly keep my eyes open. Giselle came home feeling down; she had caught the bug now and had a sore throat.

Day after day, lots of work, and we kept powering on, despite our colds. Tino provided flu tablets, and Jenny gave us throat lozenges. Giselle worked every day, often morning and night.

I wrote in my diary, '*Pain is a good reminder to care better for your health.*'

We could hear the alarm but slept on. I woke up at 6:45 am; Giselle had to work at 7 am. "Darling, wake up, quick, it's late," I called out, jumping out of bed. Giselle was right behind me, breaking all dressing and essential hygiene records. We raced to town. We broke several Olympic records and were only a couple of minutes late.

I didn't go back to bed; I had breakfast, started work early, and thought about our book idea. I tried to work out a concept that would make the content flow freely and was easy to read. I came up with a good opening and eventually wrote down a few paragraphs to discuss later with Giselle.

Jenny had good news; a parcel waited for us at the post office. Giselle's tax refund had also arrived. I went to the hotel and waited for Giselle, surprising her with our belated Christmas parcel.

Another letter had come from Shepparton, where we wanted to catch up with Bob and Joan for fruit picking. Bad news, no work available for us; we had been looking forward to picking apples, pears and peaches and sampling the goods.

We spent the afternoon unpacking the parcel, lots of sweets and things we wanted, as well as reading material. A bit more rest and it was back to work for Giselle. I had the night off.

A big repair job waited for me in the morning; someone had accidentally smashed the glass of a pinball machine. He had rested a coke bottle on the glass too enthusiastically. I ordered the glass panel from a local guy. That was the easy part; cleaning it was much more problematic as tiny splinters could ruin the playing field. I took everything apart; hunting for even the tiniest splinter took all morning.

More work, but enough time to read while guarding the shop. What was I reading now? It's a little embarrassing to say. Within our Christmas parcel, we received a stack of "Perry Rhodan", a weekly German science fiction pulp magazine. I started reading those when I was 13. That stack of magazines was the last I ever read. The supply chain had been broken.

That night, I wrote down one of my supposedly clever statements:
'When reading stops you from reading, evaluate what you read.'

•••••••••

Jenny had the dreaded cold now and stayed in bed. I was in charge of the hall for the whole day, a good time for some contemplation. Clearly we wanted to write a book, but it was easier said than done. I had written small sections and Giselle had done sketches in addition to our photos, but we lacked a good storyline.

After a couple of days, Jenny felt well enough to get up. We helped her in the shop and dismantled the Christmas decorations. Late in the afternoon, the amusement hall was back in neutral mode; it looked boring. We would have liked to add some interesting painted motives onto the walls. Instead, Giselle worked on a large sign; Tino wanted it to advertise the hall. I dug the holes for the posts to attach the sign. We had just finished when Bob walked into the 'Amusement Centre;' yes, Tino called it a 'Centre' now.

He had driven from Melbourne, unfortunately, Joan couldn't come. As Giselle had to work, I took Bob to the Golf Club where we played the pokies and talked about our next adventures. Fruit picking was still on the agenda, and even returning to Rubyvale for more sapphire digging was a possibility. We had come to the end of our poker machine budget losing money when Bob suggested trying another $5.00. Finally, and it had never happened to me before, we won the Jackpot. It may not sound much, but in 1976, $30,00 was a sizable amount. We went half / half but played on. In the end, I took home an extra $10.00.

It was raining the next morning when I drove Giselle to the hotel. Bob peered over my shoulder, watching how I fixed pinball machines, until Giselle came home. We talked with Bob for another hour before he had to leave for Melbourne.

Another working day, nothing exceptional happening. We were getting slightly bored, two more weeks before we could be on our own again. On the other hand, we planned to be back to Narooma for a second serving of hard work to earn money to fly back to Germany.

•••••••••

My dad's birthday came up, and I had time to think about him to honour his special day. He had turned 56 and was stuck in a job for the money and had lost all enthusiasm. It may be one of the reasons he had depression. I had my own ideas, of course. Having studied psychology in conjunction with my other subjects I was under the impression I was something of an expert and well equipped to evaluate my dad's depression issues. (Never a good idea.) I saw his depression as a continuation of a life that didn't take its intended route. Sent to war when he was eighteen and finally coming home from prisoner-of-war-camp when he was twenty eight drastically influenced his life.

He had dreamt of being a musician, and had played the violin from a tender age until he became a baker on his dad's strict wishes. The thirties were hard years; job security and producing food was more important than following one's musical dreams. I often asked myself, how could a young man of twentyeight, coming home from war prison, being married with one son and another one, me, on the way, become a family man?

I was born nine months after he came home. His dreams were shattered, replaced with plans of a peaceful family life, work, having enough to eat, and trying to be happy. As a kid, I saw and felt his frustration but I didn't know what those breakdowns meant. Happy Birthday Dad - be happy.

A few days later, practising guitar, I was alerted by massive motorbike noise, the typical Harley-Davidson rumble. The 'bikies' had arrived. Worry was written over Jenny's face. "Are you worried?" I asked.

"Yes, but I know some of them. That guy over there is a teacher. I am just worried it might get out of hand." She didn't need to worry; even though the guys looked like a fearsome bunch, they were better behaved than some of the young guys who frequented the hall. I stayed around to help until we closed up, no incidents, all happy.

Our feet were itching; we wanted to go. Giselle worked with double pay; it was Australia Day. At night she cut my hair, another $5.00 saved. From that day on, we continued to cut each other's hair. "Sorry," to the hairdresser community.

Tino had asked me if I could give him repair or fixing lessons. "Sure, let's start now," I said and went to the hall to pick out a pinball machine to fix.

I showed Tino how to adjust contacts, and solder broken wires. I left him to it and spent the rest of the morning writing down new ideas for books. We constantly had new ideas and dreams. I wrote them all down, as most ideas could only be realized in Hamburg. Our first idea was a book about Hamburg from the perspective of travellers who came back and rediscovered their hometown.

Giselle and I had successfully lived a new life for the last two months, developed lasting friendships, and invented ourselves further. We were feverishly waiting for the next instalment in our adventure. In our minds, we had left Narooma already.

Bookings for the hotel had stopped, Tuesday would be Giselle's last working day. We could leave as early as Friday to be ready for a shopping trip to Sydney before driving to Shepparton. A surge of energy passed through our veins.

Come Wednesday morning, we were woken up way too early. "Yes, what is it?" I grumbled. "Sorry," Tino called out, "Could Giselle work one more time?" I turned to Giselle; I didn't have to say a word; she was already out of bed and into the bathroom. I crawled out of bed, and not much later dropped Giselle off at the hotel. The next morning we were sleeping in, no phone call to wake us up, and no knock on our door. Work had finally stopped.

After lunch, Giselle started to shift our belongings back into the car, and I flushed out the radiator, attached new hoses and fitted a new thermostat. A ten-minute test drive went well, driving up and down hills; the car kept the right temperature.

At dinnertime, Tino handed over my final payment, plus a bonus. Giselle had received her money and a bonus as well. Happy all around! Even better, over dinner, we all had a good talk, and some remaining animosities were ironed out. Everyone was happy to have us back the following year.

Chapter 14

One Pear at a Time

We celebrated our last breakfast in Narooma with a second cup of coffee before shifting the rest of our belongings into the car and cleaning up our room. By noon we were ready for take-off. After lots of hugs and kisses, we left our home of two months behind us.

We waved Narooma goodbye heading for Sydney to meet up with Mark and Karin who had arrived from Hamburg and were staying at a hotel in Kings Cross.

We arrived safely at Bondi Junction, just in time to visit our favourite Chinese restaurant before going to Bernd's place. He was home and opened a bottle of Champagne to greet us in style. At night we went to see Mark and Karin. He was his usual self, greeting us with, "I told you not to walk into the bush by yourself," referring to our adventure at Dean's camp. "Nice greeting Mark, and nice to see you as well," I said, "What else is new?" The bantering went on for a while, but we still had a good time and talked until after midnight.

I went out early to buy something yummy for breakfast. That was something I missed when we were travelling. I loved going for a morning walk to the shops, buying a newspaper and fresh bread rolls.

Giselle and I love breakfast; we would sit for way too long, talk, dream and plan our future together. That morning was no different, and we enjoyed the serenity of having Bernd's unit to ourselves.

Next on our list was a beach Mark and Karin wanted to visit with us. Not sure what their fascination was with topless beaches; maybe it was a photographer's interest. We couldn't care less if someone was topless or not, as long as it was a nice beach. We couldn't find them. Later in the afternoon, we called and agreed to catch up at night for dinner. We had another evening of argument-filled discussions. As much as we enjoyed their company, Mark always found a way to trigger arguments. We were not sure if it was deliberate or it was his personality. He was not so argumentative when we were friends in Hamburg. Maybe it had something to do with Giselle and I being a couple. He often questioned our goals, and even our happiness while we defended our lifestyle.

Next day, after a last Chinese lunch, we finally separated from Sydney for another year, planning to be in Shepparton by Tuesday. The farmers where Bob and Joan were working had changed their minds; they needed more pickers after all, and were expecting us.

We were more than happy to be back on the road; nothing else can compare to that feeling of freedom. We stopped driving for the night at Yass, a small town 280 km away from Sydney. As fantastic as Sydney was, we preferred less busy locations. Nothing beats the open road, fresh air and freedom - pure happiness!

Leaving Yass early in the morning, we arrived in Shepparton by 5 pm, a leisurely drive.

As we arrived, the farmer's wife came out to greet us. She had been waiting, a bit worried we wouldn't come. She showed us where we would sleep. that cabin would be our home for the next few weeks. The room contained only two chairs, a table, and a little bar fridge, and no bed, which was just as well.

For the next hour, we transformed ourselves into cleaning machines, creating our kind of comfortable living place. We moved the foam rubber mattress from the car into our new home, added a tablecloth to the fifties style laminate table, dressed the bare ceiling light with a pretty self-made lampshade. Spreading some personal knick-knacks around the room completed our set-up. It looked homely; mission completed and inmates happy. Time for a rest and a cup of tea. We had plenty of tea bags and coffee sachets. When naughty Giselle worked in the hotel, she confiscated surplus supplies. We had finished our tea, without guilt attached, when Joan and Bob arrived with their tractor and a few trailers with boxes full of pears. They had finished a full day of pear picking and were sweaty and exhausted. No wonder, it was 35 degrees in the shade that day.

Hugs and kisses; how pleasant it was to see them again. An hour later, we sat once again in their luxury caravan. Over dinner, we caught up and found out what to expect from the fruit picking adventure and how much we could earn.

It sounded more challenging than we had envisaged. Joan and Bob could only pick 2 to 4 boxes of pears or peaches most days. The boxes held one cubic meter. For each box packed with pears, one earned only $6.17 and peaches $7.00.

They told us about the 'gun picker' working on this farm for many years. He could pick nine boxes by himself, and on the weekends, he brought his wife and two kids. They were flying through the trees.

Our goal was to pick six boxes a day. Considering that accommodation was free, and we could eat as much of whatever was grown on the farm, we were happy.

What is the saying, 'No rest for the wicked'? Not sure if that was applicable for us, but we had to get up at 6 am.

The air was crisp, not to say cold and wet. Actually, it was mainly wet from heavy dew and being among high grass and tree branches with wet leaves.

The farmer allocated a tractor for us. After a short driving instruction, we were underway with four bins in tow. Let the fun begin. We also had been given one bag each. The bag hung in front of our chest. It had an opening on top and a flap at the bottom to drop the pears out. We also had a steel ladder each. That thing was heavy, not a light aluminium one; no, it was a cumbersome steel ladder, nearly too much for Giselle to carry from tree to tree. Finally, we received a template, a piece of thin sheet metal with a hole in the middle, representing the size of the pears to pick. Anything too large or too small would be sorted out and discarded. Now we were ready to pick and take photos of our new adventure.

It didn't take long to recognize this adventure meant hard, muscle-aching work. Narooma was child's play compared to this fruit picking business.

We knew we could leave at any time but we enjoyed ourselves too much and vowed to stay the whole season despite the tough work.

We managed four boxes on the first day, despite many interruptions, a long lunch, and taking photos. We aimed for six boxes the next day.

Getting up the next morning was hard, muscle pain everywhere, but once we got going, it felt good. By lunchtime, we had already filled four bins. After lunch, I picked by myself; the farmer needed Giselle in the shed to sort pears. The farmers liked us; the wife brought us lots of books and an old Singer sewing machine.

Everyone had fun with the gun picker, Joe the Italian, who sang all day long. Often the other pickers joined in or made jokes, "Can someone switch off the radio?" which resulted in Joe singing even louder.

We had established a good routine. Getting up at 6 am for a start at 7 am. It was still cool, and we could work without getting too hot. Our goal was four boxes before lunch and 2 to 4 in the afternoon, depending on our mood and fitness. After lunch, it was hot, and we went slower, but even with more rests and drinking litres of Staminade, we managed eight bins, our best result yet.

At night we heard there were some disputes. Union representatives had visited the farmer and instructed that we – yes, we travelling German tourists - had to join the union; otherwise, we would not be allowed to work.

Neither of us was inclined to join anything, let alone the union, but it was not worth the trouble to revolt; we paid $2.00 each and became union members. Bob explained that the dispute was much more severe than we thought. If the farmers didn't employ union members, they would not be allowed to sell their produce. Our sense of justice took a serious blow. Union membership should be voluntary, not forced by blackmail.

We had been picking for a few days, and even though we could pick eight bins, we were happy with six or seven for a more comfortable situation, allowing for a refreshing lunch and even a quick shower to cope with the heat.

By now, we felt like experienced fruit pickers, not to mention we were union members, which amused us somehow. Being experienced made a lot of difference to the number of boxes we could pick in a day. We had learnt the best position for the ladder and how to change it quickly. We could spot the right size of pear from a mile away. No more templates.

On some days, we had to pick for the export market; our pears would end up in Europe. There were special rules for picking; the bins were lined with paper, and the pears were picked with the stem attached. It was 'Gently – Bentley' all the way, no bruising allowed. Naturally, that slowed us down; however, we were compensated by a 'no size restrictions' rule - anything goes.

It had been raining the whole night, and it was still raining at 6 am. We stayed in bed looking forward to a day off. No such luck. Joe came to let us know that the rain had stopped. 'Thanks, Joe, we can see that,' I thought.

"We need to pick the peaches today; you can start on the first line," he instructed us. The sun had come out, and the wet leaves on the trees were glittering in the sunlight but working in that picturesque scene was far from beautiful. I picked the first couple of peaches from the lower branches and thought it had started to rain again. Giselle looked at me; we were not sure if we should laugh or swear. We did both and kept on picking.

We stopped after lunch, showered, dressed presentably and drove to town. We had received our first big cheque. Fruit picking had earned us the proud sum of $265 which we deposited straight into our bank account.

We caught up with Bob and Joan and went for dinner at a Chinese restaurant with a boring name, 'New China Restaurant.' It was licensed to bring your own liquor; we liked that, it was cheaper to buy wine at a bottle shop.

On Sunday we took the day off. The farmers had invited us for lunch. It was Joan's birthday, the reason for this grand occasion.

1.03.1976 - A new month and a new week, and we stayed in bed a bit longer. Giselle had a toothache, and we didn't sleep well. The farmer gave us an address for a dentist. Giselle got an early appointment thanks to the pain; without pain, there were no appointments open for over a week. Personal note, 'always say I am in pain when asking for a dental appointment.'

Half an hour later, Giselle appeared in the waiting room; one of her back teeth had a new filling. It wasn't cheap, not like the dental hospital. Giselle had to pay $18, or the cost of picking three bins of pears. She took the rest of the day off. I picked three bins within 5 hours to make up for the cost of the dentist.

Joan and Bob had asked us to come to Sheppartons's Drive-In. What a treat to watch a movie, we hadn't seen any movie since watching TV in Narooma. We went in our car and followed Bob and Joan's car into the drive-in to make sure we parked where we were supposed to park. Next to each parking bay was a steel post with a speaker attached. Once parked, we opened the window and hooked the speaker to the inside of the car.

The first movie was starring an Australian actor we didn't know, but which stuck in our minds ever after. It was Jack Thompson, and the movie was "Sunday Too Far Away." The story was set on a sheep station and was about gun shearers, their bonuses and union involvement; a great movie.

The picking business went on. Day after day - some days, we felt like stopping, only to pick even more the next day.

Bob and Joan had their last working day. Bob couldn't stand it anymore; he was packing, nearly fleeing the scene. That night, we had our last dinner together. They had become more than good friends; they were the same age as our parents and often had similar concerns about our safety and goals. They planned to drive to Cairns for the winter, where most likely we would meet again.

We had to pick pears for the export market again. That time we couldn't resist; we marked a few pears with our initials. We were in our funny mood that day, playing basketball, throwing pears into each other's bags, and tried our hand at cricket as well. I am afraid we wasted a few pears that day; with pears exploding in a satisfying splat on our makeshift cricket bat.

After a quick shower and a cup of tea, we went to town, buying spare parts for the car, ice cream, and chocolate to compensate for our hard work. At the grocery, Giselle noticed a young guy looking at us. He approached us with a smile on his face, "Hi, Germans seem to be everywhere." He must have overheard us talking in German.

His name was Ralph, only 24, and from Basel, Switzerland. He and his wife Ute had lived in Shepparton for the last two months. Like us, they came to earn money for their trip around Australia. They had started with picking but changed jobs after one month. Ralph worked in an abattoir, and Ute worked at the local fruit-canning factory. They needed money more urgently than we did. When they visited Sydney and the Taronga Zoo six months earlier, their car was robbed. Their possessions were gone: money, bankbooks, passports, and camera equipment. They were devastated but determined to press on with their goal to travel for two years before going back to Switzerland. We had their current address and would visit them later that week.

We took a well-earned break from picking. I was fixing the car yet again; it was still overheating. I knew the cost of a new radiator was $50, too much when translated into bins of pears. We learnt one could buy a reconditioned radiator.

We had another day off; the remaining trees were not ready to be picked. Instead, we went to Ralph and Ute's place and found out we had a lot in common. Photography was one of their hobbies, but their particular interest was reptiles: snakes, lizards and goannas.

When we returned, the farmer's wife had brought us a yoghurt maker. It was surprisingly easy to use. One only needed a small quantity of yoghurt as a starter and milk, and the next morning one had fresh yoghurt. It became one of our favourite desserts, freshly-picked fruit, stewed, with homemade yoghurt.

The next day the picking continued, and that night we were exhausted. We had to climb high, and it was a balancing act to grab a few pears. We had stretched our bodies to the limit. Why did we punish ourselves? We stubbornly persevered, not only for us and a few more dollars but also for the very friendly farmer's family. They probably wouldn't find anyone else that late in the season to pick the last fruit.

I had suffered a painful shoulder for a few days and had it checked for free at the hospital. The excellent doctor thought it was overstretched and prescribed rest and painkillers. I didn't need the painkillers at that time but we decided they could come in handy on our travels, and they were free.

Before going back to our quarters to rest my arm, we bought a new radiator after all.

As to the doctor's order, no fruit picking for me. Instead, we walked to the post office. On the way, we talked about how familiar this strange country and surroundings had become. We behaved as if we had lived there forever. We wondered how adaptable we were, considering our upbringing in a different country and city far away.

My shoulder wasn't painful anymore, but we had one more day off before picking again. We were keen to earn a few more dollars to fill the dent the radiator had made in our bank balance. We also needed two new tyres. We planned to work to the end of March, stay a few more days for sightseeing, before driving to Melbourne.

Giselle made use of the Singer sewing machine while I pulled out the old radiator; it really didn't look good. In went the new radiator, and as a precaution, I fitted new hoses as well. I kept the old hoses as spare parts. A short test drive showed no overheating.

We had a late start the following day, but picking went well to about lunchtime. After lunch, we had to pick the last few lines of pears. Once done, the season would be over. It would provide us with enough money for our final purchases. We were keen to buy heaps of dented canned food from the local canneries for less than half price to last us three months.

We had received more worrying letters from our parents. Mark, who we knew was constantly stirring up arguments, had told my parents, that "We had lost touch with reality." Nice statement, and coming from Mark, it was no surprise, but my mother passed it on to Giselle's parents, and now our parents were concerned. It would take a few letters to claim back our reality.

We considered ourselves real enough and we also thought we had something special; our deep love for each other. It was not one of us leading the other. We were of like minds, planned everything together and achieved what we planned, even if it sounded far-fetched like our goal of buying a house. For us, it was a reality we could achieve.

It was the official end of the picking season. Joe would stay; he was also the farm manager. His main job was to cultivate new trees and prune the old ones.

It was a special day, we had conquered the picking world, and our reward was to hit the road again. There were always tingles of excitement in our flesh and bones when we started our next adventure.

We went over to the farmhouse for the final pay check and asked the farmer's wife, "Could we please live here for another week? We would like to have a look around and maybe pan for gold?" She gave us the OK and we didn't even have to pay rent.

· · · · · · · · · ·

A beautiful sunny day awaited us. No more picking – hurray! We had planned a big shopping day and having already compared prices, we knew where to shop. It took us until well after lunch to buy everything. We couldn't resist; we lined up our travel provisions and took a photo.

All those tins had to be packed into our car. The space for the spare tyre had once again become our storage cellar. We had bought a gold pan too, and a new sieve for gemstone washing. All set up, ready to go, but first we were keen to explore the country around Shepparton.

Our discovery tour started on a Sunday. We picked up Ralph and Ute and ventured out to Rushworth, a historic gold mining town. Did they leave some gold for us? It was the first long drive we had made in a while. So far, so good, the engine didn't overheat, and the car was running very nicely.

We didn't know where to look for gold. Like novice tourists, we asked someone and received appropriate directions. We found the place easily which should have alerted us that there would be nothing to find. Another problem was no running water, only a smelly puddle of dirty water.

At least we could try our gold pan. It wasn't pleasant, and we gave up after 20 minutes. It's a wonder we lasted that long; it must have been the gold fever. The result was dirty water and two specks of gold. There was gold, but not enough to warrant looking for it.

The next day we questioned the farmers about gemstones, gold and anything worthwhile. They knew of a location to find jasper, which was not highly ranked as a gem, but perfect for tumbling.

Feeling energetic, we drove to Violet Town, only 40km away, arriving by lunchtime. Not a soul to be seen, it was rather eerie. Travelling through that area was a strange experience due to the colour of the dried-out landscape. But we liked the old houses and the old Violet railway station, even if it felt like a ghost town. Somewhere on this railway line there had been a train crash with nine people killed. We took a few photos and left. On the way out, in the rear mirror, I saw two men crossing the road, probably ghosts.

Continuing our discovery tour, looking for jasper, we drove further to Corop, probably another ghost town.

We were always on the lookout for unique photos for our book. But this scenery, even though we liked it, would look dull. It was dried out, brown with a few dead trees in between. Not sure if Corop could be called a town; it was only a few old houses.

We didn't see any jasper; could we even have expected a heap of jasper in the centre of a village? A woman was standing at a farm gate; we stopped and asked her, "Excuse me, would you know where we can find jasper?"

"Yes, drive on for another mile and you will see a large rock of jasper on the roadside," she said.

"Thank you," we waved and drove on.

She was correct; we found a massive rock of jasper. Now what? I took our geological hammer and tried to hack off a piece. Not a good idea - that rock was hard, and sparks were flying. We gave up and searched until we found some manageable sized pieces. We took what we could carry. Some pieces were big enough for bookends.

When we arrived back at the farm, we found a stack of books in front of our door. The farmer's wife had found books about opal mining and where to find them. She had told us about White Cliffs and Lightning Ridge, two mining towns we wanted to visit.

At night we met up with Ralph and Ute and discussed diet. We still had our macrobiotic diet in mind, but not on our plates. I was keen to explain the yin and yang philosophy and principles. Giselle and I liked the diet but even more so the lifestyle philosophy. We saw ourselves as yin and yang, and loved the concept of plurality. Yin and yang, dark and light, female and male, one needs two of everything for life to exist. It also meant those two parts are equal, and therefore men and women are equal. Giselle was fiercely independent; to even suggest that men were the more significant gender was plain nonsense to her. I liked that and thought the same.

Our diet ideas did not overly convince Ralph and Ute. He was a haematologist, and needed more scientific explanations than eastern philosophies. In his view, blood does not change by eating the yin or yang way. I was sure one could change the body and blood composition with diet; blood sugar was one example.

The following morning, waking up earlier than Giselle, I had to make good use of April Fool's Day. I got up and opened the house door, providing a clear view of the farm surroundings. "Schatz, wake up, quickly - a dingo!" I shouted. Giselle, still half asleep, jumped up and rushed to the door, standing next to me,

"Where - where, I can't see it?" "April – April," as we would say in Germany. I was happy with my effort and went back to bed, followed by Giselle boxing me.

Our time in Shepparton slowly came to an end. We spent another afternoon with Ralph and Ute at a nearby river and tried our hand at fishing. Ralph was pretty good at it, and this time I got lucky. I caught two fish, and we had them for dinner.

Most of Saturday, we spent packing, arranging and re-packing all our goodies into our car. We had not carried so much food, books, stones and equipment before. The rear of the car was visibly lower. The two large boxes full of apples and pears didn't help either, but they would provide fresh fruit for a long time to come.

Those last few days, we had mixed feelings ranging from melancholic though to happy and excited. It had been a long time, and looking back, it was fun. How lucky we had been with the farmers; they couldn't have been more friendly and supportive.

For the final time we met up with Ralph and Ute to say goodbye. They would have loved to come with us. We promised to stay in contact and hopefully meet up in Darwin to travel the West Coast down to Perth with them together.

At the last moment, Ralph showed us a leather belt and bag he had made. Giselle wanted to buy leather for herself before we left on Monday.

Chapter 15

Moving On

We left on Monday, and the first stop was a leather-craft shop where we bought leather and a few essential tools. Did we have too many creative interests?

That was it, good-bye Shepparton, we headed to Melbourne. We couldn't wait to meet Rita again. Simone and Dean were in Europe. We deliberately made it a leisurely trip, going slow, not over 50miles per hour. We didn't want to arrive at Rita's place too early; she needed time for herself after work and wouldn't feel like cooking for us. We went to Mc Donald's instead.

We arrived at Rita's place at 7 pm. "When did you arrive in Melbourne?" she asked.

"Around 4 pm, we had some shopping to do," Giselle said.

"What took you so long? You should have come for dinner," Rita said.

"We didn't want to inconvenience you," was my honest answer.

This time, we also met her youngest daughter Maria. We were glad she was there; without Simone, it felt different but Maria made up for it, and we had a good night.

We got up late and looked out the window to check on the weather. It was not pleasant; we should have slept longer. At breakfast, we planned our day and headed back to the city. We had a list; 4 books, 1 or 2 New Zealand Tiki pendants out of jade, a couple of sheet music books, and music cassettes with Australian folk music.

It was cold, wet and simply miserable. The shops were a warm refuge, but we couldn't find any Tikis, at least not the real ones. Someone gave us a plastic one, and he also told us that the real ones cost around $300. At that point, we abandoned our search.

We arrived back at Rita's place for dinner and spent another evening together. Unfortunately, Giselle had a bad toothache, and we considered going to the dental hospital together; I also had a broken tooth which was bothering me.

Next morning we paid the dental hospital a visit. Everything went splendidly. The doctors were efficient, and after an x-ray, Giselle received a new filling which fixed her problem for good. My problem was fixed for good as well, but a bit more dramatically. The broken tooth had to come out. Easier said than done, they had to do some serious digging with an instrument resembling an ice pick. I was released with a swollen cheek and minus one tooth. We walked around for a while to forget our latest ordeal and even visited the National Art Gallery.

We recuperated for another day before saying goodbye to Rita. We were still in Melbourne when we came to a sudden stop. One of our new rear tyres had a puncture. We had driven into a nail. I quickly changed the tyre while Giselle took a photo of our yellow van and me. It didn't take long, and we were on our way, no further dramas. We arrived in Bendigo, found a caravan park at Kangaroo Flat, and settled down into our warm car home for dinner.

Next morning we found a space close to the art gallery to park for free. Other tourists had also parked there. One was a VW bus we thought we had seen before. It was a young couple, probably our age. We wanted to go over to say hello, but something stopped us, and we waited, walking to the gallery first. Looking back, we saw the young man walking away from the VW bus and the girl going into the car with another older man. We laughed about our suspicion and joked, "Beats fruit picking."

The art gallery had beautiful pieces, even sculptures by Henry Moore; we were suitable impressed. On the way back to our car, we noticed another man disappearing into the VW bus with the girl. It appeared to be a thriving enterprise.

Before we left for Swan Hill, we had a look at a typical tourist attraction, an old tram and pottery, which completed our sightseeing tour. From Swan Hill, to continue our sightseeing, we went straight to a Settler Village type of museum but gave it a miss because the entry was $2.00. We loved driving, enjoying the scenery, and taking photos, but we usually avoided tourist attractions.

Next on our list was Mildura which was another 250km. About halfway, we arrived in Robinvale, not that we wanted to go there, we had never heard of it, but we were stopped. It was a fruit fly control border.

There was a large sign, Fruit Fly – and no fruit or fly was allowed to go past that border. We got worried. Would we have to pay a fine or throw out our two boxes of pears and apples?

"Are you carrying any fruit with you?" the guy asked.

"Why, is there any problem with fruit?" I played the innocent tourist, which is easy to do when one has a strong accent.

He was nice enough and explained the fruit fly issue to us. We had no idea it was that serious, and we admitted to having two boxes in the back of our car. Now he wore a worried expression.

We got out of the car, opened our rear door and showed him the boxes. That's when Giselle took over; maybe a bit of female charm could swing the issue in our favour.

"We bought the fruit in Shepparton, and we had no idea we would have difficulties with it. Look," she said, "they are heavily sprayed; I am sure there are no fruit flies on them."

I don't think he was convinced, but he inspected the fruit and asked, "Where will you go next?"

"To Broken Hill, stay for a few days and travel on to White Cliffs and Lightning Ridge," I answered. He murmured something like, "That sounds safe enough". We couldn't believe our luck; he let us keep our precious fruit.

Having overcome that obstacle, we drove on and made it to Mildura and the Apex Caravan Park in time for coffee. We kept sitting in the sun until dinnertime. Sometimes it is nice to sit, soak up the sun and relax.

It had rained all night long, and it was still raining. We managed to stay dry on the way to the shower block. Back in the car, we had a cold breakfast, it was too hard to boil water in our car, the gas bottle being under the cover on the roof rack. Bad luck, we stayed in the car waiting for a break in the weather. It came by 11 am, and we took our chance to leave the park. After 10 metres, we got stuck in the mud. A French couple, who had camped beside us, gave us a push.

We drove into the town, went to the bank, took out some cash, bought fresh produce and had our broken tyre fixed. Afterwards, we noticed a wine cellar which was what we needed. We tasted a few of their wines and bought a bottle of sherry and port. Next came the art gallery, which had an exhibition of Ernst Barlach, a German artist, and another German, Käthe Kollwitz. We knew her from Germany but had no idea she was known in Australia. It wasn't a cheerful exhibition but we enjoyed it. We had not heard of Ernst Barlach and were happy to discover he had studied in Hamburg.

It was another night of heavy rain, but it stopped for us to have breakfast next to our car. One hour later, we were in Wentworth where we visited an old jail and even spent 30c each to get in. It was actually called 'Old Wentworth Gaol,' not 'jail.' It had an impressive looking entry, not that the prisoners would have noticed.

We talked to the caretaker, he wasn't busy, and we were the only visitors. Wentworth had a rich Aboriginal history; the police and settlers killed many of them. The goal was built in 1879, but with more goals built in nearby towns, the Wentworth Goal's population declined, and it closed in 1928.

Having completed our history lesson and once again feeling anguished by the demise of the Indigenous people in those early days, we drove on to the junction of the Murray and Darling Rivers.

Broken Hill was our next destination. The landscape was serene all the way, hardly a tree and only a few bushes and grasses, basically a desert with its own unique beauty.

We went straight to the post office; picked up a few letters, a film and one little parcel from my mother. She had sent us a homemade knitted white poodle, it had a purpose; one could hide a toilet role in it. Cute, kitschy and we used it as our bedroom decoration. The rest of the mail we kept for later after we found a caravan park.

The following day, we had a few critical issues to attend to involving the police. Our car registration was due, and my driver's licence as well. At the police station, they told us to drive to the Department of Transport where they told us we needed a car inspection first, and sent us to a service station. Not much later, we received our new registration and a new licence for me. The licence was cheap, only $10, but the registration set us back $121.00; we nearly fainted. It was the first time we had paid for car registration and had no idea what to expect.

We recalculated our budget, and because we couldn't foresee any other significant expenses, we could compensate easily enough. We went to a nearby lake for a picnic lunch. It was an elevated spot, high enough for a scenic view. A lizard was sitting close by; he looked like he wanted to steal our lunch. I took the camera out, but the lizard disappeared into the bushes.

Next stop, Silverton; it sounded interesting enough and was mentioned on the tourist map as something to see, but in the end, it was another ghost town with a couple of ruins.

Shortly before lunch, we went to the post office, mailed our letters, and picked up more mail. One letter was from Peter Alexander. We had forgotten about the Christmas story competition we wrote in Narooma. We were excited; even though we couldn't remember what the big prize was. But it wasn't to be, we didn't win, we only qualified to receive a signed portrait from Peter Alexander. How funny, receiving a photo in a remote town in the middle of the outback of someone who wasn't even in our field of interest. "Just what we always wanted," I said to Giselle amid our laughter. But it got much better; the other letter was from a well-known magazine in Germany, the Stern. We expected a 'Dear John' letter, but the Stern was interested in our slides. We were beside ourselves. We had written them from Narooma as well. They certainly took a long time to answer and we hadn't expected a reply anymore, let alone a positive one. But here we were, our first inspiring lead into our photography and writing careers. There was only one problem, they wanted the photo material yesterday and all our slides were in Narooma. We raced back to our caravan park and wrote a letter explaining our situation.

Meanwhile, we visited the Mineral Art and Mining Museum, expecting something ordinary, instead found it exciting and informative. We took photos of the old mining set up; after all, following the confirmation from the Stern, we were even more focused on taking stunning photos, feeling like professionals on a mission.

We also had a look at a gallery in town with paintings we liked. We didn't know the artist but were taken with his style, particularly his figures. His name was Pro Hart; the gallery owner told us he was a local, lived close by, was quite a character, and had even worked in the Broken Hill mine.

"Why don't you pay him a visit?" he said. How could we resist that? We went around to his property, parked outside, and went into the courtyard. We noticed a Harley-Davidson parked there and the large double front doors were wide open. We went in, "Hello, anyone home?" No answer, we tried a few more times, but nothing. He either wasn't home, or he didn't want to talk to us.

We would have loved to meet him. He must have liked music; we saw a large organ in his gallery; it was a Rodgers Electric Pipe Organ. Never mind, we gave it a miss, it was getting late.

Was it Friday already? Time to move on to our next destination. But before heading for the opal fields of White Cliffs, we wanted to bushwalk in the Mootwingee National Park, known today as Mutawintji. We drove to town first to post our letter to the 'Stern.' The town was unusually quiet, and when we came to the post office, it was closed, actually all shops were closed. I asked a passer-by, "How come all the shops are closed?" I can only guess what that guy must have thought; he stared at us with an expression between bewildered and amused, before answering, "It's the Good Friday holiday." How could we have forgotten Easter?

We didn't waste any time and drove straight on to Mootwingee. As we were driving, some emus ran alongside the car, showing off how fast they could run. They seemed curious; maybe they wondered what we were doing there in the middle of nowhere. Whenever we stopped, they came closer to the car to have a good look at us. Why didn't we take any photos of that? Probably we were too perplexed by their behaviour.

•••••••••

A ranger was in charge of the Mootwingee National Park, he showed us where to camp. We liked the setting, lots of picnic tables with roofs, and many walking tracks in all directions leading into mountains as well as bush terrain.

We were slightly apprehensive; there were way too many people there already. We preferred fewer people but we shouldn't have worried. Once two buses left for the day, we had the place pretty much to ourselves. Some other campers stayed far away from us, sitting around their campfires; someone played the accordion. We settled down for the night, our favourite relaxed time of the day. It was such a profound feeling of freedom, sitting next to our car while it was getting dark, enjoying our meal and listening to the noises of the night, and not a worry in the world.

We were up bright and early, actually not that bright, but early enough to do what we had planned for the day. We had checked the different walking tracks, and were brave and chose the one reserved for the experienced bushwalker. It would be a long walk, four to five hours. We were ready to go, packed up with cameras, a few apples, lots of water, and a hat to combat the sun.

A quick look back to our car, we always felt uneasy leaving all our possessions behind and hoped the rangers made sure everyone behaved well.

At the start of the track we found fantastic caves with Aboriginal rock paintings. The track continued into rocky bushland and high grass. We climbed up and down many hills and canyons. Rather than a graded walking path, most of the track was only marked out, and we had to manoeuvre where to step to reach the next mark.

Taking photos wasn't easy. Being in magnificent scenery does not always translate well. How does one capture the vastness of a place like that? How does one convey the emotions it stirs up? The light was challenging as well. Through the eye of the camera, everything appeared bleached out. It was always better in the afternoons as the light was warm and the shadows provided an interesting contrast. But we were not keen to walk around the bush in the afternoons. Snakes seemed to like that time and often defended their territory.

We marched on, rested on rocks, soaking up the sun and marvelling about this beautiful remote outback. We nearly forgot that we had to track our way back.

We came to a little dam; how did they manage to get the mortar transported to hold the rocks in place?

It was an impressively constructed rock wall, strong enough to dam a large amount of water, and it was part of the walking track, not super high, but still not for the faint-hearted.

It was also the midpoint, and we knew it would take us another two hours or more to get back. We thought we were clever and would find a shorter track. We did, but it resulted in a few anxious moments when we thought we were lost again. At least this time, we had enough water with us. We arrived two hours later back at the camp, tired but happy.

A few new people were setting up camp; most of them were our age and from all over the planet. We were at peace; everyone was friendly, there were stories to tell and experiences to share.

I handed a cup of tea to Giselle, smiling, no words needed; we were both at happiness level ten and intended to stay there. Later at night, the camp ranger showed a movie about Aborigines, a befitting end to a beautiful day.

We were packed and ready to leave the campsite for a slow discovery drive to White Cliffs. The road was in good condition, and we made quick progress. The park ranger had told us that many roads were flooded. After an hour's drive, we took our usual break to sit outside the car with a cup of tea. We watched an eagle gliding in slow circles and eventually diving down, landing not far from us on the road. Maybe there was some road kill. I quickly set up the camera with our 300mm lens, but I was too late. Slowly, gracefully, the eagle lifted and took up its position high in the sky.

We arrived in White Cliffs shortly before lunch. It reminded us of Coober Pedy but less harsh and forbidding. It wasn't much of a town, a post office, a pub, a few houses, and some underground dwellings. We did find a good opal shop; the owner probably hoped we would buy something and gave us the whole tour, explaining about the different types of opal and the uniqueness of the white opal from White Cliffs. Or maybe he liked us because he gave us a few pieces of rough opal, a nice souvenir.

We found out something else, much less to our liking; according to him, the roads to Lighting Ridge were flooded. He showed us a couple of alternative roads on a map, which we could try but he couldn't guarantee any of those either. Apparently, four-wheel drives had passed the road successfully.

We went to the pub at night and heard a few tall stories about opal discoveries, and someone invited us to look at his mine.

After breakfast, we drove straight to an old mine called Clancy. We appreciated the historical value, but there was nothing really to look at. The main thing was that we knew what opal mining was all about. We went back to the caravan park to ask the owner if she had heard anything new about the road. She hadn't but advised us to try driving it; we could always come back and stay another night at her park. Giselle glanced at me and we both thought the same. It sounded as if she hoped the road would be blocked!

We filled our tank, and off we went driving across the country, all dirt roads, some with a bit of water but still safe to cross. These conditions continued until we got to a section 50km from White Cliffs when our luck ended. That was fun; let's go back and try another section. We tried, but it wasn't any better, there was no other way; we had to go back to Broken Hill and take an alternative route, a 600km detour.

The next day, we caught up with what we wanted to do in Broken Hill. Finally we posted the letter to the Stern magazine. Next, a bit of shopping, and back we went, on the road again. We had to drive back to Mildura. We drove all day and into the sunset, literally. We ended up in a tiny town called Balranald, 140km away from Mildura.

As soon as we arrived at the caravan park, Giselle put water on the stove to boil potatoes; she wanted to make fried potatoes with eggs. I got spoiled that day; I was allowed to shower and relax, resting in our comfy car bedroom. One hour later, our "Bratkartoffel," fried potato comfort food feast, was ready to be consumed.

Breakfast, and we set off. We talked non-stop, mainly about our dreams. What would we do once we were back in Hamburg? Would we still like Hamburg? Would Stern give us a chance to publish a book? Questions about money triggered more ideas and plans.

I had made up a list of people who still owed me money. How could we extract it from them? Particularly Herr Rehbein, one of my many clients, I had fixed his machines and helped him when he was in dire straits. Why was he not paying off the money he owed me? Very disappointing. He was doing one good deed; he still supplied my parents with brandy. At least he had stayed in contact.

With talking, planning and driving, the time went fast, and before long we had reached our next stop, West Wyalong, another little town we had never heard of.

We walked to town from the caravan park, but didn't explore anything else. Our mission was to reach Lightning Ridge. In the morning, we filled up our car, bought a new hairbrush - which must have been very important to us - and left town.

Our first stop was Forbes where we took a short walk to stretch our legs. The town is famous because of 'Ben Hall,' a bushranger who was killed nearby. We knew of him from a magazine with Ned Kelly on its cover; it contained stories about Australia's most famous bushrangers.

The next town in our sights was Parkes to see the radio telescope observatory which received the live television images of the Apollo 11 Moon landing in July 1969. We could see the dish from far away; it was like something out of space. We had never seen a telescope dish before and attended a tour and slide show to discover that it was the largest dish in the southern hemisphere. We had seen enough, and went on our way, arriving eventually in Dubbo, where we stayed for the night, ready for the final stretch to Lightning Ridge. We only stopped when we saw a guy on a horse, a real cowboy, moving cattle to greener pasture. Giselle took a photo out of the car window. Only later we realized he was wearing shorts. Would American cowboys wear shorts?

We arrived in Walgett in the late afternoon. We spent the rest of the evening at our campsite. I was playing guitar and had finally learnt to play harmonics. A young Aboriginal kid came up to me and asked for a biscuit. We felt sorry that we didn't have any biscuits. We offered him bread, but he only wanted biscuits.

We talked a lot that night about how to help aboriginal people. But even that seemed wrong to us; we can't tell them what to do; how could we help?

According to our map, it was only 60km to Lightning Ridge. We arrived by 11 am, went to the post office, and picked up a card from my mother.

We had anticipated Lightning Ridge would be like Coober Pedy or White Cliffs, but it was far more appealing. It was definitely greener; there were trees, some interesting-looking shops, and even a bottle house.

We chose the caravan park closest to town and had lunch before heading out again for a long walk around town.

Someone asked us if we had been to the pool already. "No, we haven't; where is it?" That's how we found out about Lightning Ridge's sulphur hot pool, supposedly with healing qualities. We had to give it a try next day.

At our customary long breakfast, we went wild with our ideas of what to do in Hamburg. We thought it would be a great idea to open up a macrobiotic restaurant. We had it all mapped out; location, size, menu, and other food items we could sell specifically related to macrobiotic. Being satisfied with our planning efforts, we went for a walk. Something was going on; people were dressed formally and walked in the direction of some kind of hall. Slowly it dawned on us; it had something to do with wartime. We hoped it was not directed against us. We didn't have to worry; a bystander explained about Anzac Day.

"Thank you for letting us know," I said.

"Are you German?" he asked.

My accent had revealed our identity; I felt a bit like a spy in a foreign country but was surprised by his next comments. He seemed to admire the German soldiers, not the atrocities of the war, just the normal soldiers. That was new to us; we had been called names from time to time but never had heard anything that could be construed as positive. He must have noticed our surprise, "It's a soldier thing," he said and left it at that.

We stayed for the whole ceremony. It was a sombre occasion; even so, some old soldiers were pretty drunk and could hardly stand straight.

Having digested that new experience, we walked to the hot pool. Not for any specific healing reason, simply because it was next on our list. As it turned out, we loved the pool; we didn't bring our bathing suits and were sitting on the edge, dangling our legs into the hot water.

"How good does this feel?" I said.

"I love it; let's go back tomorrow for a swim."

Next morning, we went straight back to the pool. We were the only ones; people were working, digging for opals. We felt spoiled having the hot pool to ourselves. Carefully gliding into the pool, we slowly and gradually were up to our necks in hot, smelly dark water. It took a couple of minutes to get used to the heat. We had noticed the day before that no one was swimming; it was more for relaxing and combating painful joints and muscles.

After a few minutes, gliding through the water or resting on the edge of the pool, we felt slightly dizzy and departed the hot water, still feeling lightheaded.

Not sure if it did us any good as we felt weak and tired. I would have liked an ice-cold shower to be shocked back to life. Back in Hamburg, I went to a sauna weekly, and the invigorating feeling going from the extremely hot sauna to the icy cold pool or shower was fantastic. But no cold shock at the Lightning Ridge pool. We found out later the water came from the Great Artesian Basin and was approximately two million years old. The thought of having a bath in two million year old stinky water makes it so much more special.

We didn't do any physical activities for the rest of the day; instead, we indulged in dreaming and planning more about our future, our constant topic. Another conclusion we had with this hot water infused brain activity was to fly back to Hamburg rather than make the return journey into another huge adventure. Our focus was now on getting back to Hamburg as quickly and cheaply as possible.

We wandered around the township, checking out different opal shops. It was hard to know what to buy, and we still had only rudimentary knowledge about opals. Considering our budget, we could afford only triplets. They were pretty, but it felt like a cheap substitute because we knew they were only slivers of opal sandwiched between plastic and a clear top of quartz. What to do?

We succumbed to the lure and bought two triplets, marked at $25 each, but after ten minutes of extreme haggling, we bought both for $40.00. Maybe we were still ripped off, but at least we didn't feel it.

At night I became engrossed in a book we bought, "I, the Aboriginal." It was about an aboriginal boy who had a traditional upbringing and subsequently trained to become a medical assistant.

Time to leave Lightning Ridge but not before we visited the bottle house. It triggered all kinds of creativity as to what to do when we finally owned or built our own house. Bottles would have to be a part of that, in combination with other environmentally friendly materials. We knew of mud bricks, straw bale walls, and other weird and wonderful building materials. Naturally, we had bought a book about those types of houses for inspiration. The biggest drawcard was we could build a place like that ourselves. Not sure if it was allowed in Germany, but surely it would be possible in Australia.

On the way out, we stopped at the Spectrum Opal Mines. We didn't buy any opals; we bought three kangaroo skin rugs instead. They would keep us warm in our travels and make great gifts for our parents.

A few kilometres later, we left NSW behind and crossed into Queensland. The road was pretty bad. On one occasion, we thought the car had broken an axel. We must have hit a rock; a loud bang and crash stopped us in our tracks. We drove on and arrived in St. George in time to buy a steak for dinner. The town looked so bleak; we needed animal-sourced strength to cope. Everything was dirty and derelict, not even particularly old, and to make matters worse, rain was threatening. Is it true that everything looks better in the morning? In that case, it was. Blue sky and sunshine, but no reason to hang around, and we left for Roma.

On that road, we must have seen at least ten dead foxes. We didn't stop to look at them until we had a car problem. The radio made strange noises. We stopped, and the radio stopped playing when we cut the engine. "Must be something with the battery," I said to Giselle and checked under the bonnet. It wasn't the fan belt or alternator; instead, it was the earth wire to the battery; it had broken off, too many washboard roads. It was a quick fix; the radio started playing, obviously a good sign. When we were getting back into the car, I spotted a dead fox a few metres away.

"What a beautiful creature," I said. "I can't leave it lying on the road." I dragged that poor fox by its beautiful tail into the bush. "If we were less sensitive, we could skin those foxes and sell the fur," I said.

"I never could do that," Giselle said.

"I know, it's sad to see them lying on the road," I said. We took a photo of the fox; it looked as if it was sleeping. In Roma, we saw a car with a foxtail on the aerial; we knew where it came from. I guess we could have done that, cutting off a tail, but why would we? It's not a trophy.

We parked in town, went for a discovery walk, and visited a winery which had a dark-looking wine cellar stacked with large wine barrels. We didn't buy any wine, too expensive; but bought another flagon of sherry and settled down for the night, dreaming about our next place to visit.

The road to the Carnarvon National Park had its difficulties, which we mastered well enough; even so, it meant I had to fix the exhaust pipe again. As I was lying halfway under the car, I noticed I had company. At the edge of the dirt road, hidden in the high grass, was a large goanna checking out what I was doing. I had fixed the exhaust pipe and the goanna seemed satisfied with my work and waited for me to take a photo before disappearing into the surrounding bush.

We had successfully completed our transformation from city dwellers to bush travellers. There was not much that could tip us off balance anymore. The last stretch of the road before the National Park was the worst but, as seasoned bush travellers, we took it in our stride. We crossed two creeks, the water nearly reached the door but we managed without getting our feet wet and arrived late in the afternoon.

The park had free camping facilities, but we needed a 'permit to camp.' We booked ourselves in from the 30.04. to the 3.05.

We camped among strange looking palm trees which we learnt were Carnarvon Gorge Cabbage Palms. Actually, there were many other palms and ancient cycads as well. But for the moment we were admiring the park from the spot where we had parked our car. We were in a valley surrounded by rainforest and rugged mountain ranges, with walkways disappearing into the wilderness along creeks and canyons. There were Aboriginal rock paintings to discover, and for anyone fit and energetic, you could walk and climb to the top of the ranges.

We couldn't wait to discover nature's treasures, but first things first. We lit a campfire to stay warm and have our dinner in comfort.

I ventured out to the toilet and shower block but came back quickly; there was no hot water. Maybe taking a shower in the middle of the day when it was warm would work better. We relaxed, sitting beside the fire, playing guitar, eating dinner, and hand-fed the possums.

We woke up early eager to start exploring but decided to stay in bed. It was cloudy and cold. By 8 am, we were brave enough to face the day. Slowly the clouds cleared and we were ready to track up the mountain range. First we walked along a creek, among palms and mature eucalypt trees, climbing over rocks and broken-down logs, slowly getting up along the sandstone cliffs, climbing higher and until we reached the top. Other walkers had beaten us to it and sat close to the edge admiring the view. They were from different countries: Canada and the USA, but mainly from Europe, France, and England, but no Germans.

As fantastic as the view was, it wasn't clear enough for great photos, still too cloudy and hazy. We took close-ups of the surroundings instead. After a little picnic, we tracked back, arriving at our camp in the afternoon and rushed to the shower while there was still a bit of warmth in the air.

Having survived the cold shower, we were warmed by the campfire and a hot dinner and hand-fed the possums and kangaroos. By 8 pm, we were snuggled up in our warm bed.

Another cold morning greeted us, but it was less cloudy than the day before.

Giselle had designed a leather bag but had difficulty stitching it together. We needed to buy better leather tools, at least a few stronger needles, and a poker to make holes in the leather.

"Do you know what design you want to do?" I asked. We studied her drawings of three designs.

"One or two designs for carrying the gemstone cases, one design as a small handbag with a long strap to wear over the shoulder and another one, a long rectangle, to carry as a handbag, will be made from soft leather," Giselle explained, "I can't wait to get to Rubyvale to see if we can sell them."

That was our plan; Rubyvale miners carried around small black cases for their faceted sapphires around. Surely they would be interested in buying Giselle's protective, strong leather cases. But first, we needed better tools and more leather.

We went for another long hike, this time following a creek bed. We were the only hikers on the track, surrounded by an atmosphere of stillness. Unworldly forces propelled us forward as if our lives depended on it. We had to cross the creek a few times. There was no real track, only markers on trees to find the way back to the camp. We climbed over large rocks and through narrow canyons but came to a dead-end unless one was a professional climber. We took a rest, sitting still on a rock or tree trunk to soak up the surreal stillness and the relaxing sounds of the water bubbling, birds singing, screeching, and insects buzzing. Time stood still. We headed back to restore our grip on reality.

Back at the camp, we prepared ourselves for a lazy afternoon, playing guitar, reading, drinking coffee, everything in close proximity to the warming campfire. For dinner, we had spaghetti and nothing much else. By 8 pm, we had run out of firewood and settled down in our bedroom, doing what we were hilariously good at, 'talking', planning our future, reading and making fun of what we read. We cracked ourselves up by harshly criticizing the translation of a book by Patrick White, 'Voss.' The translation was by a well-known German author, Heinrich Boehl. The funny thing was, we hadn't even read any version of that book yet. We had the English version but only had read what it was about, and somehow we couldn't imagine that Herr Boehl could successfully translate the book into German without having been to Australia.

Our critique was harsh indeed; even so, it was for fun; I thought I would ask Herr Boehl, "Have you actually read the book?" Once I said that out loud, we couldn't stop laughing.

I woke up laughing.

"What are you laughing at?" Giselle asked.

"I just remembered last night," I said. "Let's get up; it looks good outside; we could do another walk."

One hour later, we went on our way. The first part was easy; a well-trampled bush path led us into a dense forest, walking amongst tall palms, thick undergrowth of bushes entwined with dead, broken, fallen trees interrupted by towering eucalypt trees. It was a long track, crossing creeks and climbing rocks. We returned to the camp about four hours later, feeling in harmony with this amazing nature.

After a good rest, we decided it was time to move on. We were keen to get to Rubyvale. The rest of the afternoon, we cleaned up the car and ourselves.

Washing our hair was called for, but washing hair under a cold shower was an experience one should avoid. Both of us ended up with headaches, and I had earache for over an hour. Never mind, we survived, and after dinner, all was good again, and the night progressed even better. There was a notice on the toilet block there would be a movie shown, starting at 8 pm.

The movie was about rainforests and Australian trees and explained why fire was essential for tree species re-seeding. Aborigines always knew how to light fires to regenerate life rather than destroy it. We didn't understand it completely at that time but it was enough to appreciate that aborigines were the caretakers and experts in cold burn-offs.

It was only 6:30 am when I woke. I tried to wake Giselle; she was still asleep and answered only slowly and timidly to my 1000 kisses. From that day onwards, I always woke Giselle with 1000 kisses. Never stop a good habit.

By 9 am, we were on our way, our first stop being Rolleston, only 100km further on. It was just in time, because the exhaust had come loose once again. We stopped at a service station, and luckily they had the clamps I needed to tighten the exhaust pipes together. Most small towns, farming communities, or rural service stations had what one needed. They may not find it straight away but they knew it was somewhere in their old timber sheds.

Finally, and hopefully, I fixed the pipe for the last time, and on we went to Springsure, a 'dried out little town.' We asked a local how the town's name came about. He laughed, "It's named not surprisingly after a reliable spring close by."

"Thank you," was my doubtful answer.

An hour later, we arrived in Emerald and it felt like being back on home turf. Everything was the same as when we left last year. We stocked up on fresh food before driving to our final destination, Rubyvale.

Chapter 16

Fields of Dreams

Rubyvale had changed; the old dirt road crossing in the middle of town was now a brand spanking new sealed road. That was not the only change; there were also new buildings. We stopped at the post office; the same ladies were still in charge; they even recognized us. We had one letter and one developed slide film waiting for us.

That night we stayed at the caravan park; we longed for a long hot shower. But first, we ate some of the fresh bread and salami we had bought in Emerald; that and a cup of tea, reading the letter and looking at the slides got us over the shock that Rubyvale had a sealed road.

The shower was as delicious as the bread and salami; one could always trust the caravan park's old steam engine to provide plenty of hot water.

Warm and tired, we went into our car to sleep. Giselle fell asleep, but I couldn't; I had to sort my thoughts. What would we do, who would we see, and how long would we stay?

Wednesday the 5th of May. After a relaxing breakfast and pondering our next steps, we ventured away from the caravan park. First stop, the post office, but no new mail yet. Next, turning into the road where Rudolf and Susanne lived. How would we be received? Would they treat us as friends or dismiss us as tourists?

Fifty metres away from the new sealed junction, the road turned to gravel. It was not often one greets a gravel road with a cheer but this time it was a reason for excitement; it brought back the feeling of familiarity. This was Rubyvale for us: bush and connecting gravel roads. We had hardly parked our car when Rudolf came out of his gem-cutting hut, followed by Susanne, warmly greeting us. Other people joined in and greeted us; Bob, one of Rudolf's gem cutters, and another couple we had met before.

Coffee for all, and one of the wonderful pleasures of living in a remote bush town; time to talk, time to enjoy company, and time to relax.

We shared our stories and, in return, were updated with what was new in and around Rubyvale. Yes, there had been changes, mainly regarding the popularity of Rubyvale with tourists. The area where we camped last year was now busy with tourists, hardly worthwhile going there. But before we even had the chance to worry where to camp, Rudolf told us we could stay at Ryan's camp.

We were invited for lunch. That was our opportunity to hand over our presents, a couple of jasper pieces and one of our gold melting pots, which really was a rarity. Rudolf surprised us in return by giving us a beautiful cut garnet.

We took off after lunch and arrived not much later at Ryan and Kath's camp. After welcoming us, and more coffee and talking, Ryan showed us a spot for building our camp. It was only 20 metres away from their place, and we could use their bush toilet, shower and play with the cats and dogs. They invited us for dinner; what a glorious freeloading welcoming day it was!

We set up our camp, unloaded the roof rack, and used the tarp for our camp roof. We felt settled, and showed up for dinner in time. The dogs stayed next to us, happy to see us again.

We played guitar; Ryan had acquired a few new chords, and I was playing pieces I had learned. There was much to tell and to show. Ryan gave us a present; a star sapphire and a zircon he had cut himself on his new faceting machine. It turned into a late-night, full of new ideas, resulting in our decision to stay at least one month and for me to learn to cut gemstones. Giselle would work on her leather craft.

Waking up early, we couldn't wait to start digging. Ryan showed us where we could dig undisturbed not far from the camp. I put together a rudimentary rig for washing the dirt without exhausting ourselves as we had before. After a few test runs, it worked fine, and we even found some zircons.

In the afternoon, we went back to the post office. Three developed films had arrived and a surprise positive letter from the German Stern magazine. They wanted to see our slides as soon as we were back in Germany; a good excuse for celebration.

Sitting at night, watching the fire, eating, drinking wine, cats lying on our feet and all that in the middle of the Australian bush, how much better could life get?

Does one lose reality when one lives in peace somewhere remote from the rest of society? Is it healing to have a rest from the unrest? We opted for staying well-rested for many more months to come.

Ryan needed help carting water to where he had his mining shaft. It was required to wash the gravel coming from the mine. He worked all day underground with his brothers, jack hammering and shovelling dirt into a bucket, which was pulled up by an automatic winch and tipped into an arrangement of sieves, looking a bit like an oversized washing machine. He found gemstones all the time, but he was looking for the big ones.

After helping Ryan, we drove to Emerald. Giselle bought leather and tools needed to work on her craft, and I bought a case of beer and other supplies. On the way back, we checked for mail again. My mother had written that my brother Herbert had severely dislocated his shoulder. It didn't look good, with tendons torn and possible nerve damage. He was a very active guy; I didn't think he would be able to play soccer for a while.

Kath invited us for a glass of wine; how could we refuse. Ryan had a movie camera and asked us if we could do a few films for him, showing his mining contraption, the camp and his stones, basically his whole operation to show to his mum in New Zealand.

The following day, more digging for gems, and even better, it worked. The result of one day's digging was impressive. We had unearthed small sapphires, zircons and blackjacks and some were large enough for cutting.

At night we had a different experience altogether. Rudolf invited us for a movie night. There was a 'movie drive-in' close to Emerald. Who wouldn't drive 45km one-way to watch two movies? The movies were pretty bad, but the experience itself was worth it.

Waking up late, it was Sunday; the day people visited each other to hear the latest Rubyvale gossip. Max came to visit us; we knew him vaguely from the previous year. He was Austrian and, if one believed the grapevine, he was a lazy bugger. He had lived there for a while but hadn't done much digging or anything else for that matter. We liked him; he had done a lot of reading and travelling and loved to talk. We mainly discussed lifestyle pearls of wisdom and philosophy.

The topic for that afternoon was that people who worked from 8 to 5 'to earn a living' had no time to think of creative ways of how 'to earn a living'. Naturally, we agreed; after all, that's what we were doing, taking out time to discover what life had to offer.

Max was quite enthusiastic about our choices and felt that he was on the same track; even so, he hadn't discovered what he wanted out of life.

"You need a loving partner; creating a life together with someone brings out the best in you," was my comment, thinking about the yin and yang philosophy that one by itself cannot exist.

"Not easy to find someone out here to share a life with," he answered.

"Did you come here by yourself or with a girlfriend?" Giselle asked, her intuition talking.

"I came with a girlfriend, but after a while, she didn't like it and we broke up," Max said.

He visited us sporadically over the next few weeks. We usually discussed contentious topics like religion, politics and lifestyle choices. Neither of us believed in religious institutions and instead believed in spirituality and how everyone should follow the 'Golden Rule,' of treating others as one wants to be treated.

·····•·····

Giselle had been busy cutting out designs for leather tobacco pouches as well as gemstone cases. She had finished two, one for Rudolf and one for Ryan.

It was Monday, and we had planned to work hard to get rich quick. But even with our enthusiasm, four hours of digging didn't make us any richer. Never mind, for the remainder of the day, Giselle did her leatherwork,

"We can probably earn more money selling leather pouches than looking for sapphires," I said.

Max came around a few days later with his friend, Fred. He politely introduced us, "Fred has a speedboat, and we will go water-skiing tomorrow. Do you want to come?" Max asked.

"Yes, sounds great," we said. "Where do we meet?"

"Be at my place by 8 am; it's only a bit further on from where Max is living," Fred answered. He was into barefoot water-skiing, and we were keen to watch; it was another opportunity to take unique photos for the Stern magazine.

That night when talking to Kath, she opened up, telling us about trouble in her relationship with Ryan. We stayed as supportive as we could without taking sides. We wished she hadn't told us but understood she needed to talk to someone. We would have no chance to hear Ryan's story; all we could do was to stay out of it. Their relationship appeared to be a happy one from the outside; it made us reflect on our loving relationship. People often remarked on how happy we were. Did they mean it, or were those remarks tinged with scepticism?

Getting up early, we left the camp in time to get to Fred's place by 8 am. Kath and Ryan waved us goodbye, looking happy, as if nothing had happened. Nothing had happened; Ryan had no idea that Kath had unloaded her problems.

Fred, his wife, and Max were ready to go. After a quick stop in Sapphire, buying rations, we continued our high-speed pursuit. Fred seemed to be in a hurry; we reached speeds of 120km per hour with his speedboat in tow. We asked him about it later and the police had never stopped him. Police presence on the open road was a rarity.

We arrived at a huge dam; no one else was present. No wonder; there was nothing else for many miles in any direction.

The boat slid into the water, and minutes later, we were racing at high speed over the water with Fred barefoot skiing behind us. We quickly gave up taking photos; too bouncy and being sprayed constantly with water, we feared for our cameras.

It was fun, all right, but we left after a barbeque lunch; water sport wasn't high on our agenda. We could have participated, but our excuse was the water was too cold, and for beginners like us, it would have meant spending more time in the water than out. Fred was wearing a wetsuit and was comfortable and full of adrenalin.

On the way back, we visited Rudolf and Susanne; they invited us for dinner. While Susanne was preparing dinner, Rudolf opened up to us.

What was going on, had someone opened the floodgates for confessions? Rudolf was not happy with Susanne, despite having three kids together. He felt she was holding him back. He wanted to go all-out and expand the business. Rubyvale was ready for the tourist market, and he wanted to be selling gemstones with hefty price tags attached.

Susanne was much more careful, and we understood why. Rudolf had a broken back from his mining adventure days, was in pain, and had a problem walking. No wonder Susanne was holding back.

Something else intriguing emerged. We had sensed a glimpse of it when Kath opened up to us, and here it was again, a bit hidden, but a picture emerged. Something was going on between Kath and Rudolf. How could that even happen in a small community with no place to hide? At dinner, all was well, not a hint of disharmony.

· · · • · • • · · ·

We knew about the struggle between the big machine miners with their bulldozers and the little miners who wished to protect Rubyvale's lifestyle and innovate in the tourist market.

The small miners had formed the Small Miner's Association and planned to build a large complex, creating a showcase for the gem fields, making Rubyvale the centre for quality sapphires and gem cutting.

The big miners were not interested; they came with their bulldozers, going for the quick buck, leaving utter devastation behind them. To make matters worse, Taiwanese buyers bought large amounts of sapphires, and took them out of the country, paying no duty and eventually selling them back into Australia as Taiwanese sapphires with inflated prices.

We took it easy the following morning; we had a lot of news and concepts to digest. How would we handle Kath and Rudolf's emerging, secret love affair? Taking sides is always problematic; one never has all the facts. We liked everyone in this outback soap opera and decided on neutrality.

Even more intriguing was our deeper insight into Rubyvale's politics. There was no doubt on which side we stood; we loved the small miners' idea and lifestyle and vowed to assist Rudolf for the time we were there. That day we stayed at our cosy camp. I studied a book on gem cutting, and Giselle did more leather craft. I found the concept of cutting gemstones quite logical; it reminded me of when I did practical work sessions during my studies, setting up a milling machine. I felt confident. The gem-cutting book explained the various cuts and how to apply them. Another ability needed for gem cutting was patience, one of my strong points.

The next day after lunch, we visited Rudolf to deliver Giselle's leather bags. He loved his tobacco leather bag and used it straight away. Encouraged by that, we hoped for more orders and sales. Another guy who was visiting Rudolf liked the bag as well. He was interested in a leather case for his gemstones. His name was Steve, and to our surprise, he was the president of the Small Miners' Association. Originally from Hungary, he had lived in Austria for a while and spoke perfect German.

Steve was without his car, and we took him back to his camp. It was quite an impressive set-up, with two large water tanks connected to guttering from a large shed. The shed roof covered a sizeable army-style house tent and a kitchen and workshop. He had a kerosene fridge, a diesel generator and even a washing machine.

We stayed for a couple of hours talking. Steve had lived with aborigines and told us about telepathy, pointing the bone, fire practices and about their many tribes. He explained the concept of 'walkabout' and why it was important for aborigines as a rite of passage. We wanted to hear more and left Steve with a promise to visit soon.

After weeks of relaxed travelling, Rubyvale turned out to be not as idyllic and tranquil as we thought; it was rattled by intrigue, politics and divisions and was far more complicated than it appeared to the uninitiated.

We had a disturbed night. What troubled me is not worth writing about, but it included racing to the bush toilet. Giselle experienced something more interesting. I had heard Giselle crying in her sleep and gently woke her up.

"Are you OK, darling? Are you dreaming?" I asked.

Giselle was sobbing, "We were back in Hamburg, and everything was terrible, we didn't like it at all but we were not allowed to come back to Australia."

"It's OK, darling, we will work it out as we always do," I said. Giselle seemed calm again and drifted off to sleep.

Now I was awake, playing all kinds of scenarios in my mind. It had never occurred to either of us that we might not like Hamburg anymore.

Getting up late, we were putting in a whole morning of digging. It is surprising how digging for sapphires can calm the mind. We went back to the camp admiring a few gems we had found. We didn't plan to go back digging; we were invited to a party which meant we had to look our best and needed to wash our hair which was a lot of work without running hot water. We boiled kettles full of water, enough for the two of us to wash our hair and the rest of our glorious young bodies. This exercise took nearly all afternoon but we were sparkling clean, refreshed and ready to party.

The party started well, with plenty to drink and eat. Rudolf and Susanne had outdone themselves with cooking and preparing everything. Loud music, dancing and lots of friendly people completed the perfect picture of harmony.

As the night progressed and aided by people having too much to drink, the intrigue continued. The trust our friends had placed in us was puzzling. They made us into something we were neither equipped for nor comfortable about. It started with Rudolf telling us more about his romantic longing for Kath, not something we wanted to know. Not much later, Kath wanted us to pass on a message to Rudolf that she loved him. We felt as if we were back at school, only this kind of playing around was much more serious and probably dangerous.

We relayed her message, and Rudolf was overjoyed; he felt the same. As it was a party and everyone was talking to everyone, Rudolf went to speak to Kath. Ryan, who we found out was a jealous guy, to put it mildly, must have objected to Kath spending time talking to Rudolf. We were unsure when it happened, but Ryan must have pulled Kath aside to talk to her. The problem was, he didn't only talk. Ryan was a big guy, very strong, and what he had done was apparent to everyone when Kath presented herself amongst the partygoers with a black eye. This situation was out of control; and was not something we wanted any part in.

We arrived back at our camp in the early morning. Straight to bed was the only thing left to do, and waking up late was the consequence.

We replayed last night's movie. It was bad, but not that bad; actually, it was a great party. Most people had fun and had absolutely no idea about the little interlude between our contestants.

We also spent a considerable time talking to Steve and Wally. One couldn't find two more different people to talk to. Steve was an educated and well-travelled guy with an aura of importance and authority; even so, he looked like a bushranger.

On the other hand, Wally, who we knew from the previous year, was an energetic, fun guy with little education but plenty of energy. He was born and lived in Hamburg, close to the harbour and red-light district. He still spoke a Hamburg harbour worker's dialect and he walked like he had been on the sea all his life. At fourteen, he got himself hired on a ship as a deck boy. In the late forties, no one cared about their age if someone wanted to head out to sea. When the ship reached Sydney, Wally "jumped ship." Years later, building his life in Rubyvale with a beautiful wife and kids, he was still 'as happy as Larry,' proudly declaring his independence from ordinary society.

Another guy, John, who was Ryan's brother, also talked to us at great length. As we knew, he was good at divining, either for water or sapphires. Apparently, he couldn't wear a watch, because if he did, the hands would turn backwards. He gave us a few tips. He was not one of those diviners who used a willow twig; he used a piece of wire or a coat hanger. He also used a pendulum, not with a crystal, but with a piece of corundum. We got pretty excited about the possibilities one could achieve with a pendulum, not only for finding sapphires but also for everything that needed a positive or negative answer.

Later that morning, we talked to Kath and Ryan and they behaved as if nothing had happened. We started digging at our little plot and tried out our corundum on a string to check if there were sapphires where we were searching.

"I can't feel anything," I said.

"Let me try," Giselle said. She held the pendulum over different sections of gravel.

"Look, it works," We saw the pendulum swing right or left at different gravel sections. We knew the pendulum could be subconsciously influenced. To prevent that, we tried it blindfolded. It worked, but it did not influence our fortunes. The only benefit was we searched more carefully when the pendulum indicated sapphires. And that's when we found a beautiful, well-sized white zircon, something rare. Had the pendulum shown us the way?

Back from digging, Kath came over to explain in detail what happened last night. Ryan confronted her, asking if she was having an affair with Rudolf. Kath answered 'Yes,' and that's when Ryan lost it. There was no excuse for his behaviour, however Kath was not having a real affair, at least not in an intimate sense. It was in her mind; it was a failed fairy tale. Giselle and I thought Ryan must have been under the assumption that Kath had slept with Rudolf.

All morning we were digging hard but produced nothing. The pendulum wasn't helping our endgame; it took too much time and interrupted our workflow. Two Taiwanese gem buyers interrupted us. They wanted to see our stones but were not impressed. They urged us to "Dig deep, dig deep." They promised to come back, not that we cared. We were convinced those guys were smuggling sapphires out of Australia. We had taken on the new role of protecting Australian sapphires for the small miners.

It was dark when the 'happy couple' came back from Emerald. Ryan had bought mining shaft drilling equipment and a truck with a drill on the back. He explained that as well as drilling his shafts, he would earn money by drilling for other miners. We liked his enthusiasm and business inventiveness. We wondered, 'Why can't they be a happy couple, so much potential?'

We had Ryan's film camera with three rolls of film and were looking forward to playing movie directors. The first scene was in Rubyvale, filming the post office and surroundings. Giselle was the actress who left our car to walk over the road to the post office. Next came Rudolf's place, his gem-cutting hut, and a cutting demonstration.

It's hard to believe, but the two Taiwanese dealers came back a few days later. We looked at each other in disbelief; they bought all our small stones. Yes, we were officially rich now; they paid $35 in cash. As a reward, we stopped digging for the day and relaxed in our newfound glory. At night we visited Wally and listened to the old-fashioned German music he loved so much.

We needed leather and drove to Emerald, walking into the same shop where we had bought leather before, but the price had increased from $15 to $45 a hide. We didn't buy anything. A bit further was a printer shop. We always liked the old print drawers to store the different sizes of letterings. We asked the owner if he had some. He did but wanted $10.00 each, too expensive for our liking. We performed 'being poor bush dwellers' in need of a break and he gave us one drawer for free. Giselle had one like that in Hamburg, full of little mementos. We didn't intend to keep this free one; it was meant as a present for Rudolf and Susanne. We bought paint, sandpaper and a brush to make the print drawer presentable. They loved it and would use it for displaying their precious gemstones.

Saturday was washing day; we got our act together and headed out to the nearby dam. It was like in the old days, not that we were around then. Squatting at the edge of the water, pounding and scrubbing one piece of washing after the other, all with the modern help of Omo.

Sunday morning and visitors rolled in again. Rudolf was on his way to Steve but came to let me know he had set up a workbench for me, and I could start cutting on Monday morning.

We were sure what happened next had something to do with Rudolf. One hour later, Steve visited us and wanted to talk about something important. He had a proposition, and it sounded most interesting. He had to be at the Rockhampton Hospital for a week, maybe longer, and his question was, "Do you think you could live and look after my camp while I am gone?" Just a short glance and Giselle and I knew, "Yes, sure, we'd love to."

"You can use everything at the camp and all you have to do is feed Bidi, my dog, and my three cats, Don Juan, Missis Mafu and Fufu; there is nothing much else to do," Steve said.

That was perfect timing, particularly with me starting to learn cutting. Giselle could stay at Steve's camp doing leather craft, protected by the dog and the cats, while I concentrated on learning to cut gems.

Everything always seemed to fall into place for us.

Chapter 17

The Faceting Game

We were at Rudolf's place by 10 am. Giselle looked forward to doing her leather craftwork at a proper workbench. Slightly hesitant but excited, I viewed my designated workbench. Giselle worked behind me, and Bob the master cutter in front of us.

I felt confident while reading about cutting but it looked more complicated when sitting in front of the faceting machine.

First, I had to learn how to glue a rough gem to a stick, called a dop stick. The dopping compound was heated shellac. It worked well; I tried it a few times to get the hang of it. It was quite amazing; a gemstone could be cut and polished without flying off with some shellac. I will refrain from explaining what came next, only to say I made a mistake which took the rest of the day to rectify.

"Never mind," said Bob, "making mistakes is the best way of learning."

"Thanks, Bob, very encouraging," I answered, slightly cynically.

Late afternoon I started the polishing process which was tricky as well. One speck of leftover abrasive grit nesting itself on the polishing disc would result in scratches and one had to start again. I had to re-start a few times. Bob came to the rescue, but he had the same problem. He investigated the gem closely and noticed the scratches were fine lines embedded throughout the gem and had nothing to do with polishing. My confidence was restored.

I had been so focused on my tasks, I hadn't noticed that Giselle had finished a couple of bags.

The second day involved cutting the crown, which turned into another problem. I did not have enough space left to cut the recommended angles. Clever as I thought I was, I lowered the angles, but that resulted in making more unconventional changes. As Bob mentioned, learning by mistakes was the best. Considering that, I did very well.

We were invited for dinner again. Giselle had helped with the preparations. I arrived at the dinner table proud as punch, presenting my first gemstone, cut and polished. It exceeded all my expectations. Considering the problems I had and the poor quality of the gem, the end result looked surprisingly brilliant. "Any gem cut properly will look stunning," said Rudolf. Many gemstones were machine cut with uneven angles, making them look dull compared to my effort. He showed us a few examples; I loved my first effort even more after that.

The next day we went to Steve's place; he showed us around, pointing out what to keep a watchful eye on, like his temperamental kerosene fridge. What a luxury, he had a fridge, but it needed constant attention, adjusting the flame to stop it from freezing or melting.

The generator also needed special attention, and of course, we had to know where the dog and cat food was stored and how much to dish out to his pet family.

Back for more cutting, unfortunately the new gem flew off the dop stick.

"What happened?" Bob asked.

"I don't know; the stone just came off," I said.

"It shouldn't - was the wax hot enough when you applied it?" Bob asked.

"Yes, I'm sure it was; what else could it have been?" I asked.

"Did you clean the stone with methylated spirit?"

"Hmmm, I think I only wiped it," I said. That was the problem but I couldn't be bothered to start fresh, it was already 4 pm, and we went home.

Next day was the moving day, we arrived at Steve's place early. He showed us the last few things we needed to know, said goodbye to his dog, Bidi, and left us to our devices.

Bidi was deeply upset and sulking. He even barked at us but eventually he became friendly. We stayed the day to settle in and get the animals to like us. After feeding them, they loved us. When we woke up on the first morning, Bidi did not recognize us, or he tried to get our attention to go walking with him. Steve had told us Bidi was not going to the toilet close to the camp. What a good dog. After the pets had their breakfast, they once again loved us. "The way to a pet's heart is definitely through their stomach."

Giselle felt comfortable staying at the camp with Bidi for protection while I went off to 'work' with a heavy heart, not wanting to be separated from my darling.

Cutting went well and I finished a second gem. I felt like a professional cutter; customers must have thought I was part of the team. I liked that.

Work stopped at 5 pm; I rushed back to Giselle. We had our first dinner at the new camp, sitting by the kerosene lamplight, eating, and sharing what we had achieved that day. Bidi was lying at our feet, and the cats relaxed nearby.

Bidi had accepted us, no more barking in the mornings. Same with the cats, but they never showed apprehension towards us. They were more concerned about whether there was something to eat.

After breakfast, I kissed Giselle goodbye, again heavy-hearted, but I promised to be back early. I took Giselle's leather bags; Rudolf had already sold two and needed more on display. Thinking of how little money we spent in Rubyvale, we would have plenty of money left for the rest of our trip

I finished a small gem in record time, no point to start another one; I hurried home to Giselle.

"Look at this beauty," I showed Giselle my latest achievement.

"Beautiful, we need to buy a case for it. I've got the leather case for it already."

On Sunday we couldn't even sleep in. Bidi liked us a lot which is why he decided to wake us at 6 am. No lazy Sunday for a professional gem cutter; I was now ready to cut one of our large topazes. I went to work and Giselle, who had come with me, used Rudolf's typewriter to write letters.

I made good progress but quickly learnt that each type of gem needed a different approach and a large stone was slower and harder to cut and polish.

We had coffee and cake with the team, before returning to 'our home.' Bidi went berserk with happiness to see us. Not having owned a dog before, we had no idea about their behaviours; it surprised us how quickly they become accustomed to a new owner. He was a good dog, well behaved, and listened to us, even if we spoke German. Clever dog.

Amazing how fast one could slip into a routine. Each morning, first feeding the pets, then breakfast and off to work. Giselle was doing her leatherwork or writing letters, and I kept cutting gemstones and learning in the process. That last day of the month was no different. I finished my topaz, which turned out to be my best gem so far, not only in quality but also in size and general appearance.

• • • • • • • • •

It was June, my birthday month. We had no idea how long Steve would stay away; there had been no news from him. We had to compliment him on the trust he had in us. All his worldly possessions were at his camp, with us as caretakers, and he knew nothing about us.

That morning, I started cutting one of our amethysts and had finished it by 3 pm. As usual, I couldn't wait to get home to Giselle.

Six am, and I had to get up; "Bidi, what are you doing to us?" Who is in charge here? Stupid question, the dog, of course.

We went to Rudolf's together. Whatever I was cutting on my sub-standard machine, I had to be extremely gentle; one quick movement and the angles would shift. We returned early to our camp which was fortunate because the fridge was smoking badly. I cleaned the burner, cut off the wick, and fired it up again; better, but still smoking. I checked the flue; it was clogged. After cleaning it, we had a functioning fridge again. Happy with ourselves and our fridge-fixing achievements, we settled down for dinner, some beers and a game of chess.

"Bidi, go back to sleep," I yelled. "Woof," was the answer. I guess it meant no. After I dragged myself out of bed, I checked on the fridge. It was working too well. Everything was frozen, including the milk and eggs.

After our frozen breakfast, we went together to our workplace. I wanted to attempt an emerald cut. Bob warned me it would be too hard to get the parallel lines straight on my machine. I knew what he meant, but it worked reasonably well with my super gentle approach. Before we went home, we bought ice cream. It went straight into our super fridge, and we had it after dinner.

Leaving Giselle at the camp, I delivered five of Giselle's leather bags to a shop called Capricorn Gems, before another day of cutting. Our business was taking off; Giselle's leather bags were flying off the shelf.

That night at dinner, we talked once again about Hamburg until late at night. Would we still like it in Germany where everything was so restrictive and bureaucratic? Could we work in a regular job, be separated for most of the day, come home tired, eat and watch television? Not likely. We had better ideas for our life.

Next morning, we arrived at Rudolf's at 8 am. I started cutting, and Giselle went with Rudolf and Susanne to Emerald for shopping. Away from prying eyes, I attempted to modify the cutting machine for better handling. I fixed it and even managed to get parallel cuts without problems. The day went quickly, pleasantly interrupted by a surprise phone call from Giselle to tell me how much she loved me, and before I knew it, she was back.

At the camp and after dinner we fired up the big diesel generator and watched the movie we had filmed on Steve's projector. It wasn't very good; some scenes were not even in focus. We watched some of Steve's movies instead. His films were mainly work related when he was a project manager in Gove and Weipa at a bauxite mine and aluminium smelter.

· · · · ● · ● · · ·

Hardly a day went by without discussing our future. Living together as we had for the last two years had changed us. If we went back to Hamburg to live, we envisaged getting a shop for leather craft, gems and jewellery, as well as books and photography, and if we had enough space, for exhibitions of photography and works of art. Maybe we even would get a dog.

Do people with dogs ever sleep in? Up early walking the dog but Bidi couldn't find a suitable place to do his business. Finally, after thirty minutes, he had mercy on me. I went back to bed snuggling up to Giselle, and we slept for another hour.

Arriving at Rudolf's place, he greeted me with, "Can you have a look at Bob's cutting machine and see if you can rebuild his touch control system?" "Sounds interesting; I'll give it a go," I said. Bob wasn't working, but had allowed us to take his machine apart. I opened the black box; it contained a meter, a couple of lights and some knobs.

"Look at this," I said. "There is nothing to it, only a small printed circuit board. Should be easy." It didn't take long and I had it worked out. Most of the parts were readily available, standard resistors, capacitors, transistors, and one IC, which in 1976 was state of the art. It had no markings, but I knew there were only a few choices, and wrote out a list of what to buy.

Walking the dog the next morning, the cats were following us. I thought it was unusual and even more unusual, one cat was missing. Where was Fufu, the youngest little cat? She was nowhere to be found. I woke up my darling to let her know. We were both upset but hoped she would show up soon. Giselle stayed home and I left for work. Rudolf was unsuccessful in buying the electronic parts in Emerald; he had to order them. I had finished work by 4 pm and went straight home. Fufu had still not shown up.

I woke up with a toothache which I had off and on for a while and decided to be brave and face the dentist. I had the feeling I would lose yet another tooth.

Giselle and I drove to Rudolf's to call a dentist in Emerald for an appointment. I was lucky, wasn't I? I couldn't back down now; we left after a cup of coffee.

Hesitantly I walked into the dentist's room. What I saw didn't exactly fill me with confidence. Back in Hamburg at my usual dentist, everything was clean, polished, grand and with the newest equipment. Even when I had to go to the Dental Hospital in Brisbane, it looked professional. What I saw in Emerald filled me with anxiety. Let's call it basic, a standard room with an older dentist chair and suspicious-looking equipment, reminding me of jackhammers.

The dentist was a jolly guy; an Indian with a strong accent. I had a hard time understanding him, but to be fair, he probably had a hard time understanding me.

After a minute of examination, he concluded the tooth had to come out. It didn't take him long, maybe because he didn't have to reach far for his instruments; he had placed them conveniently on my chest. I barely survived the injection. Had he hit a nerve with that long needle? I could feel the pain from the injection in my toes. Waiting a short time, he preceded to pull the tooth, but in the process, broke it off and continued with a variety of prehistoric instruments digging out the ruins of my once-proud tooth. When I came out, Giselle hardly recognized me. My t-shirt was blood-stained, my glasses were bent, I looked like I had escaped a war zone.

Surviving the ordeal called for ice cream.

"I have another appointment on the 29.06 at 10 am for two fillings; and then I should be good," I said.

"Oh no," Giselle looked worried.

"Don't worry, it can't be any worse than today." We couldn't get home fast enough. After dinner, we made a hot water bottle, went to bed and read a book we bought about pottery. We had extended our ideas about an art and craft shop in Hamburg to include pottery.

All workbenches were busy at the cutting shop the next morning. Susanne served coffee and later lunch for everyone. It was how we liked it; a harmonious, creative working environment.

In the afternoon, we went back to our camp; we were keen to dig for sapphires again. We had some ulterior motives as well. Previously, we hadn't given much attention to the blackjacks we found, but as we were now thinking of doing jewellery, we liked the idea of using blackjacks in rings. Blackjack, or the proper name, Black Spinel, is a softer gem typically used in men's rings. It was easy to cut and polish, a basic square or rectangle shape with a large tabletop.

Who was back for the next morning's pet feeding session? Fufu, who else? Certainly not Steve.

Each day when I came home, Giselle's first words were, "I love you," followed by "Show me what you have done," and together, we admired the freshly-cut gems. Once that mutual admiration session was sufficiently celebrated, it was Giselle's turn, and we admired her work. That afternoon, it was a new leather bag she was making for my birthday; a rather elegant leather cover case for my 1976 diary. I wasn't allowed to use it yet; it still needed additional work.

We survived another cold night; it was warm enough under our blankets with the help of a hot water bottle. Outside, it was freezing; it was zero degrees. How refreshing.

Nearly a month had passed since Steve's departure. Would he turn up this week? Both of us went back to the cutting shop. Giselle picked up mail from the post office; our parents had written. My mother's letter was full of worry that we would stay in Australia. Her concerns called for a reassuring answer. I wrote saying we wanted to get married and had decided on a small family affair wedding as soon as we were back in Hamburg. Surely this would reassure our parents.

I didn't go cutting at all the next day. Instead, we had a camp-cleaning and washing day. I cranked up the generator and connected Steve's washing machine. That old thing was still working. It was one of those prehistoric machines without a spinning cycle; instead, it had a manual press attached to it. We used it to squeeze the water out of our washing before hanging it up on a long washing line. The design of the washing line was quite innovative; it hung low enough to peg the washing, and for drying, a long wooden pole was used to lift the washing line high and dry.

The people from a neighbouring camp came over and brought meat for the animals. It took us by surprise, and obviously, we asked, "How much will it cost?"

"Nothing, we often bring Steve fresh meat when we come back from kangaroo shooting," he answered.

"Kangaroo meat?" I asked in disbelief. It had never have occurred to us that people fed kangaroo meat to their dogs.

"Yes, sure, the dogs and cats like it; everyone is doing it here," he explained.

"And of course, we keep the good parts for ourselves," he continued.

At night, our pets had a change from their usual dried and canned food diet; they tucked into the kangaroo meat like there was no tomorrow.

Waking up early, Bidi was hauling and barking like mad. Six am, what the heck was going on? I untied him and off he went into the bushes. Maybe some kangaroos, or diarrhoea? Anyhow, he didn't come back. After breakfast, I drove straight to the post office; hoping my birthday mail would be there. Lucky me, three letters had arrived. I stayed in town until 2 pm finished off a lovely topaz before driving back to have coffee with Giselle. My darling read the letters aloud and revealed my cash presents.

My birthday was still two days away, but Giselle had given me her present already. A hard case jewellery box and the fitting leather bag, as well as the diary leather cover I had seen half-finished.

Bidi interrupted our cosiness, he was back, and he stank. He must have rolled himself in; let's call it excrement. It was raining as well; the combination of being wet and stinking was not befitting my birthday mood. We had no choice other than to stand in the rain and wash the dog. One washing cycle was not enough; we rewashed him, but he still had a suspicious odour hanging around him.

For dinner and my birthday party, Rudolf and Susanne invited us for Wiener Schnitzel. Having enjoyed the dinner and a few glasses, Rudolf revealed the electronic parts for the touch control had arrived. We couldn't resist, and I started to put it together while we continued to drink wine. A couple of hours later, the big moment arrived. Testing commenced but it didn't work. "Don't worry," I said, "we did it very fast; it must be a wrong connection."

We went through the whole process again, double-checking everything. I fixed one connection and exchanged an old transistor for a new one. Ready for testing, but it still wasn't working. It was late at night. Susanne had gone to bed but Giselle kept us company, encouraging me in my belief I would find the problem. And I did! I had forgotten to separate a connection on the circuit board. I felt hopeful now.

"It's going to work now," I said.

"Sure it will," Rudolf said, in a slightly slurred voice. We had finished a flagon of wine, and it was past 2 am; it simply had to work. I connected everything to his machine again.

"Look, it works, magic, how good is that," I exclaimed.

"It does, and it's very sensitive... thank you," he said and opened a bottle of Champagne.

We slept in on Sunday. But I was keen on getting back to Rudolf, to see if he had started to cut with the touch control yet. Giselle stayed at the camp.

Rudolf was experimenting with his new toy, Bob and I looked on to see what it could do. There was no difference between Bob's expensive system and the one we had put together.

I went home early for a relaxed Sunday with Giselle and surprised her with $10 cash for two leather bags which had sold in the morning's trade.

Happy birthday to me. It was my official birthday, but having indulged in birthday activities on the weekend, it was another typical cutting workday. Later, we picked up a hot apple pie, and enjoyed it accompanied by coffee and good conversation.

The next day was my dental appointment, and I wasn't looking forward to it. When I went in, I said to Giselle, "It can't get any worse than last time." I was right; the only thing worse was the cost; I had to part with $26 and had three brand new fillings in exchange. The last day of the month and Steve was still a "no show." We were getting restless but determined to stay to allow me to learn all I could about cutting. Eventually we would have to leave, even if Steve did not show up. We had already arranged for the neighbours to look after the animals and check on the camp.

We went to Rudolf's for a lazy night in front of the telly. Television was a rarity for us. It was a movie party atmosphere; people met, had drinks, and watched telly.

Next morning we slept in; the long night of TV had made us tired. We went back to Rudolf's in the late afternoon; he was working on his generator which had packed it in. I joked we had caused the problem by watching too much television. Rudolf was not in a funny mood; without the generator, there would be no cutting gemstones.

He had replaced a burned-out part, but still nothing worked.

"Can you have a look?" he asked me.

"Sure, love to, let's take it step by step," I said. I was in my fixing element.

I examined what he had done and did some voltage check-ups. I was sure he had done something wrong because I measured 415 volts on the output. It was a three-phase generator, and each phase should have only 240 volts. Luckily, he had nothing important connected and it only blew a few light bulbs. It was going to be a long night. The generator had been re-wired and fixed by too many people too often, and standard rules of logic were no longer applicable.

I suggested taking everything apart and doing a completely new setup. Rudolf hesitated but agreed we would start on it with fresh energy in the morning.

Coming back the next day, I took everything apart and started re-wiring. A couple of hours later, I started the generator, and 'drum roll!' it worked perfectly. Everything looked so much neater and would be easier to maintain.

We had almost forgotten about Steve, but surprise, finally, after four weeks of no contact, Steve had called Rudolf; he needed fresh clothing and we should post it to Rockhampton Hospital. He would be back in Rubyvale in about a week.

The next morning I was back in town, first to the post office, to put Steve's parcel in the post, followed by more cutting.

I noticed everyone had a new dop stick transfer block.

"Nice, they look good; where did you get them from," I asked Bob.

"Rudolf ordered them for us," Bob said and went on working.

I was put off; Rudolf knew I would have loved to buy a transfer block. The mood at Rudolf's place had changed, and not for the better. I went on cutting, concentrating on my work. Giselle had come with me and went into the house to keep Susanne company.

After lunch, when we came back, and I used cutting powder I had bought in town, Rudolf directed his anger at me. "Why did you buy that crap? You can get it much cheaper in Germany," he shouted. I had no idea why he was angry; obviously, we were a long way from Germany.

Giselle must have heard us arguing; she didn't take it well if someone was treating me poorly. She came into the cutting shop and got stuck into Rudolf big time. She told him a few things about his bad temper, negativity and never listening, and why was he so full of himself?

His reply was surprisingly calm; "If someone wants to be my friend, they have to take me as I am," was his answer. "If I am in a bad mood, I don't feel like being nice, take it or leave it," he continued.

"Are you feeling happy that way?" Giselle asked.

Rudolf shrugged and the argument stopped. It was already late afternoon and we went back to our camp, feeling exhausted. We didn't like arguments or confrontations; it took a lot out of us. We talked about the incident until we had it solved, at least in our minds.

Slightly hesitant, I went back next morning. Rudolf greeted me in a friendly manner, all problems seemed to have been forgotten, and I started working on my next gem. Later, Susanne told me he had experienced a bad pain episode.

Chapter 18

The Enigma called Steve

We had barely finished our breakfast when out of the blue, Steve turned up. His beard a bit longer but looking happy and healthy. We had to wait to greet him; Bidi went berserk with happiness to see his 'Daddy' again.

That day we sat down with Steve and started to talk and talk and then talked some more. We didn't stop talking for many days to come.

Steve was an engaging character, about fifteen years older than us, slightly scruffy looking with a lot of life experiences behind him. Originally from Hungary, he lived in various European cities before settling in Australia. His mother had escaped from Hungary to Austria after the war when Steve was only ten. He grew up in Austria and spoke fluent German and a few other languages. In 1956, he arrived in Australia.

We were under the impression he wanted to teach us young folk about life, or maybe he was just eager to show himself in the best possible way. He didn't stop talking and we didn't mind; we were interested in what he had to say and kept listening.

He owned three blocks of land in Gladstone and a block of land with a rented-out duplex in Cairns. He must have been reasonably well off, having worked around Australia on large construction sites as a project manager.

Conversations started harmlessly enough but soon escalated into deep discussions. We had a lot of interests in common such as spirituality, psycho phenomena and conspiracy theories. Among these countless conversations were many stories which sounded suspiciously exaggerated. We realised Steve's stories were a little enhanced but exciting to listen to and always contained snippets of profound wisdom. It was those bits of wisdom in which we were interested.

Every night over the days and weeks, when we went to bed in our car, we talked for another hour, digesting his stories and keeping the valuable bits and filing them away in our minds. Actually, this technique was one of his memory improvement talks to us, or was it a lecture?

He explained how he could recall and extract 'everything' from his memory by visualizing a large filing cabinet and filing various memories, ideas and so forth into different drawers. If he had to remember something, he went to the appropriate drawer in his mind and retrieved the file he wanted. That one story would have taken him a few hours of talking. Explanations were deep, interchanging techniques with strategies and adding more stories to make his point.

We learnt a lot and listened to his every word with an open mind. Our fact check technique of discussing the day's events at night and sorting the facts from the fiction ensured our continuous learning experience.

We acknowledged we were learning new facts and growing in our awareness, enabling us to see the bigger picture and recognize there were many different perspectives to everything. To go through life, one had to understand other people's views and even have the ability to put oneself into someone else's shoes.

Steve lived for a while with Aboriginal people up in the far north. He told us about those experiences and enriched our understanding of aborigines. Those stories explained how they knew and understood the world in great detail. It included thought powers like telepathy, meditative states and extraordinary survival strategies.

We moved from the topic of Aboriginal mystics, healing powers and so forth to the subject of meditation, visualization and especially to telepathy and telekinetic practices. We had a few of our own stories to tell. Giselle and I liked meditation and visualization and had had our own experiences. I told Steve about the time when I meditated in my unit in Hamburg and floated out of my body. There was no stopping Steve; it was a topic close to his heart on which he claimed to be an expert.

He introduced us to a deeper level of knowledge into the 'Akashic Records' which were a collection of all universal events, thoughts, words, and emotions, absolutely everything that occurred in the past, present and maybe the future. Knowing about those records is one thing; to believe they exist and by practising deep meditation one can access them is a different kettle of fish.

We were willing subjects, lying still in meditation, trying to reach the Akashic Records. Amazing what a mind is capable of when one concentrates on specific matters. We either convinced ourselves or managed to get glimpses of the records about ourselves. Steve explained to master it takes many years of devoted meditation practice and a selfless, pure mind which was not motivated by greed or negativity.

Again, we could live with these requirements which sounded reasonable. However, the glimpses into our records, including those from previous lives, helped us learn more about our purposes and motivations. We concluded it didn't matter if those records were real or not if, by working with that concept, more awareness was triggered and it thereby served a valuable purpose.

In retrospect, I wonder where Steve acquired his knowledge, but we knew he had books about theosophy. He never mentioned those books, but much later, when we bought a book by Helena Blavatsky, it was evident Steve had read those books. He recited them, interweaving his own ideas or theories about 'supernatural powers' in great detail.

We loved talking about supernatural powers, and our experiences. I still found it fascinating that I grabbed eggs out of a pot of boiling water without burning myself. We attributed our experiences of apparent superpowers to the natural, peaceful lifestyle in which we were immersed in the bush and by being far away from general civilization.

All of his constant talking over several days must have worn Steve out, and a few days later, on the 13th of July, he came down with a cold. It had to be the 13th, of course.

It didn't prevent him from continuing to talk. We cared for him with herb teas and chicken soup. We applied naturopathic cures, the ones we knew from our parents. Those techniques were conceived originally by Father Kneip, the father of naturopathy in Germany. He favoured hydrotherapy, phytotherapy, the healing with botanical medicines, exercise, nutrition and a balanced lifestyle which remains today the basis for naturopathy.

As a child, I dreaded the 'wickel.' Whenever I had a cold or sore throat, I was confronted with the dreaded wickel. The first level of application was an ice-cold cloth of linen wrapped around the neck, followed by a woollen scarf, also wrapped around the neck. This combination created a mini sauna to fix a sore throat or cold. The combination of body heat, cold linen and a woollen scarf caused an artificial fever to burn out all those nasty critters, as my mum explained to me. My mum never suppressed a fever or gave me painkillers. Fever was seen as a healer, and only when it rose too high would my mum place cold towels on my feet and head to draw out the heat. Steve didn't mind those treatments because he knew them from his mother.

We hardly noticed the days going by. Giselle didn't do any leatherwork, I had stopped cutting and we hadn't written any letters. Deep discussions occupied all our time. It may have been one of the most intensive and lengthy discussions we ever had with anyone.

Steve's cold didn't slow him down; quite the opposite, it widened and intensified our topics which included all kinds of natural cures and the mental power to heal oneself. Steve knew about the mental power to heal or kill from when he was living with Aboriginal tribes in North Queensland. According to him, he had witnessed an Indigenous person die because of the practice of "bone pointing."

We had similar views on this matter for several reasons. My experience came from my grandmother when she 'talked away' two warts I had on my hand when I was little. Obviously, I totally believed her which must have triggered some kind of healing or immune response in my little body. Bone pointing was the reverse process; for Indigenous people, deep into a traditional lifestyle, it was a death sentence when a medicine man pointed a bone.

Interestingly, negative spells seem to have a stronger effect, probably because one's fear will aggravate and intensify the initial bone-pointing event. If one can worry oneself sick, can one also worry or think oneself healthy? We believed so.

At times we strengthened our mind powers with supplementary physical applications. Our excuse was Steve needed to overcome his cold. As good as mind power and cold applications were, sometimes one needs hot red wine with rum. We would have added spices but we didn't have many, and only added ginger and chillies. It turned out to be a potent mix and maybe it was what 'healed' Steve.

While we helped Steve get better, cared and cooked for him, he was excellent in return, paying for everything we bought during that time, the food, the whisky and the wine.

Our neighbours were very kind too, they brought us another kangaroo, already skinned and ready for consumption. This time, it was not to be used as pet food; it was meant for us, specifically for Steve.

We still had hesitations about eating a cute animal but the neighbours assured us it would be good for Steve to have a strengthening vegetable kangaroo stew, at least as good as chicken soup.

We went shopping and came back with everything needed to cook a stew. Steve was happy; he felt like he was home in Hungary, preparing goulash. Instead of using seasoned beef, we would use seasoned, open-air-hung-cured kangaroo.

Saturday was the day we finally would eat home-cooked kangaroo. It took us most of the day preparing our Kangaroo Goulash feast, and we still had mixed feelings. Steve was resting but kept talking, dishing out cooking tips.

We couldn't face cutting up the kangaroo without drinking copious amounts of red wine. To add extra taste to the stew, at least half a bottle of red went into it as well. We used our cast iron camp oven to cook our stew for probably much too long.

At night time, the feast began. Each of us had at least two large servings. It tasted surprisingly good. I was not sure if it was the kangaroo or all the ingredients we had used. Perhaps it was all the red wine we drank that made the stew taste so delicious.

I woke up in the middle of the night; Giselle was asleep but moaning and groaning.

"Wake up, darling," I said, "Are you OK?"

"I feel sick; I have to go to the toilet," she said.

I helped Giselle out of the car but she fell unconscious on the way to the toilet. I was worried and quickly carried her back, laying her on the bed. She regained consciousness, looking at me with a concerned expression.

"Don't worry, it's all good; I am here, try to sleep," I reassured her. Calmer now, she dropped into a deep sleep.

I watched my darling closely; her breathing was normal, but she had a slight temperature. As worried as I was, I thought everything would be fine as long as she slept. She kept sleeping all day, only waking up from time to time and having sips of water, and me reassuring her and myself at the same time. 'Surely nothing could be wrong,' I thought.

In the afternoon, I noticed her temperature had increased. When she woke up, she wasn't coherent. I didn't like it at all and became increasingly worried. I decided to take her to the Emerald hospital as Rubyvale had no doctors. I went to Steve and asked what he thought and he agreed it would be advisable to take Giselle to the hospital. Giselle's symptoms were not like a cold, and we suspected it could be something to do with eating the kangaroo stew.

I rushed back to the car, desperate to get on our way to the hospital. I opened the door and looked over to Giselle. A rush of fear came over my whole being; I saw something I had never seen or experienced before. I was paralysed for a moment and kept on staring at Giselle. She was lying on the bed surrounded by a cloud of white haze, which was a slivery, white foggy substance floating and pulsating around her body.

"Schatz," I called out but there was no response. I leaned over to touch her forehead and the cloud dissolved and gradually disappeared. Her forehead was hot, but not too hot in my limited experience, and she was breathing even though it was shallow. I stroked her head, "Everything will be fine, I will drive you to a doctor, don't worry, you will be fine." I thought there was a slight response. I didn't tell Giselle I would drive to a hospital; I thought it would sound too dramatic and worry her even more.

I gently drove off, trying to avoid bumps on the gravel road. It was about a 60km drive, mostly gravel, and it took slightly over an hour.

I knew where the hospital was and pulled up right in front. Giselle was still asleep and looked normal, not surrounded by a haze anymore. I ran to the entry and yelled for help. It worked; a nurse rushed out. I told her about Giselle. She phoned the doctor, found a wheelchair and we hurried back to the car. When I tried to carry Giselle out of bed, she woke up and helped me get her into the wheelchair. We entered the hospital, the doctor had arrived, and Giselle was wheeled away. I was told to wait. I must have waited for about fifteen minutes, worried but also thinking about the white haze I had seen. I was now sure it was her aura but had no idea, 'Was it a good or a bad sign?' At the time, I was distraught, believing it had something to do with dying. I couldn't think straight.

A nurse woke me up from my worried state.

"Yes?" I asked.

"Your wife has to stay with us tonight," she said. "We will know more by tomorrow when we get her blood results. We have given her something for the fever."

"Thank you, can I see her?" I asked.

"It's better if you come back tomorrow and let her sleep. There is no need to worry," she said.

I was too spaced out to argue, thanked her and left. It felt awful leaving Giselle behind, 'Did I do something wrong? Should I have stayed and waited at the hospital or maybe waited outside, sleeping in the car to be close by?' I kept driving slowly back to Steve's camp.

Next morning, Steve and I went back to the hospital together. I couldn't wait to see Giselle and Steve had to remind me to drive slowly. He also had to be at the hospital for a check-up appointment at 10 am.

We made it in time, Steve went for his appointment, and I was allowed to see and talk to Giselle. My darling looked weak but so beautiful, like a little girl. I wanted to take her into my arms and not let her go ever. She smiled a tiny bit, "I am feeling better but I have to stay here for a few days," she said.

"Have they found out what it is?" I asked.

"No, they don't seem to know; they have taken more blood but had to send it to Rockhampton for testing. I should know tomorrow," she said.

A nurse interrupted us. I had to leave but was allowed to come back at the visitor's time.

"Your wife needs to sleep," she told me. There it was again, I had a wife now. I didn't correct her; it felt nice to be married.

Steve and I stayed in town and did some shopping before getting back to the hospital. We stayed with Giselle from 2 pm till 4 pm. She had gained a bit of strength and was intrigued by my story about seeing her aura. With Steve present, we discussed the aura topic at great length. One of our conclusions was that training oneself to see an aura would be easier in the dark. Would I have seen Giselle's aura if it had been daytime? We couldn't answer this intriguing question. We also couldn't answer why I had seen it.

I was very happy Giselle was getting better. At the same time, I noticed Steve was still not well, he looked exhausted, and it was time to drive him home. He went straight to bed. I was the only one still standing.

Steve woke up pretty sick. I put a pot of tea and something to eat next to his bed. He assured me he would be all right. I drove back to Giselle and stayed with her till 4 pm. She was much better and reading whenever she wasn't sleeping and even managed to walk a few steps. There was still no news about her blood tests.

Back at the camp, I looked after Steve; maybe he had something similar to Giselle's illness on top of the cold he had before. I knew he had a lot on his mind, all to do with the Small Miners' Association and their conflict with the big machine miners. He was stressed but didn't talk much about this specific topic, only hinting at leaving soon and travelling to Cairns to his property.

The next morning, Steve felt better and looked well rested. I left him to his own devices and drove to Giselle. She had improved again and was strong enough to walk around unaided. She wanted to leave the hospital which sounded like she was getting back to her feisty self. The blood works had been received; the doctor told us there was still something not right, and he had ordered a follow-up test. Giselle needed to stay another day or two. We were not worried, and hoped we could be together again soon.

By the time I arrived back in Rubyvale, it was night. I drove to Rudolf's place first, and the next drama started. Susanne told me they had received a call from Giselle; she had asked him to drive to Steve's camp to get me to call the hospital. She was in a state of panic.

I called the hospital, Giselle had no phone in her room, and she had to use the phone on the floor. I could hear her crying even before she came on the phone.

"I have blood cancer," she blurted out, "Something is wrong with my blood."

"What happened? Why do you think that, did the doctor tell you?" I asked.

"They took more blood, and when I talked to the doctor, I asked him if it could be cancer, and he said, we can't rule it out, or something like that."

"Please, darling, don't worry, I am sure it's not cancer, and they don't even suspect cancer; they can't say 'no' if they haven't specifically tested for it." We talked for a while.

"Are you better now?" I asked.

"I think so; please come early tomorrow morning," she said.

"I love you, don't worry, I will be back early; I am sure all will be good."

By the time I finished the phone call, Rudolf had arrived. I thanked him and told them Giselle had misunderstood the doctor and went into a panic, but she was better now.

When I returned to Steve, I told him the whole story, and he reassured me it was all good, because if the doctor had suspected cancer, he would have answered differently.

I decided to believe my and his arguments and stay positive, which didn't stop me from worrying but made it bearable.

I arrived early at the hospital. Giselle was calm and smiling, she had talked to the doctor again and her blood tests were better. Nothing indicated blood cancer;

only some factors were still too low. Most probably, she would leave the hospital tomorrow.

I left her early, as I had to be at Robert's place to test a cutting machine he had offered to sell to me. I took an Ultra Tec machine for a test run, cutting a gem for over 2 hours. It wasn't much better than the one I had learned on. Never mind, if I pursued serious gem cutting, I would buy a new machine.

Back at the camp, Steve told me about his latest news. He had discussions with members of the Small Miners Association. He had decided to leave Rubyvale and that part of his life behind him. I had the feeling it was affecting him more than he let on. He had shown us architectural drawings of a Small Miners Centre building which probably would not go ahead without him.

When I arrived the following day at the hospital, Giselle was already waiting at the entry for me. Her final blood works had shown improvement and she was allowed to leave. They gave her a copy of the latest result and asked her to follow up with more blood tests once a week, starting next Tuesday.

We stayed in Emerald for a while, checked out leather and tools, and did some shopping before driving back.

Steve was visibly happy to see Giselle was better. To celebrate, I had bought a Sara Lee cheesecake. Not sure if it was the right food to improve Giselle's blood but it made us happy. Giselle was tired and we had an early night, happy to be able to snuggle up together.

Giselle slept well, and we stayed in bed till 9 am. Steve was busy sorting and preparing papers. I brought him a cup of tea. Something intense was on the agenda; he looked worried.

I left Giselle at the camp to rest; I had to drive to Rubyvale, checking for mail, buying rations and visiting Rudolf. I only stayed for 10 minutes at Rudolf's place. I thanked him for the opportunity he had given me and picked up my cutting materials. He was happy with the generator I had fixed and the cutting sensor I had built. In other words, we acknowledged our positive effects on each other and didn't dwell on some minor disagreements.

When I arrived back at the camp, it was crowded. At least ten cars were parked close by and many people were sitting with Steve in heated discussions. Giselle stayed in our car and I joined her; we had no business interfering.

Even when the people left, Steve didn't tell us anything specific, only that we would escape Rubyvale soon.

"I think Steve wants to protect us which is why he's not giving us details," I said.

"I think so too; I overheard a few things about bulldozers and shooting incidents. Time to go," Giselle said.

That day, we didn't find out anything else. Steve stayed in his tent; we could see him writing. I had finished filming what we wanted for our movie and used Steve's film splicing equipment to put the three films together, becoming the proud owners of a nine-minute movie. I did the same for Ryan, but his version amounted to fifteen minutes. It even included scenes from down in a mining shaft and filming underground with a floodlight.

The following day we were woken up by the sounds of many cars pulling up.

"Looks like another meeting," I said.

"Must be important to come on a Sunday and so early," Giselle replied.

We stayed well away from the activities, hiding behind our panel-van. By the time we finished our breakfast, the meeting was over.

Steve looked exhausted and he still gave us no details; he only said, "Let's start cleaning up the camp, could you help please?"

Of course, we could. Cleaning up was one of our specialties.

"Where do you want us to start?" I asked.

"The generator needs a good clean up, and for the moment a general clean around the camp," he said. He went back into his tent, working out prices for items he wanted to sell.

It was definitely serious. We were preparing to leave. I was sure it was traumatic for Steve, but we felt invigorated: a new adventure was about to start.

Monday and yet another early morning meeting took place. We were not concerned any longer; we were excited to move on and make new plans for our future.

To amuse ourselves, we drew a plan for our modest future house. It was only a tiny house on a 500 square meter block of land. The house itself worked out to be 96 square meters, a modern open plan living design, but at that time we had no idea it would become modern. We designed it for optimal space usage.

Once the meeting was over, Steve finally sat down with us and explained the next steps.

We would continue cleaning and selling everything of no use to him or the camp's new owner. He had sold his camp to one of the guys from the meetings. We were under the impression the camp was just the building, tanks and tent, but apparently Steve owned the land on which the camp was situated.

Later, he told us in no uncertain terms we would have to leave in the middle of the night without letting anyone know. For the rest of the day, it was cleaning and sorting stuff into boxes to be sold separately

We took a quick trip to the hospital for Giselle to have more blood tests and back to the camp to continue packing. Some boxes full of tools had been sold already. Association members were snapping up the bargains. People arrived, bargained, and bought whatever was available.

Steve started to relax and was in a better mood, even excited to leave everything behind and start a new life and future. He even talked about a girlfriend we didn't know he had.

He had sold more or less everything; only the diesel generator and some personal items were left. He showed us what he had received for all his goods; he had cashed in $4,000 and a further $1,000 worth of cut sapphires.

He was generous as well, and gave us his slide projector, a flashlight, books, some pearls he had dived for in Broome, and something called a tektite, a fraction of meteor debris which had made its way through our atmosphere.

It was already late but Steve wanted something special to celebrate and asked me if I would drive to Anakie to buy a bottle of Johnnie Walker. How could I refuse? I managed the 40km return trip in record time and we celebrated one hour later.

At night we fired up the diesel generator to power the slide projector, and whisky at hand, watched the movies we had made and most of our slides.

The next morning we sorted and cleaned the tools Steve wanted to take with him. He found willing workers in us, but we always benefited. On this occasion, he gave us a tool for pumping up a flat tyre. We had never seen such a contraption. To pump up the tyre, one had to unscrew a spark plug and screw in the attachment.

After lunch, we went to town for a phone call to the hospital. We were not overly worried but there was still a touch of apprehension. The doctor was happy which meant we were happy. Giselle's blood results had further improved but he still wanted the tests to continue.

Steve had received a letter from Donna, his girlfriend. He was overjoyed and even read it to us. She wrote about a new commercial project close to Dampier in Western Australia. A large company was going to build a new city and start a new mine. Steve had been instrumental in similar constructions in North Queensland and was excited about this new project.

His girlfriend was living there in the north-west. He asked us to come with him to Western Australia and work there as well. It would be an exciting project, real pioneer stuff, and the money was exceptional, while living was cheap. He even was excited about the climate, a dry heat, which was good for his joints that had been affected by having polio as a child. We hadn't seen him so happy for a while.

Steve's situation further improved when the new owners of the camp came over for a chat. Steve liked them and they promised to look after his camp and the cats. There was no way we could have taken the cats with us; only Bidi would be at Steve's side.

Steve had finished his final list of items for sale. We wanted to drive to Anakie anyhow and we took it on ourselves to be the list distributers. We only had ten copies so it was a quick job to spread them around.

When we came back, Steve was in the process of selling Ryan his Grundig reel-to-reel tape recorder for a couple of sapphires. It was a fierce battle but Steve got the better deal. More people arrived, and the haggling continued. Still, no one took a bite on the expensive diesel generator.

While Steve was busy haggling, we cleaned his Toyota 4 wheel drive and prepared it for the big trip. Steve promised we would head off at the end of the week.

I kept cleaning and serviced an outboard motor for Steve's dinghy which he would take on the roof rack. He had lots of fishing gear and diving equipment. Not sure where he would sleep, most of the space in the back of his Toyota was filled with his survival gear.

In the afternoon, the Small Miners Association secretary came to visit with a mysterious suitcase. Soon after, a few more members showed up. Steve had no idea what it was about, neither did we, of course. Once everyone had settled down, the secretary gave a little speech in honour of Steve and handed him the suitcase which was meant as a present for his work as president. We laughed, in secret obviously, not everyone had our weird sense of humour - but to give someone a suitcase as a giveaway present seemed hilarious, "Here you go, pack your stuff and bugger off."

2.08.1976 – Monday, and the diesel generator had still not sold. Steve was desperate and we decided to do something about which we had only talked. It was time to use our superpowers.

We sat down, meditating to streamline our thought powers. We visualized, in deep concentration, sending out thought waves for someone to come to buy the generator. It wasn't just for fun; we took it seriously. We anticipated people coming and we stayed in deep concentration, visualizing, meditating and projecting for over an hour.

In the end, I wasn't quite sure if I was still meditating or sleeping. We were exhausted but promised each other to hold positive thoughts while we kept working around the camp.

Late in the afternoon, we heard a car coming. At first, we didn't give it much attention. Steve talked to the guy in the car, but when they went over to where the diesel generator was standing, we knew our meditation had worked. Sure enough, after starting the generator and a few more checks, the guy was happy and took out his wallet. Steve called us over; they needed help to lift the generator into the ute. Operation superpowers complete!

Steve couldn't wipe the smile off his face; he waved a bundle of banknotes in his hand and disappeared into his tent. At dinner, Steve indicated we might leave within the next two days.

Waking up in anticipation we would leave soon, we began the final clean up. Steve seemed to wait for something; we were not sure what. Finally he announced we would leave the coming night. He told us to set our alarm clock to 3 am, to leave the camp by 4 am.

It was getting exciting. "We should have a decent hot shower before we leave," I suggested to Giselle. "Yes, please, let's go." And off we went to Rubyvale, and made it to the post office in time to get them to forward our mail to Cairns. Next, we filled up our petrol tank to the rim before we could relax and have our well-earned hot shower.

It was pretty late, nearly 11 pm, when we set our alarm clock. Steve said 3:30 am should be early enough to get up.

Chapter 19

Life is a Beach

Rising at 3:30 am, we were still tired, having not slept very well. A cup of tea, a light breakfast, packing up our gear and we were ready to go. Now came the hard part, saying goodbye to the cats. They seemed to know something was up; they behaved oddly. Steve had tears in his eyes and we felt sad too. Bidi was excited to be allowed to sit on the front seat. 5 am, and we had left Rubyvale behind us. No one saw us. We had vanished into thin air.

We followed Steve at a safe distance; it was a gravel road, and we tried to avoid the dust. Our first stop was Clermont. We had a quick break to move our legs. For the next stretch we changed position, Steve followed us and swallowed the dust. We were heading for Charters Towers, nearly 400km of dirt road. When we arrived, our carburettor was on its last legs.

We parked in the middle of town; there was hardly a soul to see. We found the only open restaurant. It had been a long day and we were not in the mood to prepare dinner, and deserved a good meal before settling at Charter Towers Caravan Park.

Giselle had a shower while I opened the car bonnet to have a go at the carburettor. I took it apart and back together; the engine sounded good again. The only problem was I had two screws left over. I didn't worry; I planned to buy a new one in Cairns. I was sure I could keep it going until then.

Charters Towers looked like a forgotten country town. Where was everyone? At church? We went for another walk, looked at the closed shop windows, found an open pub and had a beer before leaving on the road to Townsville.

Townsville came as a shock. It felt hectic and had too much traffic. We had planned to stay overnight, but neither of us felt comfortable enough and we left in a hurry, driving for another 20km.

We found a small bush track, which looked like it would make a good camp for the night, away from the highway. Having unpacked chairs and our gas bottle to make a cup of tea, a car arrived. It was a farmer, telling us we couldn't stay there. It was a track they frequently used, and we had parked right in the middle of it.

Never mind, we left and found something suitable a little further on. Now we could have our cuppa.

It was 10 am before we made a move but we didn't get far. The police stopped us. It always feels strange when the police stop you. It must be a sub-consciousness guilt trip. What had we done wrong? Did the farmer complain? No, it was the police in their role as 'Police, your friend and helper' informing us the road to Cairns was blocked. A truck carrying a massive load of steel had tipped over on a small bridge and was blocking the highway. It would take all day to clear. We were much too relaxed to let it bother us and drove closer to the coast and camped right on a beautiful beach. It was paradise and we were the only participants in it.

We slept like babies and were brave enough to have an early morning dip. We wanted to make it to Cairns, another 400km trip and we needed to be fresh. We arrived in Cairns by 4 pm, checked for mail, went shopping for fresh bread and milk before driving to Ellis Beach.

In the past, Steve had owned a section of Ellis Beach. He knew the area well and where we could camp for free; even so, the neighbouring caravan park owner wouldn't like it. Steve warned us the owner might come and tell us to leave, but we shouldn't worry; he would deal with it.

Here we were, camping right on the beach under coconut palms and surrounded by lush vegetation, literally only ten metres from the water.

Giselle and I felt like Robinson Crusoe. Not sure how Steve felt, but he seemed in good spirits. He loved the hot beach sand, it soothed his aching back. Steve wasn't the only one with a backache; I also had one. While packing Steve's car, I must have pulled a muscle.

Despite the ultimate serene, relaxing and nearly tranquillizing environment, Giselle and I were slightly on edge. Not in a negative way; it was a feeling of restlessness. We wanted to do something; we loved our own company, and with Steve around, we felt constricted in our behaviour. We were eager to start working on Steve's house but he hadn't even mentioned it.

Sure enough, the owner of the caravan park came to visit, and he didn't come for a cup of tea. He was angry, "You can't stay here and camp; you have to pack up and leave now," he declared.

What came next was funny; we were sitting and sunning ourselves, wearing only swimsuits, but Steve stood up and took on the role of a prominent company director. He took the park owner by surprise when he told him he had owned the beach and his company was working with a German travel company to buy a large stretch of the beach and turn it into a tourist resort. Steve told him the spot where we were camping was the main interest because of a natural spring with endless sparkling clear water in close proximity which would be used as a water supply for the resort.

The park owner was visibly perplexed and impressed. Steve continued, "Please meet Dieter; he acts as the solicitor for the German company and his secretary, Giselle. They have come only five weeks ago from Hamburg to start procedures."

"Nice to meet you," I said and shook the park owner's hand. Even with a well-known short phrase, one could detect my German accent. I certainly didn't have to put on a pretence. Giselle too gave a polite nod, "Nice to meet you."

Steve went on explaining about the resort and finally asked, but it was more a request, to stay two more weeks to complete our research.

I couldn't believe what I heard, "Yes, sure, stay as long as you like, and let me know if you need any help or information," the owner said and left, wishing us a good day. Our holiday on Ellis Beach was secured.

The following days went by quickly. Steve's dinghy became one of those pleasant holiday experiences one would never forget. We attached the outboard motor and skippered over to Double Island a few times. Steve had diving equipment and Giselle could use a wetsuit, flippers and goggles he had kept from a former girlfriend. We went diving, dressed up in diving gear, looking at corals and pretty fish.

Camping on Ellis Beach was already a secluded, peaceful experience. Double Island, however, was a different reality altogether, a natural environment with no signs of civilization. We were the only ones coming to the island in our dinghy. Once it was moored safely, we were island natives. The water was as clear as glass, fish an easy target. We only ever speared one or two, depending on size, enough to still our hunger. Sitting on the beach with a fire, grilling the fish, we contemplated island living. Could we live on an island, far away from all worldly troubles? Probably not. While it was fun to daydream, it was reassuring to have a dinghy to take us back to civilization.

• • • • • • • • • •

Our deep discussions with Steve had not stopped but changed to a more competitive nature as we started questioned many of his statements.

Our diet and nutritional status had been diminished, mainly because of alcohol consumption. It was our fault, but it was easier to blame Steve. I don't think we would have drunk as much on our own, the same for sweets, cakes and the like.

Health was one of the main reasons we browsed for long times in bookstores. We were reading half the books without buying them. We read about diet, healthy lifestyles, herbal remedies, and related topics. I half-read a book about massage and thought it could be worthwhile to learn. I had experience with reflexology and learnt a lot about it. Combined with my knowledge about the macrobiotic diet, and the wisdom I had inherited from my grandmothers about herbs and spiritual healing, it was even more appropriate to learn about other natural healing modalities. Giselle and I believed we would be able to heal ourselves if we had enough knowledge.

For the moment, however, I was still suffering from a sore back. Steve suggested visiting a chiropractor. I resisted, not because of any medical reason, but because it would be something we could not afford, but Steve booked an appointment anyhow. He felt guilty because I had done most of the heavy lifting to pack his car.

We arrived at the chiropractic clinic while Giselle stayed back guarding the camp. The chiropractor's name was Neville. Steve was first; it didn't take long, maybe 10min. He came out happy and his backache was nearly gone. Now it was my turn, and I hoped for a similar apparent quick recovery from days of backache. According to Neville, I had two vertebra out of place. Lying on a unique chiropractic table, Neville pushed on my back, and a table segment gave away, intensifying the push. After a few pushes and some probing around, I was allowed to get up. I didn't want to disappoint him, but I couldn't feel any improvement. He told me what not to do and to take it easy for a couple of days. If it was not better in three days, I was supposed to come back.

Giselle wanted to hear all about our treatments. Neither of us had ever been to a chiropractor before.

"How was it? Are you any better?" she asked.

"The treatment was fine, but I am not really any better. Let's wait a few days."

Even though Steve was better, he was keen on going back; he seemed to like Neville. Sure, I liked him too but I wasn't sure whether his treatment would be effective and to go again, I would have to pay $7.00.

Giselle and I discussed the financial burden of this new and unplanned activity. "I think you should try a couple of times; your back is more important than money," my beautiful Giselle told me. How could I refuse? I didn't even try to resist, and Steve and I went to see Neville again. On this visit Neville found even more vertebra out of place and each of them was put back in its proper place, so to speak. He also sold me a belt which had a little pillow attached to press on my spine. It felt good wearing it and helped with the pain.

As I still had pain and Steve liked the treatment, we returned a third time. Neville found even more vertebra out of place; by now, I started to question how many vertebra I had that could possibly go out of place. To my surprise, after this treatment, my back felt better, probably too good, because I carried equipment when we were packing up our camp, and sure enough, my back complaint came back.

Steve drove me straight back to Neville, but it was Saturday, and he had the day off. Instead, his father, who was blind, attended to me; I was greatly impressed by him. His treatment was excellent and took much longer; he must have adjusted every bone in my body. It felt better for the next few hours but then slowly deteriorated. I ended up in agony. Back I went on Sunday and Neville agreed to see me and went to work. I walked out of there poorer but my back was much improved. I also kept using the support belt whenever I lifted something heavy.

Steve went into Cairns every day but didn't tell us the whole story about his house and bank problems. It was a complicated dispute involving the bank, people who rented one of the units and the builder of the duplex who was also a partner in the project. Steve wanted to get rid of the tenants who were not paying their rent; they had not looked after the place and it was in a disgraceful condition.

After a week of bad news and Steve being depressed, he came home one afternoon loaded with yummy food and drinks to celebrate. He had come to an agreement with the bank. Finally, the unwelcome renter had agreed to leave. It wouldn't be long now before we could start renovating.

Whenever Steve was under stress, he became aggressive. Arguing was a game for him, but not for us. Giselle and I never argued about anything and we didn't see the point of arguing with Steve either. In a way, Steve made us realize that most arguments were a waste of time and energy. We became skilled in not becoming trapped into endless arguments.

A couple of days later, when the troublesome renters had moved out, we were able to inspect his house. It was a mess but nothing a good clean up and a lick of paint couldn't fix.

· · · · ● · ● · · · ·

Time to leave our beach paradise. We would live in Steve's house while renovating. It took all weekend to shift; we made sure to leave our beach camp in pristine condition.

The first night at the house, we slept in our car because the unit was not fit for human occupation. We were having dinner sitting outside and drinking Mu-tea which was unknown to Steve. We also had introduced him to tahini, sea salt, miso, and tamari soy sauce.

Before starting the renovation, Steve wanted to have an insurance guy look at the unit. We decided to take the opportunity to explore more of Cairns.

The following day, we had breakfast on our own. Steve was nowhere to be seen. He made a brief and exciting appearance around 10 am. "All good now, we can start renovating." There was no time to muck around; we were cleaning like mad to make sure each of us could sleep in a cleaned room. There were three bedrooms to choose from. The kitchen and bathroom were a total mess. How could people live like this?

Steve cleaned the house roughly from the outside with the help of a garden hose, spraying and washing off dirt and cobwebs. By night-time, it already looked acceptable. We brought our mattress and camping chairs into our room and set up Steve's stereo equipment and slide projector in the living area.

Steve was in a good mood and went shopping and we knew what it would mean. He bought a bottle of whisky for a celebration with good food, music and we watched our slides.

"Here we go again," I said to Giselle, "What's he up to now?" We had cleaned like crazy; everything looked great. The paint on most walls was good, and we all agreed we didn't need to do any painting. At night, however, Steve changed his mind. He wanted to have the whole unit painted inside and out.

"Maybe he received extra money and can now afford to buy paint," I said to Giselle.

"I wonder what else he will come up with?" Giselle asked and continued, "We need to work out when we must leave for Darwin so we don't stay here too long."

"As soon as we receive mail from Ralph and Ute as to when they will be in Darwin, we can make our move," I replied.

Steve had bought everything we needed: tins of paint, brushes, rollers, fillers, sandpaper, and masking tape.

Giselle painted the tricky stuff; precise handling of a paintbrush was her forte. She painted the doors and window frames in oil. My job was more straightforward; I painted the walls and ceiling with a roller and a roller on a broomstick for the high parts and the ceiling.

We worked with the stereo playing while Steve worked outside in the heat, painting the outside of the house. We kept on painting for days. Steve went away a few times to settle more money and council issues. It must have worked out well for him; he waved a bundle of money at us.

The unit looked pretty good. We also met the neighbours, and they were impressed.

"They'll probably ask Steve to paint their unit," Giselle said.

"Not by us, that's for sure," I said.

We had a rest from painting, time to bake my special chocolate cake. Bidi's food tin became the baking tin, and I baked it in the freshly super cleaned electric oven. The smell of cake overlapped the scent of the fresh paint. Steve came back in the afternoon, happy to be treated to a lovely cake. He had brought prawns and a lobster.

The renovation was nearly completed. We had leftover paint and painted a few more walls, even in the garage. Steve had picked up our mail. One of the letters was from Ralph and Ute; they were in Darwin but only until the 25th of September;

we needed to get a move on. We talked to Steve, and he promised we would be done in a week.

"Why would it still take a week?" I asked Steve. "I thought we were finished?

"I have promised the neighbour to paint his garage as well and they want us to have a look at their artefacts from New Guinea. Maybe we can buy something for a good price? he replied.

"OK, let's paint the garage," I said.

Steve went to town and left the garage job for us. When he returned, we had finished painting. He presented us with a special edition bottle of Champagne marked '100 Years Cairns' to thank us for all our work.

At dinnertime, Steve had another surprise; he gave us $200. It was unexpected and we really appreciated it. It's for buying a new carburettor," he said.

We drove around to buy a carburettor the next morning, but no such luck. No carburettor in the whole of Cairns. They had to order one and promised it would be in store by Thursday, at the latest Friday. We had heard such promises before but tried hard to think positive. We also went back to the unemployment office. They explained we would not get any money. Fair enough.

Steve had found a few more walls for us to paint at the neighbour's place. He wanted to keep them happy; they were the ones who actually paid rent.

On Thursday we drove to the Ford dealer; the carburettor had arrived. Another trip to the post office, and a walk to our favourite bookstore and where we bought a couple of books. One was called 'Discovery Behind the Iron Curtain' which discussed mind powers and Kirlian photography (which uses a technique to capture electrical discharges on to a photographic plate.) The other was about spiritual powers and guidance. It had paranormal themes and was by someone who called himself Lobsang Rampa. We already had a book by him, entitled 'The Third Eye.' The author claimed his body hosted the spirit of Lobsang Rampa, a Tibetan Lama.

I also fitted the new carburettor; it worked straight away, no adjustments needed. I kept the old one for spares.

Last day of painting, everything was finished by 3 pm. I helped Steve pack tools and equipment into his car and "Crack!" I had done something stupid. I was hanging from the top of the Land Rover, trying to push a heavy box deeper into the car when my back gave away again. Now I really was in pain. I kept lying on my back for the rest of the day, Giselle by my side.

Still in pain the following day, I called the chiropractor, and he was able to see me. It felt better after the treatment, but I kept resting until lunchtime to make sure.

After lunch, we all went to the neighbours and had a look at their New Guinea artefacts. They had fantastic pieces but too large or expensive. We stayed drinking beer for most of the afternoon and were educated about the various pieces and their meanings.

Steve bought a few pieces and so did we. One, was a community betel nut mixing bowl, while the other was for a single person and looked like a larger eggcup.

Steve told us he had tried betel nut. Apparently, it is a drug, a stimulant, like coffee, but more potent. It is addictive and eventually stains the mouth and lips red.

Our time in Cairns was ending; with all the renovations behind us, there was nothing much left to do.

We had booked our car for a service to make sure it would be fit for the next adventure. We stayed in town, looking for the best deals on food items to carry with us. We found some excellent deals and rewarded ourselves with a Chinese meal, blowing the money we had saved.

At night Steve cooked fresh fish which we had with salads and a glass of wine. Everyone was happy and we mapped out the next stretch we would travel together.

We thought we could leave the next morning but Steve hadn't told us he still had to level finances with the neighbours and he was waiting for a delivery of topsoil and grass. It arrived the following day. The landscape guys did a quick and thorough job. We thought it was for beautification, but it was something the council required. The back part of his block was too low and it flooded easily.

Now it was really all done, some more packing and cleaning and early to bed for an early rise.

Chapter 20

All the Way to the Top

Friday the 17.09.1976 We were on the road again. We took it easy. Our goal was to reach Forsayth where we wanted to show Steve the old gold mine. We arrived 450km later by 7 pm and camped right at the mine.

When we woke up, Steve had started digging. We joined him and kept digging for the next 3 hours. We found more gold melting pots and a few bottles as well. When does one stop; when is it enough? We left Forsayth about 11 am and headed for Normanton.

Steve came up with strange accusations on the stops and short rests. He seemed desperate to find a problem within our relationship. He came up with statements like, "You are too happy to be true, or too close and you've lost your identities."

We tried not to argue with him. We had been together with Steve for a long time; if he didn't understand our love and happiness was real, there was nothing we could do.

In Normanton, 360km later, we filled up our cars, and drove to Burketown, a tiny isolated outback town. We camped alongside the river in a shady spot under a tree. We saw a handmade boat carved out of a tree trunk. The whole atmosphere of this place was remoteness, out of this world. Had we left this time, civilization and the planet behind?

Travelling on, it was our turn to take the lead. We must have made a wrong turn and eventually arrived at a cattle station. Steve was upset with us and his mood went downhill, again accusing us of all kinds of things we were supposedly doing wrong.

We didn't mind. We liked that cattle station. The owner was an eccentric Danish guy. He had renovated an old farmhouse, and we appreciated his creativity in only using materials found among the broken-down sheds.

He sat in front of a heap of rusty bent nails and straightened them when we met him. That's what we called dedicated. He had a few young people helping him run the farm. We also talked to an Aboriginal fellow who wanted to know where we were from. We tried to explain but he gestured up to the sky. He wanted to know which direction we originally came from. When we left, he offered us something to eat on the way. It was a piece of dried buffalo meat.

One of his guests informed us the farmer was a Danish prince. Not sure it was true but it sounded exciting.

At night we camped somewhere remote. Steve kept accusing us of things; we hardly knew what he meant. Maybe it was his way of expressing sadness that our time together was coming to an end. We agreed to part ways the next morning.

When we mentioned separating in the morning, it was as if Steve had forgotten about the previous night's accusations and arguments. In the end, he agreed but suggested we should travel together to Borroloola because It was not safe to travel on our own. The roads in that region were treacherous, there could be bushfires, and we would have to cross a few creeks. His plan was fine with us.

Our next combined stop was the Doomadgee Mission, where we filled up with petrol at the highest price we had ever paid in Australia. We also had a flat tyre which was fixed in no time by an Aboriginal mechanic. He didn't even talk to us, just smiled, took the wheel off, and ten minutes later came back with the tyre fixed. At that time, we had no idea of the criticism of the conditions at the mission. I don't believe by 1976 it was still a functioning mission; it was a primarily an Indigenous community.

We stayed for a while and Steve even paid for our petrol and gave us cash. There seemed to be no animosity left that morning as we went on our way to Borroloola, another rough and dusty 400km trip. We drove ahead of Steve. If we became stuck, he would rescue us with his four-wheel drive which had a winch.

Our first stop was at a creek we had to drive across. I hopped out of the car, walked down to the creek, and walked through the flowing water without any problems. The current was mild and less than a foot deep.

"All good," I called out to Giselle, went back to the car and crossed the creek without any problems. This scenario repeated itself a few times. It was always the same, a slow-flowing little stream with clear, cool water, easy to drive across.

We came to another creek; I didn't bother getting out of the car. "Looks OK, doesn't it?" I said. I didn't expect an answer and drove down into the creek. We didn't get very far.

"Oh no," was all Giselle and I could say. We had to laugh even though it would have been serious if we had been on our own. We knew Steve would arrive in a couple of minutes.

The creek was much deeper than the others we had crossed. The water came into our car and covered the floor. The engine had stalled; water had run into the exhaust. Steve arrived but didn't share our light-hearted mood. He was fuming; how could we have been so stupid? He was right but we wouldn't have crossed the creek if we had been by ourselves. He drove down into the creek, crossed it and backed up to winch us out. He stopped while our car was still on an incline to let the water run out.

We still thought it was funny. It was hot; we took out the floor mats to let them dry in the sun and made a cup of tea. By the time we had our tea and Steve stopped complaining, the car and everything else was dry, and we could get on our way.

No more creeks after that incident, even that was funny. We promised ourselves never to be careless again. A short distance from Borroloola, we had another puncture. I quickly changed the tyre, hoping to get it fixed in Borroloola.

We were up early that morning. Was it intuition? When I stepped out of the car, I noticed we had another flat tyre. I pumped it up with that gadget Steve had given us. It still looked good after breakfast and our final separation from Steve.

Everything was fine; no one held any grudges. We exchanged addresses and promised we would create a photo album featuring him at his Rubyvale camp and our tour together. It was meant for his mother. Before we went, he gave us a spare petrol tank; he was worried we might run out of petrol on those long stretches we had to drive.

"Bye, Steve, and thank you for everything," we said. It was a sad departure; after all, we had a good time together, and the few arguments were already forgotten.

· · • · • · • · · ·

The Borroloola service station had just opened when we arrived. They fixed both tyres. They warned us we could encounter bushfires on the way to Daly Waters and we should tell the police we would be driving that route and check into the police station at the other end. It sounded serious and was a new one for us, but it made sense. The police seemed less worried; "It's only a grass fire, stay on the road, stop, close the windows, have a wet cloth over your face, and wait until it has passed," they explained.

We felt reasonably assured and went on our way. It was a slow 400km drive. The road was a sand track with deep grooves. If we saw a fire coming towards us, it would be hard to turn around. Roads like that were more suited for four-wheel drive vehicles. All we had in our favour were high profile tyres, well suited to sandy tracks and roads.

It must have been a couple of hours later when we noticed smoke coming from the direction in which we were driving. We were getting worried but reassured ourselves that we were on a sand track and the vegetation on both sides was sparse.

"Should we drive on?" I asked.

"Let's go slowly and have wet towels ready," Giselle said.

We had a large plastic insulated flask with cool water and towels ready and continued our drive. It didn't take long before we could see more smoke and fire and the wind had increased. We drove on.

The change was sudden; we didn't even have time to take photos. We saw the flames coming, stopped the car and covered ourselves with wet towels, too stunned to panic. One moment the fire was in front of us, coming from the left but not crossing the road, and a minute later it had passed us. The wind and noise were more frightening than the fire.

And then ... quietness, it was all over. It was only a low burning grass fire, a 'cold fire.' It didn't feel cold when we got out of the car. The air was hot but amazingly we could touch the ground where the fire had burned the grass.

We stayed for a while, had a cold drink, then a cup of tea, before driving on. We arrived in Daly Waters without further interruptions. Not sure what we expected in Daly Waters but there was nothing, only a pub where we had a lemon squash. We told the guy in the pub about our ordeal, but he wasn't impressed, "Yeah, a bit of a grass fire," he called it. There was no police to report to either, so we left for Katherine, another 280km.

We arrived late and went straight to the caravan park. We couldn't wait to have a shower. The shower was pretty ordinary and to stay one night in our car was $3.50, the most we had ever paid for a one-night stay.

We wondered how Darwin would look one year after Cyclone Tracy had devastated the city. The previous year when we were in Tennant Creek, the roads were still busy with trucks delivering portable accommodation and Darwin was still off-limits for tourists. We left Katherine early and arrived in Darwin by lunch-time. Our first stop was the post office and, as promised, Ralph and Ute had left a letter for us. They were camping at a caravan park outside Darwin. "Let's stay in town for the day; we can see them tonight," I said.

Our next stop was the hospital; it was easy enough to find. Giselle wasn't worried, she felt well, and we went because the doctor in Emerald had told us to do so. We went to the hospital's reception area, where Giselle presented her letter and a copy of her last blood test, "Could I have a check-up blood test, please?"

The nurse looked worried; "How do you feel, dear?"

"I feel good, no problems at all; I just need a check-up," Giselle said.

The nurse waved to a wardsman and gave him some instructions. He raced off and came back with a wheelchair.

"Don't worry, dear, hospital regulation, the wardsman will take you to get your blood test. Off they went, leaving me behind. I took a seat and waited. After a while, I began to feel anxious and tried to keep myself busy reading old magazines. Finally, Giselle was wheeled back, not to me, but straight to the exit. I ran behind her; even more worried now, needlessly, of course. As soon as we were outside,

Giselle stood up, "Everything is fine, all is back to normal," she said. Time for a hug, and back to the car, where Giselle told me how worried everyone was about the previous blood test.

We still had enough time to drive around Darwin, taking photos and listening to a group of Aboriginal guys in front of a pub singing and clapping with their cans of beer. It sounded terrific. We wondered if it was original Aboriginal music.

Darwin had not fully recovered. There were still signs of destruction but also many new buildings. We had no idea how Darwin looked before the cyclone and couldn't compare. People confirmed a lot of buildings had been pulled down and new buildings had been constructed to be cyclone-proof. The cyclone had changed many regulations of the building codes. It must have been the reason why Steve had to exchange all the roof nails with screws on his duplex.

We bought a bottle of wine and shortly afterwards left Darwin for the caravan park. The manager didn't want to let us in but when we told him we would sleep in the car and had friends waiting for us, he granted us entry. We parked our car right next to Ralph and Ute's panel-van.

Six months had passed which accounted for the exuberant greeting. Who was talking first was hard to determine and unimportant. We settled down on our camping chairs, opened the bottle of wine and the talkfest began. First on the agenda was their new travel partner. They had bought a cat, a cute little black one. Would it run away? No, it was on a leash. I had never seen a cat on a leash but it worked; she had grown up with a leash and accepted it as her everyday existence.

Next came the catching-up phase; Giselle and I dominated the conversation. We had many experiences to share. I showed off my self-cut gemstones and Giselle her leather bags before we dived deeply into the spiritual phenomenon and mental power stories. Top of our agenda was telepathy.

I told them about my struggle with Steve when he was influencing me mentally and I was influencing him. On one occasion, while we were having dinner, I could hear, Steve's voice in my head telling me to pass the salt. I rejected his 'voice' and concentrated my thoughts on him passing me the pepper and to my astonishment, he did.

We knew from reading spiritual books that a big no-no was using mental powers for negative reasons. As much as we were into positive thinking and integrity, it seemed easier to test thought powers by using them for something negative. Giselle and I had many moments of apparent thought reading experiences between us. Even though we loved those incredible exciting phenomena, we nevertheless admitted our wonderful experiences could have a perfectly normal explanation.

Ralph and Ute had a game, I can't remember what it was called but part of the game was to guess the colour of the opposing player's card. It was a game where telepathy would definitely be helpful. Giselle and I trumped in the game; we had the colours correct 80% of the time. We were intrigued; could we read minds? Probably not, but we were convinced we could sense thoughts and mental pictures to a degree which was good enough for us.

It was way past midnight when we stopped talking; the bottle of wine and another one had been consumed – it was time to sleep.

We were up early to beat the heat. By the time we arrived back in Darwin, it was unbearably hot, a scorching and sticky day. Giselle felt dizzy, which was an excellent excuse to have an iced coffee. Feeling better, we checked out tyre shops. We had had too many punctures for comfort and decided to buy two new ones. For the rest of the day, we checked for bargains on tinned food and took photos of everything remotely interesting.

By 3 pm, we were back at the Howard Springs Reserve caravan park. Ralph and Ute were about to go for a swim, and we joined them which was exactly what we needed before we left for Katherine. Our aim was to camp somewhere at the Victoria River. We only had a quick stop at Katherine for another iced coffee before we were on our way again. The day seemed to get longer, and the sun didn't want to go down. We arrived at Victoria River at 5 pm, but it felt like 4 pm. It was time to go for another swim and set up camp. We tried our hand at fishing but had no luck. Ralph tried to catch a lizard but it bit him on his hand. 'Karma,' I thought. But the lizard didn't want to let him go. We managed to open its jaw and set Ralph free and the lizard, of course.

And what did we do at night? Serious discussions about reincarnation with us believing it, and Ralph and Ute remaining sceptical. And why shouldn't they be because we had no proof, only great stories. The bulk of the reincarnation stories came from our parents after the war. Everyone had a story about dead soldiers appearing to their mothers.

I remembered from my school days our teacher telling us similar stories. My mind was made up then; I liked the idea of reincarnation which was very comforting. Reincarnation or eternal life was indeed a compelling option. We also believed in karma and the law of cause and effect. These beliefs helped us to stay within our positivity and integrity ideals.

Another crazy hot day, we swam in the river before breakfast. As we left our camp, it was so hot we didn't even open our car windows. We drove with wet towels around our heads.

Chapter 21

The Wild West

At the Western Australia border, we set our watches ninety minutes back, went for a quick swim in a dam, before driving to Wyndham. We needed petrol, but no such luck; the only petrol station was closed on Sundays. We had to stay in Wyndham to continue our journey the next day.

Wyndham had woken from its slumber; we filled up both vehicles and topped up our jerry cans as well. It was uncomfortably hot, and we hardly stopped for sightseeing - there was not much to see - but Ralph had his eyes peeled on the surroundings. He had a sixth sense when it came to spotting reptiles. Whenever we stopped, it was for lizards, snakes or for Giselle and me to take photos of wildflowers.

Ralph and Ute taught us a lot about reptiles and soon we knew how to distinguish one from another. Still, we kept a respectful distance whenever we saw a snake.

We arrived in Halls Creek but drove on a few more kilometres until we found a place with a waterhole to camp for the night. We jumped into the water to cool off.

"Stay behind me," I said to Giselle. The water was cloudy, not refreshing and one couldn't see anything, maybe a crocodile waited for its dinner. Actually, sweet water crocodiles were not in the habit of eating humans.

Not really refreshed but less dusty, we settled down for the night. It was dark quickly, and we had our dinner around the campfire.

It took us another two days to drive 700km to one of our main destinations, Broome, having stopped only at Fitzroy Crossing and Derby.

Close to Fitzroy Crossing, we noticed a broken-down caravan. Ralph went to ask if we could help. I drove barefoot, and before I could walk on the hot ground I needed my thongs. I placed them in front of the car door when Ralph called out that they were getting help already. He returned to his car and we drove off. Later, I noticed I had left my thongs behind. Never mind; I had another pair.

In Broome we camped close to the beach between the dunes, a secluded spot. Waking up early, we raced to the beach where we stayed all day. Swimming was pretty much out of the picture; one would have to go too far out but walking on the beach was perfect. Giselle spotted a water snake, it didn't look very friendly. Following this sighting, we avoided the water and only went in for quick splashes.

Hang-gliders were being pulled up from the beach by a sand buggy. Once they were high enough to catch the upwind generated from the dunes, they circled the beach until they slowly lost momentum and landed again. We had never seen a hang-glider in action and took way too many photos. The glary conditions on the beach made taking photos awkward, but it gave us a new idea for a story, hang-gliders in Broome. We constantly came up with new projects, and had a notebook full of future projects; all described how we would go about it.

At night, when we had arrived back at the camp, the police were waiting for us.

"You can't stay here; camping between the dunes is not permitted," the police officer stated in a stern voice.

"Sorry, we didn't know, we had no idea," and for good measure, I added, "We are from Germany, travelling around Australia." They were friendly and after we talked for a while, they allowed us to stay for the night.

Friday 1.10.1976 - After breakfast, we drove to the nearby caravan park and paid our due. We made the best of it, they had a laundry; everything which needed washing was washed.

For the rest of the day, we went on a Broome discovery tour. We thought the pearl fishing was still booming but only a couple of old boats were left in the harbour. One of the newest buildings in Broome was the Civic Centre; not sure what was going on there, but no one was around to ask.

After a couple of days in Broome, we were eager to drive on, but we knew we wouldn't make it to Port Hedland; six hundred kilometres on a sandy road was too far to go in one day. We made sure we had enough petrol and water because there was nothing in between the two towns, other than one roadhouse. The road conditions were pretty bad. It was sand, often called washboard roads because of the rippled road profile. The broken-down cars and caravans on the side of the road were testaments to the harsh conditions.

Having filled up on iced coffee at the only roadhouse, we drove to the fascinating sounding eighty-mile beach. We stopped at a rest spot and instantly felt disgusted; it looked like a rubbish tip. We tried obliterating this scene from our minds and made our way over the dunes to see the beach.

It was surreal, like a scene from a horror movie. We expected something horrendous to happen at any moment. It was not that the beach looked dangerous; it was desolate. But, if there was a beach on Mars, this would be it! Beach, water and nothing else as far as one could see, combined with stillness and a silvery-white shimmer from the sand. To reach the water, one had to walk a long way and the water was only shallow. Was there something missing? Yes, life. There were no birds, no animals, and no people other than the four of us. Once again, we felt like the only people on this planet where at any moment something could happen, the suspense was in the salty air.

We walked back quickly. There was no real reason to hurry, but we needed to see our cars to be sure aliens had not taken them. Alien was probably the most suitable description of this out-of-this-world beach. One can guess what we talked about that night.

We survived the night and went for another walk on the beach in the morning. It was fascinating to be there, despite its eeriness, but there was nothing more to do. We left the beach and the rubbish behind and made our way to Port Hedland. Midway along the road, we saw the caravan which had broken down at Fitzroy Crossing. What a big yet small country, one met the same travellers again and again. The driver came over to us and handed me my thongs. He spotted that I had left without them and knew we would meet again.

Port Hedland was a shock for our sensitised minds. We had lived in the bush for too long without civilization, roads and buildings. It didn't help that we couldn't find a caravan park. Luckily, a service station owner allowed us to stay for the night next to the toilet blocks. Not very romantic, but at least it had running water.

A drive-in movie theatre was in viewing distance; we could see the screen and follow the story. No sound, of course, but watching that movie from afar was the highlight of our one night in Port Hedland.

The next morning, Ralph and Ute stayed at the service station while we went to town, exploring and taking photos. We hoped to pick up mail but nothing had arrived. We drove back to the service station, had a tea, and went back on the road again.

Close to Roebourne, a former gold rush town, 200km away from Port Hedland, we found a place to camp. Wherever we camped, we were invaded by millions of flies and had to eat under a mosquito net to make sure we didn't swallow a bunch of flies. Still, it was a peaceful spot, and we stayed another day relaxing, with shade and a little lake to cool down. We deserved a break before attempting the last 1500km to Perth.

Travelling down the West Coast with Ralph and Ute had become a cheap exercise. On our own, we wouldn't have been confident enough to camp free wherever we wanted. On the flip side, we would have stopped more often to explore the surroundings.

Not far from Nanutarra, we found a river and camped close to it. Dinner was under mosquito netting again and was followed by a long discussion about the third eye and if seeing into the future was possible. If so, we agreed we all would play lotto. However, what we strongly believed in was intuition which was not the same as seeing the future. We trusted our intuition to guide us in the right direction with our lifestyle.

The next day we travelled to Canavan, another 400km stretch; we drove a couple of times into the surroundings to check for reptiles. We continued for a couple of days, went to the Billabong Road House and further on to the Kalbarri National Park.

The next overnight stay was close to a roadhouse, and at night it was surprisingly cold and windy. We parked our cars rear to rear with a tarpaulin over the top creating a cosy place to discuss a book we had read, Lobsang Rampa's prediction for the years following the year 2000.

After stops in Geraldton and another small town, we finally arrived in Perth, found a caravan park and enjoyed our first hot shower in a week. Sufficiently scrubbed-up, we could face civilization and the big city atmosphere.

Chapter 22

The Sun Sets in Perth

We set out to find Gabrielle and Henry's place. It took a while to find their location but when we did, we received a warm, loving welcome.

We were staying at the Swan Gardens caravan park in the suburb of Medland. It was a quick drive from Medland into the city but also to Kalamunda, a very pleasant leafy suburb where Gabrielle and Henry had bought their house. If one goes by the adage, a view is everything; they had found the perfect place. It was elevated and had a panoramic view over Perth city and the most glorious sunsets one could imagine.

"Let me show you the house," Gabrielle said. She walked us from room to room, seven in all. They may have been pensioners, but they didn't downsize. A large kitchen and dining room, two bathrooms, plus another spare toilet. From our perspective, it was a palace. Towards the end of the hallway, we arrived at the bedroom Gabrielle had in mind for us.

"This will be your room, it is close to your private bathroom, and you can stay as long as you like. The other bedrooms are for our grandchildren when they stay overnight."

"Gabrielle, I hope you don't mind, but we are accustomed to sleeping in our car. Is that OK?" I replied.

"No, you must sleep here, we prepared everything for your visit," she insisted.

"It is so nice of you; we will use it as our day room and use the shower, of course, but we prefer to sleep in our car." I replied.

It went on for a while but Gabrielle finally gave in, all was fine and the animated discussion ended with a request, "As long as you bake a cake for Henry."

"Of course I will, I'll make two if you like, and I will set up Henry's gem cutting machine."

They wanted to hear our stories and see our gemstones, but having joined a silversmith club, they were eager to show us their latest pieces first. Later, in the afternoon, we had to interrupt our conversation and drive back to the caravan park to let Ralph and Ute know we would stay in Kalamunda.

Henry had explained the shortest route to the main road which led straight to the caravan park. We only stayed a short time with Ralph and Ute; they would visit us soon.

As it happened, Gabrielle and Henry had a mountain devil (a small reptile) as a pet; we had never seen one before, and it certainly would be a treat for Ralph and Ute.

The next few days were filled with feverish activity. I was looking forward to setting up the gem-cutting machine with Henry. He had a workshop in his double garage. It didn't take long, I explained everything to him and the general set-up was finished. He had shellac ready, and we sorted out a pretty zircon to fit onto the dop stick. I adjusted the setting for a basic diamond cut. So far, so good; however, the cutting did not go smoothly. The machine was an early model, over twenty years old and unfortunately it was not stable. Henry's mood took a dive; being able to facet his own gems had become a pipe dream.

We kept at it for a while which helped Henry to get over his disappointment. He observed how patient he would have to be and how long it took to produce a perfect cut.

Henry had crafted silver rings and bracelets with uncut gemstones which looked very beautiful. Giselle and I liked his robust designs and suggested he could develop his own unique style of jewellery. His machine was packed up and retired for good.

As soon as Henry and I finished playing with our toys, I went to the kitchen and baked the promised cake. It was an urgent matter, Henry needed his cake, and that was it.

In the afternoon, Ralph and Ute came for coffee. Gabrielle presented my cake, but only half of it; she had put the other half aside to make sure Henry would get his fair share.

It was time for the mountain devil to make an appearance. We were sitting outside at the edge of the terraced gardens. In retrospect, it was not the best location to show a prize possession. Ralph had a hard time closing his mouth. Out of the blue, someone showed him what he had been searching for.

"I can't believe it; I have never seen one. Where did you find it?" he asked Gabrielle.

"On one of our field trips, looking for amethysts, not far from here," Gabrielle replied.

"I still can't believe it. Let me get my camera," said Ralph.

The mountain devil seemed comfortable being handled and passed from one person to another. Giselle put him on her chest, wearing him as a brooch. The little guy must have liked it; he didn't move.

Ralph came back with his camera equipment. He handed a few lenses to Ute and started taking photos. He placed the cute devil into the rock garden next to wildflowers to capture the best possible shots. It looked like the photos had been taken somewhere in the wild. Who knows what was going on in that little creature's mind? Was he planning an escape and only waiting for a good opportunity?

Ralph couldn't get enough photos and I took some too. The photo session had been going on for at least half an hour. Our attention must have dropped away when we were talking about other things. Ralph had finished changing lenses.

"Where is he?" Ralph asked while getting ready to set the light meter for his camera.

Yes, where was the little bugger? He was gone. We jumped up as if stung by a swarm of bees, frantically looking everywhere. Down on our knees, crawling along the narrow garden path, searching every niche, under plants and behind rocks.

Gabrielle, who was in her kitchen, must have observed us and hurried out, "What happened?"

"We can't find the dragon - it just vanished." I said.

"It can't be – no!" she cried out. She was furious and couldn't handle the situation. She went back to the kitchen, crying.

Giselle and I felt guilty; it looked like it was our fault. We had invited Ralph and Ute, both reptile enthusiasts, and now Gabrielle's prized possession had miraculously disappeared.

In our mind, we were sure it was bad luck, and of course, we had taken our eyes off the little fellow. Gabrielle was suspicious. She didn't say so, but one could read her face like a book and, no surprise, after one hour of more intense searching and giving up, Ralph and Ute left. They said goodbye but couldn't find the right words. "Thank you for having us," was all they could say.

Once our travelling companions had left, no one mentioned the incident again. It was like it never happened, and the next day they took us out for a drive to a nearby dam and national park. They had forgiven us, a lesson for us in not holding grudges.

At night we went cultural, and watched Lakme the Opera on television with Joan Sutherland, a harmonious night of culture together.

Straight after breakfast, we went to town. For the first two hours, we took photos. Later we concentrated on getting everything we needed for driving across the Nullarbor Plain. The Eyre Highway is about 1,700km long; we needed to be well prepared. In case of water shortage, we bought more water containers. Food, of course, we stocked up on rice pudding and the like. And finally, a few more books by Lobsang Rampa. We knew it was fiction but it was compelling reading. We did what we always did, reading and sorting out ideas from the books and fitting them into our lifestyle.

We arrived back late in the afternoon. Giselle had promised Gabrielle she would cook a German meal, Sauerkraut, what else? Henry must have loved it; he had three helpings.

The goodbye was emotional. We were good friends and had become even closer; we even had met their sons and grandchildren. Would we ever see them again? Living in Perth was like living on another planet; it was too far from everything. Even if we decided on settling in Australia, it would be on the East Coast.

Gabrielle cried, Henry was composed, so was I, and Giselle shed a tear as well. There was no reason to prolong the pain; another adventure was waiting. Ralph and Ute were waiting already in front of the caravan park. They had it easier, no one to say goodbye to.

Chapter 23

The Nullarbor Plain

We left Perth without any hassles and drove with occasional stops in Northam and Merredin, and finally camped outside Southern Cross. So far, so good, more or less one straight stretch of 370 km, six hours of leisurely driving, stopping, taking photos, looking for lizards and bush flowers.

Ralph picked up a stumpy tail lizard; it looked like a pine cone and was harmless enough for Ralph to take it with him on holiday. He would release it later before coming back into civilization. Giselle and I were not sure if it was a good thing to do, poor stumpy, he might never see his relatives again. Do lizards have family feelings? According to Ralph, reptiles recognize people.

That night, we still had fresh veggies. Giselle cooked up a storm, cauliflower with rice and steak. And checking the contents of the Esky, we found four cold-ish bottles of beer. For the night's entertainment, it was television. Ralph and Ute had a small portable TV. We were out of reach of a signal most of the time, but this evening we were still close enough to civilization to pick up a signal.

We raced towards Coolgardie after a quick breakfast. We looked around the little town, checking out the shops for old bottles and found a garage instead. We bought petrol and had a look at their bottle collection. Many old bottles were lying around, not sorted or displayed on proper shelves. Obviously, this was no justification for us pinching three little bottles. How could we do it? I thought we belonged to the good guys.

We didn't drive to Kalgoorlie, maybe we should have, we drove toward Norseman and stopped about 20km out of the town where we set up camp for the night.

It was still daylight. Ralph and I went target shooting; old tins were lying around everywhere. We saw a few lizards as well and took photos. By the way, no one ever mentioned the mountain devil.

I was waking up to the sound of music. It was Giselle; she was singing beautiful songs with 'off the cuff' lyrics. Even the flies must have loved it; they came in swarms. Giselle stopped singing, not because of the flies, but because we drank our coffee under the fly screen netting.

We stopped in Norseman to buy greeting cards to impress the folks in Germany. It was not every day one crossed the Nullarbor. The name, means 'no trees.' Actually we saw some trees which we liked; they looked like giant bonsai trees; it was how the wind had formed their canopy.

On one of our stops, Ralph released the stumpy lizard – good luck, little guy.

We stopped at Balladonia for no reason other than to refill our tanks before we drove another 30km until we found a spot to camp for the night.

Giselle and I were always happy; "How come we are always happy?" I asked.

"We have no reason not to be happy," Giselle replied.

Who could argue with this wisdom?

"Sometimes I think we are living in a dream, and I don't want to wake up," I said.

"If we wake up, it will be even more beautiful when we realize it is real and true," Giselle answered.

"I love you" was all I had left to answer.

· · · · ● ● ● ● · · · ·

We really stepped on it and ended up not far from the border of South Australia. We nearly ran out of water. Luckily, there were a couple of spots with water tanks on the roadside. The first one was empty but we were in luck on the second one. Ralph stopped a few times for his regular lizard photography and, on one occasion, even a brown snake. At the end of the day, we had driven 500 km.

The next day we continued to an actual place called Nullarbor, off the main highway. We thought it might be an old town, but there was nothing.

It was Sunday already; where had the week gone, and we were in South Australia. Ralph and I checked the cars. My car was severely misfiring, one of the plugs was burnt, I cleaned it, but would need to fit new ones soon.

The next morning Giselle woke me up with opera style singing; I nearly fell out of our bed if that had been possible in our van. We had breakfast in our 'bedroom' which we called 'The checkered breakfast saloon' because of the surrounding checkered fabric. There was a reason we couldn't sit outside; the flies were still unbearable.

We aimed to reach Port Augusta. It looked doubtful when the car started badly misfiring again. We had no choice; we drove to Kimba, where I bought six new sparkplugs, contacts and an air filter. The old filter was clogged up with all the fine red dust it had collected. It didn't take long and the car was driving like new. We made it to Port Augusta with time to spare.

We found a pleasant caravan park and paid for two nights. Glorious shower, is there anything better than having a hot shower after one week without one?

I don't think so. Giselle played housewife and did the laundry and I played husband, reading the newspaper. Giselle thought I had done enough work fixing the car.

After dinner, we went to our 'neighbours' and watched telly on their mini TV.

Next morning after breakfast, laundry and car maintenance work continued. The dust had penetrated absolutely everywhere. First, the brakes; taking off the wheels and cleaning the brake drums and pads. The racing gearshift came next; it hardly shifted anymore. That component was definitely not suitable for driving on dirt roads. I took it apart, cleaned and greased it. I even took the headlights off which were covered in red dust, cleaned the reflectors, and finally gave the car a wash. Our baby was smiling again, and we drove around Port Augusta and used the soft afternoon light to take photos.

Both cars were ready for the next stretch. Our goal was the Flinders Ranges National Park, a short two-hour drive. We wanted to stay the night but decided to drive further and camp wild to save money. We had a shower the night before, which should last for a week.

Our camp was at the foothills of the Flinders Mountain range, and there was even a waterhole.

Ralph and Ute were happy as well; they had seen many different lizards and even a tiger snake, not that Giselle and I were enthusiastic about that one.

We yearned to be on our own again. As nice as it was to travel with friends - and they were really good friends - we preferred to do our own thing.

We liked our camp, surrounded by trees, some pines, lots of ghost gums and paperbark trees. The hills around us were the right height for exploring and long walks. We took two long walks, one in the morning and one in the afternoon; in-between, we had long rests to recuperate.

We continued our exploration walks the following day. In the afternoon, Ralph and Ute were getting ready to leave the camp the next day.

We were greeted by a rainy morning which added to the sadness of saying goodbye. We hoped we would see each other again one day.

We cleaned up the camp and left as well but only to drive to a nearby spot for a good view to take photos. In the afternoon, we went to the National Park camping grounds; they had great walking tracks to the most beautiful vantage points. Dutifully, we paid our $2.50.

The following day we were greeted by sunshine, perfect weather for our trekking, camera and water bottle at hand. At the start it was easy, a well-walked sandy track going straight ahead amongst the trees. It went through a pass in the mountain range, only to change to a steeper rocky track into a valley where we found an old cottage, left behind a hundred years ago by the first pioneers. The next section turned out to be hard work; it was steep and went up the mountain range. We were not the only ones doing the walk. We met people who were on the way back; they had found the climb too difficult. Now we were even more determined to go all the way. One hour later, we were standing on the top.

This country was ours now; no one else was present. We were standing on top of the world, and as far as one could see, it was beautiful, serene, and peaceful. Nothing was disturbing our reality; for a moment, we had inherited a peaceful world, without war or conflict, without cruelty or money worries, replaced by an endless horizon of glory. We stayed in what felt like a deep meditation for over an hour, simply existing, breathing and not thinking, until another reality interrupted.

"I am getting hungry, let's head back," I said.

We walked back slowly, taking the experience with us and keeping it for the rest of the day. Not even a long shower, coffee and a late dinner could match our inner peace.

1.11.1976 – Monday. We had no idea that a new time zone - Summertime - had started and we were late getting up. Our watch showed 9 am, but as we heard on the radio, it was already 10 am. Not that we were in a hurry to get anywhere.

We planned to drive deeper into the desert. One could assume we had seen enough desert having crossed the Nullarbor, but it was a different type of desert. We saw it as a one-day tourist drive.

Now we were on our own again, our attention returned to our future goals. The topic of where we would live was at the forefront of our minds. We had to go back to Germany, first and foremost for our parents but also, if we decided to live in Australia, to finalize our last affairs and possessions.

Our main goal for the next year was flying home, writing and publishing our book, unless something came up in the meantime. Having discussed our future plans for most of the day, we came back to more immediate goals: travel to the Snowy Mountains, Sydney, and back to Narooma.

We also had noticed something else: we were getting tired of travelling. We longed for a home and space to work on our book and other projects. Our travel bug was not bugging us anymore; we were keen to explore our future life together in a more permanent set-up, other than a panel-van.

The next day we went back to Port Augusta; we needed supplies for the rest of the trip. A few developed slide films had arrived and we spent the rest of the day sorting slides and deciding which would be suitable for publishing.

The weather had changed, no more dry heat, it had been raining for the last couple of days, and it was colder. We travelled on and stayed one night at Mt Remarkable National Park before driving to Burra Burra, where it finally stopped raining. We were addicted to the sun, and we needed it after the last few rainy, cold days. We were getting closer to the Barossa Valley and stopped at Nuriootpa. The first decent winery was ours. We tasted the wine but bought a bottle of cherry brandy and one of whisky instead. There was a reason for this over-the-top spending spree; Giselle's birthday. We promised to stay awake for this momentous event. Most of the night, we listened to the radio; it had a great program, explaining everything about California's rock scene. At midnight, I congratulated Giselle; we had no Champagne but had a nip of cherry brandy instead. We listened to the radio for another hour; they talked about the Rolling Stone's history which made us realize how little we knew, having grown up in Germany.

Giselle's birthday was celebrated by sleeping in; we were too tired after listening to the radio for half the night. For the rest of the morning, I kept singing, "Happy Birthday to you."

We left late to get to our next destination; it was only a short distance anyhow. The scenery again reminded us of Germany, probably why so many Germans settled there and started growing wine. We had the same feeling last year when we drove through the Barossa Valley.

This time we looked at old cemeteries and found German names everywhere. Whole German communities had come to settle, even Lutheran churches and graveyards reminded us of the German history in the Barossa Valley. We always assumed the name 'Barossa' was German but the valley was named after a Spanish battleground where the British reached victory over the French. It was named by Colonel William Light in 1837.

We arrived at Tailem Bend a couple of hours later, and found a restaurant for Giselle's birthday dinner but it didn't meet our expectations; we were looking forward to Sydney for a well-deserved festive dinner.

Our next goal was Bendigo. We made it and stayed at the Dower Recreation Reserve and Caravan Park, and we have the receipt to prove it. The afternoon consisted of drinking coffee and writing letters, and acknowledging that taking time out, drinking coffee or tea, was one of the main attractions of long-term travelling.

We stayed two nights in Bendigo; it was the first anniversary of our engagement and happiness was still our main agenda.

I quote a paragraph from my diary of that very day.

'We are one year engaged and still totally in love. More in love than before, or to be specific, every day has added more love to the already abundance of love. Adding all this love together, it had become so huge, that we may have to buy a trailer to carry it with us. If anyone doubts our love, they surely have no problems living their lives without us.'

We went back to the city and walked everywhere, camera at hand. Finally, we sat down in an uncomfortable café. Obviously, we had looked for a comfortable one.

In 1976, the coffee scene we were used to in Europe had not arrived in Bendigo. Being strengthened by bad coffee and a bickie, we walked around until it was time to invade a Chinese restaurant to celebrate our engagement with a decent dinner. We hoped to see a movie after that, but the only one they were showing was 'Gone with the Wind,' starting in one hour; we gave it a miss.

The next morning we left early for Rushworth and travelled further to Violet Town until we arrived in Benalla. We went straight to the post office and collected a pack of mail. We looked for a café where we could sit, drink coffee and read our letters. Giselle's birthday letters and our engagement anniversary mail from our parents had arrived.

Out came our notebooks, calculating our growing budget. It looked good but the more money we had, the less we wanted to spend. Looking into the crystal ball, calculating the money we hoped to earn in Narooma, plus selling our car and probably more cash gifts from our parents for Christmas, we should be able to afford plane tickets and take cash home with us.

11.11.1976 – Thursday. Believing in numerology, we saw that day as something special. We didn't know much about it, just the basics and how it related to us. Giselle's ruling number was 11, which is supposed to be a master number. We were thrilled with that; it sounded like a good thing. My ruling number was 3, which is ruled by a lot of thinking; yes, that's me. Astrology was another subject we investigated. According to astrology, Giselle, a Scorpio, and I, a Cancer, were the perfect match.

We went back to the post office just in case more mail had arrived, but nothing. On the way back to the car, we couldn't believe our eyes. Who was walking on the other side of the road with their mother in tow? Ralph and Ute! How is it even possible in such a vast country? It must have been because it was the 11th of the 11th. What other possible explanation could there be?

We travelled together and camped 'wild,' but it was not the same as our earlier trip. With the mother around, the topics of conversation were muted and focused on weather, scenery and kangaroos.

Planning our route at breakfast, we would go our separate ways soon. We were headed for the Snowy Mountains while Ralph and Ute wanted to show their mother as much territory as possible in the short time available before she had to fly back to Switzerland from Sydney.

We said goodbye once we had found a place where we would stay that night. It belonged to the Kosciusko National Park, the area we wanted to explore, close to Corryong.

When they left, we revelled in the beauty of our camping location which was absolutely stunning. We had parked our car five metres away from the edge of an icy cold creek, among green shrubs and tall trees. It could not have been any more peaceful. The serenity reminded us of when we were on top of the Flinders Ranges, only this time it had a more romantic feel to it, close to what we knew from a German forest. We could easily imagine a deer coming out of the shrubs, walking to the creek to drink. A touch of Walt Disney. Instead, a water dragon passed by our car to disappear into the undergrowth along the creek edges.

We had no choice; we had to stay the night at this perfect spot. "We could build a house here," I said to Giselle before going to sleep.

We woke up a few times during the night; the weather had become nasty, rainy, windy and colder. We braved the weather and had a quick wash in the creek, but the rain became heavier, and we had to hide in our car for breakfast. By 11 am, it cleared up and we went walking. We tried to walk quietly; we had heard this was wombat territory. At that moment, we wished for nothing more than to see a wombat. The weather didn't look promising, and we walked back to our camp. Unfortunately, more people had discovered our spot; two more cars with camping gear. And to add to the insult, it started to rain heavily, "I don't think we will build a house here after all," I said.

At night, we heard strange noises and the car was shaking. When we looked out, we saw two wombats walking away. Bad luck, I had no flashlight and it was too dark to take a photo. Still, we were thrilled to know wombats were not just a myth.

We braved the ice-cold creek once more for an invigorating morning wash. After a coffee, we drove to Jindabyne, a well-known ski resort. However, we were not in the snow season and it wasn't busy at all. We did see some German-style houses. We posted our letters and went back to the National Park. We drove as close as we could to Mount Kosciusko where we parked and walked an eight kilometre track up the mountain.

It was incredible scenery; we were already at the height of 1700 metres and surrounded by snow from the last season. I managed to chase Giselle with a snowball, and yes, it was cold. We both wore beanies and our warmest t-shirts, jumpers and jackets.

Everything looked rough and rocky, with plants sticking out of the snow; it was a bizarre experience for us, having been travelling for such a long time through the outback and deserts, to be confronted with high mountains and snow. We marched on along creeks, snow and rocks. The pass itself was well trodden; heaps of tourists walked it every day. On this occasion, there was no one we could see ahead of us but there were other walkers following us. It was getting colder by the minute and clouds were moving in fast. Not your typical Sunday morning walk. The last thing we needed was to be stuck somewhere in bad weather. We stepped it up and reached a mountain hut after the 8 km walk. We didn't take long to admire the view; too cold, cloudy and misty. Up there, snow was everywhere. We went back quick-smart and arrived in one piece but exhausted at our car. We drove to a nice spot where we stayed overnight.

We talked a lot that night, it was a great day, and we had the feeling we had seen all we wanted to see and were ready to get back to civilisation. We would have loved to be able to teleport to Giselle's comfy unit.

Our feelings had changed; it was as if our minds and bodies mysteriously knew our two years of travelling had ended and it was time to go home. Our focus had changed. We were looking forward to the benefits of civilisation such as excellent coffee, good food and stimulating company. Even working in Narooma was something we looked forward to. We often talked about how it would be when we were back in Hamburg, visiting old friends, seeing old places. What would have changed? How would we like to live in a city after such a long time living in the bush? Would we be able to readjust? We hardly had listened to news, new music or watched new movies. What had we missed? We had lived in our own reality and would need to be able to adjust to a new one.

We drove through the rain; there was a touch of melancholy in the air, a distinct feeling something was coming to an end. Our first stop was in Cooma; we filled up the tank and ourselves for lunch. It would have been a quick drive from there to Narooma, but of course, it was much too early, we needed to go to Sydney first, and Canberra was on our way.

We drove on to Canberra; it was less than two hours. Our first stop was the General Post Office. By the time we were back at our car, another hour had gone by, and we still had to look for a caravan park, which took us another hour. We had bought fresh bread and other goodies and were looking forward to a nice dinner, reading our mail and checking two slide films which had also arrived.

We decided to stay in Canberra for sightseeing and photos and would then drive straight to Sydney.

Luck was on our side, the rain had stopped and we enjoyed a lovely day of sightseeing. We picked up more mail at the post office and arranged for all mail to go to Sydney. When we went to our bank, we got worried; something was wrong with our bankbook. Money was missing. They kept our bankbook and we received a receipt, but it was an odd feeling leaving the bankbook behind. They told us we could pick it up in Sydney at our branch in Bondi Junction. What could we do? No choice; we tried hard not to think about it, and stayed for another day of sightseeing.

Canberra was behind us, and we were driving at 55 miles per hour towards Sydney. After a quick stop in Goulburn for petrol, we arrived in Sydney, Bondi Junction.

Had our bankbook arrived? Marching into the Commonwealth Bank, just before closing time, and with mixed feelings, they took us by surprise and presented us with our corrected bankbook. They had calculated the interest for the whole year and added $49. Surely the windfall was a good excuse for a celebration. We shouted ourselves a McDonald's burger and thick shake. "Would you like fries with that?" Sure we would; we loved those skinny fries.

The bank and McDonald's were now in the brand new Bondi Plaza Shopping Complex. There was everything, even a café with real coffee, not the instant stuff we had been drinking for the last two years.

Dragging ourselves away from that modern shopping paradise was not easy. One could say we had been deprived of retail shopping for two years. Eventually, we managed to leave and arrived at Bernd's house. It was a happy reunion and we settled down in the lounge and didn't stop talking till we went to bed at midnight.

Bernd was living with his new girlfriend; her name was Julia. She was English, a few years older than Bernd, and had lived in Sydney for the last ten years. She worked in fashion, buying the latest fashion wholesale and selling to boutiques.

We really liked her and got on well. She liked most of the things we did: yoga, meditation, and the esoteric. Bernd wasn't into these things but Julia also had a sporty side; they played tennis together and definitely liked to party. It was all very harmonious and they invited us to stay as long as we liked.

The house they lived in felt spooky, and Julia thought there were spirits in the attic. The room we were supposed to be sleeping in had a strange vibe. We laid our mattress on the floor next to a table which had a large candle standing in its centre, and went to sleep. A couple of hours later, we were woken up by a loud bang; the candle had dropped off the table and landed next to my head.

It wasn't funny anymore; it could not have happened by itself. We didn't want to sleep in that room any longer. Julia had woken up as well, "I knew there was a spirit in there," she said, "You can sleep in my office if you don't mind the mess." We didn't mind at all.

After the ghost encounter, the rest of the night was uneventful. The breakfast topic was about ghosts in their various states of appearance. Julia claimed she could feel their presence. They had looked around the attic and had seen many candle holders. Julia thought they were used for occult sessions. We didn't think so; the way she described them, with seven candles, it was probably a menorah; it was likely Jewish people owned the house. Nevertheless, there was still the issue of the candle magically dropping from the centre of the table and thus defying the laws of physics.

It was fun discussing ghosts and their possible impacts, and we continued this theme until we came to the topic of drug-induced phenomena. Julia was particularly enthused by Castaneda and his experiences with mescaline. She had all his books and gave them to us to read. Another book we both had read was 'Behind the Iron Curtain.'

After breakfast, Julie and Bernd went to work and left us to do our own thing. We didn't like being freeloaders and wanted to pull our weight. First, we cleaned up the kitchen and later did all the washing. In-between, we went shopping, Giselle wanted to cook something for dinner. And of course, we bought more beer. Walking back to Bernd's house, we met Imay, a Japanese karate guy we knew from when I trained karate and he had come a few times to visit us when we still lived in Bondi. He was on his way to Bernd's place; he wanted to cook a Japanese meal on Friday night.

Back at Bernd's place, we met some neighbours from the house next door, a small block of four units. We knew one of those guys already, Peter, originally from Holland. We liked him; he was into similar music and played the guitar. He worked for the council, cutting grass and he was also into another variety of grass. As one might expect, he was a gentle, relaxed person.

Later, Peter came down, bringing his guitar and I brought out my guitar as well, and a few more people joined us, not playing but drinking beer and enjoying the warm afternoon accompanied by the sounds of guitars.

Giselle hadn't started cooking yet which was good because Julia came home and brought food and started cooking for all of us. Giselle and I sat back and relaxed into this friendly neighbourhood atmosphere.

The following day we drove to the city to buy souvenirs and check our mail. We bought two records; one was by Sherbet, an Australian rock band. We thought we had to buy at least one Australian record, and we would keep it for us. We were looking for a suitcase, but first we bought a travel bag to take on the plane. Just the idea of getting ready for travelling back home brought excitement. We truly were ready to get home and see our parents, my big brother Herbert, who always had looked out for me, my sister-in-law Heike and Marco, my nephew.

That night we went to a big party, everyone brought something and there was no shortage of alcohol. There was also a specific smell in the air from consuming something other than alcohol. Joints were passed around left, right and centre. Dancing styles were represented from the hardly moving to the exotic. Julia was channelling a ballerina.

By Monday, we had recuperated, and it was time to drive back to the city, check for mail, and finalise tax issues. Whenever we worked, we had paid tax which we were supposed to get back. However, the most critical issue was to ensure we would be allowed back into Australia if we stayed for a prolonged time in Germany. We needed a three-year re-entry visa and to arrange it, we had to hand in our passports. We were assured there would be no problems. We also bought one more metal trunk; we had way too much luggage; we would ship the trunks and take the rest in suitcases by plane.

Tired after a long day of bureaucracy and shopping, we relaxed by watching television and drinking beer.

The following morning we went sunning ourselves on Bondi Beach, and in the afternoon we walked all the way to Bondi Junction and bought another suitcase. We had the luggage situation organised; we only needed our tickets now.

Two days later we went to pick up our passports, we could leave the country with a 3-year re-entry visa. We didn't write about it to our parents; it was just for our security. We had the feeling we would come back eventually to live in Australia but we had to give living in Germany a fair chance, even if it was just to please our parents.

Once we had our passports, we went straight to Qantas and booked our flights. We knew it would be expensive, but nothing we could do about it. At least we could tell our parents we would be back in March, or to be precise; we would leave Sydney on the 4th of March at 4:30 pm and arrive in Frankfurt on Saturday the 5th of March, at 9:45 am, and finally, arrive in Hamburg at 11 am. The tickets were $640.00 each.

The other cost would be for shipping two metal trunks. We called a transport company, Kuehne & Nagel; they would pick up the trunks on January 15 and ship them to Germany for $150, inclusive of insurance. The ship would be in Hamburg on the 7th of March. A great weight had lifted off our minds.

Trying to fill up our car, we found out there was a petrol strike in Sydney. There was still no petrol the next day, but not to worry, everything on our to-do list was ticked off. There was nothing else to do other than to relax, and relax we did.

At nights, we were sitting in the lounge room watching old movies on television presented by Mr Television himself, the great Bill Collins. Julia loved him, or should I say, she always cracked up laughing the way he presented Hollywood films. She couldn't get enough of it.

Most mornings, we strolled to Bondi beach, pretty much just across the road. In a few days, we would drive to Narooma, and even though, it was work related, we saw it as an extension to our holidays.

We also met up with Jens, Bernd's friend. He worked as a therapeutic massage practitioner. I squeezed him for information, as I had looked at a few books and was thinking I might want to learn massage as well. It would work well with providing nutritional advice and reflexology.

Chapter 24

And Time Stood Still

Petrol was available, the strike was over, and we had a full tank again. We made one last trip to the city centre, to the General Post Office to pick up our mail and set up mail forwarding to Narooma.

After finding somewhere to park, we walked over to the post office and collected our mail; one letter was from my mother. It was relatively light; she usually wrote more than five pages. I thought I would have a quick look to see what this letter was about.

How is it possible that one's life can change completely from one second to the next? I read the words but didn't understand what they meant. "Schatz," I called out to Giselle and read her the first line of my mother's letter. It was addressed to me, and me only, which had never happened before; Giselle was always included. *"Lieber Dieter, du wirst deinen Bruder nie wieder sehen, er ist tot."* No warning, no gentle leading into it, just the brutal truth spelled out in one sentence. – *"Dear Dieter, you will not see your brother again, he is dead."*

It couldn't be; I was stunned and couldn't think. Giselle started crying whereas my brain seemed to revolt. Everything slowed down around me, sounds became muted and the voice in my brain increased; *'My brother is dead.'* "It can't be," I said to Giselle. "How can it be true? He is only 33 years old."

We sat down on a bench and finished reading the letter. My brother had died on 26.11.1976. He had been playing soccer and finished early as he didn't feel well. He drove home, and as he opened the door to his unit, he collapsed right in front of Heike. He had a heart attack and was dead. His funeral coincidently was on 3.12, the day we received my mother's letter.

We felt utter helplessness; we couldn't do anything; it was unreal, a nightmare. I thought if we could throw away my mother's letter, we wouldn't know and everything would be fine, as it had been only a few minutes ago. Now, life had changed and no amount of positivity would make a difference.

I felt like I was having an out-of-body experience or dreaming, and if I just could wake up, it would all be good. Giselle was holding me close. Slowly the realisation set in, my brother had gone, and we were here in Australia and couldn't help our parents, or Heike and Marco. If we were feeling drastically disturbed, overcome with sadness, how bad would it be for them?

"It's strange," I said, "Nothing has changed in our physical reality, everything is fine here and if we didn't know, it would still be fine. The difference is only one letter." I was rambling on while Giselle was holding me.

One minute we were happy and excited about seeing everyone in Hamburg again, and now it felt like we didn't even want to go back to be confronted with the cold and heartless reality of Herbert's death. Tomorrow we would drive to Narooma and work as if nothing had happened.

It took a while for us to think straight. We slowly walked back to the car, still bewildered. Back at Bernd's place, we packed up our belongings to be ready to leave the following day. I was in remote control; the body knew what to do while my mind was absent.

Bernd came home, already in party mood, but we had to tell him. He tried to console us and we understood there was nothing much to say. We asked if we could make a couple of phone calls to Germany. "Yes, sure, go ahead, no need to ask," he said. We knew it, of course, but felt we had to ask. It was a good time for calling; it would be 9 am in Hamburg.

I called my parents first, "Hello, hello, can you hear me," the usual start of an overseas phone call. It was my mother, she didn't say much and I wasn't much help, only repeating myself, "You have to be strong, just be strong, we will be home soon and will help you. Just be strong. We have booked our flights. Be strong, I am sorry we can't come home earlier. You need to be strong," I kept repeating.

I wasn't sure how much my mother understood; the connection was not the best.

"We are just getting dressed to go to the funeral," my mum said. They had to go.

"Bye Mum, bye Dad, we love you, be strong, we will be home soon. Give our love to Heike and Marco." Click, and that was it.

My mother said one more thing which I found odd at the time: *"Herbert hasn't even seen our new curtains."* It seemed so out of place, but on reflection it was understandable in the light of the shock and dislocation of the ones left behind and Mum's expectation of proudly showing Herbert the new curtains would not happen. Suddenly, inexplicably, he was gone.

Giselle rang her parents next. They were also preparing to go to the funeral. They sent their love.

Those phone calls and telling Bernd about my brother's death made it more real for me. And now Julia came home, and we talked about it even more.

It didn't get any better with talking, but one was somehow preoccupied. Julia mentioned it would be good for us to throw ourselves into work once we arrived in Narooma.

Yes, we had to keep ourselves busy. I was feeling so sad for my parents. I knew I would be coping; I had Giselle by my side. My parents had only themselves which was not enough. My dad had suffered depression previously and would be devastated. Their own recovery from the loss and grief was dependent on them being strong and providing support for Heike and Marco. And maybe to a small degree, they would be reassured by our promise to be home soon.

Our brains slowly fired up again. "When we get home, we should get married straight away which may lift their mood," I proposed. It wasn't an actual proposal; Giselle and I already knew we would be getting married; it wasn't a question. We always talked about everything and made up our minds together. We would write in our following letter that we were planning to get married in March.

We left early, saying goodbye to Bernd and Julia straight after breakfast. We had talked to Tino on the phone; he wanted us to meet in Batemans Bay, about an hour's drive from Narooma. He had opened a new amusement hall and a milk bar in Batemans Bay and several machines had to be repaired on the spot. This arrangement was fine with me; working would take my mind off my brother's passing.

•••••••••

We arrived in Batemans Bay at lunchtime. Tino was thrilled to see us and we were greeted warmly. He invited us for a coffee at his friend's milk bar. We told him about Herbert. He was visibly overcome with sadness; there was no need for him to express his empathy, "I am so sorry" was all he could muster to say. I think people who are older or have children feel empathy and share their sadness much easier than younger people. For a parent to lose a child would be the worst nightmare. Jenny and Tino had four children and Tino had siblings and felt the shock of death profoundly.

"You don't have to work, have a few days off and settle down," he said.

"No, thanks, Tino; I'd rather work and keep busy; let me get my tools."

Tino showed me two pinball machines and a jukebox with problems. It wasn't much, and I could fix them without needing any spare parts.

We drove on to Narooma. It felt like home and everything was prepared for our coming. Jenny noticed something was wrong and we told the whole sad story again over another coffee. Having drunk so much coffee, we were well stimulated, slightly shaking, but probably feeling a little better with all the attention we were receiving.

They showed us the caravan Tino had acquired for us; it stood close to the kitchen in their backyard. It was modern, immaculate and had plenty of space. It had a fridge and a gas stove, plenty of cupboard space, and even a wardrobe. Yes, we could live there quite comfortably.

In the afternoon we had surprise visitors. Bob and Joan were staying at the caravan park close to Tino's amusement hall. They were sitting at the milk bar waiting for us, such a pleasant surprise. Naturally, we had to let them know about my brother and how sad and strange we felt. I think all the talking, the activities and outpourings of emotions helped me start breathing again. Unfortunately, Bob and Joan were leaving the next day to their new destination. It would have been nice to have them around for support. We regarded them as our Australian parents; they had kind of adopted us.

It was already late when we unpacked our car and shifted everything into the caravan except the empty metal boxes.

I felt I would be all right, I had no right to be too sad; my sadness would not even count compared to the catastrophic sadness my parents, Heike and Marco were suffering. For them, Herbert's death was more than sadness; it was devastation. In our case, we could live as always; we could have our dreams and goals and go on as if nothing had changed. We were also too far away to feel the full impact of what happened.

During the next few days, we established our day-to-day routine. It was fixing or taking a machine into the workshop for a total overhaul. If nothing much had to be fixed, I was serving behind the milk bar.

Giselle had the opportunity to work at next door's restaurant or in town at the motel, cleaning rooms or serving in the restaurant. However, like the year before, it depended on tourists and bookings.

On Giselle's days off, she decorated the amusement hall and painted the windows again with Christmas motifs. We did everything to keep busy.

I thought a lot about Herbert; it was like our whole childhood replayed in my mind. I was also puzzled I couldn't feel anything in my mind or body that my brother was no longer on this earthly plane. Having immersed ourselves into spirituality while living in the bush, I had the belief I should have felt something. Maybe a departing message, even a dream, would have been sufficient to satisfy my present beliefs. But there was nothing.

My brother was six years older. He was my big brother, someone who looked out for me when we were kids. On an emotional level, we were very close. The mental aspect, love and respect for each other came later in life. I remember one incident; I would have been three, when Herbert found a bullet in one of the bombed-out bunkers. We were home by ourselves and he hit the bullet with a hammer, shooting himself through the leg. I cried more than him and he calmed me down before asking a neighbour for help. He often came to my aid when I was in some kind of strife.

I listened to him as well; when I found my grandmother, with her head in the gas oven, I was in shock. It was not a pleasant sight or experience for a kid. When my brother came home late at night, I started to let go and cried. Herbert told me to stop crying, and I did and never cried again for decades.

All those memories were rushing through my head and working for Tino was more than work now; it was my escape valve.

One night, I went into a deep meditation to contact my brother. It seemed to work; even so, one never knows if it is all imagination. I must have meditated for more than half an hour when in my mind I saw Herbert slowly walking toward me. As he came closer, smiling at me, I asked questions but whenever I asked something, he faded away. If I stopped asking, he came closer. I wanted to know how it was on the other side or wherever. After trying a few times, he gave me a last smile and faded away.

The next day, I felt better, more relaxed and concentrated on my work. Tino's truck had been loaded with a few pinball machines and other arcade games the night before. Everything would go to Batemans Bay. Some machines needed fixing, and new ones had to be installed. At lunch, Tino shouted a Chinese meal at the golf club and afterwards, we worked past 6 pm. Getting back late, Giselle and I played pool with Tino's older kids, which we did most nights.

The first week in Narooma had passed, Christmas was getting closer, and we thought someone might want to buy our car before Christmas. We hoped to get $1300, the same amount we had paid two years ago but we would be happy with $900. Car prices had gone up.

Whenever we had spare time during the day, we smartened up the car, added a touch of paint and made it more presentable. The demographic for our car was young surfer guys. Even if it was fake, the car looked sporty and the yellow colour with black trim made it look fast. The plastic pretend turbo air vent on top of the bonnet made it look even faster and the racing floor shift gear completed the fake picture.

We gave ourselves another week before we considered hanging up a note on Tino's amusement hall window that our car was for sale, with a photo, of course.

Tino had the truck ready for another machine delivery trip to Batemans Bay. He had a bad knee and it was my turn to drive the big truck, though I didn't have the licence for it. I had never driven a truck, and I wouldn't say I liked it much either. Anyhow, we arrived safe and sound. Unloading and setting up the machines didn't take long. There was no other work; all other machines were working well.

At night, Giselle and I looked after the amusement hall and milk bar from 6 pm to 10 pm. We had the faint idea to maybe open up an amusement hall in another seaside town. The money seemed reasonable and the main work was at night and in the holiday seasons. It would give us time for our creative pursuits while earning enough money to live on. A milk bar could be extended to selling Giselle's paintings or the jewellery we wanted to create. On the other hand, we were not sure if a little seaside town was our preferred lifestyle. We also had a yearning to live in the country, with the idea of being self-sufficient, having a large organic garden and living by selling surplus vegetables, creating jewellery and paintings and possibly photography and selling stories and photos.

While having those ideas, or rather dreams, we realised everything we dreamt was in Australia rather than Germany. If we talked about Germany and living there, it was about starting my repair business again which I knew I wouldn't like for long. The truth was we were deliberately setting ourselves up for failure as an excuse to return to Australia with the blessings of our parents.

It was only a few days before Christmas and Giselle had to work many more hours. It was non-stop work for everyone, even the kids worked in shifts behind the milk bar, and I helped in the milk bar at night and made repairs during the day.

During those hectic holiday times, Giselle had lots of late work. Also Tino asked if she would be able to do a sign-writing job for him. He needed four new advertising signs. Two signs were for Batemans Bay and the other two were for Narooma, one of those was "Office Rooms for Rent." Tino had built a first floor on top of his existing amusement hall, which he wanted to rent out as offices. A lawyer already rented one office which we found amusing. A lawyer on top of an amusement hall seemed slightly seedy.

We didn't have time to offer the car for sale before Christmas with all the work activities. We thought it wasn't a good idea anyhow. None of the tourists would buy it and they were the ones flocking to the amusement hall.

Christmas was a quiet affair which we liked; we needed a rest. Jenny and Tino were invited to a relative's party, but we declined their invitation; we preferred to be on our own. That year, we didn't feel like Christmas. We had received Christmas mail from our parents, and late in the afternoon, we closed the curtains in our caravan, lit a few candles and read our mail. It was sad, but we still felt happy within ourselves. It may be true that money doesn't make one happy, but it can help. In both letters were generous money gifts which would help us with our new start in Hamburg. I had written to my parents not to send money, they should keep it for themselves or for helping Heike and Marco, but my mum had still sent $50.

We still couldn't get used to the low profile New Year's Eve celebration in Narooma. Like the previous year, we went with Jenny and Tino to the golf club. And like the previous year, thirty minutes after midnight and after a quick dance, the club closed its doors, and we went home to bed. And so it was the year came to its sad end.

· · · · ● · ● · · ·

1.01.1977 – Saturday – New Year. It was the first day of the New Year, the town had woken up, and the hall was chocker block full of tourists. Tino's family, including me, pitched in, and Giselle was working at her two jobs flat out every day.

As busy as we were, our thoughts focused on what we would do in Hamburg. Our minds were already in Hamburg; we needed our bodies to follow.

I wondered if it would be possible to start my business again. I had written Christmas cards to former clients out of curiosity to judge the responses. Slowly but surely, we received one letter after the other. Some voiced their disappointment, not about me leaving Hamburg, but that I had sold my business to a complete loser. I recognized this was why some of them had not paid what they owed me.

Other letters were encouraging. Herr Schramm had written a long letter; he wanted me to start as soon as possible. Apparently he didn't trust anyone else except me. We had received many similar letters and felt validated about the possibility of starting the business again. Giselle even suggested doing an accounting course and being the manager, sending me out for repair jobs while she would do everything else. We were quite enthusiastic about the whole thing. Amazing how fast we could change our minds.

One of the most informative letters came from Herr Rehbein. He owed me a few thousand dollars. He had paid only a fraction of it to my parents. Part of his payback was in the form of alcohol. Obviously, my parents didn't store those spirits; they were all consumed with our blessings.

According to Herr Rehbein, Peter, the owner of my business, worked reasonably well but he became less reliable as time went by. The final breakdown happened in February 1975, seven months after he bought my business. Part of the business was buying poker machines and selling them to clients. So far, so good, the downfall, however, was he couldn't handle the money. He had received payments for the machines but had not paid the wholesaler which resulted in having over 40,000.00 DM in his account. Maybe he was an addicted gambler already. In any event, he took the money to Hamburg's red-light district, started gambling and lost the lot.

Naturally, it was one reason I hadn't received any more payments. This sad story didn't end there. Dear Peter had the keys to all the machines he was looking after. Two hundred keys, all labelled, with names and addresses, and constantly updated when new machines were installed. Those keys could not be found anywhere, even when the police searched the workshop; he either lost them or sold them. The clients had to change the locks on their machines. No wonder they didn't hold me in high respect; even so, I could not have foreseen those problems. I had trained him for all aspects of the business but not for gambling addiction.

Herr Rehbein was looking forward to me coming back and so was Herr Schramm, who urgently wanted to have a holiday and wanted me to look after his business. On top of those two clients, I knew a few more who were interested; it was enough to start the business again with Giselle's help.

・・・・・・・・・・

We had to be in Sydney on 17.01 to deliver our two metal trunks for shipping. We were sorting and packing. The sorting part was the fun part. The aim was to sell everything we didn't want to take back to Germany. Giselle had sold T-shirts, dresses and even a pair of shoes to her co-workers at the hotel and restaurant. Whenever Giselle came home at night, I was waiting in suspense to hear how much money she had sold the items for.

Finally we had put up leaflets, 'Panel-van for Sale.' We started with an exorbitant price of $1600 to see if we would get any responses. The other value items for sale were our two guns. We wouldn't need those and wouldn't be allowed to take them into Germany anyhow. I also wanted to sell my guitar and Tino would give me good money for some of my tools.

We had received a letter from Ralph and Ute. They had been trying for a baby for a while, and finally, Ute was pregnant. They had booked a flight back to Switzerland for March.

Everyone was flying home. Gerd and Heike, our friends from Brisbane, also were on the way back. They booked to return by ship as the last holiday before commencing a new lifestyle in Austria.

・・・・・・・・・・

Jenny and Tino's kids were still on school holiday and I had taken Ricky under my wing. He was the second youngest son and had problems learning to read and write. He could read individual letters but couldn't string them together. I was sure he had dyslexia, but there was no special teacher in Narooma to support him. I taught him the basics to fix pinball machines. He was already better at soldering than Tino. He also, maybe intuitively, understood the concept of electricity and which connections were needed to make something work.

However, the critical aspect was that he felt appreciated and taken seriously. I worked with him most days during January. His sudden interest to learn must have come as a surprise even to him. By teaching him, I noticed when I explained specific words on an electrical diagram, he remembered them and could read them by the structure of the word, like a picture. We were sure Ricky could be taught to read if someone had taken an interest.

Anyhow, the rush was on to get our trunks packed in time for Sydney. Tino interrupted our urgent mission. He had a request, would it be possible for us to stay until the second week in February? We agreed readily; it would allow us to make a few more dollars.

Once he had left, we finished loading the trunks. We had a good feeling; everything was well packed to survive the long trip. Tino's two older boys helped us carrying the trunks into the car, ready to leave the next day.

We left Narooma at 4:30 am; it was still dark. By 5:30, the sun was rising; the roads were empty and we had made good progress. By 10 am, we arrived in Sydney. I had to buy spare parts for Tino at the company where I had worked in early 1975. I said hello to the guys; they thought I was looking for my old job back before I enlightened them.

The next stop was Kuehne & Nagel, the transport company. We received a pleasant surprise; it was cheaper than the quotation. It was a German company and even the guy who did the bookwork was German; maybe he gave us a discount, it was only $125.00 including insurance.

We drove to the Qantas office to pay for our tickets. We should have paid before, they had a price rise, and we had to pay 10% more. We were not impressed.

We could relax now. The only possessions we had left were our hand luggage, a suitcase and the car. We had booked the car for a full service and a roadworthy certificate to be able to sell it. We slept at Bernd and Julia's place and picked up the car the following day with all the proper papers.

We left Sydney, stopped in Batemans Bay, fixed a couple of pinballs and arrived In Narooma late at night. We dropped into a deep sleep until we were woken by Tino knocking on our door. He needed me to fix a couple of machines and had a letter for us. It was from Ralph and Ute; everything went faster than they thought. They had sold their car in Brisbane with their camping equipment and would fly home on the 27th of January from Sydney. They beat us to it, being home earlier than us. They would move in with Ralph's mother.

We were happy we would be able to move back into Giselle's unit. It was still let out, but the couple who lived there would move out by the end of February, giving our parents a few days to clean and hopefully fill the fridge with yummy food and Champagne.

That night, before Giselle went to work, I quickly played a few tunes on my guitar before saying goodbye to it. Giselle had sold it to her boss at the restaurant. Our caravan home looked empty.

When I opened the amusement hall the next morning, a young guy was waiting to get in. He wasn't interested in playing games; he enquired about our car. He had seen the leaflet in the window. I had to compose myself not to show my excitement. Would we be lucky to find a buyer so quickly?

I locked up the hall and showed him our panel-van, parked at the back of the hall. His eyes lit up; he loved it and did not attempt to hide it. He was a 19-year-old guy living in Narooma. Perfect!

Giselle had seen us and came out as well. "Darling, can you open up the hall? I am taking someone for a drive to show the car," I said. And off I went, driving the young guy around Narooma. We stopped at the beach, and after he had shown me his driver's licence, I explained the racing gearshift and let him have a go.

He wanted the car so badly he could hardly contain himself. There was, however, the small matter of money. He didn't bargain or even mention anything about the price. He simply did not have enough money but declared boldly it would be no problem; his mother would make up the difference. However, there was another slight problem, his mother was on holiday in Hong Kong but would be back in Brisbane by the 28th of January.

"Could you talk to your mum before then?" I asked.

"Yes, she calls me every night; I will explain everything to her," he said.

"OK, you let me know when you know more," I said.

"Sure, I'll call you tomorrow," he replied.

It was fantastic news, except for those minor problems attached to it. I rescued Giselle from her temporary milk bar duties and told her the good news. We promised ourselves not to get too excited and continued with our workday duties.

The next day came and went by without hearing anything from our new friend. After we hadn't heard from the young fellow (not a friend anymore) for two more days, we buried our hopes. He called on the third day, he wouldn't be able to raise the money.

"Thank you for letting us know," I said, letting him down easy. We were tempted to lower the price, but something told me he wouldn't have bought it anyhow. I was sure his mother wasn't happy about her precious young boy buying a panel van. Everyone knew what guys like him would be doing in that car.

We changed our tactic, we would approach second-hand car dealers directly. We knew panel-vans were hot properties and car dealers were keen to have one in their yard. They wouldn't give us what we wanted, but it would be an easy and quick sell.

The tourists slowly disappeared, giving us more time to visit car dealers. They were interested but didn't want to part with their money. We would wait until we went to Bateman's Bay where car dealerships were much larger.

Tino had more pinball machines he wanted stripped and readied for a complete overhaul. Each machine took two days to be stripped, overhauled and put back together again. Ricky was still on school holiday and it was an excellent opportunity for him to learn and give me a hand. Giselle helped by covering the cleaned playfield surface with a clear plastic liner and painting jobs.

Tino needed me for Batemans Bay a few days later and I took our car to ask car dealers if they were interested in buying. The first stop was Moruya, the first dealer was not interested, but surprisingly enough, the second dealer offered $1000 cash in hand. I didn't show my excitement and told him I still had to go to Batemans Bay for a job and I would let him know on the way back.

I called Giselle from Batemans Bay although I wouldn't be able to sell the car that day. Tino's windscreen had been shattered and he had to leave it to be fixed. We decided to accept the offer, as long as the dealer didn't mind about us needing the car to drive back to Narooma and come back to him by Monday.

On Monday, Tino and I went back to Moruya. Tino went to get his car and I went to the car dealer. He was glad to see me. He must have needed our car; maybe he would have paid more. Never mind, I signed over our beloved panel-van. I gave it a pat on the bonnet and said, "Thank you for driving us a couple of times around Australia." I left the car dealer's office with a bundle of $50 notes in my pocket.

Business had slowed down; Tino didn't even bother to open the hall before 4 pm. The season was well and truly over but Tino was adamant we should stay a couple of weeks longer to overhaul all the machines he had marked.

Jenny and Tino had to go to Sydney for a couple of days, undoubtedly another reason he wanted us to stay longer. We felt confident as provisional amusement hall operators. We took it seriously enough; even though we knew there wasn't much to do. Every day we opened punctually at 4pm and closed at 10 pm. We drank more milkshakes than we sold and played pool for the rest of the time.

We were ready to leave Narooma behind us. A few more days of applying the final touches to Tino's machines, including polishing them with Mr Sheen. Tino missed us already and worried about how he would survive the next season without having me on standby.

Countdown - 26.02.1977 - Saturday. We woke up early; excitement in the air. The night before, we had dinner with the family one last time. Tino thanked us for all we had done for him and his family. We returned our heartfelt thanks: "Thank you, Tino, we wouldn't have been able to travel for two years without you."

A last look around the caravan, ensuring we hadn't forgotten anything. When we stepped out of the caravan, Tino had his car ready. We loaded our suitcase, hand luggage and said goodbye, trying hard not to get emotional. Off we went with Tino driving us to Sydney.

We were nostalgic; only a few days left in Sydney, and we would leave Australia - would we ever return? The trip was a leisurely affair. Our first stop was in Batemans Bay. Tino said he needed a coffee but we thought he wanted to make sure his machines were working. We arrived at Bernd's place in the afternoon, in time to sit in the backyard having a beer with the neighbours. Tino loved the convivial atmosphere. What was not to love? Young people were having a good time, and Tino joined right in. At night we took Tino out for dinner. It was shortly before midnight when we finally arrived home. We slept in Julia's office. Tino slept in the spooky room but we had removed the candle. The next morning we said our final goodbye to Tino and went straight for a long walk on Bondi beach, feeling melancholic. It was the end of an important episode in our lives.

Before we left Australia, we had to freshen up on our tan. After all, nothing is more important in Germany than to show up looking like you had just arrived from an expensive ski holiday. We had to show off somehow in case our adventure was not sufficiently valued.

The same afternoon, Elle, a distant relative of Bernd's, arrived on his doorstep from Germany. She would stay for a few weeks. Where would she sleep while we were still residing? It had to be in the spooky room. Hopefully, the ghost liked her and nothing terrible would happen. When she mentioned hearing voices and feeling a bit strange, no one said anything.

Monday was not a preferred day for a 'leaving Sydney party' but it had to be done and Giselle was cooking. We went to our favourite shop at Bondi Junction and bought ingredients for that last dinner. It had to be a German meal, not because we wanted it, but because it was the overriding request from our guests. It also had to be easy enough to pull off for 12 people. We bought premium mince for preparing a 'Falschen Hasen,' which in English terminology was a meatloaf and we ate it with vegetables and potatoes. Shopping and preparation took us the whole day. Actually, I shouldn't even say 'us,' as Giselle did all the hard labouring.

The last meal and the party was a huge success. It happened around a large dining table and the diversity of people made for great conversation. And it wasn't idle talk; there were engaged discussions about conspiracy theories, interwoven with politics, switching to music and the best record ever, and back to what is better, nuclear or solar power.

The gathering could have been called a United Nations party. There were the neighbours sitting in for Australia, Netherlands and Sweden. Julia was English and she brought a business friend from Ireland. An American guy and a jolly Mexican outperformed us all, judging by voice volume. And there were four Germans, Bernd, Elle, Giselle and me who were well accustomed to having deep discussions. Everyone was participating in the seriously deep, often frivolous or hilarious discussions. No one showed any ill feelings, even if views attracted a lot of contra or laughter.

I made my voice heard in regard to nuclear power. I was against it; I was sure the problem of waste and possible fatal disasters could never be avoided. I was in favour of solar energy. The American agreed wholeheartedly but was too grounded in reality. His counter-statement was, "Dream on, baby; it will never happen. As long as money can be earned from coal, oil or nuclear, they will not go for solar." I often thought about this statement and how long it took before solar eventually became feasible.

The going-away party had brought reality into the foreground. The fact we would leave our beloved Australia caused a sudden sadness. We were happy to be going back to Germany and seeing our parents. Between the sadness and happiness, we felt melancholy, excitement, and stress, even a fear of never being able to return to Australia. Sometimes we even felt resigned, with thoughts of settling down in Hamburg, getting a job, and relaxing.

The following days were filled with beach walks and sunning ourselves, interrupted by trips to the city or long walks to Bondi Junction, including a couple of more lunches at our favourite Chinese restaurant. We went to Bondi Junction a few times. We loved the new shopping centre; it had everything we enjoyed; record stores, bookshops, and a good café.

Coming back to Sydney in 1977 was like the city had been reborn especially for us. Coffee had become mainstream and we could hang out, buy a book, go to a café, read, talk while drinking freshly brewed coffee, have a cake, and, yes, eat it too.

The Bondi Junction shopping complex also had a movie theatre. I still remember one of the movies we watched during our last week in Sydney, 'The Goodbye Girl,' with Marsha Mason as the Girl, and Richard Dreyfuss, who received an Oscar for Best Actor. We loved that movie, and of course, we loved the happy ending. Some movies need a happy ending.

Finally, the waiting was over, our tan looked impressive, and we were ready to take that step back into the future, a new future in the old country. And for the first time, Giselle and I were unsure of what the future had in store for us. We had spent endless hours talking about it and had all kinds of ideas and visions but they were all of the uncertain type, a mental space where anything could happen. We knew we could do it; we had such a solid relationship, now even more strongly forged by having lived in the smallest of spaces for the longest of times. We knew one thing for sure, we belonged together, in body, mind and soul.

The day before we left, we met Gerd, a guy we had seen the last time in Bondi before going on our road trip. He had been to Germany and had arrived back with a purse full of Deutsch Marks. What a coincidence, we had all our cash dollars, and we seized the opportunity to cut out the middleman, the money exchange. We levelled the exchange rate and had now more Deutsch Marks than expected, and Gerd had more dollars.

Chapter 25

Back in the Old Country

Bernd and Julia had driven us to Sydney's Airport. On the way into the Customs zone, Julia called, "I will visit soon." The last wave and we were gone. The flight went by with hardly a memory left until we arrived in Frankfurt, in a cold, sterile, and what felt like hostile German correctness.

Nothing was specifically bad; we were overreacting to surroundings we were not used to anymore. The German language sounded harsh and impersonal. People were dressed in greys and browns, increasing the bleak atmosphere.

We had landed in a vast, busy airport in a strange and cold environment. Giselle walked behind a woman dressed in a beautiful fur coat, and she touched it which would have been OK in Sydney but not in Frankfurt. The woman was enraged and reacted accordingly with harsh words and icy looks.

Giselle sobbed, "I want to go back." I felt the same, the difference in atmosphere was palpable and we felt its impact. The short flight from Frankfurt to Hamburg helped to compose ourselves and get back into a positive mood.

Landing in Hamburg felt like coming home. We had stopped freaking out and were looking forward to taking our parents into our arms. We collected our bags and walked out into the arrival hall. There they were, our parents, Heike and Marco. Can one look both happy and sad at the same time? There hardly was anything left of Heike; she had lost weight, was dressed in black and looked broken. My mother was dressed in black, looking lost and utterly sad, and my dad wore a black armband on his jacket and had tears in his eyes. Giselle's parents looked sad, reflecting the overall gravity of what had happened.

It hit us like a brick. We couldn't escape the sadness and the reality of what had happened. It was as if my brother had died again, only this time for us and we felt heavy-hearted.

We shared hugs and tears and slowly made our way out of the airport to the car park. Heike took Marco and us in her car. My dad drove my mum and Giselle's parents and we all went straight to Giselle's apartment, only a couple of minutes away.

The apartment looked great; obviously, it was spotless, and it appeared large to us. After having lived in a panel-van for two years, Giselle's one-bedroom apartment was the ultimate luxury. We were happy to have such a 'large' cosy, beautiful apartment. The only renovation planned many moons ago was to remove the old bed and build a platform bed with shelves underneath.

But we were not thinking of renovations when Giselle and I walked into our beloved apartment; instead, we were overwhelmed with our emotions of sadness, helplessness and deep empathy.

It was the afternoon and, therefore Germany's traditional coffee time. Our mothers had prepared cake, coffee, and Champagne but we all agreed to start with a 'first aid' brandy.

Not long after, the smell of freshly brewed coffee wafted into the living room from the kitchen. The brandy beforehand and the promise of fresh coffee, cake and Champagne lifted all our spirits.

Our mothers talked first, describing how, for the last week, they had scrubbed and polished, cleaned and redecorated until the apartment met their high expectations. Apparently, and I will not repeat my mother's words, the toilet was indescribable; a chisel would have been handy for cleaning rather than a scrubbing brush. We acknowledged their excellent efforts with tons of praise, thanks, hugs and more brandy.

Marco, who was nearly nine, obviously had no brandy, and seemed the least affected by the deep sadness hanging over us. We heard from my mother that he hadn't cried much. Marco would need more time to understand and come to terms with the fact his dad would not return.

Our parents were not the only ones who were prepared for our arrival. We had a few things up our sleeves as well. Presents were in order and a pleasing way to lift the mood.

It was Marco's turn first. We had bought an original rugby tricot from a well-known Sydney football club for him. It looked cool and he liked it. Our parents and Heike received a kangaroo fur, and we had one for us as well, used as a seat cover. Giselle had her favourite rocket chair, which she had from her 'Oma,' and the fur was perfect for it. Of course, there were other presents; we had a Southern Cross Opal brooch for Giselle's mum and an opal necklace for my mother and Heike. Both dads received a tie clip decorated with an opal.

We found out more about Herbert and the funeral. While it was not a happy topic, my parents seemed to feel good talking about it.

The big elephant was in the room as well and it had nothing to do with Herbert's death. It was all about us: would we stay and live in Hamburg?

It was our cue to start talking about ourselves. Yes, we wanted to stay, and we wanted to get married straight away. Not waiting, but getting married in the next two to three weeks. The wedding announcement went well. The atmosphere became lighter; there was a touch of happiness in the room. Everyone was involved in working out the earliest possible date, and we settled for the 18th of March.

We also revealed we would try starting my business again, explaining I would do the manual work, and Giselle the bookwork.

We knew those steps would help our parents believe we wanted to stay. We were not telling lies; we tried to convince ourselves we could do it. Only if our efforts failed would we go back to Australia for plan B, our dream to buy a house with some land and live a self-sufficient lifestyle.

It was getting late and we were tired. Having lightened the spirits of all attending, it was time for us to relax and get used to being back in Giselle's apartment.

We slept like babies. Waking up was an experience in itself. We were disorientated, but after a few moments and seeing aeroplanes taking off and landing at the nearby airport, we knew we were back in Hamburg.

We craved a German breakfast. I ran down quickly, or rather, let the lift do the running and went to the nearby supermarket to get fresh, crusty and delicious smelling bread rolls and 'Aufschnitt,' small goods like pepper salami and other meats. Our parents had stuffed the fridge with lots of goodies but we needed fresh German bread rolls.

What a glorious feeling, we had our first breakfast while sitting in front of the large double window with views of the airport.

No time to lose, breakfast was our favourite time for planning, and despite the jet lag our brains were in overdrive. First of all, we needed to buy a car, some clothes and other necessities, and get ready to be married. The car was the most essential to be able to get around for shopping, visiting people and driving to the local council to book the date we wanted for our wedding.

How long did it take to buy a car? We knew where to go for second-hand cars and it wasn't far. The same afternoon, we had a car, a little Opel Gemini. We saw it, we liked it, and we bought it.

We had our little secret reasons for wanting the wedding early. One could call it calculated, but there were certain benefits to getting married. Giselle wanted to start sewing and needed a sewing machine, a perfect wedding gift. Another reason was married couples paid less tax than single people.

In Germany, people also paid a church tax, starting from the moment one earned a taxable income. To stop paying the tax, one had to exit the church, which we did; we didn't feel like paying tax for belonging to a church.

We had decided on a small private wedding. Giselle's dad stepped right up to the mark and announced without hesitation he would pay for the lot. We would choose a restaurant to our liking, and I can't remember why, but we wanted to eat 'Bambi,' Rehbraten or in English, 'deer.' How could we?

Having a car made everything easier. We were zooming around like there was no tomorrow. One of our stops was at the nearest council office responsible for our suburb. They were supportive and friendly, even showing us the room where the little wedding ceremony would happen. The 18th of March was free and we booked it on the spot. It would be a civil marriage ceremony, signing papers, with our family present.

We drove to our parents to show off our little car, it added to the reassurance we were staying for good.

Next on the list was to visit Giselle's grandmother. Giselle loved her, but I hadn't even met her yet. She had been lying in a nursing home for a few years with severe hip and leg problems. She was over ninety years old. I couldn't even imagine how one could live that long just lying in bed, more or less waiting to die. She didn't even have a television, not many visitors or activities other than reading and sleeping. I felt sorry for her but was enormously surprised by her resilience when I met her.

We drove to the nursing home, which was close to where my parents lived. She was so pleased to see us and beamed with happiness. And she was funny, alert and talking well, not at all what I had expected.

She didn't seem depressed about her situation, or at least she didn't let on. She clearly loved Giselle, and after looking at me for a while, I received the approving nod, with an appropriate comment about the way I looked, with my long hair and beard. "My Heiland," she said, which meant Jesus, my Saviour. "You two will have a very happy and long life," she predicted. Giselle had told me about her grandmother; she could see into the future, laying cards for people. One story was that she laid out cards for Giselle's older sister which was also the day she stopped reading cards. She never revealed what she had seen, but clearly, it couldn't have been good. Giselle, of course, kept pestering her to read the cards for her and one day she did. She smiled and only said Giselle would live a very happy life.

We were both happy to hear our happy life being reconfirmed but were shocked by her next question and statement.

"Will you have children?" she asked, looking straight at us.

"No, Omi, we don't want any; there are so many other things we want to do," Giselle answered.

"I waited for you to come back and to know if you wanted children. Now I can die," was her short and matter-of-fact reply. She didn't seem to mind too much and asked us what we wanted for our wedding present. We told her Giselle wanted to learn to sew and needed a sewing machine.

"I will give you one for your wedding, but you have to buy it, and I will give you the money."

We were still stunned by her comment that she 'could die now' and, therefore, were slightly subdued in our happiness at receiving a sewing machine.

She touched my face and said, "My Heiland has come," I had been confused with John Lennon before but never with Jesus. We kissed Omi goodbye and left for a shopping centre opposite the nursing home.

Our target was Karstadt, a department store and part of the large shopping centre. We found a very knowledgeable sales lady who explained the different sewing machine brands, their pros and cons. We still had no idea which brand to get and settled for a pretty orange one.

Having picked what we wanted, we shopped for books, coffee and cake. German cakes are the best, at least for our accustomed taste buds. We never found a cake we liked in Australia; most were too sweet. Would we stay in Hamburg because we liked the cakes and bread rolls?

We continued shopping for clothes and shoes; we had to look civilized, no more cut-off jeans and wearing thongs. However, we settled for a pair of worker's jeans for each of us. We liked them; they were in fashion and called Latzhosen or overalls in English. For buying our wedding outfits, we went to the city, looking into well-known boutiques and fashion houses. I found a trendy black suit, a white shirt, and a nice tie at a Thomas i-Punkt shop. It took longer for Giselle; she knew what she wanted but finding it was another story. Finally, in a small boutique, there it was, a hot red little number, beautiful, stunning, and sexy at the same time. We would look pretty cool on our wedding day.

All that was missing was booking the restaurant. We had found the one we were looking for; it meant driving there, checking their private function room and booking the venue.

The next day we drove to the area where the restaurant was located. We picked it for its old-world charm; it was as beautiful as we remembered it. All it needed was an old fashioned butler walking through the door to greet us. It wasn't a butler who welcomed us but a waiter dressed in black with white gloves. He showed us the private dining room; it was fit for a king. We loved it and discussed the menu and the serving order. That didn't take long either; we booked it, paying a deposit, with the rest to pay on the day.

Only one week had gone by, and we had already achieved the most urgent bookings and arrangements. In between those time-consuming tasks, we had also spent hours on the phone.

I called my past clients and people who owed me money. The main person was Peter, the guy who had bought my business; I hadn't been able to talk to him but managed to find his address. He owed me over DM10,000. We would be home free if we could retrieve even some of this amount. A similar amount was due from clients and past friends who had bought but not paid for my furniture, stereo equipment and other items.

I was sure most people believed we wouldn't come back. Bad luck, we were back, and we needed the money they owed. We didn't want to worry about retrieving our money before the wedding but we had to let them know we were coming for it. Our tactic was to be friendly and upbeat, and judging by the phone conversations we had, it would be successful.

There was a girl I urgently wanted to get hold of, and as lovely as she was, she didn't pay for my stereo equipment and we wanted it back. She sounded happy to hear from me and had no hesitation handing back the Hi Fi equipment. Giselle and I showed up at her door; she invited us in, we had a lovely talk and a drink, and at the end, we relieved her of our stereo equipment.

Giselle had her own stereo system but now we installed my system. It sounded fantastic but was way too big for such a small apartment.

We created a new plan and the next day we implemented it. We drove to our favourite shopping centre, to a B&O – Beomaster - music shop and traded everything we had against a new B&O quality system. The record player was exquisite, the speakers outstanding, and so was the rest of it, the tuner and the cassette player.

•••••••••

There is an old German custom called 'Polterabend.' On the night before a wedding, relatives and friends sneak up to your front door and smash porcelain for good luck. The groom opens the door, welcomes the guests and cleans up the mess. We wanted some of this good luck tradition.

Considering the size of Giselle's apartment and the fact we had not yet contacted many friends, we only invited two couples.

One was Rolf who had become a good friend and support for my parents. I met him when I was 17 and a keen visitor to Hamburg's life dance clubs. We hung out together for a couple of years until I moved on to different venues not frequented by Rolf. He eventually married, had a child, divorced, and at the point of our polterabend, had been together with a pretty young lady for a few weeks. We invited them and we were sure they would be the right people to smash generous amounts of porcelain. The second couple was Rudi and Sabine. I knew Rudi from night school and we had stayed in contact.

The smashing porcelain business was not that easy. Just one plate would not be sufficient for good luck; one needed a mountain of the stuff.

Those two couples didn't know each other. The important thing was they had time and could come on short notice and didn't owe me any money.

Giselle's best girlfriend would have been a good addition but she lived in London.

The day of the polterabend had arrived. It started loud enough, but we were well prepared and had covered the entry door and surrounding walls with cardboard to avoid damage.

Rolf and his girlfriend arrived first and they did at least five minutes of severe porcelain crashing. They were allowed in and were rewarded for their efforts with Champagne. We hadn't met Rolf's girlfriend before, a happy, fun blond girl, eight years younger than him.

While we were drinking and talking, we could hear more smashing. I had, of course, fulfilled my duty as groom to be and cleaned up the mess but left the box with the broken porcelain standing outside – a big mistake.

We opened the door, but no one was there. We were only greeted by broken porcelain. I quick smart cleaned everything and took the rubbish inside. As soon as we had done so, there were more crashes, and this time, it was Rudi and Sabine. We were happy; the smashing was over, we stored the luck we had received for when we would need it, and went on partying, eating, drinking and being merry.

Ten minutes later, there was some more smashing with no one showing up, and the noise went on for another hour. Some of the neighbours must have been alerted and took the opportunity to get rid of their old porcelain. Thank you.

Rolf, pretending to go to the toilet, sneaked out and tipped out what I had cleaned up one more time for good measure.

We celebrated until midnight before we put a stop to it, making sure we would be fresh enough for our big day. It was a happy night, helped by the drinks, our candlelit room, the aroma of the food and desserts and with us talking about our adventures and our guests filling us in on what had been happening in Hamburg in the two years we were absent.

We had noticed lots of changes; in politics, music, new restaurants and clubs while others regrettably had closed.

We had also noticed more police on the road, apparently looking for members of the far-left Baader-Meinhof gang. My dress code and hairstyle had attracted some comments and suspicious looks which we couldn't understand at first. After a week of watching and reading the news, we noticed what was going on in Hamburg and throughout Germany. I still had my long hair and beard, and my jeans and t-shirt outfit probably didn't help either. I was shaken by an incident when I was walking back to my non-suspicious, boring beige Gemini from shopping; two police officers stopped me, armed with machine guns.

"Step away from the car. Put your hands on the bonnet," one officer said. I couldn't say anything; an instantaneous fear response must have paralysed my voice box. After the officers checked for weapons, but were disappointed not to find any, they appeared more relaxed and I found my voice.

"What's going on?" I asked.

"Papers, please," was the answer. After a few minutes, the officer handed back my identification passport and the car ownership certificate.

"Everything is fine; sorry for the inconvenience," he said and off they went.

Later that night, we heard on the news they were looking for a guy assumed to be in Hamburg. It wasn't me. I trimmed my beard to a more respectable look, hoping not to be bothered anymore.

With my beard trimmed, I was now ready and acceptable in society, and could be married.

Friday, the 18.03.1977 started with the alarm going off, ensuring we did not sleep in. The sun was shining into the living room. We had our breakfast at the window, still in our underwear. No one wants food stains on their wedding dresses. After a hearty breakfast, the day could commence; we were ready as ready could be.

Thirty minutes later, we looked at our reflections in the mirror of the entry hall cupboard. A bit of self-appreciation goes a long way.

"Wow, you look fantastic, and very sexy if I may say so," I said to my darling wife-to-be.

"Thank you, you may," Giselle responded, "You look pretty hot as well."

Time to go. A taxi was so obliging to pick us up and drive us to the council office, but not before we had picked up a flower bouquet from a florist for Giselle to hold. We went out of the car, striding the remaining distance to the council office entry, where our parents and Heike and Marco waited for us. Rolf was busy filming.

It was time to go up to the celebration room. It was a reasonably large room, we could have invited more people, but it would have meant providing a party for all. We had Herbert's death in our minds and a big party was not called for.

How were my parents and Heike and Marco feeling? One could see they were trying hard to keep a happy face. Our thoughts and feelings were distracted by the impact of our ceremony and the concentration to say yes at the right moment, but it seemed to be over in about one minute.

Congratulation and hugs, a big kiss for Giselle and we were downstairs again, waiting for Heike's car to pick us up. My dad took Giselle's parents in his car. Rolf was driving behind us, filming the cars departing from the scene.

Rolf may have been disappointed not to be invited; after all, he had provided support for my parents while we were in Australia. Be that as it may, we thought it was better to be a family-only event.

We drove to our lunch destination; our planning had worked well, and everything was on time. The Restaurant Rundel had been in the Rundel family ownership since 1840 and we loved the stylish decor and atmosphere; it could have been a setting for a movie.

Our room was lavishly decorated with flowers, and 'class' was oozing from every corner. We were led to our place at a large oval table. Each high back chair was comfortably upholstered and an artwork in itself.

Starting with a toast to wish us all the health, wealth and happiness in the world, we, as the bride and groom, answered by saying thank you and also how we were happy to be back in Hamburg. We were not lying; we were happy to be back with our families. Those feelings didn't exclude our dream to go back to Australia.

Slowly, over Champagne, soup and the main course of deer roast, the mood lifted. Heike had a cheeky present for us; unwrapping our gift, we found crocheted baby booties filled with DM 5.00 pieces. Money was our preferred present; the baby booties were the cheeky addition and not on our agenda. Our parents each gave us an envelope with a card and more welcome cash. Everyone seemed happy; a lighter mood slowly came over us.

Our celebration meal ended with a Black Forest Cake and coffee. On the way out, Giselle's dad picked up the tab. He looked happy; he was proud he could provide such a luxurious experience for our special day.

The celebration didn't stop there. We drove to Giselle's parents' home where we continued to party. And yes, being in a private, cosy, and relaxed atmosphere, it started to feel like a party. Towards the evening, there was no sombre mood anymore. Everyone was laughing and sharing funny stories. There was even singing and both dads showed off their skills on the mouth organ. It may not sound like much but it reflected a very happy intimate and beautiful togetherness.

We went home by taxi late at night. Arriving at our doorstep, I carried Giselle into our apartment before we consummated our legal obligation of marriage. We were aware of the precarious tradition of some religions, the requirement that there must not be any contraception; however, as we had left the church for monetary reasons, we considered ourselves free from any obligation. Heike's gift, the baby booties, would not be occupied in a hurry.

Waking up and proceeding to have breakfast, we remarked we felt exactly the way we had felt the last couple of years; happy and in love. To be married had left no visible or emotional impact. It was more a case of now that's done, let's move on; we need jobs or the re-opening of my business to sustain us.

We didn't want to disturb anyone on a Sunday but come Monday morning, we pulled out our list and started calling people for either money retrieval or checking if old clients would consider becoming my new clients.

For fun, Giselle also checked the Saturday papers to look for possible jobs. She thought working in a boutique and being involved in decorating and designing the look of a shop could be a suitable role for her. We took notes and addresses; we wanted to look at the boutiques first before Giselle would make her move.

I managed to book a few appointments to see people who owed me money and a couple I wanted to talk about getting back into the amusement machine business.

A couple of days later, we had our first success. One client, Torsten, had given me his first instalment, and promised to pay the rest within the next four weeks. To keep him happy, I quickly fixed one of the broken jukeboxes he had in his garage. I didn't charge him and I think it was the trigger for him to part with his money.

He had been employed initially by one of my clients who tragically was killed in an attempt to rescue someone lying on the street on a rainy, stormy night. He stepped out of his car to check, and didn't see the fallen power lines. He was electrocuted when he touched that person and was found lying next to the first victim. The result of this most unfortunate incident allowed Torsten to take over part of the business.

I also met with Herr Rehbein. He was pretty frank about his unwillingness to pay but offered to pay us in spirits. In other words, he became our drug dealer. We started with a selection of fine wines, whisky, rum, brandy and gin.

The next appointment was not as happy but revealing. I met Hans, a mechanic I knew from when I wanted to sell my business. He had been one of my preferred choices and had been keen to start his own business. He was more cunning than I had given him credit for. He waited on the sidelines and slowly picked up my clients as Peter went downhill with my business. I didn't like what he had done but was appreciative he had come clean and told me what was going on. Another two guys I knew had done the same. The situation right now was that quite a few mechanics worked freelance. They worked out of their car and garage which resulted in fewer overheads. Hans had a final message, direct, but delivered in a friendly way. Everything worked well within the present amusement machine industry, and a newcomer would not be welcomed.

It was clear he meant me; no one would help or support me to get back on my feet. Still, he must have liked me and gave me a the names of people who might need my help. That's what I did next, I called a Herr Westak, and he knew of me and was keen to meet. He had worked for himself for the last couple of years, mainly in Hamburg's red-light district. He took me to a bar the same day where a topless lady greeted us. He fixed one of the poker machines and asked the lady behind the bar to show him his favourite porn movie. It was funny; it was a cartoon style orgy with well-known Disney characters performing unspeakable acts. I was driving around with him for the rest of the week and was reacquainted with the amusement business scene and with what I knew already, I didn't like it, to put it mildly.

After my week looking into the current state of the industry, Giselle and I decided that I would definitely not embark on self-employment in that industry ever again.

It was time to contact our many former friends; we made sure to mention our ample alcohol supply. They were only too happy to visit, even if it was only for a typical German coffee hour get together, followed by moderate alcohol consumption.

Our first post-wedding guests were Mark and Karin. They knew we were keen to write and publish a book and Mark offered to set us up with his photography agent who also represented artists of different modalities. It sounded promising.

Another friend we invited was Norbert with his girlfriend Sabine. Norbert was a friend from a time before I met Giselle, and he was another guy who trained karate with Mark. He also played the guitar and we all liked Ry Cooder. Health was another topic we liked to discuss; he had a medical perspective studying medicine.

And, of course, there was Susie, the girl responsible for the Christmas party where Giselle and I first met. She was together with Stephan, one of Bernd's old friends. They had planned a party for us in a couple of weeks and wanted to invite all kinds of old friends. We were not even sure we liked the idea; there were some people I wasn't keen on meeting again.

We laid down our new goals for the coming weeks. The first decision was not to go ahead with creating our own business. With this possibility out of the picture, we decided not to stay in Germany which was quick and came as a relief because we were already having nightmares we were trapped and couldn't go back to Australia.

We knew we couldn't let our parents know yet; we hoped over time they would notice we were not happy and were yearning to go back to Australia.

How could we earn enough money to go back to Australia and buy a house and land? We quickly needed well-paid jobs. We had driven around Hamburg and looked at boutiques. One boutique in a fashionable suburb was looking for a staff member matching Giselle's criteria.

It was as if Giselle had made the job materialise. We had visualized how and where it could be. And, as if by magic, exactly where we thought it should be, it was. At that time, Giselle was not ready to apply as she had no papers or recommendations with her; but she still walked in and asked to talk to the manager.

The owner, a woman in her thirties, was attending her boutique on that day. I was waiting outside and through the shop window I could see the ladies talking in an animated manner. They must have clicked because Giselle took dresses off the hangers, arranged them into different configurations and even placed a bamboo stick into the window with a dress hanging on it.

Not much later, Giselle came out; "I got the job; it's great; I can treat it as my shop, decorate and design it the way I want, and hopefully sell lots of dresses." A kiss was in order, and we walked to a cafe around the corner to celebrate.

Giselle would start the following Monday. The money was good, the working time not so much, 10 am to 6 pm but she was looking forward to earning money, and me doing the cooking.

Now it was my turn to find a job. I had someone in mind, a family business. Their name was Mendig; I knew Frau Mendig senior and had previously fixed jukeboxes for her and her son. This time, I was interested in her son's business; he, his wife and a partner had at least ten play halls, similar to amusement halls but concentrating on poker machines. I hoped he would remember me. But first, I wanted to try another reputable firm, a wholesaler with a repair shop. The firm was Reider, my former wholesaler; I had bought a lot of poker machines from them. I made an appointment; they wanted to see me the next day. It sounded promising; maybe Giselle and I could start new jobs on Monday.

Friday morning, I turned up at Reider's. I was greeted in a friendly way by Herr Reider and the repair shop manager, the accountant, and the general staff manager. Maybe I was more important than I thought.

We talked for fifteen minutes about Australia before they gave me the third degree. The only thing missing was the water torture. They had one question after the other, all having the same focus of trust. Could they trust me to stay in Germany? I tried to weasel my way out; I didn't want to lie to them. But as they were getting more serious, I was getting more relaxed and started to laugh. Needless to say, it was the wrong move. They made me wait outside their office for a while before giving me their final ruling.

As I suspected, they would love to have me for a senior role in their company but they felt I would return to Australia. I couldn't blame them. I drove back home to tell Giselle.

We had a relaxed weekend, driving around Hamburg looking at places we knew from three years ago. One place was a shop and we wanted to see if it still existed. It was located in a suburb close to where I used to live,

To our surprise, it was still there and looked the same as it always had. It was a health food shop specializing in macrobiotics, called Schwarzbrot, meaning black bread. We were keen to return to a healthy natural diet and continue studying natural health.

We bought nearly half of the shop, brown rice, of course, as the stable of the macrobiotic diet. They also had many different herb teas, several types of miso and tofu, organic vegetables, and even cakes and bread. We bought a few books as well, mainly about nutrition and herbs, iridology, homeopathy and reflexology.

On Monday, I took Giselle to her work by car. I kissed her goodbye and wished her luck on her first day. She would come home late; we roughly calculated 7 pm when I would have the dinner ready. I would be the cook, preparing our macrobiotic meals.

I spotted a phone booth close to Giselle's workplace and called the next business on my list, Mendig. "Is this the right number to get in contact with Herr Mendig?" I asked.

Yes, it was the correct number, and I could hear the secretary saying, 'A Herr Luske for you.'

"Herr Luske, what can I do for you?" I heard you are back. We talked for a while before I asked if there would be a job for me. He said 'yes' and wanted to see me straight away. I knew where he had his office, at the back of a large play hall, close to the central train station in Hamburg. It took me only ten minutes to see him in person.

Entering the hall, I felt like a participant in a crime movie. Next to the entry, someone was sitting minding the premises. He must have been waiting for me and pointed to the back of the long hall. I passed many rooms separated by plexi glass panels, each room occupied by two poker machines. The hall was dimly lit, which added to the movie atmosphere. Who would be behind the door; would I meet the big crime boss?

No big crime boss here, only Herr Mendig, his wife, his partner and the secretary, busily counting money. Crime after all? No again, they were counting the proceeds from the poker machines, probably the weekend takings. Counting and rolling up coins was one of the occupational hazards of the industry. People have suffered from repetitive strain injury from all this counting and packing coins into paper rolls.

Frau Mendig was the outstanding character; she looked like an out-of-work Hollywood movie star, with lots of gold jewellery and wearing a fur coat.

The first thing Herr Mendig said was, "We are getting a coin counting machine next week." It sounded like an excuse why they were still doing manual labour.

Herr Mendig, stylishly dressed, was very keen to have me on board. As I found out later, he was looking for a mechanic but having difficulty finding one he could trust.

Why was trust so important? Mechanics had full access to the money on every machine they maintained. I had earned his trust when I had my business and I was conscientious and whatever I did was totally above board.

What followed was swift: Herr Mendig agreed to take me on and I agreed to his terms and generous wage. He also hinted there might be bonus payments for emergency call outs or openings of new halls. I would start working the next day. He asked me if I would have time to drive around with him to see all his halls, the workshop and the storage facilities for old and new machines. "Yes, I've got all day," I said.

As I expected, he drove an excellent big Mercedes with all the comforts such a car offered. It had a telephone, a bar, and Persian carpets on the floor. Our first stop was around the corner, an ordinary multi-storied residential house where he owned a first-floor unit. It was supposed to be a workshop, but it was stuffed with broken machines of various types, shelves with useless parts, workbenches covered with I don't know what, and finally, a small semi-clean space where Herr Mendig's other mechanic was trying to fix something. He introduced us, "Herr Siemers will let you know about our working routine; I will be back in fifteen minutes," and he left.

"What is happening here?" I asked Herr Siemers. He explained he would love to turn the mess into a proper workshop, but he never had the time. He continued explaining about the hectic work schedule. He had threatened to resign if another mechanic was not employed. We planned to make the unit into a proper workshop and dropped the formal German way of addressing each other, using our first names instead. His name was Harald, and so the Harald and Dieter team was established.

Herr Mendig arrived back and handed me a list with addresses of all the halls, and we set off in comfort to visit one after the other.

Each hall was different, depending on the suburb and the people who frequented them. The hall we came from, the one with the office, was slightly elegant, with dim lighting and yellow coloured plexiglass between the rooms and it even had chandeliers. Other halls were simple and well lit, with various degrees of decor.

One thing they had in common; players were treated well. The manager would walk around and offer coffee or soft drinks to regulars and even snacks. Some people came every day to lose their money. It was pretty sad to see, particularly in poorer suburbs.

At night, Giselle and I couldn't stop talking. Giselle was happy with her job; it was easy for her. She had already re-designed parts of the shop and sold some dresses. Travelling by underground to and from work was boring and a waste of time but it couldn't be helped. I needed the car to get to my work, and drive to different places before driving back to the office to pick up the firm car. Harald and I were provided with a small box-type station car, a Peugeot, which was handy for transporting poker machines.

I took advantage of the firm car in the coming days and bought the timber for our platform bed. I know it's a bit naughty but I often did private shopping while driving to the different repair jobs. I told myself Herr Mendig wouldn't mind as long as I did my work to his satisfaction. I had already introduced Harald to some of my repair habits. Whenever we attended to a machine, we quickly cleaned the glass inside and out and replaced broken light bulbs. We made a huge difference to the look of the hall; even the Mendigs had noticed. They were happy and even encouraged us to suggest more improvements.

It also happened one of the halls was close to where my parents lived. I often dropped in for a quick coffee to make them happy and keep me awake.

The platform bed turned out to be a "real beauty," to use an Australian expression. I used all my hidden skills of timberwork (which I didn't know I had) to build the frame, shelf and hinged platform.

Happy with my creation, Giselle swung into action with her exceptional design skills. She knew how to cover everything with fabric. She used corduroy; without showing any visible signs of how it was stretched and fastened. The new-look niche with the inbuilt platform bed had transformed the unit. The shelf under the bed was filled up with books and knick-knacks and a few glass-framed photographs completed our unit makeover.

In between my working hours, I contacted former clients and managed to extract money out of them bit by bit. It wasn't easy, and we were not mean buggers, but I knew my 'Pappenheimers,' which is a German expression meaning, "I knew that lot." In our case, it meant we knew they had money but didn't want to part with it.

A couple of guys owed money for furniture but they were clearly unable to pay. They had moved to different addresses without my precious furniture. To get them out of our minds, we told them to "forget about it" and were rewarded with a heartfelt "thank you."

There was, however, still Peter; he owed us big time. We knew his address; it was not a nice suburb. We hoped he would be home when we tried to track him down one Saturday. We drove into the low-class housing estate, found his unit and rang the bell. Someone opened; it was his wife, with two little kids looking from behind her. I never had met her before.

"Is Peter home?" I asked. "Could I talk to him?"

She turned her head and shouted, "Peter, ... for you"

Peter appeared; he recognized me instantly, took a step back, recovered his poise and came to greet us. He didn't invite us in; he came out and closed the door behind him. It wasn't a good sign.

He lived in a building where each unit was accessed from an outside staircase. We stood outside, leaning against the staircase railing and listened patiently to Peter's version of his downfall. It was pretty much what we knew, only slightly embellished not to sound too ghastly. However, the result was the same; he was declared bankrupt. I looked at Giselle, there was no reason for us to talk, and no, we were not that good with telepathy; it was apparent we would never get our money. I had checked all the figures and Peter owed 11,500.00 Deutschmarks. We would have loved to have the money back in our possession, but no such luck.

I asked him if he had taken anything out of the repair shop. I knew there were many valuable items. There were a couple of pinball machines, one 'AMI Continental' jukebox and about ten amplifiers for various jukeboxes. Amplifiers are often too hard to fix at the venue; I used the spare ones in exchange, then took the broken ones into my workshop where I had the appropriate instruments to fix them.

I started to build up hope again.

"Yes," he said, "I took a lot of stuff out; it's all here in my storage room in the basement."

I hardly could believe my ears. Peter went inside and picked up a key and we followed him down to the basement. Even he seemed more confident as he unlocked his storage room door.

My heart dropped a couple of feet; I couldn't see anything worthwhile to sell.

"Where are all the amplifiers?" I asked, "Didn't you take the jukebox?" No, he must have grabbed a few boxes of virtually nothing. I picked out a couple of chrome emblems for an AMI jukebox as a souvenir.

After that, we didn't expect anything anymore; but we didn't want to make it too easy for him. We asked him to send us money whenever he had a few dollars, even if it was only $50. He agreed and promised to do that.

"Is there anything you could give us now as a first instalment?" I asked, without any expectation whatsoever. To our surprise, he produced DM200. We were stunned and hardly needed to say thank you but we did, "Thank you, keep it coming."

On the way back home, we changed our plans. There wasn't any way we would allow this setback to depress us. We decided we would stay longer in Hamburg than planned to save up the money we needed to buy our dream property in Australia.

In a way, we were happy; we had our money retrieving action behind us. We refused to worry any longer about Peter.

Marco, my nephew, had his birthday party in early April and our little family came to celebrate. It was a lovely afternoon which was not as sad as expected. We bought him a model aeroplane. I promised to help build it, but I can't remember if we ever did. Heike and Marco lived far away from us, and we didn't see each other as often as we would have liked.

We were busy, but I found time to book a silver craft course. We couldn't wait for our first lesson; the course started in late April. We also had sorted, numbered, and titled hundreds of slides most nights and handed them over to Mark's photographic agent. The agency was interested in Australia and promised to pitch our slides and possible short story to magazines.

We had sold some photos already to Stern magazine. We had a meeting and they liked our slides and picked a few and probably would buy more in the future. They paid handsomely. There was, however, an opportunity on the horizon; they were interested in my work. They had scheduled an article about poker machines and needed background stories and photos. They asked if I could take my camera to work and take photos, particularly of broken machines. The following day, I added my camera gear to my toolbox.

A play hall had been broken into that very night. There are times when one has to make the best of a bad situation. The police had departed and it was my job to inspect the damage, take out the broken machines, replace them with new ones and clean up the mess. I couldn't have ordered a better photo opportunity. I must have done over 100 shots. The 'bad guys' came through the toilet room window and smashed their way into the main hall where they left a mess of broken machines and empty cash boxes. They must have been interrupted; out of about 30 machines, only the first nine were broken. I didn't rush to Stern magazine; I wanted a greater variety of photos first.

Finally, and more than a month after our arrival, Susie's big party went ahead, with us as the main attraction. It started harmlessly enough, a couple of drinks, finger food and catching up with old friends. We had a good time bathing in the limelight, and Susie did a fantastic job inviting a wide variety of people. Then, slowly and progressing over the next couple of hours, the conversations changed from harmless and friendly to attack mode. We were amazed at what we learnt about certain people that night.

At first, we didn't notice, we thought some people were asking strange questions and slowly it dawned on us: some of them felt attacked by our presence, by what we had done, and how happy we were. Only close friends mentioned they would love to have the courage to leave everything behind and start an unknown future. Most of the other people thought we were irresponsible and didn't do anything worthwhile for Australia's society during our two-year stint.

We could have countered with arguments but could not foresee any fruitful outcomes from those discussions. Instead, we moved away and talked to the more relaxed visitors. Giselle had fun catching up with her old girlfriends and those old neighbours of mine were friendly and interested to hear about our adventures.

With the party out of the way, we promised Susie to meet up again soon. She knew how to handle a sewing machine and Giselle wanted to get some tips. Wouldn't it be a proper married couple activity, the girls sewing and the boys drinking beer?

Even so, we needed to save money; we saw any expenditure as an investment in ourselves. The silver craft course had started, and we loved it. Both of us took to it like fish to water. I had most of the skills already from my practical work experiences and Giselle from being involved with interior design and decoration.

Giselle knew how to swing a hammer and came up with great ring designs. The course was well structured right from the word go. The first session was all about the material, tools and how to use them. Exhilarated, we finished the first class, talking to other participants on the way out. One guy stood out, he was tall, taller than me, had long blond hair and looked like he was on our wavelength. He was a wholesaler for Red Indian Silver craft, often travelling to America to buy silver to sell in Germany. His wife had a pottery in an arty suburb, close to where I used to live. They sounded like an exciting couple to get to know better. We had lots of things in common; art and creativity, travelling and we were all against nuclear power, a prominent topic at that time in Germany. "Nuclear Power – No Thank You" was a popular slogan and sticker.

My work was shaping up well. I had initiated opportunities for my colleague and I to attend lectures whenever a new poker machine came on the market, great for getting a day off work on full pay. Herr Mendig was sceptical at first but I convinced him it was necessary to learn about the new machines. Those lectures were suggested to me by no other than Herr Reider, the company boss who didn't hire me. He was happy I was with Mendigs and hoped I could encourage my boss to always buy from the Reider Company. We received our first invitation to a one-day poker machine seminar not long after. Food and drinks were provided and even special tools for those new machines.

Talking of interruption, one of the ongoing problems with poker machines were fake coins. It not only affected one place; it affected the whole industry. We had two such events simultaneously; we hardly knew what to attend to first. A coin from an Eastern-bloc country fitted into the machines, mimicking a $1.00 coin but was only worth a couple of cents. It started innocently enough. We noticed a few of those coins when we fixed machines. After a few days, the news went around; everyone had the same problem. The "fakers" fed the poker machines with fake coins, pressed the payout button and received real coins. It took about two weeks before we found a way to adjust the coin slots to stop those coins and trained hall managers to spot this kind of play behaviour.

At the same time, or maybe a week later, other fake coins made their appearance, skilfully manufactured masterpieces of metal with a razor blade inserted to trick the magnets. The counterfeit coin was masquerading as a $5.00 coin. That's pretty serious money. It took us a few weeks to get that under control.

I saw it as a photo opportunity, taking pictures of fake money spitting out of those machines. I had my photos and my story; the question was: would my work be good enough for Stern Magazine to buy?

I had a great job; driving around Hamburg and no one checked where I spent my time. The bosses were happy with my work; they even commented the business hadn't run so smoothly for a long time. I had the freedom to play photographer while working, and to top it off, about once a month, we had a day off for a seminar with good food.

And, there was more; I had discovered a few rooms used as a storage facility located next to a play hall belonging to the Mendigs. I couldn't believe my eyes. Four rooms, plus a kitchen and bathroom, were stuffed with old poker machines. Herr Mendig was highly apprehensive about letting go of those machines. He worried 'naughty people' could use them to figure out how to cheat.

I had a different idea and it could be a good one. And there was every chance it would make me some money.

I contacted Herr Westak. I knew he was looking for old machines to sell to faraway countries. He had just come back from Dubai of all places and he desperately needed more poker machines to sell. I had no idea how he had established such weird business contacts, but I couldn't see any harm in it; it wasn't as if he was an arms dealer.

Setting up a deal between Mendig and Westak was the perfect solution for all parties concerned, me included. Westak would get his machines and Mendig would get rid of them without fearing it could backfire.

I told Westak about those hundreds of machines and he was instantly happy. The next step was discussing costs and my percentage.

The next morning, after the regular meeting at the office, I asked if I could talk to the boss. I said I had a friend who wanted to buy as many of his old machines as possible. I hardly finished my sentence before he interrupted to say he was not interested. I knew that would happen, of course. I continued undeterred, "He will overhaul the machines and sell them in Dubai; they will never see the light of day in Germany again." He looked at me; I could see his brain working; after all, he was a clever businessman. It seemed like an eternity before he answered,

"Let's do it."

The deal was done. I called Herr Westak from the office, setting up a meeting. Ten minutes later, it was all set in motion. Herr Mendig was happy; he mentioned there would be a bonus for me at the end of the transaction. '*Thank you, most appreciated.*' I didn't say it; I thought it; I knew I was double-dipping.

Over the next couple of weeks, I saw those old machines disappearing. Herr Westak was always smiling when I saw him. Mendig had no storage worries any longer. He, too, was a happy fellow and looked favourably in my direction.

・・●●●●●・・

We visited our parents in an alternating pattern as often as possible. However, we had to spend more of our precious free time, including weekends, helping Giselle's parents to move into a new apartment. Giselle's dad had reached the proud age of retirement. He received the obligatory watch as a thank you for his long committed service but they had to vacate the company apartment.

Naturally, we helped with decorating, painting, wallpapering and moving. Good kids as we were and skilled in the essentials of home decoration, we turned the apartment into what Giselle's parents aspired to. Nearly everything was new; the jewel in the crown was the living room, one could say; no money was spared. Everything was new, all classic robust Renaissance, Gothic style German elements which would have made any monarch proud and certainly evoked proud feelings in Giselle's parents. Once the apartment was completed, it was a showpiece, with many little extras to express their individuality.

Now, it was time to concentrate on fulfilling our dreams.

We invited Mark and Karin to thank them for setting us up with their agent who had a couple of magazines interested in our story. Having our story published and well paid for would remove the urgency of writing the book we had always planned. We also succeeded in selling more photos to Stern, including the poker machine ones.

Giselle enjoyed her work. Her boss, Frau Gartig, would let Giselle sort out new fashion ranges and invited Giselle and Marion, a co-worker, to her apartment to be models for a private fashion show. It was a large arty furnished apartment and two friendly dogs kept the men entertained while waiting for the show to commence. Giselle and Marion were putting on dresses and reappearing as models. Champagne and finger food accompanied the fashion show. Whenever most of us agreed on a dress, it would be selected to sell at the shop.

We became good friends with Marion and Hans, her husband, and often met for coffee. Hans worked as a stage-set designer and painter at Hamburg's well-known Hansa Variety Theatre, the epitome of vaudeville in Germany for over one hundred years. Many famous people performed there over the years, including Hans Albers and Josephine Baker.

Incidentally, we were in for a treat; as part of the Mendig's staff Christmas party, we were invited to the Hansa Theatre, and afterwards for nibbles and drinks at a 5-star exclusive Hotel - a classy affair.

Mark & Karin had asked us to come with them to Berlin; Mark had a job, taking photos in East Berlin. Another photographer friend, Bernd, would also come. We had never been to Berlin before, let alone East Berlin behind the big scary wall. To get to West Berlin, one had to drive through the border to East Germany and travel for two hours before reaching East Berlin, to cross the border again into West Berlin.

It may be partially forgotten but West Berlin was the democratic island within East Germany. In whatever direction one went within West Berlin, one would hit the wall. It was unbelievable something like the wall ever existed. I remember as kids at Christmas, everyone in the West would put a candle in the window to shine a light of hope to the East German people.

The following weekend we took off; five people in Mark's iconic VW Kombi bus. Coming closer to the border, we felt a touch of uneasiness. The East German border force could be unpredictable. They may not let you in, or once in, there was the fear they would not let you out again. We were given access and received instructions not to stop anywhere until we arrived in East Berlin. We drove right through; there wasn't much to see anyhow. Houses, roads and everything looked like time after World War Two had stood still.

The same impression continued in East Berlin; everything was old, buildings were not repaired, and one could still see bullet holes in buildings everywhere.

Another frightened moment was crossing into West Berlin; it took a while; they had a good long look at the VW bus and made sure we were not hiding anyone. They were puzzled about Mark's passport. They seem not to know New Zealand. It took a while for them to confirm it was a legitimate country, and we were allowed to enter.

We drove around for the rest of the day, seeking out the most prominent attractions, like the Brandenburg Gate. I would have loved to walk through the Gate to get the feel of being connected to a different time in history; King Frederick Wilhelm II commissioned the gate in 1788. The late 17th-century Charlottenburg Palace was our next stop. It was the primary residence of German royalty for decades. Time to visit friends of Mark's, where we would stay the night.

The Brandenburg Gate

Next morning we took the train to go back to East Germany, again being checked at the border crossing. For Mark, it would be a working day, the rest of us trotted along, carrying his gear or handing him lenses and fresh films. Finding something to eat was nearly impossible, and if there was something, it didn't agree with our taste buds. But the museums were outstanding, particularly the Pergamon.

Mark was in heaven, and we were his angels who carried his heavy camera cases. There were quite a few tourists, even American and Russian soldiers, who wanted to have photos taken together. Who said 'selfies' were a new development?

We looked at many other attractions, including the famous Checkpoint Charlie and finally ended up at the Kurfurstendamm, where we had something to eat before we went back over the border, drove to Hamburg and escaped the East alive.

Checkpoint Charlie

Monday and back at work, Herr Mendig must have felt confident with the way the business was running. But I was perplexed as to why he waited so long before telling us he was opening two new halls. He told us at the last possible moment; maybe he didn't want to scare us. Now we were scared! We had to stock two new halls with poker machines and pinballs, open on Friday night for guests, and on Saturday for the public.

"This week?" My question hung in the air for a while; maybe it was considered a statement.

"Yes," Herr Mendig finally answered, "all invitations are out."

"It's not enough time; we can't do it. Even transporting all the machines will take a day, let alone installing them," I objected.

"We will all help, and we will work day and night and there will be free food and drinks and a bonus at the end."

Did I hear bonus? I started to get excited. "We better get going then; hopefully, we don't have to do any other repairs." I said.

Herr Mendig had thought of everything, "Repairs will be stopped and shifted to the following week. You will transport the first load of machines and start installing them while we keep bringing the rest."

I phoned Giselle to let her know I would be home late, probably past midnight, about the bonus and that I would be late all week long, "Love you, darling, see you for breakfast."

I hurried to help load machines into my car and took off. We managed to make it in time, and yes, there was free food; I never had so many sausages and chips in my life. After the first two days, we demanded better food, received chicken and chips, and washed it down with Coca-Cola. I worried my stomach ulcer would reappear but all went well. It was fun to make a combined effort and even see the boss in his "Boss suit" doing some manual labour, wearing gloves.

Frau Mendig pitched in as well; she was the money provider. She came with bags full of coins needed to fill the machines.

Friday night at the opening, we were sipping Champagne, and that was it; we were allowed to go home and sleep. We had to be on call for Saturday.

I received my bonus, and even better; my wages were increased without asking. Giselle had good news as well; the Gartigs were talking of opening a new boutique. They wanted to be right in the middle of the city in a new shopping complex which was opening soon. It would be even more up-market than trendy Poeseldorf. They hoped to open in November to take advantage of the Christmas season, and Giselle would be the store manager and receive a wage increase.

Things were certainly looking up; we could save enough money for a house in Australia. We were constantly adding to our high yielding savings account. The interest rate was 8% or even more at the time.

In the meantime, we had become fine little silver crafters and completed a few pieces of jewellery. The class was only once a week and we had decided we would keep going as long as we could.

Frank had become a good friend, and we loved Haniga's pottery. All four of us were creative and politically engaged. There was an election, and with the combined force of us four, we voted for a new party, "The NO Nuclear Party," maybe it was a forerunner of the Green Party. Needless to say, they didn't stand a chance against the biggies.

I was not on a comfortable footing with general politics. I was sure our political system had done a lot of good, but looking around the world, it hadn't solved hunger, poverty, crime, drugs, or aggression. In the seventies, we were inundated with bad news about nuclear war. Pollution was also a big topic and had been for a long time.

Julia, Bernd's girlfriend, also had a strong sense of activism which involved doing something about pollution, nuclear power and her main topic, feminism and equality.

She was on her way to England and wanted to do a quick stopover on her way back to Australia and to see us in Hamburg.

It was late autumn when she arrived; the days were getting shorter. Hamburg looked at its best, with golden, red and yellow autumn leaves and more romantic-looking canals than Venice. The visual highpoint of Hamburg is the Alster, a lake in the middle of the city, with a backdrop of stately buildings and churches. No high-rise buildings to be seen; luckily, parts of the inner city survived the war which could not be said for the rest of Hamburg. During the war, the Alster was camouflaged by dragging a painted tarp over the lake, confusing the bombers.

We took Julia everywhere; we loved showing off our city. Every visitor wants to see Hamburg's red-light district, the famous Reeperbahn, where the Beatles found their edge. We asked Norbert if he would have time to come with us; we offered to pay for everything.

We picked him up mid-morning, introduced him to Julia and drove around many beautiful suburbs ending up in Blankenese, an affluent part of Hamburg, at the river Elbe and not far from Hamburg's harbour. Traditionally, it was the area where seafaring captains, wealthy industrialists, shipbuilders, and the like had their houses. It was 'the place' to live, and it was beautiful.

Blankenese is on a hillside, with the river at the bottom, terraced houses with great views and narrow passageways to walk down to the river. We had lunch at a spectacular and rather expensive restaurant. We wanted to sit outside and sat on the terrace marvelling at the river view and later about the food, the coffee, and the cake.

It was hard to leave; it had an exceptional tranquillity and a reassuring atmosphere; surely, sitting there, sipping coffee or Champagne, watching the ships pass by, nothing bad could ever happen. But we had to leave; it was time to show Julia the bad bits of Hamburg. Not terribly bad, of course, just bad enough to have a giggle and pretend we knew nothing about what was going in the song, 'On the Reeperbahn Nachts um Halb Eins' sung by Hans Albers and also a film title, translated as, "On the Reeperbahn at Half Past Midnight".

Giselle told the story about her beloved grandmother and her connection with that song, the movie and Hans Albers, the famous actor. Giselle's Oma lived only a couple of blocks away on the harbourside of St. Pauli. Every day, Oma went for a walk, and when she became aware a movie was being made at the Grosse Freiheit, starring Hans Albers, Heinz Rühmann and Fita Benkhoff, she wanted to be part of it. It didn't take long; the movie crew needed more extras which is when Giselle's Oma was cast in the movie. Her "role" was to sit in a venue as part of the audience. Yes, our family had been touched by stardom, even if it was only by 6 degrees of separation.

I had my own story of being close to someone famous, and I was waiting for the right moment to tell it. We were walking along the Reeperbahn, pointing out well-known clubs and institutions like the Police Station, an old building which had played many star roles in crime movies. Not everything on the Reeperbahn is sleazy. As a child, I went with my parents to the Operettenhaus, a performing arts theatre. Further on was the St. Pauli's swimming hall where I had my first swimming tournament, and I came in third place, and I will stick to that; even though, only three kids swam in my age group. That wasn't remarkable, but what was remarkable was I was allowed at the tender age of eight years to take the underground train and saw the light of day again at St. Pauli's train station, and what a light it was.

Julia wanted to hear more. "Did you see the Beatles when they were playing here?"

"No, I was too young, and I had no idea the Beatles were here. But a few years later, I got to know the guy who let them play at his clubs. That guy, Bruno Koschmieder, owned a few clubs and was good at converting old cinemas into dancing clubs. He also 'liked' young boys, and had his eye on me and made tempting offers which I refused. This was as close as I ever came to someone who had contact with the Beatles.

After our fill of the hardcore environment, we ventured to the 'Munich Hofbrauhaus' to have a hearty meal of sauerkraut, potato mash and sausages, followed by a half litre stein of beer. The music was going full blast, and people were dancing on the tables. What could we do? We had to join. We danced the night away or at least for half an hour, before calling it a night. We said goodbye to Julia the next day.

It looked like the stream of visitors was going to continue. Elle, Bernd's distant cousin, wanted to visit us. Her favourite band was playing in Hamburg, Jefferson Airplane, which became Jefferson Starship. It was Grace Slick she wanted to see and hear.

We bought tickets as well and went to the concert together. It was a minor disaster; Grace wasn't happy. She didn't sing at all for the first half-hour or so; she might have been drunk, hard to tell. Eventually, she did a couple of numbers. From a historical music point of view, it was still worth being there. The media wrote, "Slick's total lack of self-control came to a head at a show in Hamburg".

Elle stayed only for a couple of days and we mainly discussed social issues, poetry and art. She was a social worker in Duesseldorf, and we promised to visit her.

· · · · · • • • · · ·

Welcome to the most glorious, festive month of the year, December. Anyone who wishes to experience the whole Christmas spirit feeling should visit Germany or, as in our case, Hamburg.

The Christmas lights are switched on in December, and the impact is dramatic. It gets dark by 4 pm, which is when the magic happens.

Everything looks more beautiful, twinkly and glimmering, or is it the Gluehwein served everywhere? Shops stay open longer and the combined effect of happy shopping, Christmas markets, gluehwein and sausages was hard to beat. Can it get any better? It can, it doesn't happen every year, but if it is snowing, everything becomes even more magical. Snow creates such an idyllic fairy-tale wonderland that even the grimmest character succumbs to the Christmas spirit; if not, they need gluehwein with a shot of rum.

The best for us was still to come. We would celebrate Christmas Eve with our parents, and it would be at Giselle's parents' new apartment.

However, one week before was another Christmas Party, the big event in the 'House of Mendig.' As a party of 10, we walked from the office along the road for 400 metres to the Hanse Theatre. We could feel the excitement. Everyone was dressed up. The Mendig clan wore fur coats and jewellery, and the rest of us dressed as well as we could. Giselle and I wore our wedding outfits. Giselle obviously was the most beautiful one; no one could even come close. We took our seats and waited in happy anticipation for the show to unfold. We were seated on tables, not only as a support for the Champagne glasses but also for the food. We were invited to peruse the menu and to order at our pleasure ... and so we did.

The theatre itself was studded with spectacular Christmas decorations; the atmosphere was festive, elegant and classic. And there it was, for the first time, we saw our friend's artistic work. The stage, dividing panels and curtains had been painted with Christmas motives and themes of the acts we were about to see.

The guests' happy chatter and the cutlery's clattering stopped as the lights were dimmed. Spotlights came on, pointing towards the stage where the curtain slowly opened to reveal the host and compere for the night. Let the show begin.

And what a show it was, from trick poodles to acrobats, from magicians to contortionists, there was something for everyone. One had to like it, even if it was for the novelty and the experience of a former glory from a time long gone by.

Still, under the influence of the experience, we slowly walked, happily chatting, around the block to the 5-star hotel which was eagerly awaiting us. It was true, they were expecting us; the Mendigs had reserved a cosy corner for the rest of the night's festivities, consisting of more Champagne and finger food. We loved the hotel because we loved art deco, and its name reminded us of a time gone by, Hotel Reichshof. Classic, luxurious art deco, even if one can't afford to stay, it was worthwhile to walk into the reception area. But we did more, or should I say we were guests and therefore allowed to move into its inner sanctum. Simply being there in those elegant surroundings was enough to evoke happiness.

The night came to an end, and while driving home, we had to acknowledge and appreciate that Mendigs had done something they didn't have to do. It was a thoughtful gesture and made for a harmonious working environment.

Christmas Eve with our parents was coming closer. There would be presents galore, a Christmassy atmosphere and plenty of delicious food and drinks. But that was not the main point; rather we needed the evening to be unique, a night to remember.

We arrived at Giselle's parents' home. Walking into their apartment, we were instantly transported into a warm Christmas wonderland. We took off our coats and shoes and left those items in the tiny entry hall, separated by a heavy red curtain to keep the cool air out. Passing the entry hall ritual was like a ticket into a Christmas wonderland.

My parents arrived a few minutes later. I was still very protective of my parent's feelings and made sure they would feel relaxed and enjoy the moment.

What better way to relax than to start with a glass of Champagne, cheers and good wishes?

I could see the sadness harboured in my parents lifting as they sat down in the comfortable chairs. The table was laden with presents, all carefully wrapped. We were like little kids, looking in wonder at the gifts and waiting for the show to begin.

We had planned to stick to tradition. As kids, before we were allowed to open presents, we had to recite a Christmas poem. We had told our parents we wanted to have this tradition again but everyone had to get into the act.

My dad had brought his accordion; he played a couple of Christmas songs and we were singing in perfect harmony. My mother had her collection of Christmas poems and stories which she had handwritten as a school kid and decorated with colourful Christmas drawings. When it was her turn, she read out those poems and stories and because we didn't have anything specific, we took my mum's private Christmas collection and kept reading from it. Same with Giselle's parents; her mum recited the most remarkable poems from memory and her dad sang. He had a beautiful opera-trained voice and also played songs on his mouth organ.

It couldn't have been any better and more homely and festive, and the best part was still to come, the avalanche of presents.

I was chosen as Father Christmas and had the Santa hat to prove it. My pleasant role was to select a gift and present it to the lucky receiver, reading out the Christmas gift message which I did my best to embellish with funny comments. I enjoyed my role as "Weihnachtsmann."

On our way home, Giselle and I reflected how happy everyone was. It was probably the first time we saw my parents happy again.

Time to do what Germans do best, celebrating New Year's Eve, or as it is called in Germany, Silvester, after a fourth-century Pope.

Germany is one of only a few countries where ordinary citizens were allowed to buy firecrackers to create their own personal fireworks. As kids, we looked forward to Silvester all year long. It was our night. Finally, we were allowed to play with fire and make a lot of noise. Depending on our age, we were only allowed to buy crackers with minimal impact, not strong enough to blow up anything solid, but we tried. There were no limits once you were eighteen: super crackers, rockets, and crazy explosives were freely used.

And if one had an older brother, as I had, one would end up with some serious explosives. I am not particularly proud of it, but I had successfully blown up several mailboxes.

We had a few more traditions; one was mustard filled doughnuts. With doughnuts being the preferred Silvester snack, it probably was only a matter of time before someone had the glorious idea to fill some with mustard instead of jam. It was such an easy prank which no one could resist. When I was about 10, I had to help in the bakery to get the doughnuts baked. I had three jobs; dunking the doughnuts in hot oil, topping them with a sugar glaze, eating half of it myself, and the most fun of all, filling them with jam or mustard. Customers arrived with their orders, "20 Berliners (doughnuts) please, 4 with mustard."

For Giselle and me, this Silvester needed to be a traditional, fun one. We were invited to Rolf and his girlfriend's party and he ensured we would be exposed to unlimited Silvester fun and tradition.

We bought boxes full of fireworks, and so did everyone else attending the party. But I had much more fun and excitement when I was a kid. After setting off one firework after the other, we became a little bored. How many 'bangs' can one enjoy? Nevertheless, it was a fun occasion, and we could tick it off our list.

Chapter 26

The Final Stretch

We had decided to wait till Easter before telling our parents we were going back to Australia. Only after we told them could we plan how to sell Giselle's apartment and furniture to go back to Australia in September.

What would we do in the meantime? Working, of course. Neither of us had an extended Christmas holiday. Giselle went back a few days after the New Year, and the same for me.

In January, we had a dry spell of activities, but the silver craft course continued in February. In addition, I also finalized my Diploma of Reflexology and studied Homeopathy, Herbal Medicine, Iridology and advanced nutrition.

Silver craft was still our primary goal, and we had bought tools and silver already. We had designed a workspace we wanted to build once we had found a house in Australia. We didn't discuss our goals and ideas with anyone else. We knew certain people would probably tell us that we had 'lost our sense of reality' again. We strongly believed in visualization and projecting what we wanted, and we were sure everything would go according to plan.

Next to our visualisation, we needed facts. We were interested in hearing about Australia's property prices and wrote to Bob and Joan. We specified the approximate area where we wanted to buy a house and asked if $20,000 would be enough to make our dreams come true. They wrote back they would be on the east coast towards the middle of the year and would look around for us.

In the meantime, we were working, only interrupted by family gatherings for my dad's birthday and a month later for Giselle's dad's birthday. Those parties were always tricky as we still pretended we would stay in Germany.

We were still in contact with Ralph and Ute and planned to visit them. We didn't see 850km as a long-distance; we had a different perspective since travelling in Australia. Our friends thought we were bonkers to drive so far for a weekend. We drove on Germany's famous Autobahn, and managed a comfortable speed of about 140km/hour.

We arrived at the Swiss border, opened the side window and produced our passports. The border police must not have liked my appearance and we were ordered out of the car for further checks. I should have trimmed my beard. It didn't take long, and we were excused and allowed to enter Switzerland. We arrived in Basel at Ralph and Ute's place at the right time for a late afternoon coffee.

There was much to talk about and the main topic was going back to Australia. They had the additional responsibility of little Ken, their precious baby. He would make it harder for them to leave secure Switzerland and venture back to Australia. Ralph had found good work for himself; he was a haematologist and never had problems finding work in a hospital or laboratory.

His hobby was still very evident; their unit was crawling with snakes and lizards. It didn't take long and we had to cradle a giant carpet snake, which luckily was on her best behaviour. No need to worry; all creatures had their secured apartments, their terrarium.

I noticed he seemed to breed mice; I shouldn't have asked him. He demonstrated what they were for - turn away if you are squeamish – he fed his carpet snake, not something we wanted to see. Picking up a mouse at the tail and dangling it in front of a carpet snake will create a quick response. We didn't see that mouse again.

We were treated to a Basel tour the next day, a beautiful city. We ended up, where else, at the reptile club. Aside from meeting heaps of snakes, we met their closest friends. One couple had shifted their attention to tropical fish and specialized in this field. They wanted to go to Australia as well to open a shop and research centre into tropical fish in Queensland.

The following day, Ralph took us for a drive up into the mountains; Ute had to stay home with little Kenny. By noon, it was time to leave. We promised to meet in Australia, or if possible, in Hamburg.

A month later, after getting in contact with Gerd and Heike, who lived in Austria, we decided to meet them in Munich. We found a lovely café, just the right place to stay and talk for a couple of hours with the help of apple strudel and many cups of coffee. Gerd and Heike had decided to go back to Australia and buy a house in Brisbane. The big news was they would leave in a couple of months, way ahead of us.

We had a similar short trip to Düsseldorf to visit Elle. Düsseldorf was terrific, or it was Elle's company and what she showed us location-wise which made the city look favourable to us. We loved the art galleries, shops and cafes.

Our silver craft course had finished and we had a few pieces to show. One silver ring I had done with a tiny pearl was much admired by one of our friends and she even bought it. What a triumph; we had hardly started and sold a ring already. But that was it; because we couldn't work from home, we packed up our silver and tools, ready for shipping to Australia. We had bought plenty of silver. It was a good time for buying; the price was comparatively low.

Giselle's workload had increased dramatically and my darling loved it. She was in her creative element. The new boutique in the city centre was about to be opened. It was a well-positioned shop, right in the middle of the split-level centre. It was really Giselle's shop, not only the interior layout, designs and decorations but also of her input in selecting the fashion lines.

•••••••••

Finally, we received a call from a magazine confirming they wanted to publish our story. Their head office was in Munich; they would fly a journalist to Hamburg to discuss the project. It would be more than one page; and published as the main feature in one edition of their magazine *Freundin* and spread over five pages. The first meeting would be in a restaurant of our choice; all paid for by the magazine. We always wanted to go up Hamburg's Television Tower; it had a restaurant on top and a 360-degree view over Hamburg. We asked if it would be possible and it was, with no hesitation.

We had to wait another couple of weeks, bubbling with excitement, before the meeting took place. The journalist was a friendly young lady; she hadn't been to Hamburg and loved the opportunity to see Hamburg from the TV Tower. We felt the same and forgot she was there to interview us. We walked around with her and took heaps of photos, not to forget we enjoyed a nice lunch. Not much interviewing happened. We drove to our place to work on correcting the text we had written. She would use our story and her notes and would send us the final result for our approval.

Sure enough, as promised, our completed story arrived ten days later. It was well written, and most of the original text was still present; however, the journalist had exaggerated the dramatic aspect which didn't sit well with us. We toned it down and sent it back. A few days later, she confirmed with a phone call she would implement the changes and would come to Hamburg for a final talk and take photos before we would leave for Australia.

We were surprised by how long everything took, particularly when we found out our story would be published as late as March 1978.

It must have been June or July when we started to get ready for our big move. We had one metal trunk already, and we bought three more. The final clean out had started; everything was sorted into three categories, selling, charity and rubbish.

Whenever we had an assortment and quantity of items to sell, we invited people from far and wide to come around to buy our goodies. It didn't take long before our unit looked minimalistic. Books, porcelain, small furniture, lamps, shelves, and records all went under the hammer. It was surprising how many books we sold.

In May, we had told our parents we would go back to Australia, and they were slowly getting used to the idea. My mother liked Giselle's red coffee set which was very modern and we gave it to her in exchange for my parents' old fashioned coffee set which they had received in 1942 for their engagement.

Our next focus concentrated on how to sell the unit with all of the remaining content. Luck, destiny, or visualization techniques once again played in our favour. Our friend, the stage designer, had bought many of our books but it got even better. His mother was looking for a unit, and Giselle's unit was the perfect match. They took a while to think about our offer before they finally brought their mum to have a look. Mum loved it!

Our bank account looked decidedly positive; we achieved our monetary goal of buying our dream house. We loved the position we found ourselves in. We had all the essentials in our unit to stay until we would leave without the hassle of having to clean everything and having to live somewhere else for the last few weeks.

We were ready to go. We had our airline tickets. Our friends were sorry to see us go but happy for us to follow our dreams. Our parents were sad but understood our excitement. My parents, I was sure, were sadder than I could imagine. They had lost one son and now they would lose another one. No amount of positive reframing could change the fact we wouldn't be around to hug and support them.

In Giselle's case, the Gartigs were not happy. They had found in Giselle someone who had enriched their business, and who had worked with joy and creativity.

The same for Mendigs; when I told them, they misunderstood and offered more money, much more money, and a better car. I should have threatened to leave six months ago. It wasn't a threat now, it was real, and they were nice about it in the end. The secretary even said she always thought we would go back. I had talked too enthusiastically about Australia.

Other people were happy for different reasons. Herr Rehbein, and a few others like him, who still owed us money were relieved. We had no direct contact with our main money defaulter, Peter, but we wanted to be free of expectation and move on, which is why we wrote him a card. It wasn't Christmas yet but we wrote to him, 'Merry Christmas, we are leaving for Australia, see this card as your present.'

Calculating all the money owed to us, we arrived at over $18,000. Why did we leave such an enormous amount of money behind? It's simple; it would have spoiled our life. We were happy to let go and move on, starting fresh. – And we did. – No regrets.

Chapter 27

Hunting the Dream

Bye, bye lovely apartment, bye, bye Hamburg and bye, bye parents and friends.

We arrived at the Hamburg airport in plenty of time. Our fan club had assembled. Facial expressions were varied. Lots of smiles and laughter from Susie and Stephan, Frank and Haninga, Rolf and Monika, Norbert and Sabine, and they all gave us presents. Could we take a bunch of flowers onto the aeroplane?

Monika gave us something adorable, lots of clear little bottles with natural cork tops filled with substances found in Hamburg. In one bottle was a picture of her, a Hamburg Girl. But others we couldn't take because of Australia's strict regulation. There was a glass of Hamburg soil, others with leaves and seeds, and one cute one, Hamburg air, labelled – 'be careful don't open.' Unfortunately, we had to leave them behind, but we loved the idea.

Giselle's parents looked quite happy and cheerful; was it an act? Surely they had mixed feelings. My parents and Heike looked sad. My dad looked lost, it was too much for him. My mum, who I thought would be the hardest hit, seemed to have turned the corner. "We will save money to come to Australia," she said. I felt relieved my mum had found a new goal and purpose at the last minute. Hopefully, it would catch on with my dad. The final hugs and kisses, and we disappeared behind the gate.

We were glad to be on our own. Our actions had disrupted many lives, but now we wanted to enjoy our journey to our dream destination.

We welcomed the boarding activity; it snapped us out of the sad feeling. We entirely concentrated on the moment, even to the degree of admiring the leather seats in the Lufthansa plane which would take us the short distance to Frankfurt.

It was short, we had just settled down and got comfortable and we had to prepare for the landing. Frankfurt was the easy part; we had booked our luggage right through to Sydney and could take it easy. We relaxed into our excitement and looked forward to arriving in Sydney.

A faint question remained: would we really be able to find a house and land package within our budget? Had we fooled ourselves with crazy fantasies?

Sydney – 1.10.1978 - We arrived. An overwhelming ecstasy affected our whole being and became more intense once we stepped out of the airport. Everything at that very moment in time was Sydney; the air, the noise, the warmth, and of course, Bernd and Julia, who had come to pick us up.

We were home. We felt more at home in Australia than anywhere else. More at home than in Giselle's apartment. Had we really been away for more than one year? Did we have the nightmares of not being able to get back to Australia? All of it was already in the distant past.

We were smiling so hard our cheek muscles were hurting. It must have been catching; people who looked at us smiled as well. One guy gave me the familiar, what we called Australian 'nod,' the little, distinctive head movement indicating one was in the land of 'mates.'

Bernd's place looked like it always had; nothing had changed; it felt like we had been there yesterday.

We left our suitcases and went for a walk; we needed to feel the Bondi atmosphere and smell the ocean undisturbed by talking. We went along the beach past Bondi Pavilion up to Sandridge Street where we lived first. Then back along the shop fronts, checking if our favourite shops were still operating. Yes, there were changes, and it seemed busier, but we couldn't have felt more at home. Looking over Bondi Beach triggered the same feeling we had when we first arrived in 1974. We were captured by the familiar sense of total freedom and excitement of things to come.

Next morning, we woke up at 6 am, much too hyped to go back to sleep. The weather was perfect, and we went for a walk, a light warm breeze caressed our bodies and happiness warmed our insides. A quick dip completed our Bondi return.

We bought bread rolls and grapes and went back for breakfast with Bernd and Julia. They had planned a full day for us, only one event, but it was a big one, a world rodeo championship. Rodeo riders from all over the world came to Sydney. We were carried away by the country atmosphere and even ate a meat pie. We quickly recovered our composure and vowed never to have one again. Tired from the heat, excitement and jet lag, we were happy to arrive back in Bondi.

The following day, we walked up to Bondi Junction and paid our bank a visit, hopeful our money transfer had arrived. We received a new up-to-date bankbook, but our money hadn't arrived, they suggested it could take a few days.

That night it was our turn to cook. We cooked what I had cooked nearly every night in Germany, our standard rice and vegetable dish, spiced up the macrobiotic way.

We checked the classifieds to buy a car and found a few we wanted to have a look at. One of Bernd's neighbours, a car mechanic, offered to drive us and help us pick the right one.

We settled for a Ford Falcon XR station wagon from 1966. It didn't look particularly nice but the engine had been replaced and it was in good shape. There was an issue with the gearbox which our trusty neighbour wanted to fix for free. We bought it on the spot; it was all we needed, basic transport.

I loved driving that old thing; it had the gear stick next to the steering wheel. Very comfortable driving and shifting gears while you were sitting on what felt like an old couch.

To celebrate, we invited Bernd and Julia for dinner at the Bondi Steakhouse. It was possibly the last steak we ate before turning vegetarians.

Our neighbour and friend stuck to his word, took the gearbox apart, bought a new part, and put it back together; simply amazing. It would have cost more than the car was worth. We rewarded him with a carton of beer.

Back to the bank; we needed our money, but nothing had arrived, triggering a feeling of Deja Vu. We could do with some extra cash, and Bernd arranged work for me, fixing pinballs. They stuck me into a gigantic hall with hundreds of broken pinball machines. The pay was more than worth it.

Our last day in Sydney had come. We were on the road again. It felt like we had never stopped travelling, only this time, we were driving towards our future, towards a new life altogether. We went straight through to Forster, the caravan park was pretty empty, and we could pick a spot next to a few trees and not too far from the shower block. We had prepared our dinner the night before, noodle salad. Later we played frisbee. A fatal dose of frisbee fever had infected Sydney and we had become frisbee fanatics.

We woke up early the next morning, all our senses tingling with the expectation of finding our dream house. We knew exactly what we wanted and had visualized it for such a long time it had become a reality. A timber house, easy to renovate, large enough with a couple of bedrooms, a living room and a room we could transform into our art and craft workshop and enough land to have a large garden. The house would be on a hill with a view of beautiful mountain ranges. We also saw a creek or river within walking distance for a quick swim. All we had to do was find a property to match our visualization.

We drove to Port Macquarie and had a first tentative look at properties in a real estate window. A couple of houses were even below $20,000 but they didn't feel right; we decided to drive further north where it would be warmer.

We were up early and went through Grafton and further north, right up to Ballina, and had a look at Coffs Harbour and its surroundings but without knowing why, it was not for us. We trusted our intuition and drove on.

We didn't sleep well; we only dreamt about houses. No point staying in bed tossing and turning. We sensed we were on the brink of finding our place.

We checked out a couple of real estate offices in Ballina. They suggested we look first and if we found anything to our liking, they would contact the owner. It sounded like they were not interested in selling us something. The first three properties were too close to town and were standard house blocks, not what we wanted at all.

The following property was much further out in the hills. It was on two acres, and the house was being renovated. We walked around the house; no one was home; we checked the door, and it was open. We felt invited. It was a small house, with a nice view, but not enough rooms, and no bathroom, toilet, or kitchen. It didn't quite match our expectations, and it was too expensive for the size. We stayed and had a cup of tea while sitting in our car looking at the house but our excitement level was fading. We went with our intuition; it was a close match but not close enough.

It wasn't far to drive to the Gold Coast, to Surfers Paradise, where we knew our friends Bob and Joan were staying. We found them at a caravan park on Main Beach, a short distance from Surfers Paradise.

They didn't see us coming and we surprised them by knocking at their door. Joan opened it, embraced us and called out for Bob, "Guess who is here?" He had no idea and when he came to the door, he jumped out in excitement to greet us.

We had a lot to catch up on and told them all about our dreams and which type of properties we had seen already. Bob told us about the many real estate offices; there definitely would be something waiting for us. He mentioned a friend would come to visit in the morning, a real estate agent, he might know of something.

We thought being Sunday; nothing would happen, and we might as well walk along the beach to Surfers Paradise to look at the real estate office windows.

As we were about to leave, Bob's friend, Will, showed up. He had a new listing on his books which matched our dream description, but warned us it was far out in the hinterland. He mentioned names, but we didn't know places like Canungra, Binna Burra, O'Reilly's or Mt Tamborine. Bob and Joan suggested going for a drive and having a look. They knew the area well, and showed us on the map where Canungra was and the two possible roads we could take. We decided to drive to Canungra first, then to the property and come back to the coast on the second road over Beechmont. Ten minutes later, we passed Nerang, the last suburb before the mountain range.

A bit further on, Bob turned off onto a gravel road; a couple of kilometres later, we were surrounded by mountains, trees, and a river running along one side of the road. All very beautiful, but we were slightly concerned about the gravel road and the distance. It took about 45 minutes to reach Canungra, a cute little village in a valley. We also had passed an Army camp which had us concerned.

Having inspected Canungra, a few shops, a service station, a school and a post office, we turned around and drove to what could potentially become our new home. The property was 4km out of Canungra. We stopped on a gravel driveway going up a hill on the right side of the road. We liked what we saw with the house on top in the far distance. The driveway was pretty bad, washed out and closed off to trespassers with a wire between two posts.

Bob parked his truck on the driveway, and we made the long, steep walk up the hill, passing a sign, "Yardley," the property's present owner.

As we walked up the driveway, the house looked bigger and bigger the closer we came. Bob mentioned the driveway was well placed and should be easy to fix with a grader to smooth out the washed-out tyre tracks.

Our excitement level was at 100%; everything matched our visualisations. It was a large timber house on stumps. We couldn't go inside, but we could see enough from the back veranda through a window. It was empty but clean, and the rooms had very high ceilings.

From the open back verandah, one had a perfect view. To the left in the far distance, one could see the O'Reilly Rainforest. Straight ahead, a mountain range covered densely with trees, and to the right was Mt Tamborine. The house was on the highest point of the hill and, according to a fence line, about two acres. Next to the house, there was a little shed which was the original laundry which still contained a large copper in a concrete fireplace. We also saw the remains of two other sheds and a little hut which appeared to belong to the property.

There were three water tanks large enough for two people. We noticed a second driveway, which, and we hardly could believe it, was leading down across a side road to a river and waterhole. It couldn't have been more perfect. As we looked back up, we could see the house from a different angle, with the enormous

Moreton Bay Fig tree in the background. We had found our dream house; our visualisation had been manifested.

We left what we felt was our new home. We drove up to Beechmont and stopped at a picnic ground with a view over a large valley, a good place for contemplation.

We couldn't believe our luck, the mountains were nothing like the height in Switzerland, but everything around was beautiful with the added benefit of the rainforest. We had found the perfect house and also the perfect location.

We told Bob and Joan we would buy that house; it was ours. They were less enthusiastic, or rather, they were calling for caution; at least we should see the inside. We didn't mind how it looked inside; we would renovate and change it anyhow.

"Please wait a bit before you make up your mind and go back with Will," Joan said. We agreed, but we knew it was ours and we hoped to get it cheaper than the asking price.

· · · · ● ● ● · · ·

We were worried about our money; why wasn't it coming? Our first priority on Monday morning was to drive to the Commonwealth Bank in Southport. We needed the money urgently. The bank staff was sympathetic and suggested a few steps to help us. To speed things up, they sent a telegram to find out more. They believed it might be held at another bank because of the large amount transferred. They asked us to come back on Wednesday.

Will would drive with us to the property the following day. He picked us up at 10 am. He told us the owner had someone else interested in the house. Was it a ploy? We enjoyed the drive to the property. It seemed shorter a second time around.

We walked into the house and loved it even more. The high ceilings were fantastic. Every available wall was whitewashed, and we couldn't wait to paint it the way we wanted. It didn't have a kitchen as we knew. Instead, it had a niche, which the agent told us was the space for a slow combustion stove. The rest of the large room was an open kitchen and dining room combined. There was another large room which could become a living room or bedroom but we wanted a smaller, much cosier room as our bedroom to the north of the house. The bathroom was small and had no toilet. A bathtub resting on its side was waiting to be installed. Another room was perfect for our studio and workshop.

"Where is the toilet?" we asked.

"The original owners had an outhouse as toilet," the agent replied.

We thought we could do that for starters, no problems.

And then, of course, there was the verandah. It was 8 meters long, 3 meters wide, and very inviting; we couldn't wait to sit there, having a glass of wine and admiring the view.

"Yes, we will buy it; please pass on our offer of $22,000," I said.

That was it; we signed the contract. The agent was sceptical; he thought our offer was too low.

The property owner was a director of a TV station; he and his wife had planned to retire at the house but had changed their mind.

The next morning Will came around with the good news. The owner would accept $22,500. We agreed instantly. We drove to the bank and saw our case manager, and we knew he had good news. He approached us with a smile.

"The money had arrived in Australia but was held at the National Bank.

"If you can confirm the money is your savings, they will release it, and it will be in your account in a couple of days," he said.

"Thank you; that's good news," I answered, and we signed the relevant papers. And the good news continued.

"While you were waiting, there was a devaluation of the dollar, and you will receive a better exchange rate."

Overjoyed, we thanked him and walked out feeling 3 feet taller. The sun was shining on us; the universe was on our side. We were house owners with no rent to pay ever again, and it was the only way we would succeed in living a self-sufficient lifestyle.

We had told Will about our photographic skills, and as we had anticipated, he needed someone to take photos of blocks of land he wanted to sell. It was exactly what we were looking for. We could easily live self-sufficiently with a few jobs and opportunities coming our way, even before our garden was established.

A couple of days later, we drove to our house in our car for the first time. It didn't feel far away anymore. We had a good long look around our land and found out we owned more land than we thought. The land behind the fence towards the west belonged to us too; we had 5 acres all up.

While walking around taking photos for the agent, a guy approached us from the empty block next to ours. He introduced himself as Tom.

"Are you the real estate agent for this block?" he asked.

"No, we just bought this block," we replied.

"It's a good block; I was tempted to buy it and use the house as my office," he said.

"What are you doing?" I asked.

"I am a developer; I bought most of the land you can see around you, except the few blocks which had been subdivided previously. I will subdivide everything into 5-acre blocks."

"And we thought we might be too isolated," I said, laughing.

"It could be another year before blocks will be ready for sale. I will plant lots of trees, bore for water, fence all the blocks, and construct an excess road to get final council improvement," he said.

"When will you move in?"

"The contract will settle on the 30th of November; we will move in the next day if we are back from Sydney," I said.

Giselle explained our situation and answered more of his questions. He seemed to be after something; we felt an opportunity emerging.

"I see; maybe before you are self-sufficient and have a garden, you could help me out with doing some jobs?" he asked

Giselle and I looked at each other; we couldn't believe our luck, "Yes, that would be great; what would we have to do?" we asked.

"Taking photos from each block, for payment, of course. And I need help with fencing, planting trees, and watering," he explained.

"Sounds perfect. Is it OK to take the photos when we come back from Sydney?" I asked.

"Yes, no worries, the blocks are not ready yet," he said.

Everything fell into place, two opportunities in one day; lucky again. Tom must have liked us, and we liked him, a down-to-earth, no-nonsense guy.

The next day shaped up to be a busy one. We went to Surfers Paradise to see the solicitor, checked with the bank; they gave us the all-clear. Next came setting up the reconnection of our power supply.

Giselle's birthday was coming up, and we celebrated a couple of days before by inviting Bob and Joan for dinner. It was a restaurant in Surfers on the top floor of a high-rise with a great view over the ocean. We had a wonderful time; great food, and we were in such a happy mood we went on to a club for dancing.

On Giselle's actual birthday, we drove to Brisbane to check whether prices for white goods and garden equipment were lower than on the Gold Coast. We didn't find anything in Brisbane and drove to visit Gerd and Heike. They lived in an older high-set timber house, and they were home; such a wonderful reunion.

The rest of the week went in a flash. The house payment went through on Wednesday.

• • • • • • • • •

We left Main Beach caravan park early in the morning. Bob and Joan promised to drive a couple of times to our house to check while we were in Sydney. We took a stopover in Kempsey and stayed overnight, sleeping in our car. The following day, we drove the last 450 km to Bondi and arrived in the afternoon.

Bernd and Julia had separated but behaved as if nothing had happened, there was no animosity. After dinner, we settled down with a can of beer watching telly. If we hadn't known they had split up, we wouldn't have noticed.

We were planning and waiting desperately for the arrival of our trunks. Finally, a letter arrived from the shipping company; the trunks would come on 27.11.1978.

I worked again at the former job, making good money fixing pinball machines, which meant Giselle had to arrange to get our trunks out of Customs. However, the proper papers were not yet available.

On the weekend, we met Mark and Karin; they had arrived in Sydney to stay over the summer and fly back to Hamburg when summer arrived in Germany. We spent the day together, lying on the beach and going out for dinner at night. They looked forward to visiting us over Christmas and New Year. It looked like we would have a grand party. Julia had asked if she could stay over Christmas and so did Gerd and Heike. And Simone and Dean, who now had a baby boy, would also try to have a little holiday with us. We were not even living in our house and had already planned for a house party.

After the weekend, Giselle tried her luck at the shipping company again. They explained the process but advised her to get an agent, and they had one for her - coincidentally. Giselle was sure she could handle it herself.

The next step was contacting someone who could transport the trunks to the train station. The freight company recommended a guy who would be ready on call. We still didn't know when we could pick up the trunks; we had to call the harbour office on Wednesday. However, we knew the ship's name: 'Professor Schaefer.'

The freight train station department turned out to be expensive; it would cost $100 from Sydney to Southport. We didn't even know if there was a train station in Southport, and as we found out a few days later, there wasn't.

Giselle received a phone call in the afternoon from the Harbour people. It was the news we had been waiting for; the trunks could be picked up on Friday morning which meant Thursday had to be my last working day. I notified the boss and he promised to have my pay ready when I finished up in the afternoon. He thanked me and offered me more work whenever I wanted it. It was nice to be wanted but it was unlikely to happen again. With my pay packet in my pocket and good wishes for our future, I said goodbye to that episode of my life.

1.12.1978 – Friday – Punctual, we arrived at the harbour before 9 am. Our trunks were in a 15-metre long container, pointed out by one of the guys responsible. As it happened, we were misinformed; the container had been unloaded, but not unpacked. And it wouldn't be unpacked for a while yet. We gave up after hanging around for 3 hours. The Customs officer told us they would be ready for us on Monday morning.

Monday and our positive mindset had returned; we packed up our car to leave Sydney, said goodbye to Bernd and Julia, and arrived at the Harbour by 8 am. We immediately saw the container had not been unpacked. It was still waiting in a queue. The harbour workers were about to open another container, but Giselle went over to one of those guys and asked him if they could open our container first.

I don't think the guy would have listened to me, but he did listen to Giselle, and she had some excellent true stories at hand to explain the urgency and how we had to be at the train station with those trunks by noon at the latest. Blessed be the Sydney harbour crew; they thought it was all pretty funny and opened our container. Giselle had ordered the taxi truck for 11:30 am. Time was flying by, but that was the only thing flying; the work progressed at a laid-back pace.

Finally, our trunks appeared, and two Customs officers joined the crew. I am not joking; everyone stayed around the trunks and made funny comments as the Customs officer unpacked the lot. They looked at our family photos and wanted to know who those people were. They seemed to like our coffee cups, and so it went. They knew we had to get to the train station. Were they playing with us, a little bit of fun to kill the monotony of the job? They were very friendly and told us, "She'll be right." At 11:30 am, no taxi truck to be seen. I must have looked worried, "No worries, mate, he will arrive."

At noon, things started to move; even the taxi truck arrived. The Customs officers had finished and were happy. We were less happy because the trunks needed repacking, and the clock was ticking. We couldn't get everything back into the trunks; we chucked the rest into our car. The truck driver loaded the trunks, and we raced off to the train station.

The harbour crew probably knew more than we did. There was no need to hurry. At the station, stacks of goods were not loaded, and no one seemed to be in a great hurry; it was "She'll be right" all the way.

We waited until our trunks eventually were stacked into a small container before being placed onto the train. The trunks looked good, with no damage, not even the slightest dent; surely, nothing could go wrong now.

We were exhausted but relieved and left the train station; it was 2 pm by now. We drove the 400km to Kempsey, where we stayed the night in a motel. We couldn't sleep in the car; it was full of our belongings.

We left Kempsey early and arrived in Surfers Paradise before 3 pm. The first stop was our bank, where we received a new bankbook. Everything was fine. The house was paid for, and we had money left over. The next stop was the real estate office to pick up our house key. What a feeling, our excitement grew as we drove towards our dream house.

The road from Southport over Nerang to Canungra had already become familiar. We turned left at the Army camp and continued 2km before turning right, driving up our gravel driveway and stopping at our back verandah. – "HOME"

We gently stepped out of the car as if we didn't want to disturb the precious grass. Slowly walking the few steps to the house, looking around, hugging each other and saying the obvious, "It's all ours."

We took the three wooden steps up to the verandah and looked westwards to the mountain range. I held the key, showed it to Giselle, as to say, this is it, and unlocked the door. Slowly opening the door, we took the first steps into our house. We had seen it once before, but now it was different; it was ours and we saw every little bit.

We hadn't previously noticed but there was a kitchen cupboard in the living room. It was old fashioned but looked functional.

"We could paint it and shift it to the other wall," Giselle said.

"Look, I quite like the old fridge; I wonder if it still works?" I said.

"Do we have power?" Giselle asked.

I switched on the light, nothing happened. Maybe the main switch was off, and I went to check. The fuse box was on the open verandah. Sure enough, the main switch was off; I switched it on.

"Try now," I called. I could see the light coming on. We plugged in the fridge, and it worked; we wouldn't have to buy a new one. Slowly, we walked through every room, making plans about what to do on the spot.

"I feel like a kid, playing cubby house," I said.

The bathroom had an old-fashioned vanity. I tried the taps. There was no hot water, but the cold-water tap worked. There was not much pressure, and we would have to get used to the gravity-fed water supply.

"Maybe we should install the bathtub into the floor; it would give us more water pressure," I said.

"Why not? It could be fun. Is there enough space underneath the house?" Giselle asked.

A bedroom was next to the bathroom, not connected by a door, only by a window. The entry to this room was from the middle room, the coolest room, which didn't receive any sunlight. The windows opened to the front hall and back verandah.

We decided to call the front hall "the studio." Giselle drew a house plan to send to her parents.

Our new life had started.

Dieter Lüske is a writer who enjoys life and life's journey, loves working with Giselle, his wife, in their enchanted organic garden, dabbles in art and music and consults on holistic health and lifestyle topics.

He has written 3 books, has published hundreds of holistic lifestyle philosophy articles, and lives by his motto,

"By attempting the impossible - one is meaningfully occupied (D.L.)"

Dieter combines the perseverance and courage of the finest tradition of investigative & creative writing with the ability to keep complex topics simple.

He lives and works in the Gold Coast Hinterland with his artist wife, Giselle.

Dieter Lüske – www.dieterluske.com

www.ingramcontent.com/pod-product-compliance
Lightning Source LLC
Chambersburg PA
CBHW020316010526
44107CB00054B/1862